The WrestleMania Era: The Book of Sports Entertainment

By "The Doc" Chad Matthews

The WrestleMania Era: The Book of Sports Entertainment

This book is dedicated to my family and friends. To my dad (RIP), for being my biggest fan. To my mom, for <u>everything</u>. To M, for teaching me how to excel. To my friends, for their support. To Rudy, for saving my life. To my wife and my kids, for being the best things that ever happened to me.

The WrestleMania Era: The Book of Sports Entertainment

Copyrighted Material

Copyright © 2016 by MCM

DPC Publishing, Incorporated
North Carolina

All rights reserved. No portion of this publication may be reproduced or transmitted in any form or by any means, electronic or mechanical, including photocopy, recording, or any information storage and retrieval system, without permission in writing from the author or publisher, except by a reviewer who may quote brief passages in a critical article to be printed in a magazine or newspaper, or electronically transmitted on radio or television.

"The Doc" Chad Matthews
The WrestleMania Era: The Book of Sports Entertainment (Third Edition)

ISBN-10: 0692705848

Disclaimer - This book is not an official WWE publication. It is not affiliated, associated, or otherwise endorsed by the WWE. The names of all WWE programming, talent, images, likenesses and logos are the exclusive property of the owner, World Wrestling Entertainment, Inc. This book is analytical and editorial. All information contained in this book has been obtained through resources readily available in the public domain.

Editor: Corwin Metcalf
Cover Image: Chad Matthews
Back Cover Image: Matt Nelson

The WrestleMania Era: The Book of Sports Entertainment

Contact

Chad Matthews is very active on social media, posting daily questions to wrestling fans on various topics to stimulate engaging debates.

To contact "The Doc" :

Twitter: @TheDocLOP

Facebook: https://www.facebook.com/doc.lop.9

To read "The Doctor's Orders" column by "The Doc" Chad Matthews, please visit:

www.wrestlingheadlines.com / www.lordsofpain.net

To listen to "The Doc Says..." weekly podcast, please visit: www.blogtalkradio.com/lordsofpain

Books by "The Doc" Chad Matthews

The WrestleMania Era: The Book of Sports Entertainment

The Greatest Champions of The WrestleMania Era

Starrcade vs. WrestleMania: The Prelude to the Monday Night Wars (e-book)

The Greatest Matches and Rivalries of the WrestleMania Era (estimated release in 2018)

The WrestleMania Era: The Book of Sports Entertainment

Table of Contents

Prologue - "Well, why don't you write it?"

My Parallel Life with the World of Professional Wrestling

The Criteria

The Third-Tier (Profiles on #61-90)

The Second-Tier (Profiles on #31-60)

The First-Tier (Profiles on #11-30)

The Greatest of the WrestleMania Era (Profiles on #10-1)

The WrestleMania Era Wine Cellar

Acknowledgments

Prologue

Professional wrestling has never been as popular as it has been over the last thirty years. Beginning with Hulk Hogan's rise to the top of the industry and the advent of WrestleMania, it found a place in the pop culture lexicon that made it a widely accepted, albeit still controversial, form of sports / entertainment. The WWE (formerly the WWF) has led the way, making the business as much about theatricality as it is about simulated combat and expanding its viewership in the process. Subsequently, a generation of fans has grown up with pro wrestling as one of their pastimes, watching the likes of Hogan, "Macho Man" Randy Savage, Ric Flair, "Stone Cold" Steve Austin, The Rock, and John Cena excel in the wrestling ring.

Wrestling's growth has paralleled the rise of the media's obsession with sports. Football, basketball, baseball, soccer, and wrestling fans enjoy greater access than ever before to their favorite teams and superstars through television and the internet. Increased coverage has brought more in-depth discussion, creating a network of enthusiasts who are as much critics as they are devotees. Sports analysis is no longer just water cooler talk, but also a burgeoning profession legitimized by college degrees. Be it as diehard supporters of respective sports enjoying educated conversations about player legacy, zone defensive schemes, and the ideal offensive formation or be it as an employed statistician whose job is to categorize the best of all-time, find the right point guard for the pick-and-roll, and identify Wins Above Replacement Player, we have become a sports world obsessed with analytics and data.

The WWE product is more globally visible than ever. They currently broadcast their weekly programming, *Monday Night Raw* and *Tuesday Night Smackdown!*, and their monthly pay-per-views in one hundred fifty countries and in thirty languages. Websites that cover pro wrestling such as The Pro Wrestling Torch, Figure Four Online, and Lords of Pain (LOP) each draw millions of people every week from around the world. Much like ESPN, Fox Sports, and others, these sites provide news, results, and insider reports. The thirst for a constant stream of information is as strong amongst wrestling fans as it is for any sport or entertainment avenue. I know that better than anyone, being one of those rabid diehards, myself. I started watching wrestling with my grandfather when I was two years old, but my introduction to online coverage while an eighteen year old undergraduate student turned my weekly television habit into a daily obsession. The same could be said of college football and pro basketball, but there was always something about pro wrestling's combination of athletics and drama that made it a higher extracurricular priority for me.

In my early college years, I began writing television recaps of WWE shows for LOP as a hobby, later writing full-fledged critical reviews while going through professional schooling to become a doctor. Writing was my therapeutic outlet to escape from the mental rigors of the real world. During the same period, I took a strong interest in analytics, particularly as it pertained to the NBA. When I transitioned to writing subjective columns for LOP, I followed the lead of my favorite basketball writer, Bill Simmons, in combining my interest for hyper-analysis with the sport that I covered. Simmons proceeded to take his analytical approach and create a list of over ninety of the greatest to have ever played in the National Basketball Association. His amazing work, *The Book of Basketball: The NBA According to the Sports Guy*, was the ultimate fan account of pro basketball history. Inspired, I set out to write the modern pro wrestling equivalent.

I developed a methodical criterion to support my personal observations of nearly thirty years of fandom in order to definitively answer the question as to which wrestlers belong in the debate for the greatest of all-time. Bear in mind that this has never been done for wrestling before. All discussions about greatness in sports entertainment come back to one central idea: it is *so* subjective. I do not dispute that it is subjective, but I counter that it is reasonably objectifiable too. Creating a statistical method for analysis and combining it with educated opinions allows for a complete picture to be painted. So, as Simmons said about basketball in his book, I posit in mine that wrestling is "both subjective *and* objective."

Wrestlers are both athletes and entertainers. They are physical artists, trained to perform intricate sequences of grappling holds, throws, high risk balancing acts at often great heights, and hand-to-hand combat that all looks and sounds legitimate without intentionally hurting their opponents. It is dangerous. For a living, they put their bodies at risk, landing as safely as possible on thinly padded wood, off ladders, on concrete, through tables, and on/off steel platforms. Yet, to be given the chance to achieve the most success, they must also be able to establish an emotional connection with pro wrestling's audience. Wrestlers have to be actors capable of playing a character that is often an extension of their own personality to make the people care about the stories that they tell on the 20'X20' canvas.

While analytically reviewing and celebrating the "WrestleMania Era" dating back to the early 1980s, I spent countless hours researching, formulating, and categorizing the matches, the interviews, the main-events, the pay-per-view buyrates, the television ratings, and the championships won. In order to be considered the greatest, a wrestler had to be able to convince viewers that, either through verbal communication or body language, his match was worth seeing. If he got the people in the door, then he had to deliver something worthy of critical acclaim in the ring to give the paying customers a show worthy of attending/viewing again. Then, it came down to how many people actually came through the door or watched the show from home; success at the box office is a must. Since the business is not immune to economic shifts, however, it would have been remiss to ignore the longevity of some tenured headliners who stayed in the main-events through years of fiscal thick and thin. Finally, one of a wrestler's primary goals is to achieve championship gold, so title reigns were also assessed.

A five-tiered breakdown shaped the definitive list. Through a formula (to bridge the gap between eras) for championships won, a scale for main-events and headlining matches to account for longevity, a compilation of television ratings and pay-per-view buy rate data for financial success (revised for the 3rd edition to account for the WWE Network), a wrestler scoring system to reflect physical attributes and microphone skills, and a film critic-like star rating scale to account for performance, I have named the "Greatest Wrestlers of the WrestleMania Era."

My Parallel Life with the World of Professional Wrestling

I was two years old when my family and I traveled to Carlsbad, California to see my dad's parents. I remember just two things from the trip: #1 is my granddad tied my shoelaces together and sent me careening to the floor in a heap. #2 is that wrestling was on TV when it happened. The rest is history. I have followed the world of professional wrestling ever since.

As a child, I could not get enough of it. The United States Wrestling Association was on after school in Greensboro, North Carolina, where the better-known National Wrestling Alliance dominated the region's top arenas and TV on Saturday nights. The internationally popular WWE did not enter the picture until a bit later, but it quickly took over my imagination with its more colorful and kid-friendly product.

As many kids do with sports, I began to establish a deeper connection to wrestling through experiences with my father. We bonded over basketball and football as time went on, but pro wrestling came first. My dad and I grappled in the living room multiple nights per week, with the furniture acting as the ring ropes and the armrest of the couch becoming the top turnbuckle. I had the chance to spend a lot of time watching sports with him, such as the Montana-led 49ers throttling Elway's Broncos in Super Bowl XXIV and Mike Tyson's epic title loss to Buster Douglas, but the wrestling memories stand out most.

There were some awkward times around 1990-1991 when my parents divorced and my mom remarried, but the wrestling connection honestly helped smooth the transition. "Adapt and react to the best of your ability" became a mantra that I have lived by. Adapting was made much easier through the WWE's Coliseum Home Video, which my stepdad's

Blockbuster Video stores carried in bulk. Every pay-per-view (PPV) that the WWE produced was in the "Sports and Special Interest" aisle and, every other weekend, my dad and I would rent at least one. I vividly remember watching the 1992 *Royal Rumble* at his apartment, which foreshadowed one of my favorite weekends that he and I ever spent together sixteen years later in his eventual home of Orlando, Florida. I found myself rooting for Shawn Michaels, a young bad boy at the time looking to make a name for himself as "The Heartbreak Kid (HBK)," while my dad pulled for Ric Flair, that era's most prolific wrestler. I give a lot of credit to pro wrestling for giving me a healthy distraction from the tumultuous nature of everything going on around me. It would not be the last time that it served that purpose.

    I developed strong attachments to the greatest moments in the early WrestleMania Era by living them in my dad's apartment. We witnessed Hulk Hogan slam Andre the Giant, the "Mega Powers Explode" (when Hogan's team with "Macho Man" Randy Savage split), The Ultimate Warrior - my early childhood favorite - take down Hulkamania, and the rise to prominence of young guns like Michaels and Bret "Hitman" Hart. The night of *WrestleMania IX* was one of the pinnacle moments of my first ten years. After a weekend of trading Figure Four leg locks (Flair's signature move) and Sharpshooters (the submission of choice by my new favorite, Hart), we tuned in for what became critically known as the worst *WrestleMania* in history. The poor quality did not bother me. It was my first live Mania. There is no other wrestling event that comes close to the spectacle of the show that has been nicknamed everything from "Wrestling's Super Bowl" to "The Granddaddy of Them All" to "The Show of Shows" to "The Showcase of the Immortals." There is WrestleMania and then there is everything else. No sport's grandest stage, to this day, ignites my passion for sports or entertainment quite like Mania.

Basketball took over as my #1 hobby thanks to the combination of Christian Laettner's turnaround jumper to beat Kentucky in the 1992 NCAA Elite Eight, the Barcelona Olympics' USA Dream Team, and Michael Jordan vs. Charles Barkley in the 1993 NBA Finals, but it did not take long for me to be, yet again, bitten by the wrestling bug. I was lured back in 1995 when Michaels was ascending to the top of the WWE. HBK was fast becoming my all-time favorite wrestler with his highly athletic matches. He and Bret gave me a wrestling education, as they performed brilliant tales on the 20'X20', three-tiers-of-rope surrounded canvas. They put on display for the WWE that wrestling could be more than just glitz and glam. The 1980s WWE shows built around Hogan were akin to "box office blockbuster" movies. The theatrics were emphasized over the actual story, appealing to the masses just as in Hollywood. The WWE rode Hulkamania to unprecedented success in the industry using that model. Hogan's success allowed WWE owner and promoter, Vince McMahon, to buy up all the best talent in North America and absorb the regional entities that had once dominated pro wrestling.

For those unfamiliar with the history, McMahon changed the landscape of the sport in less than ten years. For the majority of the 20th century, wrestling was separated into territories – the northeast (owned by Vince's dad), the Carolinas, southern California, Texas, Chicago, Florida, Georgia, St. Louis, Toronto, Montreal, Oregon, etc. The National Wrestling Alliance was formed in 1948 to create a National Champion (though it was always referred to, just as the NBA does with its titleholder, as the "World Champion"). Each territory had a primary owner, so the various presidents would get together and vote on who the NWA World Champion should be. The champ would travel across the United States and Canada facing the top challengers and regional champions of each territory. The NWA was the entity that showed that wrestling on a national level could work.

McMahon had a strong business acumen and, having grown up in the northeast seeing professional sports franchises such as New York's Yankees, Knicks, and Jets and Boston's Red Sox and Celtics achieve great success and make a lot of money on nationally televised platforms, he saw an opportunity to take what the NWA was doing to a level similar to Major League Baseball, the National Football League, and the National Basketball Association. He had an idea for a product that he thought would appeal to more people, which would then make more money. So, Vince scoured the North American scene and found Hogan. The Hulkster was everything you would want in a 1980s hero. He was big, muscular, and tanned. He had the look of a Hollywood star and the personality to back it up. Contrast that to stars from the 1950s-1970s such as Lou Thesz or Bruno Sammartino, who were athletes, but were not the types that stopped you dead in your tracks because of their appearance. When you saw Hulk, you thought star. McMahon strapped a figurative rocket to Hogan's back and shot him onto the national TV airwaves. Wrestling exploded in popularity, more visible to the national audience than ever before.

WrestleMania came from McMahon's desire to create a yearly event that could put wrestling on-par with the Super Bowl or the World Series which, to their respective sports, are the culmination of their calendars. He wanted to blend celebrities such as Muhammad Ali and Liberace with his wrestlers. Howard Finkel, the long-time announcer who introduced the wrestlers to live audiences, coined the event in reference to Beatle Mania. With the success of the first *Mania* and the unbelievable achievements of *WrestleMania III* (record setting numbers for pay-per-view in its infancy and the world indoor attendance record that stood for over twenty-five years), McMahon's WWE was able to conquer a longstanding tradition in professional wrestling and leave, by 1991, only one other competitor standing (Ted Turner's World Championship Wrestling, which carried on the traditions of the NWA).

The WrestleMania Era: The Book of Sports Entertainment

The rise to prominence of Bret Hart and Shawn Michaels coincided with an economic downturn for the wrestling business stimulated by a federal prosecution against McMahon, who had been indicted on charges of conspiring with a Pennsylvania doctor to distribute steroids to his wrestlers (Vince was acquitted). Hart and Michaels were smaller athletes whose respective reigns as World Champion took the WWE away from its requisite bodybuilder look popularized in the 1980s. Though well-sculpted athletes remain, historically, McMahon's preference, it took several years before the company could get past the public relations nightmare created by their association with steroids. In the long-term, it was a blessing in disguise that created awareness about the dangers of the drugs, which at that time were not well known. It also opened the door for wrestlers with less size, but more talent to shine on wrestling's largest platform.

In the 80s, McMahon rebranded his vision for professional wrestling as "sports entertainment." Recognizing that increased media coverage meant that the veil of uncertainty about the predetermined outcomes in pro wrestling matches was soon to be completely lifted, McMahon opted to change public perception. It happens all the time in the business world. If you want the general population to regard what you do as different than the current view, you change the name and re-educate the consumer. Though Vince has often been criticized for it, it made good financial sense if he wanted to target a new market. During the Hulkamania era, heavy emphasis was placed on the entertainment side of the rebrand. Whereas wrestling for an hour was once celebrated, Hogan and other top wrestlers from that period routinely wrestled less than 15-minutes.

Hart and Michaels reintroduced the sports aspect. With it firmly established that wrestling was a performance art rather than a sport in the traditional sense of the word, they concentrated their attention on telling more intricate stories and on creating the most aesthetically pleasing in-ring product imaginable. Watching those two perform was like night and day compared to Hogan and his contemporaries. They were much more like Ric Flair, who had been keeping professional wrestling tradition alive in the NWA. Flair had some of the finest matches of the 80s and early 90s. The Flair-Hart-Michaels style of wrestling was, in contrast to Hogan's blockbusters, more critically acclaimed. Arnold Schwarzenegger was to movies what Hulk Hogan was to wrestling. Flair, Hart, and Michaels were Robert De Niro, Al Pacino, and Tom Hanks. Arnold may have made more money bringing in the masses, but the others won more awards catering to the aficionados.

    Through watching Hart and Michaels from 1992-1998, I developed a definition of a "great" wrestling match. They borrowed on the principles that helped make Flair and Ricky "The Dragon" Steamboat so popular with critics. I give credit to Flair for creating the modern formula for in-ring excellence because he understood that a little flash to go along with the substance was necessary in a changing world, just as the NBA knew that the three-point line, the Dunk Contest, and the "Showtime" Lakers would better adapt their product to the growing TV market. You have to change. Flair had the foresight to recognize that what McMahon was doing could be blended with the history of the game, so he borrowed from greats of the past such as Gorgeous George, Buddy Rogers, Lou Thesz, and Harley Race and added more panache to help shape a new, more entertaining version of excellence in the pro wrestling ring. Michaels and Hart were the evolution of Flair's in-ring ideals with a boost from McMahon's first-rate promotional and TV production concepts.

    I became enamored with wrestling all over again and in a completely different way by watching HBK and Bret have classic after classic in the mid-1990s. I learned that wrestling was a "combat drama" that takes the elements of struggle, heart, and desire that make for a great television show and ends the conflicts with risky sequences of unchoreographed fighting. It is a dangerous art form. People are drawn to it for the same reasons that people love sports and theater – because of the passion and the entertainment, the camaraderie and the grandeur. Wrestling combines the violence of the NFL (America's most popular sports league) with the athleticism and style of the NBA (America's second most popular sports league) and has the global of appeal of European football/American soccer (the world's most popular sport). For some reason, the fact that the winners are pre-determined in wrestling bothers some people, but I do not know why. As fans, we have no more control over who wins a baseball or football game than we do a wrestling match. The difference is that wrestling is run by promoters who have the luxury of ensuring that their versions of Lebron James and Kobe Bryant – box office draws - are on top.

There is not a group of athletes that I respect more than pro wrestlers. The physical toll that hundreds of matches per year take on the human frame is greater than in any other sport. NFL players are said to absorb the equivalent of thirty car accidents per game…and they were pads. Wrestlers endure worse and they wear what most of us do when we sleep. Bronco Nagurski, for whom the yearly college football award for "best defensive player" is named after, would have enlightened you. He doubled as a pro football player and a former World Heavyweight Champion pro wrestler.

Wrestlers have brutal schedules. Only soccer is comparable. European football season begins in August and ends in late May, while at least every other year an international tournament occupies the summers of the world's best. Wrestling does not have an off-season. For the WWE wrestler, "practice" is the house show circuit. House shows are live events that allow more personal interaction and cheaper tickets for the average fan to show their appreciation for the sport while simultaneously getting to witness the performers hone their craft. Live events were a much bigger part of the business side before TV and PPV became king, but still represent an integral part of the WWE model. A typical week for a WWE superstar would be to do a live TV broadcast on Monday (*Raw*) or Tuesday (*Smackdown!*). These TV shows are the equivalent of soccer's regular season games. They are meaningful, but there are so many of them that they tend to get lost in the shuffle. Nevertheless, they are a vital part of the "season" because they allow the promoters to see who is worthy of being involved in the crucial, money-making events of the year. There are between 12-14 PPVs a year on the WWE calendar; before March 2014, people paid up to $70 in the USA to see them and they have since been included as part of WWE Network's $9.99 (US) monthly streaming service. The stakes are higher on PPV and some are bigger than others. Summerslam (August), The Royal Rumble (January), and then WrestleMania (March/April) are the three major PPVs, with WrestleMania trumping them all.

Pro wrestling saw a resurgence in the late 1990s that eclipsed Hulkamania. It has often been referred to as "The Attitude Era." Turner's WCW, spearheaded by Eric Bischoff's television production team, made their weekly cable show, *Monday Nitro,* feel more authentic. Bischoff turned Hogan, the hero of the 80s to kids around the world that helped make Hulkamania a household brand, into a villain who turned on those kids-turned-teenagers. Flanked by former WWE stalwarts, Kevin Nash and Scott Hall, Hogan led The New World Order (N.W.O.), a group that played on the dream scenario of WCW and WWE clashing in an NFL vs. USFL / NBA vs. ABA type interpromotional war by suggesting a "hostile takeover." The war was very much happening, but it was behind the scenes and not scripted for television. WCW raided the WWE for its top talents just as the WWE had raided everyone else a decade prior.

The WrestleMania Era: The Book of Sports Entertainment

That was an interesting time to be a fan. I represented the target market for both of the modern wrestling boom periods. I was just a little kid for Hulkamania and I was in middle and high school during the Attitude Era. It was a huge difference between the late 80s and late 90s. As teenagers, counter-culture was in while pure, wholesome entertainment was very much out. The 80s was like watching one of Arnold's action films, where the story was simply "good guy vs. bad guys." In the 90s, nobody wanted to see the standard, vanilla, whitemeat babyface/good guy pulverize the opposition in the ring anymore than they wanted to see one man gun down two hundred without a scratch. Fans demanded something different. The Attitude Era was a lot more like *Stars Wars*. It was not just about good vs. evil. "Stone Cold" Steve Austin was an anti-hero, for instance. He was the Han Solo of wrestling - a bad guy that just so happened to align himself against the pinnacle symbol of evil. Vince's on-screen CEO persona, leader of "The Corporation," was akin to "The Empire." Stone Cold flipped people the bird left and right, cursed like a sailor, stabbed the good guys in the back, and drank beer in the ring. He was a bad ass. The masses flocked to him. Austin took a character that was completely counterculture and fully ingrained it into popular culture. The Rock, my favorite of that era due to his unmatched athletic ability and charisma, was like Darth Vader - he was so good at being a bad guy that you wanted to like him. He gave the WWE a second megastar in one era. Dwayne "The Rock" Johnson, now a leading man in Hollywood, is rivaled only by Hogan as the most well-known wrestling celebrity in the mainstream.

The late 90s was the most competitive period in wrestling history. NWA/WCW was no more than a pesky fly in the WWE's quest to monopolize the status of top wrestling promotion, despite the brilliant work from Flair throughout the 80s and early 90s. The WWE was king. WCW was clearly #2. Yet, the steroid trial opened the door for Turner's group. WCW created *Nitro* to go head-to-head with WWE's Monday night cable program, *Raw*, and on the heels of The N.W.O. became the undisputed #1 company for two years. Their product was edgier and better fit the times. WWE was countering with great wrestlers at the top, but the general theme of their product was cartoonish. WCW gave us fresh takes on Hogan, Hall, Nash, Macho Man, and Roddy Piper, while also providing us with things that we had never seen before in mainstream wrestling like Mexican Lucha Libre from Rey Misterio, Jr. and fresh new talents like Eddie Guerrero and Chris Jericho. In the WWE, Michaels, Hart, and Undertaker were flanked by a supporting cast full of goofy, gimmicked characters like a wrestling garbage man, clown, racecar driver, blueblood, and even a ridiculous take on the Minotaur (Greek mythology's bull-headed man) called Mantaur.

    I, personally, stayed loyal to the WWE, thanks to Michaels and Hart, but I was in the minority. It was not until Austin's character figuratively caught fire that the majority of the teenage crowd came back to the WWE product and said, as Stone Cold would, "Oh HELL YEAH!" As much as The New World Order took wrestling in a different direction, Stone Cold turned it upside down. After Mike Tyson showed up for *WrestleMania XIV* in 1998 to lend the WWE mainstream credibility and put Austin over as the next big star, the WWE was off to the races. The Rock and Triple H emerged that year, as well. Meanwhile, WCW seemingly had no idea what it was doing. They had a lot of talent on their roster, but they appeared to have no concept of what to do with it. The American Basketball Association (ABA) invented the Dunk Contest and it was a great idea. They had a lot of talent in that league, too. So did the United States Football League. Unfortunately, to defeat the supreme juggernaut of your sport, you have to have business people in charge that have a sound model for how they intend to succeed and remain successful. WCW, no more so than did the ABA or USFL, had no one who knew how to manage a wrestling business. They had a great idea – The New World Order – but they could not sustain the success that came with it.

McMahon, ever the master promoter, found something that worked, but kept searching for other things that worked like the sophomoric, but perfect for the target market faction known as Degeneration X (led first by Michaels; then by Triple H), the hardcore stylings of the Philadelphia-based Extreme Championship Wrestling, and the scantily clad crew of beautiful women that steamed up the screen. The next thing you knew, the WWE was every bit as talked about as it was a decade prior. They soundly defeated WCW from late 1998 on. It was a staggering turn of events. WCW rose to prominence in 1996 and was still dominating the ratings in what was dubbed "The Monday Night War" as of early 1998. Even when WWE started coming on strong, WCW still had a viable product to oppose them after they almost accidentally stumbled upon former Atlanta Falcon-turned-wrestling megastar, Bill Goldberg. In 2001, Vince McMahon bought WCW for a paltry $3 million. How quickly the mighty fell.

The WWE won what was an honest-to-goodness fight for survival. They were legitimately on the verge of going under in 1997, from all accounts. As a fan reflecting on that era, the WWE was fueled by the competition from WCW, giving rise to an internal competition that sparked some of the best individual work in wrestling history. The Rock was the definition of what the WWE envisioned when they coined the phrase "sports entertainment." Austin was the greatest era-specific star of all-time. Triple H was a modern day Flair. Mick Foley was a tremendous underdog on TV and a great ambassador for the sport off-camera, penning multiple New York Times bestselling books. Undertaker was completing the first of two incredible decades as the all-time most successful gimmick performer. When all was said and done, 45% of the top 20 in the WrestleMania Era either made it to the top or became prominent stars during that brief, three year period known in the WWE as "Attitude." Incredible.

There was a downside, though. With "Attitude" came a lot of poor booking decisions that led to some awful television. To hook viewers, they would do something outrageous – a strategy known as "shock TV." When the WWE was on fire, it did not matter. Unfortunately, when Rock and Austin left and the WWE completely botched the dream feud of WWE vs. WCW, the product cooled down and the mistakes became glaring. Mae Young – a Hall of Famer, but an old lady – got naked and eventually got pregnant with what turned out to be a plastic hand. Triple H, dressed as the masked character, Kane, got into a casket and pretended to make coitus with a girl that had, in storyline, been dead for years. Linda McMahon pretended to have a stroke, announcer Jim Ross was set on fire, Vince wrestled his daughter, porn star character Val Venis got his "penis chopped off," on-screen General Manager Eric Bischoff had women make out in segments called "Hot Lesbian Action," and on and on and on with TV that made me embarrassed to be a wrestling fan. I wish I was making that stuff up. It made me nearly give up on wrestling. Luckily, *WrestleMania X-8* happened. That night in 2002, The Rock battled a returning Hulk Hogan in a match for the ages that I will talk about with my grandkids in the same breath as Jordan's game-winner to win the 1998 NBA title and Notre Dame's undefeated 2012 regular season. Rock vs. Hogan solidified my status as a wrestling fan for life.

I was a freshman in college by the fall after *Mania X-8* and I needed something to keep my mind focused. Wrestling, just as it had navigated me through some awkward times in my youth, gave me a healthy distraction that wound up broadening my horizons. 2002 was also the year that Michaels came back from the injury that had sidelined him for the previous four years. He was better than ever, having a match at *Summerslam* with Triple H that was rivaled only by Rock-Hogan that year. The WWE also decided to split their roster, having accumulated the remnants of WCW to combine with their already stacked talent pool. *Raw* and *Smackdown* each hosted their own roster.

I particularly enjoyed the *Smackdown* brand, which featured in-ring performances of the highest caliber under the booking scheme of former Extreme Championship Wrestling head, Paul Heyman. *Smackdown* matches such as Edge vs. Kurt Angle, who became two of my favorites of all-time, appealed to me in the same way that Michaels and Hart matches had in the past. Angle was a 1996 Olympic Gold Medalist in freestyle wrestling for the United States and the most decorated amateur athlete ever to join the pro ranks. Along with Rey Mysterio, Chris Benoit, Eddie and Chavo Guerrero, Edge and Angle formed the "Smackdown Six" that would, on a weekly basis, combine for excellent matches.

    A sizeable portion of the viewing audience dropped off by 2003, along with most of my friends that had once been avid followers. My friend Jeff watched with me through our freshman year in college. His brother, Matt, introduced me to online wrestling coverage. The Pro Wrestling Torch, Wrestling Observer Newsletter, and Lordsofpain.net (LOP) became regular sites on my daily browsing list. I made a lot of pen pals through LOP. I came to think of these sites as the "Wrestling Media," given that the mainstream does not dedicate much critical opinion to sports entertainment. The PWTorch and Observer editors, Wade Keller and Dave Meltzer, actually started their newsletters as high school students who were huge wrestling fans. Each made careers out of providing a critical voice for pro wrestling, as well as behind-the-scenes news. They adopted rating systems to judge matches on a 0-5 star scale much like movie critics (longtime NWA and WWE manager, Jim Cornette, was said to have developed it). Their ratings opened a door to my analytical mind and I began to apply my adopted version of their system to the classics that I had grown up watching. Rating matches and studying wrestling became a hobby. I had a bevy of great talent to watch each week on the WWE shows, such as the Smackdown Six, Michaels, Taker, Triple H, Chris Jericho, and others. The internet opened the door to downloading matches from the past like Hart vs. British Bulldog in front of 80,000 people in London's Wembley Stadium back in '92, the Austin vs. Rock *WrestleMania* trilogy, Savage vs. Steamboat from *WrestleMania III*, and Macho Man vs. Ultimate Warrior from *WrestleMania VII* (one of history's most underrated classics).

After honing my star ratings scale, an opportunity knocked in 2004 while I was taking summer classes. An opening came available on LOP to review *Smackdown*, which had been my favorite WWE show since the brand split. I wrote a sample, sent it in, and got the position. For the next three years, I was LOP's go-to review man as it became a site with upwards of millions of viewers per day. I recapped the emerging John Cena's rise to main-event status. I saw him go from freestyle rapper to the face of the WWE from the summer of 2004 to the next. Cena, along with Randy Orton and Dave Batista, were the new stars that helped pull the WWE out of the post-Attitude Era lull. While I was transitioning from undergraduate to professional school, I was writing about wrestling every week. It was odd to have people seeking my thoughts on certain wrestling-related topics. It was and still is surreal. I wrote *Raw* and WWE PPV reviews in 2006, which made me one of the most visible wrestling writers on the internet. I made LOP the quickest place to get real time recaps and educated opinions for the WWE's flagship program and their PPVs. Tens of thousands were reading what I was writing. LOP's owner, Calvin Martin, would later compliment me as "one of the best ever."

Of all the storylines that I reviewed from 2004-2007, my favorite was the John Cena vs. Edge rivalry. They pushed each other to excel in a manner that reminded me of Austin, Rock, and Triple H from an era gone by. Cena became one of the top stars in industry lore and Edge a Hall of Famer. While watching and writing about Cena as he developed into the Hogan of his generation has been one of the most gratifying aspects of my "wrestling media" career, the most stunning was the tragic death of Eddie Guerrero. Eddie had been a wonderful story of redemption until his heart gave out in November 2005. His death was an important moment for pro wrestling. It prompted the WWE to implement its Wellness Policy that monitored prescription and other drug use (though Eddie was not on drugs when he died) and, in general, brought awareness to making sure that wrestler safety and health was more of a priority.

    Wrestling became less of a hobby and more of a passion during those years. When I moved to St. Louis, Missouri, on my own for the first time in my life, I targeted attending a *WrestleMania* as soon as possible. As luck would have it, Chicago – just a few hundred miles away - was the site of the next one. I was one of the 17,000 to secure tickets for *WrestleMania 22*, main-evented by Cena being passed the torch from Triple H. That was the night that Cena became "The Man" – the moniker given to the top wrestler of his generation so named because of Ric Flair's iconic catchphrase, "To be the man, you've gotta beat the man." Triple H had been the top star of the WWE's Monday night brand since the departure of his Attitude Era cohorts, helping the company through a difficult transition period. Cena helped shift the WWE back to its Hulkamania roots, with the product once again becoming family-friendly. He has been an excellent ambassador for the WWE, globalizing their brand more than ever before and taking WrestleMania to unprecedented heights. Mania has become a global pop culture event that draws people from all over the world, setting attendance records every year in stadium venues across the United States and Canada and making each host city $50-$200 million in local revenue.

    Going to WrestleMania was an unforgettable experience. My first one in 2006 was like getting a taste of a great bottle of wine; on a date night years back with Mrs. Doc, I picked up a bottle of French chenin blanc that blew us both away and we have regularly sought it out since. I have, similarly, been back four other times to WrestleMania and plan to go every few years for the rest of my life. For my second

"Show of Shows" excursion, I went with my dad to *WrestleMania XXIV* in Orlando. That was one of the top five experiences of my life. It was the night of Flair's retirement match. Just as we had sixteen years earlier when we sat in his apartment watching the *'92 Royal Rumble*, we watched Flair put on a show with Michaels. My dad passed away ten days after my daughter was born in 2012 (R.I.P.). I am glad he and I got to attend a Mania together; it was experiences like that one that fuel my desire to go back.

Attending *WrestleMania XXVII* in Atlanta was my wedding gift from my wife, Sarah. We watched Michaels, then retired for a year, get inducted into the 2011 Hall of Fame class on Saturday night and then attended the Georgia Dome show on Sunday, which was the final in-ring performance in Edge's career. Two of my best buddies from St. Louis, Drs. Jeff and Tony, accompanied me to a bit of a reunion weekend in 2013 for what I'd consider to be the best Hall of Fame Induction Ceremony of all-time and *WrestleMania XXIX* in New York/New Jersey. Then, my stepdad accompanied me to Dallas for *WrestleMania 32*. After reading the first edition of this book in 2013, he told me he would like to go to Mania with me someday. My mom later told me that he has never had more fun on a trip...and he is not even a wrestling fan! That is the awesomeness of WrestleMania, folks.

In 2010, I was preparing to open a private clinic in my hometown. Wrestling, once again, gave me an avenue to channel my stress. I started writing "The Doctor's Orders" for LOP and have been going strong ever since, offering an analytical view on current topics and an unmatched historical perspective. Along the way, I discovered that writing about wrestling is the very best stress management tool in my arsenal. I hope everyone can find constructive ways to take their minds off of the real world. Life is 10% what happens to us and 90% how we respond to it; writing, reading, sports, going to the gym

– whatever it may be – make time for it so you can be happy and healthy.

I published the first edition of this book in November 2013 as a tribute to *WrestleMania XXX* and have thoroughly enjoyed increased opportunities to write about and discuss WWE as a result. *Mania XXX* was as emotionally invested as I have been in wrestling as an adult; Daniel Bryan's improbable rise to the top peaked in the main-event by the standards to soon be defined by this book, but his journey to reach that pinnacle completely enveloped me as I again found myself in the target demographic of a new booking strategy at a time when WWE was beginning to economically boom again (seriously, check the numbers) with the launch of the WWE Network.

Back in 2011, CM Punk was given no bullet points for his show-closing promo on *Raw*, this particular episode being roughly a month before his WWE contract ran out. Frustrated by a system that he felt catered to a prototype no longer applicable to the times and with no intention of signing a new deal, Punk dropped what famously became known as "The Pipe Bomb" - a scathing review of McMahon's business model and an anthem, of sorts, for fans in-the-know. His words stirred the pot and earned him a ton of mainstream press. *Raw*, long-removed from the days when it was must-see TV, suddenly became very interesting. The "Reality Era" was born through the success that Punk achieved on the heels of his highly memorable interview.

Punk, similar in size to HBK, Hart, and Flair but whose heavily-tattooed body and piercings made him the antithesis of clean-cut, broke the mold. Aside from the famed Ohio Valley Wrestling developmental class of 2002 that produced Cena, Randy Orton, Dave Batista, and Brock Lesnar, WWE had struggled to produce fresh top-level talent. WCW's demise eliminated what had been WWE's primary source for acquiring new stars; instead of seek out the best wrestlers from the independent wrestling promotions that emerged as the secondary companies in the aftermath of WCW's death, WWE tried to pull needles out of figurative haystacks. Until Bryan main-evented *WrestleMania XXX*, the only wrestler who debuted after 2002 to achieve wrestling's highest honor, post-Attitude, was The Miz in 2011. Part of that, in fairness, was due to Cena et al being a special group, but it was also heavily influenced by a failure to develop top-tier wrestlers for almost a decade. CM Punk, recruited out of Ring of Honor, changed the perception that an "indy darling" did not have what it took to be an elite WWE Superstar. From mid-2011 to his self-imposed departure in early 2014, Punk was one of the Top 5 biggest names in the industry (and what my buddy Mattberg described as a "fan anchor" – a wrestler who was good enough to keep you engaged in WWE even if the overall product was lacking).

Bryan kicked down the door that Punk had cracked open. Despite his smallish stature, he became the everyman to a generation of fans like myself who knew the deck was stacked against him but witnessed firsthand as he did everything WWE asked him to do in order to go from just a great technical wrestler to a great entertainer who also happened to be arguably the world's best wrestler. He became the most popular star since Guerrero and the most genuinely over babyface since Austin. His "Yes! Movement," as it was termed, was a phenomenon that went beyond WWE's scope. The diehard, "internet" wrestling fan both fairly and unfairly has a bad reputation but, at its heart, simply wants the guy who most deserves it to get to the top. Bryan deserved it and the support for him swelled to astronomical levels when it briefly looked as though he was not going to be in the *WrestleMania XXX* main-event when it clearly seemed like his time to shine.

The Reality Era got its name for taking backstage rumors and using them against those that read them, what my pal and fellow DPC author, Samuel 'Plan (*101 WWE Matches To See*

Before You Die), refers to as "neo-kayfabe" – rebuilding a version of the veil of illusion stripped away in eras gone by that better suits the digital age where information is so readily available to anyone that wants it. The Authority, Triple H and Stephanie McMahon, brilliantly utilized this new age version of an old school philosophy to perpetuate the perception of Bryan's inherent disadvantages. Bryan's journey to winning the WWE World Heavyweight Championship in New Orleans was the peak of that era.

The heights reached by Punk and Bryan altered WWE's new wrestler-acquisition strategy. Triple H took over the talent development department in WWE and spearheaded the construction of their state-of-the-art Performance Center based in Orlando, giving rise to NXT. The Game has many fans excited about the future of the business on his watch. NXT exploded when it began airing on WWE Network, its presentation of a simpler, more wrestling-focused program has truly resonated with the diehard sect of the fanbase. For years, I kept openly wondering if an alternative to WWE-proper would emerge; it seems as if WWE themselves stumbled upon it with NXT.

The first class of wrestlers from the revised developmental system to emerge on *Raw* and *Smackdown* had a distinct aura about them, making clear that the changes down in Orlando were yielding significant results. Roman Reigns, Seth Rollins, Dean Ambrose, and Bray Wyatt burst onto the scene hungry to supplant the previous generations and redefine the industry's standard of excellence. Time will tell if they can achieve their lofty goal, but they have unquestionably cleared a path on which subsequent main roster rookie classes have joined them. They are ushering in their own era and forging a revised historical context for WWE. I am at a stage in my life now when I appreciate more than ever before getting to watch their journeys and talk about them in columns, podcasts, and books.

The WrestleMania Era: The Book of Sports Entertainment

The success of *The WrestleMania Era* (I humbly thank you all) sparked interest in a spin-off series that provides greater detail to the rankings you will soon read; *The Greatest Champions* was published in 2016 with *The Greatest Draws* up next on the docket. I had an e-book published about the rivalry between Jim Crockett and Vince McMahon called *Starrcade vs. WrestleMania: The Prelude to the Monday Night Wars*. I have also been working on a massive project that will take an in-depth, analytical look at the greatest rivalries and matches of the WrestleMania Era.

In 2013, I started recording a weekly podcast as part of a collaborative project with our incredibly talented crew at LOP. I do not believe that there is a better group of wrestling podcasters in the world. Personally, I had been told since I was a teenager that I had a great radio voice, so it has been a lot of fun to test those figurative waters and find that I could swim pretty well. An added bonus has been that, as extracurricular time has decreased with my clinic's growth and my family's expansion, the podcast has been a great outlet to express my weekly wrestling thoughts. "The Doc Says..." can be found on the LOP Radio station on Blog Talk Radio, airing every Wednesday, and can also be downloaded through iTunes, Stitcher, etc. If you enjoy my brand of insight via the written word, I am confident that you would enjoy my podcast too.

It is safe to state that the "wrestling bug," at least for me, has no cure. Somehow, pro wrestling managed to become a huge part of my life and helped keep me sane through the trials and tribulations. As my professional and family life has grown, writing about wrestling has become my little escape from the rest of the world. Though other sports occupy sizeable portions of my extracurricular time, I have never gotten the itch to write about them. As much as I love college football season, the NBA Playoffs, March Madness, the World Cup, and Olympics, none of them sparked a journalistic urge. Over the years, I have come to greatly appreciate historical context in the sports that I enjoy. I like to dive into the past to help put the present into deeper perspective. I often write my columns with an eye on history, having seen so much of pro wrestling lore and shared so many birthdays with WrestleMania these past thirty plus years.

The Criteria

  The first several months of prep work for this book revolved around determining the details of the ranking system. A five-tiered breakdown, including titles, main-events, box office success, critical performance ratings, and a score of the pure essentials of pro wrestling (physique, ability to verbally sell oneself, and wrestling acumen), ensured a thorough analysis. It also limited the talent pool to the WrestleMania Era. I flirted with the idea of creating the ultimate fan account of pro wrestling's entire history but, without the requisite ability to judge the skills of a past superstar through a firsthand account combined with the vast differences in pro wrestling's first eighty years versus its last thirty, it was an easy decision to stick to what I have seen. The fiscal priorities have changed so much since McMahon took over the wrestling world. TV ratings and pay-per-view buyrates, much more so than general ticket sales for a live gate, reigned supreme for much of the last three decades until the WWE Network took traditional PPV's place in the hierarchy. Statistical analysis of different eras is partly predicated on the same set of data points being transferrable from past to present. Attendance figures are available dating back to the days of wrestling's first recognized World Heavyweight Champion, George Hackenschmidt. However, you cannot accurately compare the business impact of Hackenschmidt, Jim Londos, Ed Lewis, Lou Thesz, or Bruno Sammartino to Hulk Hogan, Steve Austin, Dwayne "The Rock" Johnson, or John Cena due to the stark differences in the other data.

  I have seen arguments made that you could bring Lewis or Thesz into the modern environment and they would succeed as much as modern stars. I, personally, would (maybe) assume that to be true, but statistics do not assume. It is nothing but conjecture. What I do know, definitively, is that you could take Hogan, Austin, Rock, Cena, and other modern stars, plop them into Madison Square Garden during their respective primes and have a sellout like Sammartino was known for drawing. I have the proof. What I do not know, definitively, is whether or not we could take Sammartino, once the champion of the northeast territory for over 4,000 days, plop him in Sun Life Stadium in the main-event at *WrestleMania XXVIII* and expect him to both draw 78,000 people for the live gate and 1.3 million buyers on PPV.

In baseball, home runs, batting average, and RBIs have been accounted for since the infancy of the game as we know it. Wins and losses, of course, are the biggest era-to-era figure in team sports, allowing comparisons between the 69 win Lakers that won 33 straight in 1972 and the '96 Bulls that won 72 games. The fact that winning the World Series or an NBA title was every bit as important decades ago as it is today is a significant point that bridges the time specific gap and allows for historians to converse about Babe Ruth vs. Barry Bonds or Bill Russell vs. Michael Jordan. Wrestling does not have those types of stats.

My goal in the selection criteria was not to be purely objective, but rather to create a hybrid of objectivity and subjectivity – objective subjectivism, as I like to call it - that used available numbers across the board to help with the details. Through plain observation, a fan that studies the wrestling business can come up with the top twenty or thirty, but separation amongst those wrestlers requires a greater attention to detail. Statistics were vital in shaping the definitive list. In order to be objectively subjective, I decided to stick to an era that I have seen with my own two eyes. I have seen everything that there is to see between *Starrcade '83* to *WrestleMania 32*. Wrestler eligibility was determined solely on what he contributed to the WrestleMania Era. However, once deemed eligible, relevant pre-1983 statistics were included for wrestlers such as Harley Race or Bob Backlund whose best work occurred prior to that period.

The next big decision concerned which promotions to incorporate. I limited the initial landscape to the United States and Canada, which regularly featured the WWE and WCW. The 1980s had a strong third wheel organization in Verne Gagne's American Wrestling Association that was shown on ESPN in the flagship cable sports network's early years. The 1990s had an influential #3 in Extreme Championship Wrestling. ECW had a cult-like following that eventually grew substantially, earning its own TV deal and featuring several pay-per-views. The 2000s saw the rise of Total Nonstop Action Wrestling as well as smaller outfits such as Ring of Honor to the scene in the wake of WCW's 2001 collapse.

After careful consideration, I excluded wrestlers who made the AWA, ECW, or TNA their primary workplaces. The bottom line was that the WWE and WCW raided the best talents from the AWA and ECW with one particularly noteworthy exception: Nick Bockwinkel, the all-time industry great who made his mark in the 1970s as the sophisticated heel champion of the AWA. He was the greatest casualty of this decision. However, I did not fail to take into account the quality or importance of the work done in the AWA or ECW by any wrestler that achieved fame in the top two promotions. TNA and ROH are such distant second and thirds to the WWE in current times that the financial importance of its top stars did not compare. Thus, neither was taken into account. I likened my decision to Bill Simmons deciding to limit his ranking of basketball players primarily to their accomplishments in the NBA and the ABA, while merely making mention of standout collegiate careers.

Then, there was the issue of whether or not to separate certain tag teams. Tag team wrestling has been unable to maintain a level of consistent importance in the last thirty years, rendering its place in the eyes of the fans far less consequential than singles wrestling. Nevertheless, several tag teams have made sizeable contributions that rival their singles counterparts in modern wrestling lore. I based the choice to divide tag teams in the rankings simply on whether or not a member of the team won a World Heavyweight (singles) Championship in the WrestleMania Era. If he did, he and his partner were split. For instance, Jeff Hardy was a three-time World Champion, so he and his brother, Matt, were considered separately.

One of my biggest struggles was determining how many wrestlers to include. It came about organically, after six months of nothing but research, to go with three tiers of thirty wrestlers each for a total of ninety. Reflecting back on that decision years later for the 3rd edition, I just cannot imagine giving an accurate historical account of the WrestleMania Era by discussing merely a few dozen wrestlers; too many stars have provided too many memories.

I did not actually start writing until 2012. From June 2011 until the New Year, I did research only. The objective subjectivism first came into play with my initial rankings draft. I looked at the rough numbers, which were eventually refined numerous times (and have continued to go under my own yearly microscope), and used the eyeball test to put together each tier. It was only when I felt comfortable with the three tiers that I began writing. The final rankings were based mostly on the statistics – and there were some surprises – but remember that this list is not purely objective; it is objectively subjective!

The following is a specific breakdown of each criterion:

Main-Event/Headlining Factor

Only a handful of superstars ever make it to the elite of their sport. In wrestling, being in the top billed match at *WrestleMania* is the pinnacle, just as being in the Super Bowl is for the NFL, the Finals are for the NBA, the Stanley Cup Finals for the NHL, and the UEFA Champions' League final for the

European club soccer teams. There have been outstanding players in those respective sports that never made it to the biggest game/series and, while you cannot, consequently, consider them at the end of the discussion for the best of the best, they still deserve mention amongst the elite.

In basketball, winning an NBA Championship has become a prerequisite in most discussions about the best player ever. Karl Malone was a two-time Most Valuable Player and is the second all-time leading scorer in the NBA, but he never won a title; missing from his still incredibly decorated resume is that elusive championship ring and he should rightly be passed by many of peers who earned the premiere achievement in the sport accordingly.

WrestleMania changed sports entertainment. I once read an old school member of the wrestling fraternity suggest that there were plenty of WrestleManias before there was the actual *WrestleMania*. Yeah, and there were a lot of bowl games before there was one labeled "Super." *WrestleMania* stands alone. Sure, there were other stadium shows with 70,000 people jam packed to the last nosebleed seat, but with the "Super Bowl of Professional Wrestling" came the combination of an enormous gate along with national closed-circuit TV feeds, soon afterward, pay-per-view, and now the WWE Network. That is not to mention the national (and eventually international) media attention. *WrestleMania* is so far beyond anything that came before it on every scale imaginable. Wrestling in the main-event at *Mania* is sport entertainment's Holy Grail.

Having cards that were clearly designated as bigger than others raised the stakes, making them more profitable and increasing the competition beyond the last match or the match for the title and into the upper mid-card, where men like Undertaker have thrived for most of their careers. A super card gives added layers to the presentation than your standard, "main-event with an undercard" from the old days. People are paying to see more than just a single match, even if that single bout is the primary purchasing reason. Edge, Chris Jericho, Randy Savage, Mick Foley, and Sting are other examples of stars that made big names for themselves as headliners, but were not often counted upon to be the primary draw for their promotions.

What separates the Main-Event/Headlining factor from financial statistics is longevity. Unlike with the business data, the number of major shows headlined is cumulative. Steve Austin cannot be faulted for having a main-event shelf life of just six (off and on) years, but it also cannot be ignored. Undertaker has been headlining for over *twenty-five* years. That has to account for something and is why he is #1 in that category. You could argue that, because of longevity, Emmitt Smith was better than Barry Sanders in the NFL discussion of "best all-time running backs." Sanders retired in his prime and did not accumulate the numbers. In some ways, Sanders was superior, but longevity hurts his argument. The same applies to the Austin-Taker debate.

The other difference is parity – a balance of talent spread across a show. Wrestling has achieved it through super cards. Just as not everyone can be MJ or Lebron, not everyone can be Austin or Cena. Austin and Cena may get the bulk of the credit for the business success of their time, but other guys deserve credit for their contributions to PPV cards, as well. A super card is just a card without the secondary headliners to compliment the main-event.

The main-event/headlining statistic was shaped by a hierarchy for the major events in WWE and WCW. In crunching the numbers, *WrestleMania* was weighted as the clear cut, top card to main-event or headline, with *Starrcade* and *Summerslam* next, followed by *The Royal Rumble, The Great American Bash, Halloween Havoc,* and *Survivor Series*. Other monthly PPVs were accounted for, but on a lesser scale than the major shows.

Business Factor

Until 2014, two dominant constants had emerged on the business side of wrestling: television and PPV. I took the TV ratings and PPV data and weighted them equally for comparative purposes. Originally, PPV was separated into two categories to account for differences in availability from one era to the next: buyrates (greater during a time when fewer households had access) and total number of buys (greater once virtually everyone had access). Hogan vs. Andre at *WrestleMania III* drew a record buy<u>rate</u> of 10.2, meaning that 10% of the potential customers with PPV access ordered the event. That was astounding and will never be topped. However, Rock vs. Cena at *WrestleMania XXVIII* drew a record 1.3 million <u>buyers</u> across the globe and Rock vs. Austin at *WrestleMania X-Seven* set the record for domestic buys. In the 80s and early 90s, the buyrates were much bigger. From the late 90s onward, the numbers of buys were bigger. The rates for *Mania X-Seven and Mania XXVIII* do not even come close to 10.2, but they each earned far greater actual numbers of buys than *Mania III*.

The WWE Network changed the game, creating an interesting wrinkle for data analysis unique to the rest of the WrestleMania Era. It used to be that, for example, "The Show of Shows" would routinely double the amount of PPV buys of the second biggest drawing card of the year (often the Rumble from the late 2000s on). However, with nearly 1.5 million subscribers as of mid-2016, a similar number of people who would watch WrestleMania on the Network would hypothetically watch the Rumble too, or Money in the Bank or Hell in a Cell for that matter; to borrow a term from the PPV era, the "buyrate" for each show has become uniform thanks to the Network. Consider that WrestleMania only drew over a million buys five times and that, after the Network became available to most of the world by mid-2015, well over a million people could watch every special event.

Comparing the Network and the PPV models, then, is like weighing Redbox, an a la carte movie vendor, against Netflix, a subscription service that allows you to watch as many movies (among other things) as you want for a set fee. From 1987 to 2013, WWE was dependent upon new titles from their Big 3 PPV franchises to earn most of the revenue like Redbox is dependent upon popular new releases to drive its business. Examining that fiscal style, WrestleMania in the PPV era was like *Stars Wars: The Force Awakens* coming out on DVD/Blu-Ray. Netflix, meanwhile, thrives off the combination of new releases and original content; WWE Network is similarly successful because it offers the works – new content, archived shows, and the newest titles in their monthly special event series.

It was a brilliant, forward-thinking move by WWE, but it represents such a stark contrast to the old way that it made it necessary to formulate a system for measuring individual economic stimulation by a wrestler in the Network era, particularly as it pertained to contrasting that financial influence to that of a peer from the PPV era.

The difference in TV ratings over the last thirty years creates for an increasingly interesting discussion and must be accounted for as well. In the Attitude Era, technology had improved and cable TV ratings were king versus the Hulkamania era's dependence on network ratings. Domestic ratings, determined by Nielsen, were substantial in both periods. Today, the ratings are much smaller, but the broadcast for WWE's *Raw* spans the globe and can be accessed through so many different avenues.

In the new system for analysis, PPV buys were averaged by year to reflect the willingness of fans to monetarily invest in the wrestling product and coefficients (1-5, with 1 lowest and 5 highest) were assigned to establish a hierarchy between eras; for instance, 1999-2002 (5) was an outstandingly consistent time for WWE on PPV, while 1995-1997 (1) was their worst stretch ever. The same exercise was repeated for TV ratings. Wrestlers were then ranked according to their main-event stats to determine a Top 5 pecking order for each year and were scored based on the combination of their positions and the PPV and TV coefficients of their zenith years; Austin, for example, was the #1 star during two years ('99 and '01) when both TV and PPV numbers were at their historical peak, while his third best year ('98) saw peak TV ratings but historically above-average PPV buys. The WWE Network, due to its undeniable success in keeping fans investing and re-investing, was put on equal ground with '99-'02 in the PPV hierarchy, but abysmal ratings in 2015 and 2016 kept the TV numbers on-par with the all-time worst eras.

The other two common themes from era-to-era over the last three decades were merchandise sales and live events. Live events were not considered due to their dwindling significance to the bottom line. Though they are still important, PPV and TV remain the best ways to calculate historical rankings amongst the top stars of the last three decades. Merchandise sales were used as more of a tiebreaker in cases that were too close to call.

It was an interesting race for #1 between usual suspects Hogan and Austin, along with a resurgence from the time the initial data collection started to the time it finished from Dwayne "The Rock" Johnson, whose record setting *WrestleMania* trio propelled him from distant third to very much in the discussion.

Performance Factor

No statistic better defines "objective subjectivism" than the star ratings used to judge the quality of wrestling matches. Just as in the movies, it is an inexact science. The scale that I have developed over the years takes into account – in no particular order - the length of a match, the atmosphere (including pre-match hype), the crowd's reaction, the execution of the moves performed, the dramatic effect of the plot twists and false finishes/near falls (moments in the match where you believe that the end has come, but it does not), the wrestler's ability to sell his opponent's offense, and facial expressions/reactions.

As in the movies, a longer match allows for a more thorough tale to be told in the ring, so rarely is a five-star match (the ultimate critical achievement in wrestling) less than 20-minutes in length and more often is closer to thirty-minutes (or longer); there are exceptions, of course, but it is hard to tell a brilliant story without time. The atmosphere created by the hype surrounding two wrestlers can enhance or hinder a performance, as failing to meet, meeting, or exceeding expectations can help shape one's opinion of a match. The crowd reaction is immensely important, for the wrestler's play off the audience to help them determine what they want to do. It can also enhance a match, though I do not usually allow it to, as strongly, hinder a rating. The false finish or plot twist adds a layer of drama and helps further invest the viewer and helps the wrestlers separate the beginning of the match through its progressions to the climax. The selling, expressions, and execution by the wrestlers are prerequisite to a successful performance, as they are key elements to telling a story.

For this category, I took the best star-rated matches for each performer and simply added them together, increasing the sample size in the final rankings for the 31-60 and 1-30 tiers to include more matches. Shawn Michaels was #1, not surprisingly.

Championship Factor

Just as in any other sport, championships are vital to wrestling. Generally, there is not a more important role in the business than being the World Champion. When a wrestler reaches that pinnacle, he becomes a face of the brand. The only higher honor to achieve in wrestling is to be in the main-event at WrestleMania. In the old days, being the champion often meant wearing the gold around your waist for a year or longer. That has happened just twice in the last sixteen years. Title changes occurred more frequently beginning in the early 90s and hit arguably ridiculous proportions during the Attitude Era. Thus, a yearlong-plus title reign from pre-1991 must be weighed against the 1992-present title reigns which have been much shorter. It is not fair for Sheamus's first three reigns as a World Champ that lasted a combined 10 months to be given more credence than the single, 10-month title reign that Ultimate Warrior had from 1990-1991.

I also wanted to make sure that I gave credit where it was due to the secondary titleholders. Championships such as the Intercontinental, United States, and Tag Team titles have held various degrees of importance over the years, with the creative effort put into their respective divisions often waning from year-to-year (particularly since the Attitude Era), but they have also been stepping stones for future World Champions. The majority of the top thirty stars of the WrestleMania Era held mid-card titles before becoming main-eventers.

Since it would not reflect accurately the historical context of a wrestler if more credit was given for holding multiple titles in multiple divisions, that was another dynamic to consider. For instance, Booker T held nearly thirty titles in his career, but that does not make him a bigger star than Hulk Hogan, who held just thirteen but spent the majority of his time as a World Champion. Thus, being a World Champion was weighted most heavily, followed by the IC and US titles, and then the Tag titles. Belts such as the Cruiserweight, European, or Hardcore championships were not taken into account. Booker T still ranked seventh in the title stats, but he did not beat out Hogan.

I developed the "Title Formula" to account for the lengths of the reigns, giving maximum credit to Hogan and Ric Flair, each of whom had single World Championship reigns of over 500 days. The formula breaks down as follows:

(3 pts for being World Champion) X [(# of reigns of 119 days or fewer X 1) + (# of reigns of 120 days or greater X 2) + (# of reigns of 270 days or more X 3) + (# of reigns of 540 days or more X 4)]

+

(2 pts for being IC/US Champion) X [(# of reigns of 119 days or fewer X 1) + (# of reigns of 120 days or greater X 2) + (# of reigns of 210 days or more X 3) + (# of reigns of 300 days or more X 4)]

+

(1 pt for being Tag Team Champion) X [(# of reigns of 119 days or fewer X 1) + (# of reigns of 120 days or greater X 2) + (# of reigns of 210 days or more X 3) + (# of reigns of 300 days or more X 4)]

"Bret Hart" Wrestler Score

In Bret Hart's enthralling autobiography, he lets us in on a scoring system that he developed to assess wrestlers, breaking down a talent into three, 1-10 scales concerning his/her physique, microphone skills, and in-ring abilities. I made the decision to add his system to my evaluation because of the fact that, in order to write a thorough report of the best of the WrestleMania Era, there had to be consideration for how wrestlers would rank if we stripped things down to the basic elements necessary to be successful. One would like to assume that the cream of the crop always rises to the top, but that is not always the case due to the strong political undertones in the wrestling business. Many a great performer was doomed to a place on the card beneath their ceiling because he could not catch a break from the people whose opinions mattered most.

There is also the age old discussion among fans about which wrestlers would have been World Champions in an era when the title was awarded to different superstars with greater frequency. Take "Ravishing" Rick Rude, for instance. He was a fantastic performer and it has largely been agreed upon by the wrestling media that, if Rude's career had peaked during the second boom instead of the first, he would have surely been a World Heavyweight titleholder. He was still a Top 5 star in WWE during two huge years, but his resume is weakened by never winning the big one – even if the reason why basically boils down to "they rarely switched the championship back then." Alas, there has to be a way to even the statistical playing field.

Since the WrestleMania Era saw the breakdown of the professional wrestling scene from dozens of regional territories spread across the United States and Canada to two major promotions through the 1990s and, now, just one mainstream wrestling company, the destinies of potential superstars have been put into the hands of a very few men and women. Thus, the "Blatantly Stolen from Bret Hart Wrestler Scoring System" intends to add a component of pure skill to the equation. Not surprisingly, many of the top 30 of the last 30 years are featured in the top of this category. Yet, there are also a number of talents, such as Rude, "Mr. Perfect" Curt Hennig, Jake "The Snake" Roberts, John "Bradshaw" Layfield, and Barry Windham, who had top 20 Wrestler Scores but whose careers suffered in the other categories for various reasons.

One Last Note

The combination of the five factors makes some of the results that you will read eye-opening, at times to the point that you may want to chokeslam this book through the fiery pits of hell. Please do me this one favor, though...if you feel that way after the entire book has been read, contact me (page 4) and we will discuss your points. After all, this book is meant to evoke passionate conversation about the first of wrestling's two great questions: who is the greatest of all-time? We have a while before we get to the definitive answer. For the purpose of both celebrating history and establishing context for the all-important Top 10 ever and ultimately #1, I invite you on a journey through the pantheon of the WrestleMania Era.

The Third-Tier

#90: Raven

While I was not a part of the "Revolution" known as Extreme Championship Wrestling, I became quite fond of it as soon as the WWE released the *Rise and Fall of ECW* DVD in 2004. It took one viewing of that documentary, along with my subsequent study of the promotion's best matches, to make me a huge fan. I was particularly enthralled with ECW's most psychologically brilliant character, Raven (real name Scott Levy). He perfectly exemplified the renegade promotion, which placed a premium on unique, wildly creative personas in need of an environment fit for pushing the envelope.

After early 90s stops in WCW and WWE as Scotty Flamingo and Johnny Polo, respectively, Levy came to ECW under the name Raven (a tribute to the poem by Edgar Allen Poe and inspired by Patrick Swayze's "Bode" from the film, *Point Break*). Paul Heyman, the former on-screen manager for WCW turned promoter for ECW, saw the potential in Levy and turned him loose.

If ECW was analogous to a cult classic movie such as *The Usual Suspects*, then Raven was its Verbal Kint/Keyser Soze. The depths of Raven's psyche ran deeper than most superstars seen on mainstream wrestling television. The very appreciative and incredibly enthusiastic Philadelphia fanbase made Raven's intelligent, often poetic character a cult icon in response to his feuds with The Sandman and Tommy Dreamer.

The storylines in ECW were influential in their adult-oriented nature during an era when the WWE and WCW were cartoonish and geared toward children. Some might argue, though, that they took things a little too far at times. Kurt Angle, a Pennsylvania-born and bred Olympic Gold Medalist and future pro star, would certainly take that position. He showed up on a night when Raven fought Sandman, whose wife and son had already been turned against him by Raven's manipulation.

The feud escalated to a level that Angle was embarrassed to be associated. Raven "crucified" Sandman in a controversial plot twist that drew plenty of attention to ECW.

The best feud in ECW's history was Raven vs. Tommy Dreamer. Dreamer, ECW's hardcore folk hero, was billed as Levy's childhood friend. In their matches, Raven defeated Dreamer (literally) every single time for two years. WCW caught wind of the work that Raven was doing, saw dollar signs, and inked him to a new contract, prompting ECW to feature one final battle between him and Dreamer before he left for the big time. The crowd for that match was off the charts. I think the fans that made the ECW Arena their weekly hangout knew that they were a part of something special, but I have often wondered if any of them recognized that the style that ECW made famous was not sustainable and, thus, tried to enjoy every second of it while it lasted. On that night, Dreamer finally defeated Raven after a very emotional match.

Raven left for WCW as a two-time ECW World Heavyweight Champion and debuted in 1997 surrounded by several other wrestlers known as "The Flock" (a spinoff of his ECW faction, "The Nest"). In his story-based contract, a stipulation was included that all of his matches were contested as No Disqualification (or "Raven's Rules"). WCW had the smarts to transplant the Raven of ECW onto their show. You would be surprised how many times a major promotion failed to do the same.

It was in a 1998 match with Chris Benoit that Raven started to take off. He ultimately passed out while locked in the Crippler Crossface, but he was sadistically smiling right before losing consciousness. He may have been defeated, but all anyone was talking about afterwards was Raven. People wanted to know what he was all about.

The biggest moment of his career came during a two night stretch on April 19 and 20, 1998. At *Spring Stampede* on the 19th, Raven captured the highest championship honor of his career when he defeated Diamond Dallas Page for the WCW United States Championship. On the April 20th *Nitro*, he defended the newly won gold against the undefeated, 74-0 Goldberg. The bout was hyped throughout the show and was Goldberg's first major title match and he mowed through Raven in just a few minutes. Nevertheless, Raven was instrumental in boosting Goldberg's profile and keeping his momentum on the upswing.

The aftermath of the US title win/loss prompted the beginning of the end for Raven in WCW. He had been openly abusive to his "Flock," but the cruelty hit its crescendo after the 4/20/98 *Nitro*. One of the key members, Perry Saturn, took the brunt of the blame for Raven's defeat. His subsequent retaliation against Raven was one of the better storylines in WCW leading to one of 1998's better matches in the promotion. At *Fall Brawl*, Saturn defeated Raven, stipulating that "The Flock" disband. Just like that, roughly a year and a half after his WCW return, Raven's run as a major player ended. He fell off the face of the earth until returning to WWE in 2000 to become a record-holding 27-time Hardcore champion in the days where the title was defended, according to storyline, 24 hours a day / 7 days a week (the 24/7 rule). Sans for one very good match at *Backlash '01* against former ECW Champion, Rhyno, he never really found his place in the WWE. His last significant contribution to mainstream pro wrestling came in the independent promotion, Ring of Honor, during which time he feuded with a young CM Punk in a storyline that helped develop Punk's persona and prepare it for the WWE.

Raven's legacy will be that of a creative savant who challenged his peers with some of the most mentally stimulating storylines of all-time, making him an important figure in what is considered to be the greatest era in professional wrestling history.

"Quoth the Raven, Nevermore."

#89: The Honky Tonk Man

One word that describes why Raven's place in history is secure is "transcendent." His most relevant run in the mainstream was not long, but it was distinguished. Some men do not need a decade to put together a body of work fit for the Hall of Fame. Others do not even require five years. Yet, there is one man, who refers to himself as the "greatest Intercontinental Champion of all-time," that put together the bulk of his legendary career in one very historically significant 454 day period.

Debuting in 1986, The Honky Tonk Man garnered major attention for smashing a guitar over the head of Jake "The Snake" Roberts. Alongside annoying manager, Jimmy Hart, the evil Elvis impersonator gained traction in the ensuing feud with Roberts that ultimately helped him ascend to Intercontinental Championship-contending status. The Intercontinental title, circa 1987, was one of the hottest titles in all of professional wrestling. Coming off the classic *WrestleMania III* match that saw Ricky "The Dragon" Steamboat defeat then champion "Macho Man" Randy Savage, the Intercontinental belt was quite coveted. Savage used the notoriety from that title bout to become WWE Champion; Steamboat used it to earn the NWA World title. The IC strap was #3 in the industry.

Honky defeating Roberts at *Mania III*, especially considering that one of the more notable celebrities involved in the event, Alice Cooper, was in The Snake's corner, was an important moment. Roberts was quickly becoming the third most popular star in the WWE, so the victory over him gave Honky the momentum to be given a match for the Intercontinental title.

On *Superstars* in June of 1987, Honky cheated to win the title from the champion, Steamboat. Often in wrestling, you can sense when a title change is imminent, but that match did not give the impression that Steamboat was set to lose considering that he had chased the title for months and overcome a major storyline injury to win it. To that point, the ten previous IC champs had average title reigns of 307 days. Steamboat was champion for merely 65 days.

Looking at his face after the victory, it was not as if Honky appeared elated so much as he expressed the same emotion as the rest of the viewing audience: shock. "What," his expression seemed to question; "I won?" Indeed, Honky Tonk, "What!? *YOU* won?!" Nevertheless, beating The Snake and The Dragon in a span of three months ratcheted up his standing tremendously.

For one year, two months, and twenty-seven days, Honky Tonk was the Intercontinental Champion. The defining feud of his career – one that was very important to the history of the WWE – took place during his reign. When Honky first prematurely declared himself "the greatest Intercontinental Champion of all-time," Randy Savage took issue and received quite an ovation from the crowd despite his recent standing as the consummate bad guy. It was sort of the perfect storm. Honky was on the rise and really getting under people's skin, while Savage was so charismatic that his popularity was looking for an excuse to skyrocket.

No one could have predicted that Honky Tonk and Macho Man would have set the stage for Savage to become one of the all-time great superstars. With each disqualification or count out victory for Honky in their matches for the IC title, they had the people clamoring to see Savage win back the strap. The feud ended with a match that took place on the highest rated television program in the history of professional wrestling. February 1988's "The Main-Event" was built around the showdown between Hulk Hogan and Andre the Giant, but the second biggest match on that card was Savage's last ditch attempt to regain the IC title. Listening to the crowd during the match gave you everything you needed to know about Honky's importance in getting Macho to the precipice of WrestleMania glory (Macho won the WWE title at *Mania IV* six weeks later).

The 454th day of Honky's record setting reign was shared with the day of the first *Summerslam* PPV in August '88. *Summerslam* was hyped as having a surprise opponent for the champ. Honky's time as a top star came to an end that night, but not before he helped put over another of the era's mega stars in the making. It took just 30 seconds for The Ultimate Warrior to destroy Honky and take the title.

He once challenged Hulk Hogan for the WWE title on a network television special and was a Tag Team title contender as a member of "Rhythm and Blues," but The Honky Tonk Man will always best be known for being the Intercontinental Champion. His record stands to this day.

#88: The Rock 'N Roll Express

Heavy metal hair bands were one of the hallmarks of the 1980s, putting a new spin on the rock 'n roll genre. Professional wrestlers share a bond with the stars of the music industry, as they live a similar lifestyle of partying and performing while traveling from town to town (or at least they used to). Being kindred spirits, wrestling promoters have often worked with music moguls to bring various artists into the fold for major events. On occasion, some in the sports entertainment industry have ventured out and had success on the music scene as well.

So, it should come as no surprise that, from the "birthplace of rock 'n roll" - Memphis, Tennessee - came the spawn of wrestling and music's relationship in the team of Ricky Morton and Robert Gibson. Sporting the look of two once well-toned rockers with thinning but still glamorous hairdos ravaged by years of drinking, they made a splash in the south as "The Rock 'N Roll Express" and became one of the greatest tag teams of the decade. Their exciting style in the ring combined with the "us against them" culture of metal rock made them the ideal babyfaces. They would draw females who thought their gimmick had sex appeal (despite both being average looking) and the males would dig their association with a popular music type and their flashy, in-ring move set. Their connection to the crowds was second to none.

Morton and Gibson were trendsetters. Two tag teams patterned after The Rock 'N Roll Express included The Hardy Boys of the Attitude Era and The (Midnight) Rockers of the AWA and WWE, the latter blatantly copying them. Shawn Michaels and Marty Jannetty dressed the same as Morton and Gibson and, if you look at the things that Jannetty, in particular, did well, they were almost exactly like the things that Gibson did well. The Rockers were like a new rival band coming onto the airwaves that did all the same things as the old guard, but just rocked a little bit harder. I suppose that imitation is the sincerest form of flattery. Gibson and Morton can take solace in the fact that they were the far more accomplished duo, racking up four reigns as World Tag Team Champions to the Rockers zero.

In terms of their impact, The Hardys would make a better comparison. Morton and Gibson were stars in the NWA when the promotion was leaning on tag team wrestling to be the main or semi-main-event. Whether it was against The Russians or The Andersons, The Rock 'N Roll Express were not curtain jerkers keeping the crowd interested until Hulk Hogan or Randy Savage made their appearances (as were The Rockers). They, as The Hardys did during the Attitude Era, were involved in top feuds with or without the Tag titles on the line. They took top billing over Tully Blanchard and Magnum TA's famous "I Quit" match at *Starrcade '85*, main-eventing the Greensboro portion of the event against Ivan and Nikita Koloff. A year later, they defeated The Andersons in a classic Steel Cage match at *Starrcade '86*.

The competition was stiff for the top babyface spot in the NWA and they often took a backseat to The Road Warriors since Hawk and Animal were so unique for their time. Nevertheless, they added substantial talent to an excellent roster and were still putting butts in the seats no matter their place on the card, thanks in no small part to their rivalry with The Midnight Express. "Beautiful" Bobby Eaton, Dennis Condrey, and Stan Lane were all closer in size to Gibson and Morton, so while their stories with The Koloffs and Andersons were more of the "overcoming the odds" variety, their work with the "other" Express was a game of one-upmanship. They headlined major shows throughout the southeast through 1990's *WrestleWar* PPV, offering up some of the best tag team matches of the last thirty years. Their most high profile match came at *Starrcade '87* in a Scaffold match – a quite clever gimmick with a palpable aura of danger. No more risky a concept has ever been thought up for mainstream wrestling.

The Rock 'N Roll Express vs. Midnight Express is on the short list for best tag team feud of my time. You would be hard pressed to think of many, if any, tag team storylines that were as prominently featured. I do not think that the WWE, outside of maybe the teams involved in the Attitude Era's Tables, Ladders, and Chairs matches, has produced anything that can be in that conversation. In the NWA, Morton and Gibson's work against The Four Horsemen (wrestling lore's preeminent group, led by Ric Flair) could possibly rival it. The pace was similarly crisp and fast.

Since the conception of *Starrcade '83* gave birth to wrestling as we know it today, there have been a few handfuls of tag teams that stood out above the rest. When you consider that their performance method and gimmick was often imitated, that the emotion that they drew out of the audience was rarely duplicated, and that they won four Team Championships in a stacked NWA tag scene, The Rock 'N Roll Express deserve their place amongst the best.

#87: *"Superfly" Jimmy Snuka*

Before Hulkamania started running wild, the most popular star in the WWE was "Superfly" Jimmy Snuka. In 1983, Snuka's fame arguably eclipsed even that of the heroic World Champion, Bob Backlund; a borderline truth that must have grated on the titleholder's nerves given that Snuka had been one of his chief rivals in the years prior. The Superfly was a chiseled Polynesian powerhouse with a penchant for aerial assaults that dazzled a fan base that was becoming increasingly demanding. Tired of the so-termed "white meat babyface" that was Backlund, the people embraced the daredevil tactics that made Snuka a star. The WWE's magazine named Snuka the 1983 Wrestler of the Year ahead of Backlund and Pro Wrestling Illustrated (PWI) gave him the title of the year's "Most Popular Wrestler."

Hulk Hogan was credited with changing the landscape when he transformed the identity of professional wrestling in 1984, but Snuka had been setting the stage for the change. Superfly pushed the envelope and his high-risk style never failed to elicit one of the largest reactions on a card. Against Don Muraco (one of the last wrestlers cut from the third-tier) in a 1983 Steel Cage match for the Intercontinental Championship, a bloody, battered, and (cheaply) beaten Snuka would not stand to see arguably his greatest nemesis walk away the victor. After dragging "The Magnificent One" back into the ring, he ascended to the top of the 15-foot structure and gave his signature "I love you" hand gesture to the Madison Square Garden faithful before leaping toward the mat below and crashing all of his weight down onto Muraco. Mick Foley and Bubba Ray Dudley were in the crowd that night and used it as inspiration to become professional wrestlers. Long before Mankind was thrown off the top of Hell's Cell and Bubba was tossed off a 20 foot ladder, there was the most famous Superfly Splash of all-time.

It was through his intense battles with Muraco that Snuka earned his 1983 accolades and eclipsed Backlund as the most popular wrestler in the WWE. Backlund knew very well what the Superfly Splash from the top of the cage felt like, as it had happened to him numerous times in his own battles with Snuka. Their Steel Cage matches were regarded as some of the best contests of the early 80s, with their June 28, 1982 encounter being named PWI Match of the Year. Snuka's innovation had been the catalyst for his becoming a fan favorite after an initial run as a top heel. I wonder if it might have made Backlund breathe a sigh of relief to have such a trendsetter off his list of WWE Championship challengers, only for it to be exhaled once the October '83 Snuka-Muraco match put the spotlight on the fact that a babyface competing for the secondary title was now his crowd supported superior.

Unfortunately for Snuka, the transition from Backlund to Hogan as the WWE titleholder did not land him in the top spot. Perhaps in another era it may have worked out differently, but not as Vince McMahon prepared to take over the sport. Superfly continued to be a major asset, however, engaging in a feud with Roddy Piper. On the set of *Piper's Pit*, Snuka was the subject of one of "Rowdy Roddy's" tangents. The guest of the show, Superfly could not get a word in as Piper verbally berated him. When he finally stood up to the "Hot Scot," he was blasted over the head with a coconut in one of the most iconic television moments in WWE history. The incident set off a fierce series of in-ring altercations, which began the trend of Snuka being a set-up man for bigger stars to get to the elite level. Superfly branched off into a side story with Piper's right-hand man, "Cowboy" Bob Orton, as Roddy moved into his famous *WrestleMania* saga with Hogan.

One would have thought that Superfly would have been a more integral part of the first *WrestleMania*. He and Orton had a memorable match at the MTV special leading up to Mania, *The War to Settle the Score*. In defeating the "Ace,"

Snuka was kayfabe responsible for breaking the Cowboy's arm and putting it into the notorious cast worn for many years after it had actually healed. A rematch between the two would have been a nice addition to the historic card, but they were instead placed in the respective corners of the Hogan and Piper led tag teams in the main-event.

Snuka took a multi-year hiatus from the WWE beginning in 1985 and did not return until 1989, when he received a quick push on television to re-establish his character. From then on, he continued the role that he had shown the ability to do so well with Piper in 1984 and put over many of the aspiring headliners from the heel dressing room. He did the honors for The Million Dollar Man at *Summerslam*, lost numerous times to Mr. Perfect, and gave "Ravishing" Rick Rude a convincing victory at *WrestleMania VI*. He went onto take the first loss of Undertaker's vaunted Mania undefeated streak, helped prepare Rick Martel for a marquee match at *WrestleMania VII*, and took the fall for Shawn Michaels. Every one of the above mentioned grapplers have featured chapters in this book.

His last significant contribution to the wrestling business was helping to get Eastern Championship Wrestling off the ground as their first World Champion. ECW – once it dropped Eastern for Extreme - became very influential. In 1996, Superfly was inducted into the WWE Hall of Fame.

While not the type of star whose involvement in the WrestleMania Era jumps off the page statistically, he was one of those guys – had I been reading instead of writing this book – who would have stood out had he not been included, as in, "Why wasn't Superfly in the Top 90?"

#86: Dean Malenko

Wrestling fans have preferences for certain styles just as football fans might prefer a defensive-minded approach to one that involves outscoring opponents. Personally, I have always enjoyed mat wrestling and grappling holds. Execution of numerous holds is not necessary to have good matches, as wrestling is all about storytelling, but I like the moves. I find it easier to get invested in the entirety of the match if there are more holds. Subsequently, I could watch Dean Malenko wrestle all day. He was, after all, "The Man of 1,000 Holds."

Malenko was a consummate professional that had a virtually unmatched command of the squared circle. Bringing a style to American wrestling that had been shaped by his time in Mexico and Japan, he was able to do things not seen from many of his peers. In the mid-1990s, he initially made a name for himself by winning over the hardcore-conditioned fans of ECW. Then, upon arriving in WCW, Malenko became the glue that held together the vast array of styles in the Cruiserweight division. A lot of the high risk takers could be criticized for their matches being too choreographed at best and sloppy at worst. Malenko's combination of the strength necessary to perform impressive power moves (like the fireman's carry toss over his shoulders into a top notch gut buster), his second-to-none grappling, and his well-timed use of aerial moves added realism and legitimacy that separated his work from others.

My first exposure to Malenko was his match on the July 8, 1996 *Nitro* with Rey Mysterio. I may have tuned in that night to see Hulk Hogan form The N.W.O. after he turned heel at the famous *Bash at the Beach* PPV, but I never forgot the incredible mix of Malenko's ground game and Mysterio's high flying, lucha libre. His job description was plain and simple: have outstanding matches. He was quite good at his job. He not only had some of the best matches in the Cruiserweight division, but he had two of the best matches of that entire era in WCW. The

Halloween Havoc '96 match with Mysterio and the *Starrcade '96* match with Ultimo Dragon were amazing.

    I would rank Malenko vs. Ultimo Dragon as one of the best Cruiserweight matches of all-time. The near twenty-minute bout was also one of the best matches in *Starrcade* history, but somehow got left off the WWE's *Essential Starrcade* DVD. It was as if, in collecting opinions, everyone wrote down "the cruiserweight match from '96" and those working on the DVD mistakenly thought they meant Mysterio vs. Jushin Liger. Malenko-Dragon <u>owned</u> that match in every way except popular name value. They built the match slowly and steadily and just kept adding layer after layer until climaxing with a great series of high spots and near falls at the end. They stole the show at arguably the biggest event in WCW history. Had they had the same match at WWE's *WrestleMania XII*, they would get credit for all of eternity.

    On a near weekly basis for a few years, Malenko was having one of the best matches in North America with a variety of wrestlers, including Eddie Guerrero, Chris Benoit, and Chris Jericho. Promotions have to keep guys like him around. I wish there were more no-nonsense grapplers in the WWE today that were not forced to discover outside-the-box personalities just to get on TV. Malenko came from an era where you could just be a great wrestler and that would be enough for you to find a place – even a good place like being one of the last members of The Four Horsemen and winning the United States and Tag Team titles, in addition to the Cruiserweight Championship four times. Promotions need genuine wrestlers to balance out the entertainers and create the best product possible. When he and his friends – Benoit, Guerrero, and Saturn - left WCW to join the WWE as The Radicalz, it sealed WCW's fate. WCW had nothing left to watch that we had not all seen numerous times before.

Malenko, a second generation wrestler, made his family proud. He was one of the best performers of his generation; every bit as good as his more famous friends. He will be remembered as the consistent, week-in and week-out presence that helped make WCW a superior product for a short time during the Monday Night Wars. Daniel Bryan is probably the closest thing to him in recent memory – in terms of grappling acumen - but when I review Malenko's work, it makes me think of Kurt Angle. It is a shame that Malenko and Angle's primes did not match up, as I would have loved to have seen those two go at it. 20-minutes of Malenko vs. Angle in their primes would have been mat grappling Heaven.

#85: Bray Wyatt

This is where the historical tone changes for a few pages. #85 has, through three editions, been the place in the book reserved for a current star on the brink of solidifying his long-term place in WWE lore. One such star (Dolph Ziggler) flamed out in a short main-event run and never fulfilled his potential, while the other (The Shield) became the driving force behind there needing to be a third edition of this project.

Now Bray Wyatt is on deck and, while his track record in three years definitely suggests that he will do nothing but climb the rankings as the years go by, he still has his work cut out for him as questions swirl about his ability to adapt his character and advance his standing in a more competitive environment.

If I had to guess, I would say that he will almost assuredly maintain his Top 90 status and push for a Second-Tier spot within the next couple of years. Can you name another star in the last three decades whose first two WrestleMania opponents could equal the stature of Wyatt's (Cena and Taker)? When you are performing a peer-to-peer comparison, that kind of factoid stands out. Three prominent acts had to be removed from the Top 90 to make room for Wyatt and his contemporaries; here is how Wyatt's first three years compare to their substantial careers:

<u>Trish Stratus</u> – Originally included because of her status as the greatest female wrestler ever, the 2013 Hall of Fame inductee's influence has been called into question by the incredible women of the so-termed "Divas Revolution." After seeing what the NXT-to-WWE crop has accomplished in short order, what does it say about Stratus and her era when talents like Charlotte or Sasha Banks have arguably done more for the perception of women's wrestling in two years than they did in triple the time? Stratus never had a match anywhere near as good as even the 5th best effort from the revolutionaries; she

was never able to create an opportunity necessary to achieve something like Banks vs. Bayley from *NXT Takeover: Brooklyn* in 2015. Is it completely fair to make that comparison? I think so; and without the confidence to keep Stratus in the top female spot, can her entire resume really compare to Wyatt's headlining stats alone? I do not think so.

Jerry "The King" Lawler – Having headlined just one Summerslam and one WrestleMania (Wyatt has headlined two of each), having won an equal number of mainstream championships as Wyatt (zero), having nothing close to an indisputable advantage over Wyatt as a draw *in WWE* (considering Wyatt is hitting his prime during a much more successful era), and having a lot fewer stellar performances in an on-again, off-again WWE run as Wyatt has amassed in roughly one fifth the time (Lawler never produced anything in WWE on the level of Wyatt vs. Daniel Bryan at *Royal Rumble '14*), this was a pretty easy call (with all due respect to Lawler's overall influence on wrestling history).

The Fabulous Freebirds – This decision really boiled down to the Badstreet trio having done so little in WWE and having contributed to WCW only when it was reeling in the early 1990s. They were unquestionably, like Lawler, more influential to the history of the business than Bray and, unlike Wyatt (as of mid-2016), they actually have a championship trophy case. However, being a pioneering stable is more of an intangible accolade and The Eater of Worlds has a pretty impressive tangible resume with a pair of huge WrestleMania matches and a handful of great matches.

On that last point, we have to be careful not to over-inflate the modern era's inherent advantages. With five hours of TV to fill each week and at least one PPV-per-month combined with the fact that today's fanbase is more demanding of critically-acclaimed matches than ever before, the climate is ripe with opportunities for someone like Wyatt to rattle off 4-

star headlining performances on a much more regular and prominent basis than peers from even a decade ago (much less three decades ago). Dolph Ziggler's was a perfect example of the mid-2000s-to-present-day-resume for a long-tenured upper mid-card act; taken at face value, he looks like a huge star compared to someone like Dean Malenko or Jimmy Snuka, so you have to look deeper.

Wyatt is a different story, though. Even without a World Championship (yet), there are important qualities that allow him and his place in WWE to compare well with Lawler and The Freebirds intangibly and then to take their place at the WrestleMania Era roundtable tangibly. Wyatt has been protected from the moment he debuted, meaning that WWE has not absentmindedly tossed his character up and down their hierarchy; his ceiling has been very high and his floor has never been low. Look at his feud list from summer 2013 to winter 2016: Kane (Top 45), Miz (Top 90), Bryan (Top 45), Cena (Top 10), Jericho (Top 20), Ambrose (Top 90), Taker (Top 10), Ryback, Reigns (Top 45), and Dudleys (Top 90). Impressive, right? His work with those wrestlers was inconsistent at times, but always psychologically engaging. He is also highly unique and has rare-for-his-time charisma; with more attention to detail and greater focus, he could ascend to a level on-par with the greatest maestros of the microphone.

It is hard not to see Bray Wyatt becoming one of the greatest of his generation.

#84: Rick Martel

There was a natural arrogance to Rick Martel. Even in his days as a successful tag team wrestler in the early 80s, where he earned his initial claim to wrestling fame with two championship reigns alongside Tony Garea, he had a certain pep in his step that suggested a cocky aura. His role back then as a babyface contradicted the subtleties in his body language that made it evident to the well-trained eye that he was suppressing a darker side. Martel knew that he was good and nobody could have convinced him otherwise.

When he became "The Model" in 1989 and began thumbing his nose at the fans that had once showered him with praise, there was something very personal about it. Martel might be a nice guy, but what lies beneath is always what fascinates me about a wrestler's on-screen character. He played "The Model" too naturally for the persona not to be an extension of himself. Perhaps he was unleashing a few year's worth of frustration. It could not have been easy on his ego when, upon returning to the WWE in the mid-80s after holding the AWA World Championship for the better part of two years, he was thrust directly back into the tag division where he had already achieved the highest of team-oriented highs. The psychological self-image changes when you become the top guy. Martel may have expected similar success as the man he replaced in the AWA, who went to the WWE and became one of the biggest stars of all-time (Hulk Hogan).

Martel begrudgingly started a successful tag team stint with Tito Santana as Strike Force, a WWE Tag Team Championship winning duo that peaked during an era loaded with great tag wrestlers. They won the belts from the famed Hart Foundation and held them for five months before having their run upended by Demolition (whose proceeding reign set the WWE record for length). Having gotten himself over, Martel was then taken off television to sell an injury and remained away for several months. During his time away, "Mr. Perfect" Curt Hennig, his successor as the face of the AWA, came to the WWE and was given a long undefeated streak. How must that have set with Martel? He held the AWA title for 595 days, two hundred days longer than Hennig and 595 days longer than Hogan and yet they got the star's treatment. Hogan even won the WWE title in his first month. Like any man assured of his own self value might, Martel must have been stewing at home waiting for his chance.

At *WrestleMania V*, Strike Force reunited to take on The Brain Busters (Arn Anderson and Tully Blanchard). During the match, Tito accidentally collided with Martel, who had recently returned from his hiatus. It turned out to be little more than the excuse that Martel had been dreaming of, as he left Santana to fend for himself against the future Hall of Famers and quickly vented his annoyance to Mean Gene Okerlund at having Tito ride his coattails. The French Canadian star displayed impressive cunning. It was good timing, as he could not have picked a bigger stage. Considering that Santana was much beloved in the WWE after years of loyal service and stardom, he also could not have chosen a better target to begin his upward mobility.

In a series of matches that spanned 1989 and 1990, Martel engaged Santana intent on making a lasting impression that would one day earn him a headlining match at *WrestleMania*. The former partners traded victories, but it was the newly dubbed "Model" that most notably strutted his stuff. His attention to detail had some calling him narcissistic, but "Yes, he was a Model" and his intentions to become a top heel in the WWE were legitimized by his attire, his creative use of an atomizer to blind opponents with his own fragrance (*Arrogance*), and the critical success of his matches with Tito. During one such bout at a late '89 *Saturday Night's Main Event*, Martel put on one of his finer "runway" performances in the squared circle. It was a great match, the signature moment of which came courtesy of The Model. With his arms locked in position for a dreaded backslide, Martel's face told the entire story of the match in a 30-second struggle. He showed buoyancy, fear, anguish, excitement, and overwhelm before being pulled to the mat for the long two-count.

Martel emerged as the bigger star and reached the peak of his career a year later when he put Jake "The Snake" Roberts on the shelf with an eye injury courtesy of a spray of his cologne. It ignited a unique feud that culminated in his most high profile WWE run, which included being captain of a *1990 Survivor Series* team that swept its opposition (4-0), a then-record 53-minute stint in the '91 Royal Rumble match (a 30-man Battle Royal), and a headlining match at *WrestleMania VII*. Playing off of Jake's temporary vision impairment from the touch of *Arrogance*, the *Mania* showdown was a Blindfold match. With both men's heads covered, it was up to the sheer brilliance of the talents involved to make a challenging situation work. Martel was tremendous in his role, elbowing the mat, punching into thin air, and nearly coming to blows with the ring ropes, much to the delight of the jeering crowd. Underneath his cover, he was grinning from ear-to-ear. That was the moment that he had worked for.

All tongue-in-cheek writing aside, he was a "Model" WWE Superstar.

#83: The Iron Sheik

On December 26, 1983, the second longest WWE Championship reign in history came to an end at the hands of The Iron Sheik, a former Iranian Olympian who had successfully made the transition from amateur to pro in the same Verne Gagne Wrestling School class that produced Ric Flair. Bob Backlund had been the champion for 2,135 days, making Sheik's victory as big a shocker as there has been in the last thirty years.

With his manager, "Classy" Freddie Blassie, by his side, The Sheik was one of the most recognizable performers of the early wrestling boom period in the 80s. He had a typical anti-American gimmick, but he also had a lot of charisma. Broken as his English may have been, when he spoke, his words carried the weight of those Persian clubs that he often swung around in an impressive and challenging warm-up exercise. They still do, as Sheik's unfiltered opinions and outspoken nature are doled out regularly on Twitter. He is unabashedly the most entertaining wrestling personality using the social media outlet today (though Kevin Owens is giving him a run for his money). You should "follow" him. It will keep your life interesting.

His run with the WWE title did not last long, as he was a transitional champion to make way for Hulk Hogan. His dreaded Camel Clutch submission hold was enough to make Backlund's manager throw in the towel to avoid permanent damage, but it was no match for the growing power of Hulkamania. One month after becoming the champ, he dropped the strap to Hulkster in a match that showed his scientific wrestling prowess and ability to mix in a little bit of hand-to-hand combat to add a little spice to his game in the same way that his curled-toe wrestling boots did for his ring attire.

In 1984 and 1985, he was one of the top heels in the WWE. After concluding his feud with Hogan, he engaged in what would become his greatest rivalry. Rising up to defend the nation against The Sheik was Sgt. Slaughter. As on-screen characters, they mixed like oil and water. It was the Anti-American who incited the crowd by yelling "E-rahn (Iran) #1, E-rhan #1" and spitting after mentioning the USA versus the All-American synonymous with the red, white, and blue. As competitors and storytellers in the wrestling ring, they meshed beautifully in a series of matches that spanned the first half of 1984 and produced some of the most time-tested work of the era.

I am partial to a series of matches that tells a thorough and complete tale, like a movie trilogy that maintains the quality of the first film or even betters it. Chapter 1 in the Sheik-Slaughter story set the tone with a bloody slugfest. There were no headlocks or jockeying for strategic advantage. It was a match that sold how much the two men and their respective countries disliked each other. In those days, it was considered very much faux pas for a hero to do something traditionally reserved for a villain, so when rage got the better of Sarge to the point where he took off his combat boot and used it as an in-hand weapon, it was eye-opening. He walloped The Sheik continuously until the ref stopped the match. The NYC faithful nearly came unglued when the decision was awarded to the Iranian. Sheik 1, Slaughter 0.

Chapter 2 began with Sheik spitting twice on the Sarge and slapping him three times. Spitting on a man is the ultimate insult - the premier sign of disrespect. When Slaughter proceeded to methodically dominate the first half of the match, the crowd loved it. All three matches in the series took place at MSG, so there was a familiar feel to each one that gave it the atmosphere of a home town team vs. heated visiting rival. Imagine if wars between nations were waged between two men, one from each land, and that they were fought in an arena on one's native soil. Think of what that atmosphere might look and sound like. That was Sheik vs. Slaughter. Both were disqualified for being overly aggressive with the referee. Sheik 1, Slaughter 0, 1 draw.

Chapter 3 was one of wrestling's most famous matches. Known simply as "The Boot Camp Match," it was a no-disqualification, no-count out brawl to a pinfall finish, leaving no doubt as to who was the better man. MSG was sold out to the rafters, as was the theatre attached to it, where the match was shown on closed-circuit TV. The announcers could not even hear themselves talk it was so loud in there. Good vs. evil was, perhaps, never better personified than it was in Sheik and Slaughter's final bout. The crowd was 100% locked in to the story and they felt their own sense of victory when Sarge got the win. The series ended 1-1-1.

The WWE title win and the Slaughter matches were the hallmarks of Sheik's career. Though he would go on to form a Tag Championship winning team with Nikolai Volkoff that gave WrestleMania its first title change, The Sheik never again reached the heights of the first half of 1984, but by that point he had already confirmed his spot among the greatest in WWE lore.

#82: Shelton Benjamin

When I sat down to narrow my list, I said to myself, "There is no way I am leaving Shelton Benjamin off it." That said, I ranked him too highly (69th) in the first two editions. He has the statistics to back up his original spot but, since he never ascend higher than perennial mid-carder in a time where it was a lot easier to ascend higher than perennial mid-card status, a reflection that yielded a thirteen spot drop for Mr. Benjamin.

Here is why he was originally ranked so highly: his first Intercontinental title reign lasted eight months, which is the second longest since 1990 behind only The Rock's nine month reign in 1998. He is also tied with Steve Austin for the 2nd longest United States Championship reign since 1991. He is in good company when it comes to his "gold standards." Each reign came in an era where holding a mid-card title for any considerable length of time was rare. He also had two other runs with the IC title to go along with his two WWE Tag Team titles. His performance record, in matches for those titles against the likes of Los Guerreros, Chris Jericho, Rob Van Dam, and Matt Hardy, was pristine. When combined with his *WWE Raw* matches with Triple H, Shawn Michaels, and Kurt Angle, Benjamin proved to be one of the top *wrestlers* of the 2000s. He is a perfect example of how championships, performance, and pure talent can propel a wrestler past his peers that were on higher on the card if all factors are equally weighted.

On his *Smackdown* debut as a member of Kurt Angle's "insurance policy" to remain WWE Champion, Benjamin displayed an uncanny combination of athleticism and grappling ability. He would often be referred to, in the years that followed, as the most athletic wrestler in the business. I would take that a step further. He might have been the most athletic wrestler in the *history* of the business. The only two that come close to him are Angle and Brock Lesnar. Shelton was the only

245 pound guy that I ever saw do a springboard move off the ropes.

As he refined his skills, his partnership with Charlie Haas evolved from Team Angle to "The World's Greatest Tag Team." They were deserving of the moniker. In terms of in-ring ability, they were the best tag team in the WWE after the Attitude Era ended and it was not until the mid-2010s that any team even came close. The week after they split in 2004, Shelton got the opportunity of a lifetime. On March 29, 2004's *Raw*, he wrestled in the main-event against Triple H. That was at the height of a time when Trips was the most hated heel in the WWE, so if anyone came close to beating him, it worked the people into frenzy. Shelton held his own and looked athletically superior *AND* smarter than Triple H, at times. When the unthinkable happened and Benjamin actually won, he shocked the world. He actually beat Trips three times in the span of a month.

He won the Intercontinental title at the first *Taboo Tuesday* (soon after renamed *Cyber Sunday*) PPV, in which fans voted on matches and stipulations. The people voted Shelton in for a title match against then-champion, Chris Jericho, and won the belt. He went on to successfully defend it at *Survivor Series* in arguably the best PPV match of his career against Christian in a show stealing performance that opened up his aerial arsenal and suggested that there might not be a limit to what he could do in the ring. Only his *Backlash '05* bout with Chris Jericho was in its league.

Undoubtedly, Shelton flat out understood what it took to deliver in the ring and, after a match like he had with Christian, one could not help but start thinking about him being a main-event player down the road. He further made his case with his breathtaking work in the first Money in the Bank Ladder match at *WrestleMania 21*. He stole the thunder from the rest of the great workers involved. Edge won the match, but people came away from it talking about Shelton. Money in the Bank Ladder matches made him somewhat of a Ladder match legend. He was in five of the six MITB bouts at Manias and had the most memorable spot in three of the first four. Every time I saw him run up ladder rungs like stair steps, I was in awe.

He carried a lot of momentum from *Mania 21* into a match with Shawn Michaels on *Raw* a few weeks later. My thought on the match can be summed up by HBK's unscripted comments from the next week, in which Michaels called Shelton "the best young piece of in-ring talent I've seen in years." At one point during the match, Shelton flat foot jumped to the top rope and sprung off into a clothesline in one fluid motion. Of course, the finish with HBK catching a springboarding Benjamin with Sweet Chin Music was featured in the *Raw* opening montage for years. The only match in his career that rivaled it was his work with Angle from a few months later. When Angle was drafted to *Raw* in 2005, he stated in an interview that he thought it might be so that he could help take Benjamin to the next level – to the main-event. Though Shelton never got past the upper mid-card, his athletic exploits left their mark. For instance, he was German suplexed in the match against Angle, but rotated enough in mid-air that he landed on his feet! What an incredible athlete!

He could have been the World Champion with the right manager. He just came up in the wrong era, in which there were really no managers.

I once had this fantasy promotion where I would write the "shows" online and perform the "matches" on Nintendo GameCube's "WrestleMania XIX" game. I gave him a manager similar in personality to Don King, made Shelton my ridiculously talented Mike Tyson-type, and put the big gold belt on him for six months. I will go to my grave believing that idea would have worked spectacularly well in the WWE.

#81: Demolition

Statistical records matter, creating separation from the historical pack; they are why an Elvis impersonator absolutely deserves a spot in the pantheon of modern pro wrestling lore and why Demolition's absence from the Top 90 would have been a glaring omission. The legendary tag team held the World Tag Team Championship for 478 days (from March 27, 1988's *WrestleMania IV* to July 14, 1989's edition of *Saturday Night's Main Event*), establishing a WWE record tag title reign that still stands to this day.

Think of all the things that you could do in 16 months. With 478 days, you could go to 68 Saturday matinees at the movie theater, watch your favorite team play 243 Major League Baseball games, or sail around the world six times.

Demolition, the focal point of the tag division for three *WrestleManias*, consisted of Ax and Smash. Ax was Bill Eadie, the former Masked Superstar who had made a name for himself in the last great years of the territory days of the 1970s. Smash was Barry Darsow, a product of the Minnesota wrestling hotbed that gave us Rick Rude, Curt Hennig, and Nikita Koloff. After finding marginal NWA success in the mid-1980s as Russian sympathizer, Krusher Khrushchev, Darsow joined the WWE.

Their record setting title reign alone would put them in the conversation for the definitive best in tag team wrestling lore. The fact that they thrived at the top in a period in which the tag team division in the WWE was as strong as it has ever been was, along with a second and third title reign, what secured their place at the roundtable.

Arguments against Demolition's spot at the top of tag team wrestling's historical ladder largely have been based on the claim that they were the WWE's version of the NWA's Road Warriors. Each had a look inspired by *Mad Max 2: The Road*

Warrior. Demolition's attire was an homage to the film's antagonist, Lord Humungus (who, later, also inspired Chris Jericho's moniker as the "Ayatollah of Rock 'n Rollah"). With their faces painted in KISS-like fashion, as well, they were more a tribute to 80s pop-culture than a rip off of The Road Warriors.

Without a question of who inspired it, their look made Demolition intimidating. They had a destructive style and mastered the art of isolating challengers in their corner, using quick tags to maintain their momentum. It was intelligently executed domination. For instance, they completely tamed the British Bulldogs in a summer of 1988 title defense. The Bulldogs had been the central figures of the tag division since 1985, but found very quickly that the new champions were more powerful, more aggressive, and smarter even.

There was an intangible quality about Ax and Smash that, when combined with their hard rock entrance music, made them easy to cheer. Even with devious Japanese manager, WWE Hall of Famer Mr. Fuji, in their corner, wielding his cane to seal cheap victories against some of the signature duos of the era, the fans still wanted to cheer. In late 1988, Fuji turned on Demolition to manage a former NWA pair called The Powers of Pain (The Barbarian and The Warlord), giving the fans their reason to embrace the champions. It was a unique situation. You can count on your hands the number of times in the WrestleMania Era that top level heels have turned their backs on the dark side in the midst of a highly successful run. Steve Austin's 1997 switch is the most famous, but Demolition's took place eight years prior with them becoming fan favorites right in the middle of their record-breaking title reign. Ax and Smash were the top heel team and top babyface team all in one physical year.

It was The Brain Busters that ended their reign as champs in a 2/3 Falls match with some help from Andre the Giant and a steel chair. In late 1989, they regained the belts from The Busters, only to drop them to Andre and Haku. Anyone that got to feud with Andre was doing something right. In the midst of that feud, Demolition pioneered the popular trend of having tag team partners start as the first two entrants in the Royal Rumble match. #3 that year was Andre, who further fanned the flames of the tag title situation by eliminating Smash. At *WrestleMania VI*, Demolition regained the titles in what was the last great moment for Ax and Smash and the last hurrah at Mania for Andre. Crush was inserted into the fold as the third member of Demolition soon after, being groomed to take Ax's place when his body started rapidly breaking down. They did alright as a 3-man team, even having one of their best matches against The Hart Foundation at 1990's *Summerslam*, but it was not the same.

Ax and Smash, together, formed one of the best tag teams of all-time. Their three title reigns combine for almost 700 days, beating out any other WWE tag team's total days as champions by over two-hundred days. That is another record never likely to be broken.

#80: The Miz

"REALLY.....??"

This former *MTV Real World* star has a lot of detractors that may scoff at his inclusion on this elite list, but in a book dedicated to celebrating "The WrestleMania Era," it would have been remiss to exclude one of the few dozen superstars to have ever been in the main-event of a WrestleMania. The Miz has the resume, whether you love him or hate him. He made himself relevant in professional wrestling by channeling his natural charisma and the screen presence that he developed while on reality television at a young age into a wrestling character that was quite adept at making people dislike him. He became so good at playing the annoying heel on camera, while simultaneously showing an off-camera personality that was a big hit in media appearances, that he wound up retaining the WWE Championship against John Cena in the main-event of *WrestleMania XXVII*, which (Rock-assisted) drew 1,059,000 buys on pay-per-view (4th all-time).

I remember watching his tryout on the 2004 season of *Tough Enough*, the WWE's own attempt to break into the reality TV market in the early 2000s that originally aired on MTV. He was not a sculpted athlete and he sounded uncomfortable on the microphone, but he made the final and was given a contract. The Miz was terrible when he first started on the main roster - just absolutely dreadful - and, as he would later tell the world, his reality TV background made him a popular target backstage by people that may have been hoping that he would fail. Yet, he worked on his game, found a comfort level, settled down, and developed a highly entertaining duo with John Morrison. Their popular internet-only show, "The Dirt Sheet," gave him the opportunity to develop as a personality.

Once he found his groove, Miz quickly proved to everyone that he had incredible potential as a heel character, verbally berating John Cena in a series of promos in 2009 that had fans and management, alike, taking notice. The one lingering question remaining for Miz in 2010 was about his in-ring capabilities. He answered the call at *Night of Champions*. Earlier in the year, Miz had been a "Pro" on the WWE's next attempt at reality-based programming called *NXT* (which later became the name for WWE developmental). Hilariously, he was paired with "rookie" Daniel Bryan, a wildly popular, recently signed independent wrestler at the time known amongst inner circles as arguably the best technical wrestler in the world. The dynamic between the two naturally set them in opposition, as Miz was the more engaging talker, but Bryan the superiorly skilled wrestler. Fast forward six months and Bryan was challenging Miz for the U.S. Championship. It was Miz's chance to show what he could do in a featured match with a good back story. He delivered in spades, working a smart match that he lost via submission.

Six months later, he was in the main-event at *WrestleMania.* I was in attendance that night in Atlanta. The WWE produced an amazing promo video hyping his entrance, featuring the Nas track "Hate me now" that made him look like a huge star throwing his success in the face of all the naysayers. It really meant something to him to be in that spot. Like many stars, he was a fan first. "During (Cena's) entrance, I'm black, nobody's seeing me, nobody's looking at me," Miz said in an interview, referencing his emotions prior to his *Mania 27* match. "I see my ten best friends sitting in the front row. The friends that I watched in my living room, WrestleMania after WrestleMania; all watching me in the main event with my WWE Championship and me looking at them and going, 'we did it.' That is my moment. No one will ever be able to take that away from me and that was what it was all about."

The Miz held the WWE title for over five months. For a thirteen month stretch between November 2010 and December 2011, he established himself as one of the bonafide top guys in the WWE. Though he has dropped down considerably since then, he has still been a featured and quite valuable act in the mid-card. With his direct-to-DVD movie career and his good ambassadorship for WWE combined with his wrestling resume, I have come to describe him as a "poor man's Chris Jericho."

#79: Alberto Del Rio

Asked to name twenty wrestlers over the last fifteen years (as of 2016) who have had better careers than Alberto Del Rio, could you do it? I will save you the time; the answer is "no, you cannot."

In a reasonably objective analysis, that he won Money in the Bank and the only 40-man Royal Rumble match, headlined two WrestleManias, held the World Title four times, looked like an evil Don from a Zorro movie, and was widely regarded as a three-star (good) match waiting to happen makes Del Rio's resume difficult to equal in the post-Attitude Era. However, it is equally difficult to ignore the time period in which most of his success took place (ditto for The Miz).

WWE's struggles to build new stars beyond the mid-2000s started to become glaringly obvious by 2009 and 2010. Benjamin apparently did not seem to want it enough (ditto for Carlito); Mr. Kennedy shot his mouth off before earning the necessary clout to avoid the serious repercussion of becoming a "never was"; The Great Khali was the worst wrestler of all-time; Bobby Lashley flamed out; Umaga died young; MVP never caught a break; Drew McIntyre's wife derailed his future. It was always something.

By the latter part of the decade, WWE had two brands mostly full of talents who would have been no better than solid mid-carders in other eras, but they had to push somebody to the top; that is why The Nexus was pushed straight to the main-event and that is why Del Rio, a guy with limited personality who I saw wrestle at a house show in June 2010 to absolutely no response from the crowd, showed up two months later and beat Rey Mysterio by submission in his first TV match en route to a Hall of Fame-worthy resume.

I will be the first to say that I appreciated ADR's presentation and his abilities in between the ropes. His entrance grand and his style of dress immaculate, he was offered as a cut above the rest, reminiscent of The Million Dollar Man and JBL. Unique to each of his predecessors was his own, personal ring announcer, who would pronounce his name with great flair; I loved Ricardo Rodriguez. Meanwhile, Del Rio showed in his matches that his wrestling ability was on par with the best in the industry. He was a breath of fresh air after watching some of the mid-2000s riff raff struggle to string two sequences together. I would not call him a great wrestler, but without question a very good one. Be it against Edge, Christian, John Cena, CM Punk, Sheamus, Big Show, Jack Swagger, or Dolph Ziggler, he put together a body of work that will stand the test of time. His match against Punk at MSG that stole the show from Rock's first match in seven years and his Ladder match with Christian earlier that year (arguably the most underrated match of the century) were particularly noteworthy.

Nevertheless, Del Rio in a more competitive era simply would not have accomplished a quarter of what he did from 2010-2013, during which time he also was one half of Edge's last match and wrestled for the World Title, was in a match for a World Title shot, or was waiting in the wings for a championship bout after already becoming #1 contender at **twenty-seven** PPVs (Doc's note – he was the Royal Rumble winner at *Elimination Chamber '11* and concussed at *No Way Out '12*, forcing a replacement). He was arguably the face of the World Heavyweight Title division from 2010 until it was finally unified with the WWE Championship again, but that is perhaps a misleading accolade. If the old saying "The Man makes the title" is correct, then the title was reduced to a fraction of its previous worth by way of its being on the shoulders of less worthy men. I often referred to the World Title of that period as being on-par with the Intercontinental Title of the mid-1990s; it was still important, but had fallen far in just a few short years from being contested in the main-event between Edge and Undertaker at *WrestleMania XXIV*.

    Credit where it is due to Del Rio for his performance acumen, but I would call his stats inflated and I, thus, see fit to knock him to a spot further down the rankings than his overall statistical achievements may warrant. We could theoretically play the mix and match generation game for all ninety wrestlers discussed in this book, but you would have to admit that it is a challenge to recall as decorated a superstar who was so marginally over (as hero or villain) or who had less definable charisma. I think it is telling that Del Rio came back to WWE in late 2015 and, within two months, was barely relevant. The NXT call-ups since 2012 ushered in a more talented, far hungrier generation, rendering someone like ADR a mid-carder at best.

    I frankly wish Del Rio had not returned to WWE, as he had already proven his worth on pro wrestling's greatest platform. Criticisms of his era aside, allow me to end on a compliment and point out that any era would benefit from Del Rio in the mid-card, having really good matches and helping make the overall product better.

#78: Brian Pillman

On November 4, 1996, Brian Pillman was at home recuperating from the ankle fusion surgery that significantly shortened his career. In wrestling storyline, it was Steve Austin that inflicted the injury. The two were a former WCW Tag Team Championship winning duo pitted against each other in their first year in WWE. Austin, upon learning that Pillman would be doing a live interview from his home, decided to "break in" to Pillman's house and continue his assault. Knowing that to be the case, Pillman had his personal firearm ready and waiting.

Most fans watching the WWE were still kids and, yet, that edition of *Monday Night Raw* ended with Pillman pointing a gun at Austin and the television feed cutting out amidst a lot of commotion. WWE and WCW had enough to answer for with steroids and the "fake" stigma, so pushing the envelope with their shows usually involved very calculated moves in which the damage control could be swift. The use of a gun on a live program entered uncharted territory. Pillman looked legitimately crazy. Austin was believable as the calculating, sadistic villain. Each played their parts so well that you could not tell, especially as a young person, whether or not the happenings were authentic. The media firestorm was predictable, but the fact of the matter was that "Austin 3:16 vs. Pillman 9-millimeter" got a lot of attention.

The segment was the WWE's step into the world of "shock TV," developed to surprise the consumer into repeated viewings. Pillman created a character in the mid-90s known as "The Loose Cannon" that blurred the line between reality and television to the point where even his fellow wrestlers were often out of the loop. He was the perfect choice for the production of an eye-opening moment. Pillman was one of the most unique personas of the entire WrestleMania Era. Unfortunately, his ankle got him hooked on pain killers and other drugs and he died in 1997 before ever showing the world his full potential.

Earlier in his career, he had been an innovative in-ring performer. I wish fans of his mid-to-late 90s work could have seen what he could do in his early days in the NWA. At the 1989 (inaugural) *Halloween Havoc*, Pillman made his PPV debut in a US title match against then-champion, Lex Luger. Brian lived up to his nickname of that time, "Flyin' Brian," whizzing around the ring at a ripped 225 pounds. It was hard to believe that he was a former nose tackle, but his football playing days in college and the NFL (he wore Cincinnati Bengal striped tights) gave him a rare combination of strength and speed. Against Luger, he looked like a seasoned veteran despite being a relative rookie in the business.

As good as he looked in the loss to Luger, it was in February 1990 that Pillman went from intriguing young talent to future star in the making. On *WCW Saturday Night*, he was involved in a special challenge match against NWA Champion, Ric Flair. Pillman was the relative unknown commodity that had merely a puncher's chance of winning. When he took Flair to his limits, it vaulted him up the figurative ladder. His star continued to rise throughout the early 90s, as he feuded with Flair's Four Horsemen. At the time, feuding with The Horsemen guaranteed that you were going to get significant television time and be involved in major PPV matches.

His program with Barry Windham in 1991 took Pillman to the next level. Flyin' Brian had become one of the best young wrestlers in the world, but in several bloody, knockdown, drag out fights, he was established as more than just a finesse wrestler with aesthetically pleasing moves. He came out of the feud with a more palpable connection to the audience.

Pillman only won two championships in his career: the aforementioned tag title and the precursor to the WCW

Cruiserweight Championship, which he was the first man to hold. He had one unforgettable match with Japanese light heavyweight icon, Jushin "Thunder" Liger. In a preview of the classic styles clashes that we saw during the Monday Night War involving smaller talents from all over the world, Pillman vs. Liger was an aerial war that holds up well against Rey Mysterio vs. Eddie Guerrero, Mysterio vs. Dean Malenko, and Malenko vs. Ultimo Dragon in the all-time North American Cruiserweight discussion.

Winning the Tag Team Championships as a member of The Hollywood Blondes (with Austin) was the stage of Pillman's career where he began transitioning from just a very good wrestler to a cutting edge character. They may have been a short-lived team, but Pillman and Austin's work together was important to their careers. Pillman came out of the team as the one that appeared to have the greatest long-term potential, in my opinion; which is funny to write given what Austin became.

Statistically, Del Rio, Miz, Benjamin, and Wyatt should rank higher but, the Third-Tier being an interesting mixture of talents who thrived on various levels of wrestling's hierarchy (instead of a group of 30 first ballot Hall of Famers), judgment calls seem more appropriate. Why put Pillman ahead? Well, I asked myself if I could ever see WWE ten years down the road making documentaries about the aforementioned four others. Time will tell on Wyatt, but that is a negative on Shelton, Miz, and Alberto. The Loose Cannon, though, was influential enough to be immortalized by a documentary.

Pillman was brilliant and far ahead of the curve in figuring out where the business was going, creatively. If he had been able to maintain the same athletic superiority that had brought him marginal success as a gifted newcomer, then I think he could have ended up one of the all-time greats.

#77: Tito Santana

WWE is a brand of sport and entertainment that appeals to many different cultures, regularly featuring top stars throughout its history that were heroes amongst immigrant communities. Bruno Sammartino, for instance, was the WWE's greatest star until Hulk Hogan came along. He was adored by the Italian-Americans. Pedro Morales was a Puerto-Rican star that made it to the top, propelled by his countrymen. During the 1980s, the number of Mexicans seeking opportunities in the United States rose sharply due to an economic downturn in their home country. When the WWE's mainstream profile exploded, it was Tito Santana that gave the increasing Mexican population in America a sport hero in whom they could invest.

In recent years, we have seen the likes of Eddie Guerrero and Rey Mysterio become WWE World Heavyweight Champions due to their immense popularity, particularly with Latinos. Santana was the man that laid the foundation for them. As a headlining act in the Tag Team and Intercontinental title divisions, Tito was one of the top babyfaces in the WWE throughout the early-to-mid 80s. He was a heck of an athlete, having been a college and pro football player before transitioning to wrestling. There was something genuinely likeable about him too. He maintained a babyface persona for thirteen years in the company prior to moving on in 1993 and becoming the last Eastern Championship Wrestling Heavyweight Champion before the promotion went Extreme.

His 1984 feud with Greg Valentine over the Intercontinental title is, perhaps, his most well-known contribution to the business. They had a series of great matches that combined an old school focus on mat wrestling with a new school concentration on brawling, inside the ring and out. It seemed as if, by their second match together, they knew each other so well that they could anticipate their next moves, making for exchanges in every outing that would make them perfectly enjoyable to the fan of the current era. There were not many stars in the WWE higher up the ladder, at that point, than Santana. He was in the group including Jimmy Snuka, Junkyard Dog, and Ricky Steamboat that were behind only Hulk Hogan, Andre the Giant, Iron Sheik, and Sgt. Slaughter in the pecking order. Not coincidentally, Tito and all the rest of them are Hall of Famers.

Santana was selected for a very important duty at the first *WrestleMania*, asked to open the show and get the crowd sufficiently warmed up. So, Tito holds the unique distinction of having wrestled the first match in the history of professional wrestling's Super Bowl. He used his victory as a springboard to, later in the year, win the IC title back from Valentine before being put in the path of the fast-rising "Macho Man" Randy Savage. Tito lost the title to Savage in late '85 and clashed with him in a series of heated rematches. They were a fascinating pair to witness as opponents thanks to Savage's famous intensity combined with Tito's quick pace.

The losses to Savage marked the last time that Tito would get a chance at the IC title until 1990. When the belt was vacated after *WrestleMania VI*, Tito reached the finals of the tournament to crown a new champion, facing Mr. Perfect (Curt Hennig). The *Saturday Night's Main Event* match was short but thrilling – one of my favorite Tito bouts. They had a sequence in the beginning where they traded hammerlocks in rapid succession five times in a row; it could make you dizzy all that switching. Santana lost the match and would stick around for another few years to give back to the WWE, putting over guys like Perfect and Shawn Michaels.

In between his last two Intercontinental Championship opportunities, he formed a WWE Tag Team title winning partnership with Rick Martel. Dubbed "Strike Force," Santana and Martel were more famous, perhaps, for their break-up and subsequent matches against each other than they were for their title run. The story of Martel being injured only to come back and turn on Tito lasted about as long as their active tag team. Their on-again, off-again rivalry lasted much longer. For two years, they traded victories on television and clashed in tag matches on PPVs. It was the most high profile feud of Tito's career, given that the work that he did with Valentine took place just before the WWE hit it big. Tito won the 1989 King of the Ring tournament at Martel's expense, beating him in the finals. They had a memorable match on the October 14, 1989 episode of *Saturday Night's Main Event*. It was Tito's last storyline before slowly fading into the sunset.

Santana's legacy will be his influence on Mexican Americans in the WWE and of his titles won throughout the 1980s. I will always remember him as a likeable wrestler whose LJN action figure I still have to this day. It is pretty beat up from years of toy matches, but you can still make out his face (which looks like Han Solo's when he was frozen in carbonite). That is one of the last physical remnants of my original wrestling fandom. Everything else is just memories.

#76: Ron Simmons

Decorated athletes have always been a staple in professional wrestling, especially those that have come from the gridiron; the physicality of wrestling surely is a draw to former football players. No other athlete that had ever traded the pigskin for the tights was as big a name on the football field as Ron Simmons, the All-American defensive tackle from Florida State University. The Seminole legend rose the ranks quickly in wrestling and captured the WCW World Heavyweight Championship on August 2, 1992, becoming the first African-American to win a World title.

The 2012 WWE Hall of Fame inductee bookended his career with significant tag team success. He and Butch Reed formed Doom in 1989. Simmons immediately displayed well controlled power; the guy was *STRONG*, his high impact moves so seamlessly executed. A lot of credit should go to announcer, Jim Ross, for constantly putting over his athletic pedigree, as it shaped the perception that Simmons could be a major player one day. Doom won the WCW Tag Team titles from The Steiner Brothers and had a dominant, record-setting run as champions; their 281 day single reign was unmatched in NWA/WCW history. Simmons would later become a three-time WWE Tag Team champion as a member of the Acolytes/Acolyte Protection Agency (APA) in the final years of his in-ring career alongside Bradshaw. The APA was a focal point of the team division in the last golden age of tag wrestling in the WWE.

The biggest matches of his tag team career were a pair of Street Fights seven years apart. At *NWA Starrcade '90*, Doom faced Four Horsemen, Barry Windham and Arn Anderson, in a violent match for its time that saw all four of them bleed. At *WWE WrestleMania 13*, Simmons led his faction, The Nation of Domination, in a particularly brutal battle against his biggest WWE rival, Ahmed Johnson, and The Legion of Doom.

Simmons was a legitimate singles star in both WCW and WWE, as well. Going by the name "Farooq Asad" in the WWE, his leadership of the controversial Nation, with its similarities to the Black Panther party, earned him a WWE title shot against Undertaker at the 1997 *King of the Ring*. The Nation was one of those underrated pieces of the puzzle to ushering in a change from the kid-friendly product to one geared toward young adults in the late 90s. Farooq's last big singles match in the WWE came against the man who infamously took from him control of The Nation; one Dwayne "The Rock" Johnson.

Though unquestionably successful in WWE, his greatest achievements came in WCW. After *Starrcade '90*, it was clear that Simmons was being groomed for a larger role. Doom lost the tag titles two months later, prompting Simmons and Reed to split up. Simmons built up considerable momentum in a short amount of time on his own. At *Halloween Havoc* in October '91, they showed a video of him training at FSU and being mentored by Bobby Bowden in preparation to face Lex Luger for the WCW title. That match was a test for him to see if he could handle the main-event spotlight; in a Two-out-of-Three Falls match, Simmons earned the crowd's respect and support in defeat, passing the test with flying colors. About a year later, he got his title winning moment.

The entire presentation of Simmons winning the World title was very well done. Vader was the WCW Champion, at the time, and was a force. His style was brutal, backing up his billing as a monster. Simmons was justly billed as the underdog. Vader dominated most of the match, with Simmons catching quick spurts of powerful offense that looked all the better on a guy of Vader's size. There was great drama in the near 10-minute affair, with each of them nearly winning on several occasions. Simmons connected with a powerslam to win the title. Ross, on commentary, helped put over the moment, again adding a vocal ally to Ron's cause to be among the elite.

Simmons held the title for nearly five months before dropping it back to Vader.

Among his Third-Tier peers, he was one of the longest-tenured stars and had one of the best championship resumes; the intangible quality of his pioneering World title victory was one of the most underrated achievements of the WrestleMania Era. I like to imagine him reading this chapter of the book, smiling to himself, and then in that deep, southern African-American speaking tone saying, "DAMN! I'm appreciated." More than you know, sir….more than you know.

#75: X-Pac

Let it never be said that being friends with the right people will not do you good in your life. If you have any questions about that, ask Sean Waltman, better known as the 1-2-3 Kid, Syxx, and X-Pac in wrestling lore. Waltman became good friends with high rolling WWE stars Shawn Michaels, Kevin Nash, and Scott Hall during the mid-90s as a part of the group collectively referred to as "The Kliq" (which also included a young Triple H). He surely benefitted from his friendships backstage, which ultimately put him in position to be a key member of two of the most influential factions in wrestling history: The New World Order and Degeneration X. However, there is no question that he had a lot of talent and was one of the most entertaining in-ring performers in both the WWE and WCW for several important years.

Waltman's claim to fame was his well-controlled, high flying style in the ring. He was a very good wrestler that initially made a splash in upsetting Hall (as Razor Ramon) on *Raw* in 1993. A year later, he was given a WWE Championship match against Bret Hart in the summer of 1994; a match that is considered one of the greatest in *Raw* history. The Kid nearly defeated The Hitman on multiple occasions, but perhaps his most ringing endorsement was the commentary from Jim Ross and Randy Savage. They praised him up and down, left and right for the entirety of the match.

Waltman had a lot of very good matches in the WWE with various opponents, but with the exception of his bout with Hart, his best work generally came against other members of The Kliq. One of the forgotten classics of that era came in a Tag Team title match between then-champions Diesel (Nash) and Michaels and the team of The Kid and Razor. Somehow, the match – which had about twenty long two-counts – manages to go unmentioned in the conversation for best tag matches of the 90s. I would rank it in the top 5.

While with the WWE, he did well in a land of giants. His martial arts background helped make his work against bigger wrestlers look more legitimate. It made sense when he jumped over to WCW, following Hall and Nash in 1996, as they had a roster full of guys his size against whom he could showcase his considerable skills. Unfortunately, various issues including a neck injury kept him from maximizing his potential, though there was one night in January 1997 where we saw him put on a special match. After "stealing" the US title from then-champion, Eddie Guerrero, the belt was held up in a Ladder match at the PPV, *N.W.O. Souled Out*. There were many great matches in WCW that year, but few were better than that Ladder match. Waltman performed a jumping roundhouse kick off the top of a ladder, which was a move that required incredible timing. Had that move happened in the WWE and Waltman been more historically respected, it would be replayed over and over.

He came back to the WWE, joined DX, laid into WCW in his first promo, and fanned the flames of the Monday Night War. After setting a tone that the WWE was the place to be, he was instantly boosted to the most prominent position of his career. X-Pac was a big star as a member of DX; everything that they did mattered. He went on to beef up the mid-card with high profile matches against Jeff Jarrett and D-Lo Brown. He defeated Jarrett in a Hair vs. Hair match at *Summerslam '98*, an important night for the WWE that exemplified their qualitative dominance over WCW. He then won the European Championship from D-Lo (a supremely underrated talent from that era) at *No Mercy '98* in what turned out to be one of the best matches of his second run in the WWE. Pac proceeded to the highest profile match of his career against Shane McMahon at *WrestleMania XV*. Out of all the DX members on that card, it was his match that was the biggest. It was also, arguably, the best performance of his career as he carried a non-wrestler to a very good match.

Waltman had some huge moments in wrestling and they deserve to be highlighted. Who could ever forget the revelation that he had joined The N.W.O. as the sixth member – Syxx? Or the even more unforgettable night when he became the first man brought out to reform and reshape DX after HBK retired? His role in creating a "DX Army" that helped turn the tide against WCW cannot be understated.

#74: William Regal

William Regal could have been a World Heavyweight Champion. End of story.

His talent was evident from the time he showed up in WCW, winning the Television title from Ricky Steamboat within his first year and becoming one of the best and longest (combined) reigning TV champions ever. He made it apparent over ten years later, too, in a moment I will never forget when he confronted Triple H and verbally laid into him with a short, fiery promo that so effortlessly brought out people's emotions.

Unfortunately, like so many wrestlers, he also had demons and bad luck. His chronicles with drug abuse have been well-documented and they have sadly overshadowed the immense talent that he possessed. By the masses, he is best remembered as the Commissioner and General Manager in WWE, instead of the gifted wrestler who could talk and grapple with the elite. I am not a big fan of playing the "What if?" game, but I have often pondered what Regal could have been minus the addictions and if he had reached his prime during more recent years when, with WWE viewed globally, there has been greater emphasis on international stars.

There have been times throughout his career where he was merely a break or two away from ascending to the top of the ladder, anyway, but the chips never seemed to fall his way. When he began using brass knuckles and claiming to have been blessed with the "Power of the Punch" in late 2001/early 2002, I thought he had the main-event in his sights. His work with Edge suggested that he could quite easily step into a top spot and nobody would bat an eyelash. The influx of WCW talent cluttered the entire company, though - even with the brand split. He did find success in the tag team ranks, capturing the titles, but shortly thereafter, he was misdiagnosed with an illness when he actually had a heart problem that nearly took his life.

When he returned, he showed the range of his personality by becoming the guardian for the mentally-challenged Eugene character, prompting the aforementioned interview on HHH, but it did not lead anywhere. He built up some momentum with several critically acclaimed matches in 2005 and 2006, ultimately putting him in position to become the General Manager of *Raw*. I always thought that an active wrestler as GM would make for a great heel World Champion. He could book himself into favorable situations and dodge his primary opponents with ease, drawing tremendous heat from the fans in the process. Regal had already been a Commissioner who wrestled on a smaller scale (in 2001), but when he was the GM of *Raw* in 2008, he won the King of the Ring tournament in convincing fashion, giving him the extra credibility that he could have used to step up to the main-event. Unfortunately, he got suspended for violating the WWE's drug policy. Another missed opportunity.

So, I go back to the "What if?" He has wrestled ***fifty*** of the Top 90 wrestlers of the WrestleMania Era in the previous two decades. The only thing that most of them have over Regal is a better look. In every other aspect, be it getting over with crowds, performing in the ring, or speaking on the microphone, Regal is as good or better.

In other chapters, you will read about stars that offered something completely unique to their peers. Regal was like a larger version of Malenko, his greatest gift a supreme mastery of wrestling holds. Be it earlier in the 90s against Sting or Ultimo Dragon or more recently against Christian or Daniel Bryan, with any Regal match, you were going to get an utterly spectacular wrestling nuance. Probably the best examples came from his matches with Chris Benoit. I remember filling in on LOP, recapping a Saturday show called *Velocity*. One random week in July 2005, Regal vs. Benoit was on that program and produced a match distinct to anything that you could see in the WWE back then or today. The wrestling style employed, grappling and counter-grappling, is not typically thought to be exciting enough to fit the sports entertainment genre, but if you have a guy who can do it right, then it works because it is so unusual. 85% of the match was wrestled on the mat, with only a handful of suplexes and other moves. Any time that those two wrestled, it was a "can't miss" occasion.

Some critics might suggest that Regal does not have the credentials, outside of his obvious talent, to be considered one of the best of the last thirty plus years. To those people, I simply state that William Regal, be him a Lord guiding an Earl (Robert Eaton as part of the WCW Blue Bloods), an authority figure, an Intercontinental Champion, a member of King Booker's Court, or an ECW Championship contender, made an impression. His work always outmatched his push, as evidenced by his position here as the 74th greatest star of the WrestleMania Era.

He has become one of the most respected men in WWE thanks to his talent development work behind the scenes. Younger wrestlers look up to him and veterans admire him. Former WWE commentator Matt Striker was even known to call him "Master Regal" out of respect and reverence. You cannot quantify that sort of quality, but you also cannot deny how much it matters in the grand scheme of things.

#73: Magnum TA

It is quite possible that many fans reading this book have never heard of Magnum TA (Terry Allen). To the younger viewer of the modern professional wrestling television product, the former two-time NWA United States Champion has not been a relevant name in the industry since the mid-to-late 80s. Magnum TA was once an excellent talent destined to be NWA World Heavyweight Champion. Unfortunately, he is wrestling's version of Lenny Bias, the Maryland Terrapins basketball star taken #2 in the 1986 NBA Draft by the Boston Celtics. Bias, on the brink of a potential all-time great career, died two days after being drafted. That same year, Magnum lost control of his Porsche on a rainy night and crashed into a telephone pole just one month before he was scheduled to defeat Ric Flair for the World title at *Starrcade '86*.

He never wrestled again.

If Magnum had not suffered a career-ending injury, then he might very well have changed the course of wrestling history. The NWA was still very much a southeast-to-midwest-dominated company in the mid-80s. There was a reason why they ran the first four *Starrcades* in Greensboro and Atlanta - the south was where their product was most popular. Jim Crockett's Mid-Atlantic Championship Wrestling was the NWA hotbed and along came this handsome young man with unmatched southern charm (and drawl) with the Wyatt Earp-mustache and cowboy-styled wrestling boots. Andre the Giant gave Allen the name Magnum TA because of how much he looked like *Magnum P.I.* star, Tom Selleck. Years were spent trying to find the right guy with whom Ric Flair could pass back and forth the NWA title. Magnum appeared to be the one, possessing some of the natural "common man" qualities of Dusty Rhodes, but also the body of the modern athlete. Allen was the perfect foil to The Nature Boy's heel character.

Magnum was anything but flashy; the antithesis to Flair, who was cut from the white collar mold of the antagonist from the old northern territories. The southeast was a part of the country where the blue collar guys like TA resonated. He had that Steve Austin kind of rough around the edges, grab your lunch pail and head to the mill attitude about him. The Magnum vs. Flair rivalry could have been huge with the NWA's target markets. The potential was shown at the *AWA Super Clash* in 1985, where he certainly looked the part of a main-event talent waiting to happen in a 25-minute World title match with Naitch. They had the southern version in the 80s of that "special" feel that Rock and Austin had in the Attitude era. When they locked up, the people knew that they were witnessing two equally passionate people that were from different sides of the tracks.

The best of the best have an aura about them. Allen exhibited that presence; the look and feel of a champion. He was a great wrestler, too. Many fans might be familiar, even if by reputation alone, with his United States Championship bout with Tully Blanchard at *Starrcade '85*. That match is still regarded as one of the finest ever. The Steel Cage "I Quit" match was a bloody brawl that has stood the test of time. It was also the match that put Magnum on the road to the NWA World title, as the committee in charge of choosing a champion surely viewed his production in a high level, well-hyped situation and saw dollar signs.

Equally as impressive were his patriotic battles with the Soviet, Nikita Koloff. Any questions about Magnum's performance ability should have been put to rest when he essentially taught a novice to wrestle in a story that spanned much of 1986 prior to his accident. Their matches were so good that many assumed that they would pick back up where they left off with the US title when one of them became World Champion. It was two emerging stars of the business clashing early in their respective careers; two budding main-eventers similar to seeing Rock vs. Austin for the Intercontinental title in 1997 or a young Randy Orton go up against Edge for the IC belt in 2004. On Magnum's merits, Koloff was one of the most sought after talents in the industry at feud's end and was the one that replaced Allen in the *Starrcade* main-event against Flair.

      Simply put, Magnum TA was everything that you could want in the face of a southern franchise. Combining his unique connection to the audience with his talents, he could have supplanted Flair as "The Man" in the National Wrestling Alliance. The NWA was predominantly a heel driven institution, but in a wrestling world full of changes, Magnum could have had them plotting a new course. Had Allen avoided the crash and won the World title, the likes of Sting and Lex Luger might have been jockeying for position as the next top heel instead of becoming well-renowned heroes, The Four Horsemen might have met their match, and America vs. Russia might have lived on through Magnum vs. Koloff.

#72: Dean Ambrose

We begin our discussion of the three former members of The Shield with Dean Ambrose. In the second edition (through *Summerslam '14*), The Hounds of Justice were in the wait-and-see 85th spot, championed for their Freebird-esque influence on stables in the modern WWE product. I knew full well, though, that the third edition would be shaped by their success. I wrote then, "As of late 2014, they were each on track to break through the proverbial glass ceiling and become the foundation for the next generation of WWE main-eventers. Their rabid desire, to not just get to the top in WWE but define a new era, will surely serve them well in the near future." Indeed it has.

Though we have to be equally mindful with Ambrose, Rollins, and Reigns as we do with Wyatt not to over-inflate their Network Era resumes, it was evident from the outset that The Shield was a cut above the Zigglers, Del Rios, and Mizs of modern wrestling lore. They were like the evolutionary Piper, Michaels, and Cena grouped together, destined to push each other from within their tight-knit unit. I am known in my columns for being occasionally hyperbolic and maybe at times a little too anxious to shove something into a higher place in history than perhaps it deserves (mainly because I so greatly appreciate seeing something historic); I am also known for being happy to eat crow when appropriate. Over two years since The Shield's last match, I do not think it hyperbole to proclaim them one of the greatest stables ever or to state that they were more impactful in just eighteen months together than most acts are in their entire careers.

The Hounds of Justice crushed their debut match at *TLC 2012*, creating a non-traditional TLC format in the process. By the spring of their first full year on the roster, they had already re-defined fan expectations for the Six-Man Tag Team match. I am not sure I even would have thought to make "Six-Man Tag" a proper noun before watching them break down and rebuild the match type, but today I regard Six-Man Tag Team matches between The Shield and both The Wyatt Family and Evolution as among the greatest of all-time and consider them blueprints for future faction clashes to follow. Their *Elimination Chamber 2014* match with The Wyatts earned a "This is Awesome!" chant from the audience before the match ever got underway and lived up to the hype with a phenomenal performance. I sat with my friend, Chris, watching it on one of our "wrestling days" when we also revisited HBK vs. Taker from *Mania 25*, War Games 1992, Magnum TA vs. Tully Blanchard from *Starrcade*, and other classics of that ilk. He called it, "as good as anything we watched today." That match is a microcosm for The Shield; they were all-time-level awesome.

Since the destruction of The Shield in June 2014, all three have had plenty of success, but it is the Lunatic who remains on the Fringe of greatness while his cohorts have already reached staggering heights. Ambrose sits in the Third-Tier right now because he is their historic third wheel, the Foley to their Rock and Triple H if you will. It is still very early in the game for them, though, and there is plenty of time for multiple lead changes. You will see later who currently leads, but do not be surprised if the fourth edition of this book sees Ambrose vault ahead of at least one of them.

What makes it so intriguing is that all three are so versatile. Reigns has the traditional look of the dominant WWE babyface and has that "it" appeal that draws in young viewers but, in a changing wrestling world, he might actually be the perfect heel. Rollins has proven he can excel as the company's top antagonist but, given what he can do athletically and modern fan appreciation for in-ring excellence, there is a huge babyface run in his future. Ambrose is the most natural hero of the three in today's climate, with a multi-faceted skill set that suggests his popularity could explode to #1 for his generation; all the while, it is generally regarded that his potential as the #1 heel is limitless. As a group that once professed its central goal was "to take over the business," they are likely to spend the rest of this decade measuring their successes against each other and it will be my job to measure their successes against the rest of their all-time-level contemporaries.

Ambrose has the tools necessary to ascend quickly in the coming years. He is the most engaging talker perhaps of any modern era peer (Wyatt and Kevin Owens are the only challengers), capable of filling any verbal need for WWE; comedy, drama, go-home promos that drive PPV interest, he is like a vocal Swiss Army-knife and has the potential to become one of the greatest ever. He has also become a well-rounded in-ring performer, best evidenced by his work with Rollins and Owens; rivalries with both have easily captured the imaginations of the current fanbase and have produced some of the most stimulating, psychologically-sound matches in recent memory.

He has been one of the Top 5 stars in WWE every year since 2014; he is a former Intercontinental Champion and the longest single-reigning United States Champion under the WWE banner; he has been in the main-event of seven non-Big 3 PPVs and been on the marquee for Summerslam and WrestleMania as well; he has shown a propensity for creating new standards in gimmick matches (Lumberjack, Hell in a Cell, Ladder, and Last Man Standing); Ambrose is well on his way to an outstanding career.

#71: Yokozuna

The WWE went through a major transition in the early 90s, during which time the government was reigning in the use of steroids in wrestling. Bret Hart was chosen as the new face of the company in the aftermath as the 'roided up bodybuilder era abruptly ended and WWE needed to find a menacing challenger for Hart to accentuate an underdog mentality for their new star. Enter Yokozuna, a five-hundred pound Samoan portraying a Polynesian sumo grand champion under the tutelage of long-time Japanese heel manager, Mr. Fuji. The 1993 Royal Rumble match, for the first time, gave the winner a championship match at *WrestleMania* (*IX*). Yokozuna won the match and earned the right to face Bret in Vegas that April.

Originally, it seemed that Yoko was merely being built up to take the fall for Bret, making the new WWE poster boy look stronger and more credible. However, the questionable decision was made to put the belt back on a very trimmed down (off 'roids) Hulk Hogan. To do that, Yoko defeated Bret in the main-event at *Mania IX* by nefarious means. It was one of the two best matches of his career, but it will always take a backseat to the controversy that happened afterward. Hogan ran down, Yoko (illogically) put the title on the line immediately, and Hulkamania ran wild yet again. The Hogan experiment lasted just a few months, though, putting Yokozuna in position to actually have a historically memorable run as a top star in the WWE. He beat Hogan to win back the title at the '93 *King of the Ring* and held it for nine months.

One of the bigger storylines of his career came shortly after he won the championship from Hogan. The WWE was somewhat desperate to find someone cut from the same mold as Hulk. They had a competition aboard a decommissioned aircraft carrier (the USS Intrepid) over the summer to see if anyone could body slam the new champion. Nobody could do it; nobody, that is, until Lex Luger flew onto the ship in a helicopter and proceeded to perform the most significant body slam since 1987. Off the two of them headed toward that year's *Summerslam*, with Luger challenging Yoko for the title. The storyline was handled well, as evidenced by how supportive the live crowd was of Luger during the match in Detroit.

Yokozuna began struggling mightily with his weight toward the latter part of his title reign and ultimately died because he could not keep it under control, but when he came into the WWE, he was a fairly mobile guy for his size. He had several solid performances during his first year. His work against Undertaker at the '94 *Royal Rumble* (in a Casket Match) was particularly memorable because the two of them worked such similarly dominating styles. Something had to give and it ended up being The Deadman. Yokozuna subsequently got the chance to main-event his second consecutive WrestleMania. He joined elite company, as only he, Hogan, Randy Savage, Steve Austin, The Rock, Triple H, John Cena, and Roman Reigns have wrestled in two or more show closing matches at Mania in a row. *Mania X* was also the night that Yoko became the only wrestler in WWE history to wrestle two matches at two different WrestleManias (vs. Hart and Hogan at *IX*; vs. Luger and Hart at *X*).

At *Mania X*, Yoko dropped the WWE title back to Bret. Later that year at *Survivor Series*, he had his last high profile singles match, rekindling the feud with Undertaker in another Casket Match. After that, Yokozuna seemingly did nothing but eat. Jim Cornette, one of the best managers of all-time, was by his side as a mouthpiece to help keep him relevant, but his weight limited what they could do with him. They found a good way to utilize the name he had built during his main-event run by putting him in tag teams, first with Crush and then, most successfully, with Owen Hart. He was revealed to be Owen's "mystery partner" at *WrestleMania XI*, where the duo faced The Smoking Gunns for the Tag Team titles. He could still competently move around and execute. Owen was so good that the team worked quite well. Yoko and Owen ruled the tag team division as champions for half of 1995.

Yokozuna may not have had a lengthy run in the WWE, but it was noteworthy. His role was important in helping the WWE transition from the Hogan era to their next boom period. He won the Royal Rumble match, won the WWE Championship twice, and was a Tag Team champion. He was actually the first Samoan WWE Champion (and look at the legacy that stemmed from it). During his run as a top talent, he was in the main-event at all of the major WWE PPVs (*Royal Rumble, Mania, Summerslam, and Survivor Series*) and managed victories over some of the top talents of all-time in Hogan, Bret, Luger, and Taker. I also maintain that any wrestler that competes for a World title at *WrestleMania* is deserving of praise in historical context and he accomplished that twice. For all his accomplishments, he was inducted into the WWE Hall of Fame (class of 2012). Rest in Peace.

#70: Harley Race

Let me make one thing perfectly clear: Harley Race is one of the greatest in the history of the sport. Race was a diamond in the rough in the '70s, combining an uncanny understanding of wrestling psychology with a true grit en route to becoming arguably the greatest wrestler of his generation. He was an eight-time NWA World Heavyweight Champion at a period when there was an extensive championship committee around the country that chose which wrestler they thought would best draw money across the map. Race was to Ric Flair's generation what The Nature Boy has been to mine; absolutely one of the most respected individuals to ever grace the squared circle.

He made a name for himself in 1973 with his NWA Championship-winning victory over Dory Funk, claimed in some circles to be a legitimate match (a shoot fight) that NWA bookers expressly told Race not to lose. The circumstances found Funk refusing to drop the title. As history shows, the leaders of promotions do not take kindly to such actions from their champions (see Montreal Screwjob). Race was a man's man. I highly doubt Funk found that there was much he could do except lose as he was told. It took another four years after Race dropped the title to Jack Briscoe before getting it back. During that time, he amassed a laundry list of regional and international titles, in addition to becoming the very first United States Champion.

Race was a star around the world. When he won the NWA title in '77, he was the second most well-known star in the business (behind Andre). He was the face of the NWA until 1981, when he lost the belt to Dusty Rhodes. The loss to Rhodes turned out to be the beginning of the end for Race's run at the top of the wrestling world. His body was starting to break down and the tempo of the main-event matches was starting to pick up with more athletic workers. He still had one more vitally important feud, though.

His contributions to the modern era were limited, but imperative. The lineage being documented by this book began at the NWA's attempt to create a Super Bowl of professional wrestling, main-evented by Race defending the NWA Championship for the final (significant) time. *Starrcade '83* was Ric Flair's night to shine, but it was essential that Race put him over so that Naitch could go on to his all-time great career. Their Steel Cage match was hyped by Race placing a $25,000 bounty on taking Flair out. The match took place about 15 miles down the road from my house at the Greensboro Coliseum. Race vs. Flair, for those that have not seen it, was a torch-passing moment. Harley was the business's most appreciated star of the 1970s; Flair was the same for the 1980s. It ended with Flair victorious and newly crowned as champion, but it was the swansong for Race.

Flair was important to the future of the sport and Race recognized it. He had the respect for Flair to lose to and "make" him, if you will. Race was not a fan of the way Vince McMahon was going around the country buying up much of the top talents to make his WWE promotion national and he knew that Flair was the one true hope for the NWA to withstand the onslaught. With *Starrcade* (and Flair vs. Race), the NWA beat the WWE to the punch in creating a major yearly event for professional wrestling. Race did everything that he could to ensure its success, both in the short and long term. He was also an inspiration for any aspiring wrestler that had an appreciation for the old school. Whenever I watched Arn Anderson wrestle or do an interview, I saw a lot of Harley Race. Their styles were eerily similar, from their tough guy attitudes to the way that they would bump around for their opponents. Triple H also emulated some of Race's style.

Race was eventually forced to go to the WWE. He lost a lot of money that he had wrapped up in the St. Louis territory that Vince basically squashed, so he swallowed his pride to provide for his family and made his way up north to work for McMahon.

Here is the difference between a Harley Race and a Dusty Rhodes, once they made it to the WWE: Vince McMahon saw Rhodes as a joke – he poked fun at him in numerous ways, from naming a character that was subservient to a rich man, "Virgil" (after Dusty's real name), to making him dress like an idiot and partner with a nobody. Yet, when Race came to the WWE, Vince lined up the majority of his roster, from the dressing room to the ring, and had them all help coronate Harley as the "King of the Ring." Race was given a respectable run in the WWE that culminated in several WWE Championship matches against Hulk Hogan in 1987.

He would later go on to manage Lex Luger to the WCW World Heavyweight Championship and help Vader become the force to be reckoned with that helped keep WCW afloat in the early 90s. He managed "The Mastodon" to three reigns as World Champion.

In 2004, Race was inducted into the WWE Hall of Fame. During his induction speech, he said something that has always resonated with me. He stated that "there's not a better place on Earth than under those bright lights," in reference to the spotlights shining down on the wrestling ring.

#69: Greg "The Hammer" Valentine

Hall of Famer, Greg Valentine, became a part of the WWE's national expansion plans in the early 80s with an already impressive resume that included four NWA World Tag Team Championship reigns, two runs with the NWA Television Championship, two NWA United States titles, multiple one hour time limit draws with former WWE Champion, Bob Backlund, and a legendary Dog Collar match against Roddy Piper at *Starrcade '83*. The brutal, bloody war with Piper likely made Valentine most attractive to Vince McMahon, who saw him as just the dastardly heel that he needed to top his Intercontinental Championship division.

"The Hammer," as he was known, was an old school, second generation wrestler with a sturdy, rugged look. In 1984, the WWE was going full steam ahead with changing the image of professional wrestling into sports entertainment with Hulk Hogan as the World Champion. Valentine was firmly established by year's end as the man with the #2 title in the organization, providing balance as a more traditional wrestler.

He took the Intercontinental belt from arguably his greatest WWE rival, Tito Santana, and they had a feud that lasted over a year that I would highly recommend you revisit; I had a blast watching their matches in preparation to write this chapter. It was interesting to watch the tone change as the animosity between them grew. Initially, they were clearly feeling each other out, trying to learn the other's strengths and weaknesses. Then, Valentine won the title even though it looked like Santana had him beaten; Tito was actually celebrating with the title when The Hammer rolled him up for the three count. To add physical insult to emotional injury, Valentine locked him in the Figure Four and injured his leg. Consequently, in their next match, the heat was turned up ten degrees, as not only was Tito trying to get the title back, but he was also trying to exact revenge. That was when their matches got really good. Valentine may have been technically oriented, but he could brawl with the best of them. He and Tito had some serious fights, busting each other open with no one there to see it but the live audience.

Valentine put Tito out of action for several months and Junkyard Dog became his primary title challenger. I never much cared for Hammer and Dog's work together, but their *WrestleMania* match was arguably the biggest in their careers. The only other matches that come close for Valentine were the *Starrcade* bout with Piper and the following year's *WrestleMania 2* Tag Team title match.

Santana vs. Valentine resumed after *Mania*, with Tito ending The Hammer's IC title reign (the 5th longest in history). They had No Disqualification matches, Lumberjack matches, and Steel Cage matches, the latter of which decided the end of their feud in July 1985. The magic of YouTube allowed me to relive their rivalry, match by match, so a big thank you to "hoftitosantana." Here is an idea for a WWE Network show: have Mean Gene do a studio introduction for rivalries that did not have modern avenues (TV, PPV) for their biggest battles, maybe featuring the talents talking about them in hindsight, and then play the matches; Hammer's rivalry with Tito would make for an awesome episode.

To illustrate how big a star that Valentine was at the time, he went right from being the face of the IC title division to being the face of the World Tag Team Championship division. A month after losing the Intercontinental belt, he and his new partner, Brutus Beefcake, won the WWE Tag titles. Dubbed "The Dream Team," they engaged in a memorable, yearlong saga with The British Bulldogs that featured three major television or PPV matches (what Valentine-Santana lacked!). Valentine and Beefcake retained the titles on one of the early episodes of *Saturday Night's Main Event* in March of '86. The Bulldogs retained later in the year on another *Saturday Night's*

Main Event; the Two-out-of-Three falls match was voted one of the program's all-time Top 33 matches. In between, The Bulldogs topped The Dream Team at *WrestleMania 2* to win the straps. Other than the TLC era in 2000/2001 or when Hogan dropped down to the division in 1993, there was never a more prominently featured tag title bout at WrestleMania. The match was the main-event of the Chicago portion of the three citied-card, with celebrity guest Ozzy Osbourne in the challengers' corner to offset heel manager, Johnny Valiant. The concept of "stealing the show" at *Mania* was not officially born until a year later, but Valentine, Beefcake, and The Bulldogs definitely had the best match of the second edition.

Valentine's career started its decline shortly thereafter. He remained a tag title contender both with Beefcake and later The Honky Tonk Man (as "Rhythm and Blues"), but his role increasingly diminished as the 90s approached. His last significant feud was with Ronnie Garvin, a former NWA Champion. They feuded throughout 1989, with The Hammer forcing him into retirement until Garvin's antics as a hired referee and announcer for Valentine's matches got Greg and his long-time manager, Jimmy Hart, so fed up that they asked the stipulation from the "retirement match" earlier in the year to be lifted. The story came to an end in an "I Quit" match at the 1990 *Royal Rumble*. Newer fans should go back and watch it.

The Hammer, compared to his peers in the Third-Tier, was the second most successful champion and ranked in the Top 15 in three of the four other categories. WWE created a DVD called *The Greatest Wrestling Stars of the 80s* and highlighted Valentine among the dozen or so featured superstars. Let that plus his ranking here reinforce his Hall of Fame status.

#68: Bob Backlund

When the first *NWA Starrcade* took place in November 1983, unofficially beginning the modern era of pro wrestling, Bob Backlund was in the midst of an almost <u>six year</u> reign as the WWE Champion, dating back to February of 1978. "The All-American Boy," as he was known, defended the title against all comers, including the champions from the NWA and AWA, often in 60-minute draws that consistently challenged his endurance. He was a hard-nosed worker considered old school even in his day, but he soon became a victim of the changing times, losing the championship and leaving the company before wrestling boomed in popularity. He was a smart guy who saw the writing on the wall about where the company was headed. Accomplished amateur wrestlers like him were going to be pushed aside in favor of more charismatic, larger-than-life characters. He disappeared for ten years.

One of the cool things about wrestling, though, is that a guy like Backlund can come back and be a major player after a decade away. It does not happen in any other sport. During his time away, he must have focused on a piece of his personality that he could enhance into a successful, modern day heel because he eventually morphed from a reboot of his earlier paint-by-the-numbers, white meat babyface character into one of the best maniacal personas of the last thirty years. His interviews were perfect in their poignant pessimism, focusing on the negative changes of the wrestling industry and its fan base. When he snapped on television and used his submission hold to attack several on-screen personalities, most notably the WWE Champion, Bret Hart, he found himself back in the main-event scene with a title match at the 1994 *Survivor Series* - eleven years after his last title bout.

You cannot mistake what Backlund meant to the WWE in the late 1970s and early 1980s, but it was strange to see him out there hanging with the biggest star of "The New

Generation" after so long away from the mainstream. All the same, he did have a legitimate claim to the title. As he told us, he had never submitted nor been pinned when his reign as WWE Champion ended. His manager had thrown in the towel while he was locked in Iron Sheik's Camel Clutch back in '83. He had a point. Still, Backlund getting a title shot was like seeing the forty year old guy hitting on the best looking girl in her twenties at the bar and somehow having a legitimate shot to go home with her. Imagine being a young guy watching that happen; that is the girl with whom you want to make bad decisions. You do not understand how the old-timer even managed to get past a 30-second courtesy chat from buying her a drink. That is annoying! *THAT GUY!? Really?* You want to see him fall flat on his face; you want to swoop in and steal the girl, reminding him that his day has long since passed. From that standpoint, it made Backlund easy to dislike in the wrestling world. It made you want to see Bret show him up. It was like, "This old goat still thinks he can be the champ, huh? Well, the best in the game today is going to make quick work of this goof and send him back to the 1970s where he belongs."

Alas, that is not what happened. The WWE title was the beautiful girl in her twenties and Backlund somehow took her home. Between the matches in 1994 with Bret and the character work leading up to them, the veteran proved to a new audience that he was still better than 75% of his modern peers.

The build-up to the Submission match for the championship was pretty cut and dry back then, but if you examine the match twenty years later with a higher powered figurative microscope, then you will see some interesting things. Historically, Backlund and Hart ended up having something important in common. A "company-carrying champion disappearing from the WWE scene right before one of the most profitable periods in wrestling history" describes both men. They were both old school grapplers that hoped to uphold the traditions of the game more so than they were "sports entertainers," putting each of them in position to be Vince McMahon's castoffs to make room for the Hulk Hogans and Steve Austins of the world.

Backlund requested that his '94 title match be only able to end with the towel being thrown in, playing off his '83 loss. Owen Hart would be the towel-wielder for Backlund, giving the challenger a psychological edge over Bret since the brothers had been feuding for much of the year. In Bret's corner was Davey Boy Smith.

It was an old school style of match, in which Backlund and Hart did not waste much of their time pounding on each other for show. Since submission was the only way to win, they spent the majority of the match targeting body parts that would open the door to eventual victory via the Crossface Chicken Wing and the Sharpshooter, respectively. Critics have mixed opinions of the match, but I thought it was tremendous. I wish that we saw more of the style of wrestling seen from that match. I think it would be a good change of pace in the modern era, much like a team running the option is a welcome sight in an age in college football where it is all about the spread offense. Owen's involvement with the Bret-Backlund scenario added more intrigue to an already entertaining situation; his tears when persuading his parents to throw in the towel - after Bulldog became unable - fanned the flames of his own personal issues with Bret and allowed Backlund to win the title.

Backlund's second title reign lasted 0.001% of the length of his first, as he dropped the WWE Championship to "Diesel" Kevin Nash three days later at a house show in Madison Square Garden. Backlund could not have put him over any stronger, taking the fall in just 8 seconds.

#67: "Sycho" Sid

Sometimes, it is not about skills. That seems odd even writing it after so many years of being a critic for professional wrestling, but it is true. Occasionally, you have to strip away being analytical and appreciate an athlete for nothing more than his physical gifts. Sid Eudy, better known to fans as Sid Vicious, Sid Justice, and/or Sycho Sid, had maybe three good matches in his entire 15 year career, but he damn sure looked the part. From a business perspective, it did not matter if Sid could have high quality matches. His chiseled, 6'9" frame supporting 317 pounds put rear ends in seats, so he was a star. What else was he going to be but a wrestler? His look, along with his old school "I'm going to half yell everything that I say" promo style, won out over his (lack of) wrestling ability.

Once Sid stepped foot in the NWA in the late 1980s as a member of The Sky Scrapers (which also included a young Undertaker), it was hard to imagine him not making it big. Using the Bret Hart Wrestler Score, Sid definitely warranted a "10" for his look. His "body," as referred to by Ric Flair, earned him a spot in The Four Horsemen early in his career, which ultimately led to a World Championship match in essentially his very first big singles feud against then-champion, Sting. The main-event was simply where he belonged. He looked out of place anywhere else from that point on.

Keep in mind that physically sculpted big men were not a dime a dozen in pro wrestling back then. Sid debuted in an era where One Man Gang, Big Bossman, Earthquake, King Kong Bundy, and the like – who carried quite a bit of girth on their frames - were the norm, while more athletic looking guys like him were rare. So, when his contract with what became WCW ran out, the WWE pounced. Vince McMahon was constantly looking for the next Hulk Hogan and Sid was brought in during the summer of 1991 as a babyface to potentially become the next big player. It did not take long for him to get over. Even though the WWE changed their mind and wanted Sid to be the next heel to challenge Hogan, the fans chanted for Sid. He had a natural charisma about him; a magnetizing presence similar to Hulk's.

Throughout his WWE tenure, all fans really needed was an excuse and they would get behind him. He could flip a switch and be whatever a promotion desired him to be. His imposing figure made him a vicious (pun-intended) heel and led to the first of his two *WrestleMania* main-events. He was not a guy that you wanted your heroes going up against. It was like watching Ivan Drago fight Rocky...how could your hero beat HIM? At *Mania VIII*, he fought Hogan to a DQ loss. He only had two *Mania* matches, the other being an unsuccessful WWE title defense against Undertaker at *WrestleMania 13*, making him the only wrestler in history to have a 100% ratio of *Mania* main-events to *Mania* matches.

He went back and forth between WWE and WCW throughout the '90s. He adopted the "Sycho" nickname during his second run with the WWE, perhaps because he infamously got into a hotel fight with Arn Anderson that led to Sid stabbing him almost two dozen times with a pair of scissors (Sid got stabbed a few times, too, but he took most of the blame and got released). It fit him very well and he ran with it successfully. When he got that wild-eyed expression on his face and started laughing, you would have thought he was legitimately crazy. Maybe he was...

Survivor Series '96 was the best night of his career. He had bigger matches, clearly, but he never had a better match and never more dramatically won a World title. I remember the weekend leading up to it. Shawn Michaels had been WWE Champion for eight months. I had watched most of HBK's title defenses and at no point did you really get the vibe that the reign was over until Sid. I had this little notebook for WWE PPV predictions that I would write in the night before each one that I watched. For some forgotten intangible reason, I went against my all-time favorite that night and predicted that Sid would win.

It had a big fight feel. Madison Square Garden's adult portion of the audience was firmly in Sid's corner. HBK pulled out one of his finer displays against Sid, shaping a gem of a main-event that highlighted all of Sid's strengths. Writing of this match without acknowledging Sid's understanding of his moment's importance would be foolish, though. Far too often, HBK is given all of the recognition for the quality. That is a mistake. Sid stepped up more than ever before when he could have phoned it in and still won the title. He won the championship that night and did it with a lot of fanfare from the WWE's most important fan base. In the most famous arena in wrestling's rich history, the crowd roared with approval when Sid covered Michaels for the three-count.

Four times Sid was the World Champion. He was born to be a pro wrestling headliner, with top matches against a virtual who's who in the industry. Sadly, his career ended tragically with an uncharacteristic high risk move gone horribly wrong. Luckily, he made a brief comeback in 2012 on *Raw* to give fans something positive to remember him by.

#66: Matt Hardy

Matt Hardy had a very good career. For a decade, he was an important figure in the WWE, providing depth to the roster with his steady presence in the upper mid-card. Top wrestling companies will always need guys like him. Not everyone can be in the main-event and there is plenty of show to fill besides the last match. Matt was a guy with a great connection to the audience that could always be counted to step up when called upon for a headlining match or work hard to add to the overall quality of the show.

For a long time, he was one of my favorite wrestlers. I remember reading him and his brother's book, *Exist to Inspire,* and gaining an immense respect for Matt. He opened his own wrestling promotion, the Organization of Modern Extreme Grappling Arts (OMEGA), at the age of 23. I resonated with his drive and determination. I must have flashed the Matt Hardy: Version 1.0 hand sign (1st and 2nd finger up, ring finger down, and pinky up) in three quarters of my college pictures.

Though when I think of Matt, I mostly recall his work as a vastly underutilized singles performer, most people will remember him as one half of The Hardy Boyz, arguably the greatest tag team since The Road Warriors. The brothers from North Carolina were risk takers of the highest order who burst onto the scene at *No Mercy '99* in the first Tag Team Ladder match against Edge and Christian. Together, the four upstarts redefined what came to be expected of a Ladder match, shifting the focus away from storytelling to an exhibition in destructive visual artistry. They put their bodies on the line like few had ever done before. Their rivalry soon included a third team, The Dudley Boyz, who helped them pioneer an era in tag team wrestling simply known by three letters: T-L-C (Tables, Ladders, and Chairs). With each passing match, they found new ways to push the limit of what the human body could endure. It was truly a spectacle, as the degree of difficulty kept rising. The

Hardys were the ones willing to take the greatest physical risks, but Matt knew that there were only so many stunts that his "bump card" could punch. He always wanted to take the challenge of making it on his own.

The Hardys were a brilliant tag team. Yet, much like Marty Jannetty was overshadowed by Shawn Michaels in The Rockers, the same could be said for Matt often taking a backseat to Jeff. For instance, Jeff got more of the credit for a lot of the risks that they took, but when looking back at the TLC era, it was Matt front flipping off the platform through a table with no human cushion at *Mania 2000* and it was Matt falling from a ladder in the ring to a double stack of tables outside the ring at *Mania X-Seven*. He took a lot of risks too. And for as much credit as Jeff received for his natural creativity and charisma, it was Matt that had the keen sense for the creative side of the wrestling business along with being the better wrestler.

Matt could have been a headliner by himself. I agreed with JBL's wrestler-turned-commentator assessment that the elder Hardy was a "main-event waiting to happen." Whether it was his work in the cruiserweight division in 2003 or his run of continually putting on some of the best matches in the WWE from 2007-2008, Matt was an "always around, within striking distance of special" kind of wrestler. Though major opportunities rarely seemed to knock on his door, when they did, he never failed to deliver. He and Jeff got the chance to work together at the *25th Anniversary of WrestleMania* in a headlining match. Matt successfully turned heel on Jeff, who had been achieving the top status that Matt so badly desired. It was a natural tale to tell, with Matt unleashing a series of dark promos – the best interviews of his career - about his jealousy toward his brother.

The best work of Matt's career, undoubtedly, was his work with Edge in 2005. That was the year that he proved he could be a top-tier player. Unfortunately, it was quite an emotional roller coaster that led up to it. Edge was having a real life affair with Matt's long-time girlfriend, Lita. Hardy got released during the ensuing internet-driven melee. It was an emotionally charged story that hit home with a lot of people and gained Matt sympathy, while putting the heat on Edge and Lita. Hardy had created a bond with people in the years prior and they were on his side. Week after week, the fans chanted "You Screwed Matt" at Edge and Lita. Matt was hired back to turn the negative into a business positive.

Matt vs. Edge in a Steel Cage was one of the biggest moments of Hardy's singles career. That bout perfectly told the tale of the man that got the short end of the stick in the past giving his former friend and ex-girlfriend the comeuppance that they deserved. Lita got the Twist of Fate, Edge took the fall after a Hardy leg drop from the top of the cage, and Matt received the well-deserved hero's praise.

He went on to win the United States Championship and the ECW Championship to accompany his numerous tag team titles and, on the strength of his headlining statistics as a member of the Hardy Boyz and his laundry list of good matches, ascended to an historical level above higher profile main-event talents in the Third-Tier.

#65: Goldust

Making his first appearances in the WWE and WCW in the early 90s, Dustin Rhodes seemed every bit the "Natural" that his nickname suggested and several top notch matches with all-time greats such as Steve Austin, Rick Rude, and Ricky Steamboat gave every indication that the son of Hall of Famer, Dusty, would be following in his father's footsteps and making the family name proud. Yet, in winning the WCW United States Championship twice, he showed little of his father's iconic personality, seemingly ensuring that he was destined to be a "helluva hand" who could wrestle well enough to help others get to the top, but would never be given the chance to, himself, become a headliner.

But there was something going on inside that man's mind.

Whether it be his unusual upbringing that saw his father on the road all the time and his parents divorcing at a young age, the latter of which I can personally vouch for taking its psychological toll on a young person; or be it an addictive personality that led to heavy drinking early in his career and progressed to full blown substance abuse via the combination of booze and painkillers (a common practice in wrestling at the time made most famous by Shawn Michaels in the 90s), Dustin had a lot going on in his head. He talked in his book of the issues with his father that, at first, quietly drove him to a dark place.

Dustin must have been having some sinister thoughts when Vince McMahon approached him about a new character that he wanted to try on WWE television. To see Dustin Rhodes from the early 90s and then turn on *Monday Night Raw* in 1995 to see the same man dressed like an Oscar statue rubbing all over himself and his opponents while going under the name "Goldust" was as stark a contrast as you could ever imagine. It was like seeing the clean cut Dennis Rodman with the NBA's Detroit Pistons turn into the Dennis Rodman that everyone came to know, only taken up a few notches. It was bizarre, to say the least. The skills were still there, but the persona was significantly blurring the lines between hetero and homosexuality and preying on the fears of homophobia that were, if you will recall, quite common in 1995.

Society's view of the homosexual male has changed quite a bit since, but back then the world had neither come to grips nor knew what to do nor knew what to make of such an unusual character, groping, sometimes kissing, and frequently making sexual innuendos toward other wrestlers in a sport dominated by men grappling "in their underwear." People were incensed. Dustin was playing the role to perfection and if the WWE had a "Slammy" award for Best Performance in the Supporting Cast, then surely he would have won it in 1995 and 1996. As strange as it was, there was some critical appreciation for his artistry. The fans being outraged was really just icing on the cake since Goldust was eliciting exactly the response that Vince had hoped for.

Scott "Razor Ramon" Hall was the first major feud for the "Bizarre One." Razor was perfect because Hall, in real life, was extremely uncomfortable with what was happening between his character and Goldust; it jumped off the screen. He embodied all the ill feelings that people were expressing. Every time that Dustin touched him during their matches or segments, Razor darted away like he was fending off a man stricken with plague. According to Dustin's biography, Hall was not thinking about the creativity involved or the money that could be made, but instead was counting the days until the storyline was over. On camera, it came across very well because his legitimate feelings were resonating with people. Their match at the 1996 *Royal Rumble*, which saw Goldust defeat Razor for the Intercontinental Championship, was very good because of that dynamic. It was my personal favorite match in Dustin's career.

There was something inside the mind of Dustin Rhodes that allowed him to play that role very, very convincingly. It became a real hit for a few years and they did a lot with that character in a short time from late '95 to '99. Whether it was the unusual work that he did with Luna Vachon featuring all the crazy outfits and animated face and body paints or his transition to a sympathetic protagonist once his real life relationships with his father, wife, and daughter were exposed, Dustin showed himself to be quite versatile. As sick as he could be as a heel, the Goldust babyface character was rather popular.

He became a multi-time IC champ and won the tag titles with Booker T. Once he got his personal life under control, he became a molder of the young minds in the business, mentoring and offering advice as a guy that wanted to give back; and also leading by example during a dazzling last hurrah with WWE in the tag team division, from late 2013 through 2014.

His most significant contribution to the industry was pushing the envelope in the mid-90s. Goldust was not a character suitable for the predominantly child-geared product of that generation and, subsequently, the WWE and the USA Network were threatened by sponsors and censors fueled by groups of parents that wanted Dustin's work taken off TV. Inadvertently, he had set the tone for what would become the Attitude era. Goldust was suited for a more mature audience of teenagers and up (TV14). Because he got parents all riled up, he started the trend toward the WWE becoming something that you were not supposed to like; that your parents told you that you should not watch and that, in turn, you were driven to watch in defiance. Many starting points have been defined for the WWE's most profitable period, but the series of events that allowed for "Attitude" were started by Goldust.

#64: "Mr. Wonderful" Paul Orndorff

Paul Orndorff was one of the WWE's biggest stars from 1984 to 1986, during which time he had big money matches against some of the era's other heavyweights such as Hulk Hogan and Roddy Piper. He represents a good example of the pressures that come from wrestling professionally when the industry is rolling in financial dough. The business wreaks havoc on the human body and part of the reason why you see so many muscled up guys on television is because they need more chiseled meat on their bones to withstand the rigors of falling on a lightly covered thin piece of wood for a living. Orndorff was as well-sculpted as any of the WWE Superstars of the 80s, but to do so he had to spend an exorbitant amount of time in the gym (no matter if it was during the steroid era – steroids do not make you suddenly have a lot of muscle).

During the height of his career when he was making a lot of money challenging Hogan for the WWE Championship, he injured his arm while working out. Instead of taking the time off that he needed to heal, he kept pushing himself past the limit of what he could handle. The injury eventually forced him into retirement. It was an example of how it works in wrestling and other professional sports – you may only get one shot at glory; only one chance to shine at the top of the card where the most money can be made and the most fame can be earned. He took a risk because it was worth the quality of the rest of his life to achieve that position where greatness lives. You cannot condemn him for it, but at the same time, you wonder if he, now, thinks it was worth it. Ironically, there is no way that he would have made this list if he had not kept on. Without those high profile championship matches with the Hulkster, Orndorff would be where Don Muraco is (on the outside looking in).

Mr. Wonderful's initial claim to fame was being the fourth wheel in the main-event of the original *WrestleMania*, clearly behind Hogan, Piper, and Mr. T in star power. Orndorff's truly best work came during his storyline a year later that saw him align with Hogan and eventually turn against him out of jealousy. After becoming quite popular in opposition to Piper (the top heel of the mid-80s), he began teaming with the Hulkster, earning his trust and setting the stage for his summer '86 return to the dark side. Adrian Adonis made fun of him, insinuating that he was a Hogan clone. Orndorff was great in response, showing signs that the words were stinging before eventually snapping, giving Hulk a piledriver on national TV, and bringing aboard one of Hogan's greatest rivals, Bobby "The Brain" Heenan, to be his manager.

Orndorff vs. Hogan was a legendary feud. The Hulkster's matches with Piper, Andre, and Savage have gotten more publicity because they were featured at *WrestleManias*. Nonetheless, as Orndorff himself would tell you, "he made Hogan." There is some truth to the statement, however braggadocios it may have been. They grappled for the WWE title at three major events, though only two were televised to an American audience, both on *Saturday Night's Main Event*; the other, *The Big Event*, I call major because it drew over 70,000 people in Toronto's outdoor Exhibition Stadium (you can see it on the WWE Network). It appeared as if Mr. Wonderful had won the gold in Canada when the referee slapped his back three times while he was covering Hogan. Heenan even went so far as to strap the belt around his waist (and it sure did not look out of place). The referee would then award the match to Hogan by DQ from an earlier bump. They had a similar, hotly contested championship bout six weeks later, ending with Hogan winning by disqualification.

Keep in mind that there was no domestic PPV other than *Mania* until later that year. Had the Orndorff-Hogan matches taken place at the hypothetical *Summerslam '86* and *The Royal Rumble '87* instead of a gigantic house show and on TV, perhaps they would be better remembered, historically. Make no mistake about it, Hogan was not going to be quite as much "the irresistible force" in the *Mania III* showdown with Andre the Giant in March of '87 if he had not drawn as much money and had such a terrific rivalry with Orndorff leading up to it. Hulk had a lot of momentum because of his matches with Mr. Wonderful.

They concluded their series with a Steel Cage match in January 1987. Midway through, both of them escaped the cage with their feet hitting at the same time on the floor, necessitating a restart that ultimately led to Hogan retaining. Such endings go over like a lead balloon with today's audiences, but back then, there were so many matches that ended without a clear cut victor that having two wrestlers continue on after an initial non-finish was fiercely dramatic because you knew you were more likely to finally get an answer to the question of "Who was the better man?" It was the runner-up for '87 WWE Match of the Year, which nobody remembers because the winner doubled as the WWE Match of the Decade (Steamboat-Savage from *WrestleMania*).

Orndorff was one of a few top acts from the 80s that finished his career with few major championships (only winning the WCW Tag Team title twice), but his Wrestler Score (Top 5 among Third-Tier stars) combined with the stretch from '85-'87 during which he headlined several major events and became one of the top draws of the era solidifies his place in wrestling lore.

#63: Sheamus

Sheamus has an impeccable resume. There have been eight month periods in two different years when he was the focal point of a WWE brand. Several historically heralded stars ranked ahead of him cannot make such a claim. Since 2009, he has won the King of the Ring tournament, the United States Championship, the Royal Rumble match, the World Heavyweight Championship at *WrestleMania*, the Money in the Bank Ladder match, and the WWE Championship three times (from John Cena twice and Roman Reigns once). The native Irishman did well in four of the five statistical categories, with a bevy of headlining matches to accompany his title reigns, several very good performances in high stakes situations, and a Wrestler Score that tied him with all-time greats such as Bret Hart, Jake Roberts, and Sting. His career, to this point, actually reminds me of First Tier-superstar, Dave Batista, just without the financial impact.

The Celtic Warrior's Second-Tier ranking was unpopular in the first edition. My perspective was admittedly skewed by his impressive statistics and, though he is the most accomplished wrestler from the weak class discussed in the Del Rio chapter, the fact remains that he was part of that class of time-specific beneficiaries. The advantage he holds over ADR and Miz is that he won World titles six years apart, the victory in late 2015 when there was only one World title to win.

I have been partial to Sheamus since the very beginning, when he came out of nowhere to win the WWE title in December '09. He earned the #1 contendership on a memorable *Raw* from MSG after he had been on the brand for barely a month. His victory over Cena at *TLC* was not well-received, for it continued an unfortunate trend of WWE giving wrestlers the top prize before they had been properly pushed and/or prior to their becoming over enough with the audience to warrant it. However, Sheamus exceeded expectations and showed composure well beyond his mainstream experience level, earning himself a second run with the title after WrestleMania season ended. Taking everything into account, only Brock Lesnar and Kurt Angle come to mind as having a better first full year on the main roster.

I was especially impressed with how he carried himself at *WrestleMania XXVI* against Triple H. Only a handful of stars have been given a major match at their first Mania for a reason – they simply are not ready to handle the spotlight. Also, Trips had become his confidant, with Sheamus immediately seeking his council after years of looking up to him while coming up through the ranks in Europe. Working with your mentor increases the nervous energy that is already magnified times ten at the biggest show of the year. He seemed unfazed by the moment and seized the opportunity.

In his matches with Cena and Trips, Sheamus displayed a high level of confidence as an in-ring competitor. There are few in the game today that are smarter and more diverse workers. In basketball, experts refer to certain players as having a "high basketball IQ"; Sheamus has a high wrestling IQ. He understands the cerebral side to putting on a great match, despite what you might think when you see him. If he wanted, he could get by on just his impressive frame, unique look (classic pasty white Irishman with red hair), and natural athleticism, but he has studied the deeper, psychological context of professional wrestling.

The Great White has excelled as an in-ring performer throughout his career, but his personality has often received criticism. Some of it has been fair, but I choose to judge each superstar by their best work. Few were complaining when Sheamus was a vicious heel, developing an aptitude for taking old Irish stories and turning them into the basis for believable, villainous promos; ditto for his return to the dark side in 2015 that culminated in a Money in the Bank cash-in. It was his time as a babyface that has justly come under fire. Like many WWE heroes in current times, much of the creativity that allowed him to play such an effective heel was stripped away when he became a babyface, leaving a kid-friendly, overly positive, at times unrelatable protagonist in its place. Partly, it is a sign of the times, while it is also a knock on Sheamus for failing to properly adapt to it.

When he won the 2012 Royal Rumble match and defeated Daniel Bryan in 18-seconds at *WrestleMania XXVIII* to become World Heavyweight Champion, it seemed to confirm Sheamus as one of the leaders of the PG Era; he was a Top 5 star in 2010 and 2012. Following the formula that Cena created for a lead babyface, Sheamus to me seemed destined to be the European face of the company as Cena had been the franchise domestically; never before has WWE relied as heavily upon the worldwide audience to grow and maintain its business and Sheamus has long been the most high profile superstar amongst the international roster. However, it never worked out that way, in large part because the NXT Generation usurped the spot he had once occupied.

Bottom line: Sheamus has had a good enough run to secure his place in the history books as a dependable commodity that won a lot of matches and titles in some of the most underrated bouts of his era. The Celtic Warrior is far and away the statistical beast of the Third Tier.

#62: The Midnight Express

There have been a lot of great tag teams, but none were better than The Midnight Express. In this book's analysis, tag teams such as The Koloffs had better Wrestler Scores, The Road Warriors headlined and main-evented bigger events, Demolition had better championship stats, and The New Age Outlaws meant more to the financial bottom line, but when it came to pure performance, The Midnight Express was the best. For the better part of a decade, it was only on a rare night that the NWA/WCW would hold a major television or PPV card without the combination of "Beautiful" Bobby Eaton and either "Lover Boy" Dennis Condrey or "Sweet" Stan Lane having one of the best matches of the evening. Managed by the tennis racket-wielding James E. Cornette, The Midnight Express was my favorite tag team of the 80s.

Eaton and Condrey debuted for the NWA and made a splash with their superb matches against The Rock 'n Roll Express, with whom they traded the World Tag Team Championships in 1986. Midnight vs. Rock n' Roll, in the battle of the Expresses, provided for the most balanced tag team bouts of the decade, as the athleticism of their opponents combined with Condrey and Eaton's abilities to both wrestle technically and attempt high risks made for a potent recipe of aesthetically pleasing in-ring action. When "Sweet" Stan entered the fold, he instantly became the most physically gifted of the lot, helping some of Midnight's rematches with The R 'n R in the late 1980s and early 1990s exceed the originals.

Neither Lane, Condrey, nor Eaton had the bumping ability of an Arn Anderson or Tully Blanchard, nor were they as athletic as The Road Warriors or Steiners, but they were fluid, quick-tagging wrestlers that understood team psychology as well as any in wrestling lore. They were tacticians who were not great at any one thing, but were good at everything necessary to be successful in the ring. Their X-factor was Cornette, who was a lightning rod for crowd heat. He was their mouthpiece and ranks behind only Bobby Heenan in his ability to incite the reaction from the fans necessary to ensure that his team's matches were always high profile.

The Express vs. The Express was undoubtedly the best rivalry for both teams, but their battles with The Road Warriors were Midnight's most famous. The Scaffold match at *Starrcade '86* will be covered in more detail later, but I prefer watching their standard work together, which I always found fascinating. It is a basic tenet of tag wrestling that the heel team dominates to allow for the babyface comeback. Yet, Hawk and Animal were so dominant in their own right, with their unmatched size and strength, that it was intriguing to see how The Express was going to apply their usual strategy. Most of the time, it involved rampant cheating. The Express gave Hawk and Animal the best matches of their careers.

If they ever come out with a DVD set called "Every Man's Nightmare And Every School Girl's Dream: The Midnight Express," then I hope that in addition to highlighting the above that WWE also features their two most underrated matches against The Fantastics and The Wild-Eyed Southern Boys; the latter, which stole the show from Sting winning the title from Flair at *Great American Bash '90*, was one of the top 5 tag team matches of the 1990s.

No team had better quality matches with a larger variety of opponents. That will be the lasting legacy of The Midnight Express. I truly hated to knock them and the next entry out of the Second-Tier, but two of the three former Shield members were relentless in their pursuit of all-time-level excellence, necessitating tough decisions be made; believe me, these two demotions were the most difficult and it was in large part due to their standing as pillars of the NWA/WCW tag team scene in the 1980s. The NWA understood tag team wrestling better than WWE. For some reason, Vince McMahon has continually struggled to comprehend that tag wrestling can draw money all by itself if consistently treated like it matters. Until WCW started picking up lousy, sports entertainment booking tendencies in the early 90s, their tag team division was one of the best things about professional wrestling at the beginning of the WrestleMania Era; The Midnight Express was a huge part of that.

      Unfortunately, beyond their in-ring performance prowess, there was not much statistically verifiable about their greatness. Nevertheless, the "underrated" label justifiably follows The Midnight Express wherever you find them historically, particularly when it comes to "Beautiful" Bobby; he was also an underrated singles wrestler and a member of one of wrestling history's most underrated factions, The Dangerous Alliance. I want to be there when Cornette and The Midnight Express finally get inducted into the WWE Hall of Fame.

#61: Tully Blanchard

Back in the 1980s, the Los Angeles Lakers of the NBA took the country by storm with their aesthetically pleasing brand of basketball. They were led by an exciting, flashy, all-time great player in Magic Johnson. He was the face of the franchise, but flanking him on one side was the league's all-time leading scorer, Kareem Abdul-Jabbar, and on the other was one of the most underrated big-game players in history, James Worthy. They also had a great coach, Pat Riley, who embodied their "Showtime" image and a cast of very good, sometimes excellent role players. The Lakers were a big reason for the resurgence of pro basketball in the U.S.

Over in the Nation Wrestling Alliance during the same period, there was a group called The Four Horsemen that exhibited many of the same qualities of the "Showtime" Lakers and, subsequently, kept the NWA in the game against the WWE. The Horsemen's underrated big-time player was a wrestler by the name of Tully Blanchard. He was an integral part of the group, but he was never quite as heralded as Ric Flair, the flashy, Magic-type leader that received most of the individual honors. Nevertheless, like Worthy, Blanchard deserves a lot of credit for the success of the team. Being in a position like Blanchard in wrestling or Worthy in basketball may not have been as glorified, but fans and pundits alike still had the utmost respect for them. It was a reflection of that respect that Blanchard originally cracked the Second-Tier, but his was a resume that did not compare favorably to a group of wrestlers who peaked during boom periods and/or had more opportunities to create longer-lasting memories.

Flourishing in his upper mid-card role in the NWA, Blanchard had a lot of the same qualities as Flair. He was a natural heel; cocky, arrogant, and easy to dislike. His persona turned up a few notches was that of the athletic, good looking, and womanizing jock. He was a quarterback in college, playing on the same team as Tito Santana and Ted DiBiase at West Texas State. He had the QB swagger and it translated well in wrestling. His interviews exhibited a cool arrogance. Shawn Michaels once described Tully as one of the first "cool" heels that he had ever seen and his matches clearly drew the ever important line between good and bad, ensuring the effectiveness of the presentation for the good guy overcoming his evil ways. He was tough enough to back up his promos, but he knew just when to be cowardly. He was also great at accentuating his cockiness. Flair had his strut and Blanchard had his shuffle; both were perfect for drawing the ire of the fans. Between the ropes, he was as smooth as silk. He could execute complicated grappling sequences with ease. Blanchard might have been the most fluid performer of all-time.

Blanchard came to the Mid-Atlantic territory, where the NWA shone brightest and was drawing national recognition, and almost immediately took the World's Television Championship. The TV title was prestigious, as it was defended quite frequently and in shorter matches, changing the pace from the World Heavyweight title's longer bouts. Being TV champion required you to work faster. Modern fans conditioned for rapid fire action would have loved a TV title and they would have loved to hate a TV Champion like Blanchard.

His career peaked in mid-to-late 1985. He was in the main-event of the very first *Great American Bash*. In a Steel Cage match, he lost the TV title to the incomparable Dusty Rhodes, but it was a huge night for Tully, going on last after Flair's World title defense. That was a big deal. The Flair-Rhodes feud was legendary, but Blanchard's rivalry with the Dream was noteworthy as well. They wrestled on several other big stages, including a First Blood match at *Starrcade '86* and a unique, Barbed Wire Ladder match for "$100,000" that was the main-event of the Charlotte version of the *Bash* in '87 (it was a tour of 3 events under the "Bash" name that year).

Also of note was Blanchard's tag team success with Horsemen stablemate, Arn Anderson. Naturals who had great chemistry as partners, they won the NWA World Tag Team Championships and were the featured team of the NWA tag division until surprisingly leaving for the WWE (for monetary reasons) in late 1988. They kept on rolling as "The Brain Busters," under the guidance of the best manager of all-time, Bobby "The Brain" Heenan; in the summer of 1989, they won the WWE Tag Team Championships, ending Demolition's record setting reign. One nuance that I loved about Blanchard in a tag team setting was that, when he was getting beat up by the more popular opponent, he would expectantly extend his hand toward the wrong corner. Tully and Arn had a slew of great tag team matches during that era in both promotions.

Of course, everything in Blanchard's career pales in comparison to his all-time great saga with Magnum TA. "I Quit" matches in wrestling have traditionally been reserved for only the most personal rivalries. When you take that type of match and place it within the confines of a Steel Cage, then "personal" does not do it justice. In one of the greatest matches in *Starrcade* history, Magnum defeated Tully to win back the US title, but both men were winners in a match of that caliber. It was always regarded as the match that put Magnum on the radar to win the World title the following year, but it could have just as easily done the same for Blanchard. Unfortunately, just as it was difficult for Worthy to win the ultimate individual accolade with Magic on his team, Blanchard had Flair standing in his way of the NWA Heavyweight Championship.

If you are looking to study professional wrestling history, then you ought to make sure to watch some of Tully's work. No heel other than Flair from the mid-80s NWA was involved in more important matches. Blanchard was one of the top guys of the era. He should be remembered as a smooth talker and ring general. His induction into the WWE Hall of Fame, along with The Horsemen, was long overdue in 2012.

Appendix A
The Bret Hart Wrestler Score

#	Wrestler	Look	Mic	In-ring	Total
61	Sheamus	9	7	8	24
62	Dean Ambrose	6	9	8	23
62	Bray Wyatt	6	9	8	23
64	William Regal	5	8	9	22
64	Paul Orndorff	7	7	8	22
66	Tully Blanchard	5	8	8	21
66	Brian Pillman	6	8	7	21
66	Goldust	7	7	7	21
66	Magnum TA	7	7	7	21
70	Raven	4	9	7	20
70	Alberto Del Rio	7	5	8	20
70	Demolition	7	6	7	20
73	Dean Malenko	5	5	9	19
73	The Miz	5	8	6	19
73	Bob Backlund	4	7	8	19
73	S. Benjamin	7	4	8	19
73	Harley Race	4	7	8	19
73	Rick Martel	6	6	7	19
79	Sycho Sid	9	5	4	18
79	Matt Hardy	5	5	8	18
79	Jimmy Snuka	8	3	7	18
79	Iron Sheik	6	5	7	18
79	Tito Santana	7	4	7	18
84	Greg Valentine	4	5	8	17
84	Honky Tonk Man	5	7	5	17
84	Ron Simmons	7	5	5	17
84	Midnight Express	4	4	9	17
88	R 'n R Express	3	5	8	16
89	X-Pac	3	4	8	15
90	Yokozuna	6	3	5	14

The Performance Factor

#	Wrestler	Total Score
61	Dean Ambrose	13.25
62	Dean Malenko	13
63	Bray Wyatt	13
64	Matt Hardy	12.75
65	Midnight Express	12.25
66	Alberto Del Rio	12
67	Tully Blanchard	12
68	S. Benjamin	11.75
69	X-Pac	11.5
70	Magnum TA	11.5
71	Brian Pillman	11.5
72	Sheamus	11.25
73	William Regal	11
74	Rock 'n Roll Express	11
75	Tito Santana	10.75
76	Bob Backlund	10.5
77	Greg Valentine	10.5
78	Goldust	10.5
79	Raven	10.5
80	Ron Simmons	10.5
81	Paul Orndorff	10
82	Iron Sheik	10
83	The Miz	10
84	Demolition	9.75
85	Sycho Sid	9.5
86	Jimmy Snuka	9
87	Rick Martel	8.5
88	Honky Tonk Man	8.25
89	Yokozuna	8.25
90	Harley Race*	7.5

(Total score is based on the top 3 star-rated matches of each wrestler's career; tiebreakers were performed)
(*Race was a shell of himself after 1983)

The Business Factor

#	Wrestler	Comment
61	Paul Orndorff	Underrated Hulkamania era star
62	Yokozuna	Helped carry the load in tough times
63	Sycho Sid	Around for solid times and bad ones
64	Harley Race	Built the super card as we know it
65	Bob Backlund	Rivalry w/ Bret + #1 draw pre-Hulk
66	The Iron Sheik	Rivalries with Hogan and Sarge
67	Honky Tonk Man	People paid to see him get beat
68	Jimmy Snuka	Big time Northeast player face or heel
69	Dean Ambrose	Top 5 star in a thriving business
70	Greg Valentine	Legit top secondary player in 80s
71	Demolition	Difference makers in the tag scene
72	Goldust	All press is good press?
73	Matt Hardy	Attitude Era heartthrob with his bro
74	X-Pac	Factor in DX and N.W.O.
75	Rick Martel	Tertiary draw at a boom period's end
76	Tully Blanchard	Four Horsemen drew gates if not buys
77	Tito Santana	Brought Latin attention in the 80s
78	The Midnight Express	Ask The Road Warriors…
79	The Miz	By-product of those around him?
80	The Rock 'n Roll Express	Tag titles drew thanks to teams like them
81	Magnum TA	Was well on his way to drawing big
82	Ron Simmons	Top WCW star in weak era
83	Alberto Del Rio	The WWE machine at work
84	Bray Wyatt	Hard to quantify true fiscal impact
85	Sheamus	May have already peaked
86	Brian Pillman	Always around during lousy business
87	Raven	Influential, but not substantial $$
88	William Regal	He did little to garner added interest
89	Shelton Benjamin	Should have been in the NFL
90	Dean Malenko	Awesome wrestler; fiscal bit player

(Ranking is based on best buyrates, buy numbers, WWE Network, & TV ratings)

The Main-Event/Headlining Factor

#	Wrestler	Total Score
61	Sycho Sid	36
62	Yokozuna	28
62	Sheamus	28
64	Alberto Del Rio	25
65	Matt Hardy	23
66	Dean Ambrose	21
67	Bray Wyatt	17
68	The Miz	16
69	Ron Simmons	15
70	X-Pac	11
70	Goldust	11
72	Paul Orndorff	8
73	Greg Valentine	6
74	Shelton Benjamin	5
74	Rick Martel	5
76	Rock 'n Roll Express	4
76	Iron Sheik	4
76	Bob Backlund	4
76	Harley Race	4
80	Midnight Express	3
80	Tully Blanchard	3
80	Brian Pillman	3
83	Magnum TA	2
84	Tito Santana	2
84	Demolition	1
86	Raven	1
86	Honky Tonk Man	-
86	William Regal	-
86	Jimmy Snuka	-
86	Dean Malenko	-

(Total is based on cumulatively weighted score)

The Championship Factor

#	Wrestler	Score
61	Harley Race	49
62	The Miz	29
63	Greg Valentine	26
64	Sheamus	21
65	Shelton Benjamin	18
66	Bob Backlund	16
67	Alberto Del Rio	15
68	Sycho Sid	14
68	Yokozuna	14
70	Ron Simmons	12
71	Goldust	11
72	Dean Ambrose	10
72	Tito Santana	10
74	Matt Hardy	9
75	Jimmy Snuka	8
75	Magnum TA	8
75	Honky Tonk Man	8
75	William Regal	8
79	Demolition	7
80	Tully Blanchard	6
81	Rick Martel	5
81	Rock 'n Roll Express	5
83	X-Pac	4
83	Paul Orndorff	4
83	Iron Sheik	4
86	Dean Malenko	3
86	Raven	3
86	Midnight Express	3
89	Brian Pillman	2
90	Bray Wyatt	-

(Total score based on "Title Formula")

The Second-Tier

#60: The Dudley Boyz

The line that separates Third-Tier and Second-Tier placement is more empirical than statistical. The Dudley Boyz, Tully Blanchard, and The Midnight Express were the bottom three of the original Second-Tier. By virtue of the numbers alone, it was a very close call as to which remained, but the Dudleys were chosen because of their historical impact. Going back to our DVD test, Bubba Ray and D-Von had their set released a decade after their last relevant contribution to the industry. It has been more than two decades and we still have not seen the Midnight or Blanchard DVDs and probably never will; WCW Home Video never even released a VHS tape about either of them.

Also, consider that for a decade following the Dudley Boys departure from WWE in the mid-2000s, tag team wrestling became a consistently inconsistent hodgepodge of horribly underutilized talents, dead end gimmicks, and randomly thrown together main-eventers with nothing else to do. Their arrival in the WWE and the style that they brought with them from ECW spawned a golden age for tag teams during the Attitude Era that made them headliners at some of the biggest drawing events in history. As soon as they were gone, WWE lost interest in the genre.

Because of the singles success that their TLC era peers went on to have post-Attitude, I think they tend to be underappreciated, but it is important to remember that without them, the popularization of tag team wrestling in the 2000s could not have happened and, without TLC, the Attitude Era might have been about 25% less exciting. The combination of the Dudleys, Hardys, Edge, and Christian were a Top 5 drawing act in 2000, the only instance of tag teams climbing that high up the figurative ladder in WWE history. They were all innovators, but perhaps none more so than the woodsmen that wielded tables as their primary weapon.

The first Tag Team Tables match in the WWE was truly something to behold; that is still my favorite Dudley Boyz match. There is a unique psychology to a Tables match and The Dudleys were keenly aware of it from past experience in ECW. The best case scenario sees all involved willing to put their bodies on the line, as the gimmick is meant for destruction beyond reason. Modern varieties of the bout revolve around one big table spot at the end and several close calls along the way, but it is out of place in today's time. It was a match invented for the hardcore environment made popular by ECW and brought to the WWE by its alumni. Luckily, The Hardys were up for just about anything asked of them back in 2000.

The *Royal Rumble 2000* Dudleys vs. Hardys bout set the standard for WWE Tables matches. It was about coming up with creative ways to go through as many tables as possible within just over ten-minutes. The grand finale saw Bubba Ray fall backward off the top of the famous New York Knick player's entrance and through a stack of awaiting tables below, followed by Jeff Hardy performing a Swanton Bomb off the entrance through a prone, table-lying D-Von. The best sequence saw D-Von play "dodge the table." He moved off of a table just in time as Matt was flying toward it, but rolled right onto another table. Jeff proceeded to dive toward it, but D-Von rolled out of the way. Matt leg dropped table #1, Jeff suicide dove through table #2, and D-Von escaped unharmed.

It was like nothing else we had ever seen as WWE fans and it was very well-received. The signature gimmick of The Dudley Boyz became a huge hit, but none ever quite lived up to the original. Flames were even added, ala ECW, in attempt to equal what the first one accomplished, but to no avail. The Dudleys went on to a great run in the WWE, in part due to the success of their rivalry with The Hardys and the Table match that furthered it.

The Tables match did for the Dudleys what the October '99 Ladder match did for Edge and Christian; even in a loss, it boosted their profile well above that of the usual tag team. Those two matches put the three teams in position for the TLC era and the series of four classic Tables, Ladders, and Chairs matches that followed.

It was not until I became more educated about Extreme Championship Wrestling that I fully appreciated that the work done in the TLC era had been so heavily influenced by ECW's history. ECW's main-event scene, of which The Dudleys factored in heavily for a number of years, was all about pushing the limits. Fans of traditional wrestling may have frowned upon it, but the WWE adopted a similar approach during the Attitude Era and few raised an eyebrow. The TLC and Tables matches, like the ECW hardcore style that influenced it, is like watching a 1980s action movie – they may not be brilliant works of art, but they are _really_ entertaining. I would happily sit around on a random night watching TLCs like I would *Bloodsport* or *Commando*.

Purist historians who preferred the traditional tag match have justly made the 80s tag scene out to be far superior to the more gimmick-heavy Attitude Era. As right as they are, in general, context is often lacking when comparing eras. The Dudleys set the bar so critically high in their stunt brawls that it overshadowed their standard tag work, which was quite good in its own right. Matches against Edge and Christian, RVD and Kane, and RVD and Rey Mysterio jump out to me as candidates for the best normal tag bouts of those respective years.

When all the statistics were tallied, there were just two tag teams that received a higher cumulative score. A *WrestleMania* and *Summerslam* headlining, *Great American Bash* main-eventing duo that won double-digit championships in some of the most era-appreciated matches in modern lore, The Dudley Boys deservedly earned their spot.

#59: Ivan and Nikita Koloff

Technically, Ivan and Nikita Koloff were a tag team for only a short time and most of Ivan's success as a singles wrestler came a decade before the time period considered for placing and ranking superstars in this book. However, I do not think of one without thinking of the other. As considerable as their individual successes may have been, "Uncle" Ivan and his "nephew," Nikita, accomplished enough together as part of "The Russians" stable in the mid-80s that separating them did not sit well with my analytical mind. So, they are going in as a unit.

Ivan won the WWE Championship in the early days of the World Wide Wrestling Federation, giving him credibility for the rest of his career. Though he was a transitional champion much like Iron Sheik was in 1984, "The Russian Bear" was the man that unseated the longest reigning champion in WWE history, Bruno Sammartino. Koloff held the coveted prize for three weeks in 1971 before dropping the belt to Pedro Morales. He proceeded to become, until the NWA's profile expanded with *Starrcade*, a territory star who won (and won often) everywhere that he traveled. With the Cold War strongly raging, wrestling promoters nationwide took full advantage of the Canadian born Koloff's Soviet character, positioning him as the evil foreigner against various heroic Americans.

He won nearly twenty different versions of the World Tag Team Championship, four of which came when he wrestled for Jim Crockett Promotions (the NWA as most of us knew it in the 80s). It was in JCP where Nikita came into play. The younger Koloff was a Minnesotan that went to the same high school as Mr. Perfect and Rick Rude. He had developed a massive frame ideal for the hulking <u>WWE</u> superstar, but it was the NWA that got to him first. He was so unique in the NWA, which did not have many bodybuilders. Ricky Steamboat and Magnum TA had the best bodies in that promotion, at the time, but Nikita blew them away. Rumors eventually surfaced of the WWE's interest. The WWE had some bodybuilder-types, but none seemed to possess the work ethic or the skills that Nikita displayed in his early years.

The younger Koloff fully embraced the opportunity and the character afforded him by the NWA. When Ivan brought him in and The Russians were born, the NWA instantly had a team on their hands that could draw money against any of their established American stars. Nikita was your favorite wrestler's worst nightmare. Subsequently, when The Russians made "The American Dream" Dusty Rhodes their primary target in 1984, Nikita was dubbed "The Russian Nightmare." They took the Tag Titles off Rhodes and Manny Fernandez that fall and shifted gears toward their most epic feuds against The Rock 'N Roll Express and The Road Warriors throughout 1985.

During that time, Nikita was still a novice in the sport. He was agile and a fast learner who really went all-in with his persona (eventually changing his name, legally, to Nikita Koloff), but in '85 he had been wrestling for less than two years. Ivan was a ring general and still quite nimble for being in his mid-forties, but he could not consistently carry the team. Thus, a third member for their group was brought in named Krusher Khrushchev (later Smash of Demolition). Nikita and Krusher were both acquaintances in the real world of Hawk and Animal (The Road Warriors), so the brutal battles between the teams in NWA vs. AWA crossover matches were actually quite memorable despite the relative inexperience of most involved. I give a ton of credit to Ivan for guiding and directing those bouts.

The Koloffs and Krusher frequently used the "Freebird Rule" so that any two of them could defend the Tag Team titles. Ivan and Krusher lost the belts to The Rock 'N Roll Express in the summer of '85 in a match that well displayed the difference in psychology between tag and singles wrestling. In what was a fine performance from Ivan, "as smart a wrestler as there is in wrestling" at the time, according to guest commentator Magnum TA, The Russians dominated and worked over Gibson, in particular, for close to FIFTEEN straight minutes. The goal for a tag team match in the most basic heel vs. babyface format is for the antagonists to keep one member of the opposition at bay for as long as possible, thus building up as much heat as they can to make the eventual "hot" tag (the moment where the good guy finally reaches his partner). Rock 'N Roll were the model rivals for The Russians, who were almost universally hated throughout the NWA's predominantly southern towns. Combining the attention that Gibson and Morton received from women and the bloodthirsty, red blooded Americans anxious to see The Russians defeated was a recipe for one of the best tag team feuds of the era. When The Express won the Tag Titles just down the road from me in Shelby, NC, the people went bananas.

The Russians regained the straps at a house show in the fall, but then dropped them right back in a classic Steel Cage match at *Starrcade '85* that showed how far Nikita had come in a short time.

Nikita began breaking off into headlining singles matches in 1986. He was one of the fastest rising stars in the industry when the year began, as was Magnum TA. When they began a storyline for the United States Championship that spring, both were on the precipice of something really special that could have taken them each to the top of the sport for years to come. Nikita and Magnum battled a Best-of-Seven series of very physical matches, predicated mostly on Magnum working over Nikita's humongous arms. The crowds were going wild throughout their matches, especially the last two in the series. Nikita had gone up 3-0 to take the most commanding lead known in sports. Magnum had won two in a row heading into Match #6. Nikita ended up losing the sixth match in controversial fashion, but then winning the seventh match to capture the US title by equally as controversial means. Such was the times back then, when clean wins were a rarity when you had two guys involved that needed to be protected for the future. It was a series to remember, though.

With T.A. forced into unexpected retirement, *Starrcade '86* suddenly had no highly anticipated main-event. The solution to the newfound problem was obvious thanks to the surprising popularity that Nikita had gained while working against Magnum. Wrestling fans respect the prodigies in the business and always have. Those that put the effort in and improve in a hurry are going to be given the benefit of the doubt. So, the NWA looked to the other half of the Best-of-Seven series and saw Nikita waiting in the wings. Koloff was slated to get a crack at Flair's NWA Championship at *Starrcade*. It was not the first time that they had faced each other. In fact, some credit Koloff's match with Flair at the *'85 Great American Bash* as the one that helped Nikita turn the corner as a performer.

Matches between Koloff and Flair were similar to the Lex Luger vs. Flair matches that would soon follow. Being so physically outmatched, Flair had to work over Nikita's legs to chop him down to size. Nikita, though, would shake off the injury and toss Naitch around like a rag doll. The title did not change hands at *Starrcade* and Nikita never did become a World Champion, but he was certainly a star – that much was obvious. The WWE reportedly came calling that year with the idea of making him a primary rival of Hulk Hogan ("Russian Nightmare" vs. "Real American"), but he stuck with the NWA through his retirement.

As Nikita became a consistent headliner throughout 1987, teaming with Rhodes to form the "Super Powers," taking part in the first War Games match, and being one of the main protagonists against Flair's Four Horsemen, his body style became the industry standard and his opening to get to the

WWE began to close. The Ultimate Warrior, Sting, and Lex Luger were notable additions to the WWE and NWA's respective rosters that had better looks than Nikita. Unfortunately, the death of his wife zapped some of his drive to push for that elusive World title, as well.

Between the two of them, the Koloffs held four major NWA Tag Team Championships, had one of the longest reigns in the history of the United States Championship, held the WWWF Heavyweight Championship, held the NWA Six-Man Tag Team Championship, and headlined numerous major events including three of the most important *Starrcades* of all-time and the inaugural *Great American Bash*. Their combined resume is, obviously, quite impressive, and they did more in a short period together than most can accomplish in an entire career.

#58: Jake "The Snake" Roberts

Wrestling, as in life, has many levels and phases. The characters that you see on television can be very basic to quite in-depth. An example of a simple persona would be the foreign flag-toting, anti-American (i.e. The Iron Sheik). He gets you riled up by making derogatory remarks about the USA. For my tastes, that type of heel does nothing for me and neither does its smiling, American flag-wielding babyface counterpart. I like to see substance. *The Dark Knight* is my all-time favorite movie, mainly because Heath Ledger tapped so deeply into "The Joker" and Aaron Eckhart's role as Harvey Dent becoming "Two Face" was so complexly layered. I appreciate wrestlers who can tap into themselves and find a darker story to tell. There was never anyone better at that than Jake "The Snake" Roberts.

Blessed with an uncanny understanding of the human psyche, Roberts debuted for the WWE in 1986 and quickly made it well known that he was not your average, cookie cutter personality wearing a cowboy hat, war paint, a mask, army fatigues, or an Elvis suit. In 1986, on *Saturday Night's Main Event*, he was in a match with Ricky Steamboat. After spotting "The Dragon's" wife in the crowd, he made sure that he ended up outside of the ring right in front of her seat and proceeded to connect with his famous DDT, dropping Steamboat's head right onto the concrete floor and legitimately knocking him out. Roberts, with a definable expression that showed no remorse, then unleashed the *actual* snake that he kept in a ringside bag and tossed it on top of Steamboat's unconscious body. It was fascinating. Typical antagonists would just wallop you with a steel chair or give you a low blow or maybe even, in serious circumstances, spit on you. Not Jake. He was something else.

He did not have, what was quickly becoming by the mid-80s, the prototypical pro wrestler body. He was tall and uniquely featured with his mustache and borderline mullet, but he was no body builder. Neither was he given the stereotypical gimmick. Everything that Roberts accomplished was due to the one thing that he had more of than everyone else: an ability to psychologically accentuate the details within himself that were relatable to people. If they wanted him to be the heel, then he morphed into various takes on what I can best describe as the textbook definition of a pathological criminal whose moral compass was fundamentally different than the rest of ours; something that you might see from Hannibal Lector in *Silence of the Lambs*. If asked to be the good guy, then he would become the flawed, yet honorable "every man" with whom you would just assume share a beer as you would ask for advice.

His interviews were the stuff of legend. Nine men received a "10" rating on the microphone in the "Bret Hart" Wrestler Score (Jake, Rock, Rhodes, Jericho, Hogan, Flair, Foley, JBL, and Punk), each one of them differing in the definition behind the score. Amongst them, Roberts had the most dangerous demons - a drug and alcohol addiction fueled by a very difficult upbringing. Guys like him, if they could tap into it, had the content burned into their brains to create heartfelt or heart wrenching promo material. His 1991 mic work during his feud with Randy Savage, for instance, would have frightened even the generation of kids today that grow up playing violent video games. One of the best, simplest interviews – one that I would put up against anything ever said by any of the mic nines or tens – was Jake talking about his yearlong feud with Ted DiBiase prior to their match at *WrestleMania VI*. He embodied the qualities of each person that "The Million Dollar Man" had made grovel for his money and was subsequently his greatest rival (amongst an impressive list that included the likes of Hogan and Savage). "And how appropriate; that the money that you grovel for is your very own."

As an in-ring performer, Roberts was a cerebral genius. I know it is high praise to hyperbolize Jake as the smartest wrestler of all-time, but while there have been many grapplers blessed with a heightened sense of when and why to execute a certain move or give a particular look, none had to rely on it quite so much as The Snake. Since he was not a physical presence, he had to make up for it in other areas. Thus, he became the guy whose work you had to watch closely to fully appreciate. If you blinked, you might miss that little smirk, scowl, or gesture. The actual snake, the most famous amongst them being Damien (the python), was always there to keep the casual viewer in tune, but he was so much more than that. His understanding of what he could and could not do was uncanny. Jake knew that he could not out muscle or out wrestle his more naturally gifted peers, so he put his efforts into making sure that everything that he did in the ring had an identifiable purpose.

Even when he returned to the WWE in 1996 as a fatter, more Christian version of his former self and knew that he had very little left in the tank, athletically, he based his entire matches on hitting the DDT. The crowd would go bananas, chanting "D-D-T" as Jake desperately tried to hit his home run shot. Nowadays, the washed up guys are out there throwing dropkicks when they make their comebacks. I respect the veterans that come back to earn a little bit more money but know their limits as Roberts did that year.

In his prime, he was a "5-star" worker that never had "5-star" match. While his bouts with Rick Rude, DiBiase, Savage, and Steamboat were all excellent for what they were, none of them were given the chance to be special in a way that, say, Steamboat vs. Savage was at *Mania III*. He came about in an era in the WWE where even the main-events did not get a lot of time to play out. Many talents of his caliber suffered because of it, in terms of their legacies when being compared to the stars of today. At *WrestleMania XXVIII*, three matches were given 23-minutes or more of bell-to-bell time, with two of them going over a half hour. During Jake's first WWE tenure ('86-'92), not a single PPV or major televised match went longer than 23-minutes and only two matches in six years eclipsed the twenty-minute mark. It was not until *Summerslam '92* that a WWE match went longer than 25-minutes and, believe it or not, there were two that night. Thus, Jake had a lot of opportunities for "good" matches, but literally no chances to have "great" ones. It makes it difficult to properly assess him as a performer, much as it would be to rate Leonardo DiCaprio if the only movies that we saw him in were 90-minute action flicks.

His two best matches were against The Million Dollar Man at *Mania VI* and versus Macho Man at *This Tuesday in Texas* (Nov. '91).

In the bout with DiBiase, which doubled as The Snake's "biggest" match (second billing on the 9th most successful *Mania* in history, pre-Network), he displayed a knack for storytelling that would have fit well in today's elaborate storytelling era. It was a match about the less fortunate having someone to stand up to the evil rich man. In 1991, Roberts targeted Savage and his wife, Miss Elizabeth, during their "wedding" reception, giving them the "gift" of a King Cobra. The ensuing feud provided the iconic moment when a live (devenomed and defanged) cobra bit Savage on the arm after Roberts got him tied up in the ropes. I remember watching that as a kid and have been scared of snakes ever since. They got this camera shot of Jake on his hands and knees, smiling at the cobra, whose neck was flared out looking right back at him. The match that followed on PPV was extremely intense and dramatic.

Though Jake never won a title in the WWE or WCW, he will always be regarded as one of the top acts of the Hulkamania era. He was involved in multiple marquee matches at WrestleMania and was a fixture on WWE programming, featured regularly in top feuds from 1986 until 1992 opposite a "Who's Who" of modern wrestling history (in addition to those already mentioned in this chapter, there was Andre the Giant, Honky Tonk Man, Ultimate Warrior, Rick Martel, and Undertaker). People can question his drawing power since he played the 80s version of Mick Foley from the 1990s, setting up everyone else to be in the main-event but never getting there himself, yet he was Top 5 draw in WWE for four very important years and, in his one match that went on last as the top billed contest at a PPV (his one and only WCW PPV, *Halloween Havoc '92*), he and Sting drew a buyrate nearly double the WCW average between the summers of 1992 and 1994.

#57: The New Age Outlaws

Who was the third highest seller of merchandise during the WWE's famed Attitude Era behind only "Stone Cold" Steve Austin and The Rock?

"Oh, you didn't know?"

"Yo ass better call some-bodyyy!"

It was "The Road Dogg" Jesse James and "The Bad Ass" Billy Gunn. The New…Age…Outlaws!

The New Age Outlaws were one of the iconic acts of the 90s. I was sitting in Atlanta with my wife watching the 2011 WWE Hall of Fame ceremony live in the Philips Arena when, for the first time in over ten years, the old "Outlaws" music hit. Everyone there was thrilled. To this day, when I talk about wrestling with random fans, someone mentions the opening words to their classic theme (quoted above). They have never been forgotten. And how could we forget them? As the great Jim Ross once said, The Outlaws were one of, if not *the* greatest tag team in WWE history.

Some wrestlers debut and you know they are going to make it big, but neither Road Dogg nor Bad Ass seemed to have "superstar" written all over them. They had their good qualities, such as James being the son of an eventual Hall of Famer and Gunn having the ideal "look," but for all intents and purposes they were a couple of mid-carders for hire until the D-Oh-double G decided to come down to the ring and talk the B-A-double D to join forces with him in late 1997. Fittingly, James would refer to each of them as curtain jerkers, but noted that - as a team - they could make a ton of money. They did just that. From then on, they were self-made men. One month, they were doing nothing of importance and, the next, they were taking out and dominating The Road Warriors like no one ever had before, winning the Tag Team titles for the first of five times in the process. They got over in a hurry with their pre-match schtick and they never looked back.

How can you not appreciate guys that find something that works and turn themselves into one of the most memorable duos in history during a time when more people watched wrestling than ever before or since? 1998 was a turning point year for the WWE and The Outlaws were right there in the thick of things, headlining *The Royal Rumble* against The Road Warriors and pushing Mick Foley and Terry Funk off the *Raw* stage in a dumpster en route to headlining *WrestleMania XIV* in a "Dumpster" match. The Outlaws were in the main-event of the February PPV, too, teaming up with the original incarnation of Degeneration X before officially joining the group the night after *WrestleMania*.

Most will remember James and Gunn from their time in DX. Degeneration X "proudly" brought to "you" The New Age Outlaws for the most financially significant portion of the noteworthy stable's run. DX was a major reason why the WWE was able to oust WCW at the top of the ratings. When The Outlaws joined, it basically took two concepts that were working and turned them into one huge concept that worked really well. DX helped take Road Dogg and Bad Ass to a new level that they likely would not have reached without the faction. The fact that they rank only behind Austin and Rock in merchandise sales during that period speaks to both their own talent and their association with the revolutionary group.

Oh, the antics of Degeneration X...I may not have been the biggest fan of the "shock" TV that dominated a lot of TV time back then, but I loved watching DX make fun of everything and everyone. Their parodies of The Nation of Domination and The Corporation were some of the best moments on *Raw* in those days. My favorite DX moment was their invasion of WCW when *Nitro* was in Norfolk, Virginia. Looking back on it, that was the moment where the war basically ended. DX pulling up to the arena in a military vehicle with camouflage pants and their "S*CK IT" shirts riling up all the fans was a brash and confident move pulled off by young and hungry guys wanting to succeed. WCW could not counter that. Nobody in power there was smart enough to realize that the only way to counter fresh talent like The Outlaws and DX was with equally fresh talent. WWE beating WCW became a "when, not if" scenario from then on.

For a solid year, Road Dogg and Bad Ass were involved in Tag Team Championship matches on most of the PPVs, often in a semi-main-event position. To think, they actually did that without there being much of a tag team division to speak of. Right before they started their team, the division was as weak as it had ever been in the WWE and not much changed after The Outlaws became the focal point with the exception of the fact that they were enormously popular. They did not so much rise up to the top of the tag team scene as much as the tag team scene slowly rose up to them. As the WWE made more money, the roster expanded and some quality pairs were eventually put together to combat them, but by and large, they became one of the top tag teams ever without the help of any great tag team rivals. The most high profile team that they ever faced on PPV was The Rock 'N Sock Connection and that was at the very end of their run. Gunn got hurt just as the Edge/Christian, Hardys, and Dudleys came around, so the most memorable tag matches that they had usually came on *Raw* against thrown together main-eventers like Austin, Rock, Foley, and Undertaker.

When *Raw* had its 1,000th episode in July 2012, all the DX members (sans for Chyna) had a reunion. I think that most of the members of DX, with the exception of HBK and HHH, had looked in the rearview and seen that the group was the pinnacle of their careers. The Attitude Era was a time in which limits were not thought possible because the industry kept reaching such unprecedented heights. Subsequently, it created a lot of egotistical comments once those limits were finally discovered. The Outlaws, Chyna, and X-Pac all made some less than flattering statements after "the ride" was over, but the *Raw* reunion (and Chyna's tweet in reference to it) showed that they all, in retrospect, understood that DX made them household names.

For Billy Gunn, The Outlaws opened up big doors. He had already been a Tag Team champion before pairing with The Road Dogg, but everything from the time he and James formed The Outlaws until he left DX for the final time in early 2000 had to have been like a dream for him. The main things he had going for him were his look and his athleticism. Being a key member of an elite team - rather than having to go it alone - let him play to his strengths. He was well liked with the female audience and all he had to do to get a reaction from the guys was signal the crowd to recite DX's signature chant and crotch chop. I was there the night that he won the 1999 King of the Ring Tournament in Greensboro, which he parlayed into a *Summerslam* feud with The Rock (the second biggest match on the card). The Outlaws and DX were kind to Mr. Ass. The culture of the late 90s was ready made for a guy like him to succeed as he did.

For Road Dogg, The Outlaws were his avenue to superstardom. He had the pedigree from being a second generation star to make it in the business, but the former Marine and Desert Storm veteran was a little rough around the edges to make it to the top. I think he broke the mold of what was generally considered "making it to the top," as you would probably have a hard time arguing that he did not - even though he never won a World title or achieved the singles success that his partner did. For a guy that started off impersonating a "Roadie" and actually released a hit WWE country song ("I can't wait to be alone with my baby tonight") to morph into the slick dancing, smooth talking head of the "Dogg House" was quite a transition, but there should never have been any mistaking his ability to do it. If there was one thing we always knew about The Dogg, it was that he could cut a promo. In wrestling, cutting a good promo will provide you with a few chances. He could have gotten a poop sandwich over with his verbal skills. His highest singles honor was being the Intercontinental Champion, but I think he bucks conventional wisdom and is unquestionably a legendary figure based solely on his work with The Outlaws and DX.

One day, either The Outlaws or Degeneration X as a group will be inducted into the WWE Hall of Fame. It will be well deserved when it happens, but if you are not down with that, then I am pretty sure these guys would have two words for ya...

#56: Andre the Giant

At 7'4" and 530 pounds, Andre the Giant was destined to have neither a long career nor life. His size resulted from a condition called acromegaly, in which the pituitary gland overproduces growth hormone, causing organs, muscles, and tissues to become larger than intended. Andre's life expectancy was over three decades shorter than the average. Yet, he made the most of his time on this earth, personally and professionally. He was as famous for his ability to down a hundred beers, a case of wine, a bottle of Jack Daniels before dinner, and a bottle of cognac after dinner (and still be the designated driver) as he was for his record-setting match with Hulk Hogan at *WrestleMania III*. He lived to the fullest extent possible in his forty-six years.

The very first inductee into the WWE's Hall of Fame, Andre was wrestling as we know its' original nationally known superstar. When the sport was split into regional territories, the NWA's World Champion would tour the country, facing the regional titleholders, but none of their faces could be splashed on the pages of the Topeka (Kansas) Capital Journal or the Greensboro (North Carolina) News & Record and invoke reader thoughts of "I know who that is" in the same manner as the man once dubbed "The Eighth Wonder of the World."

There had and never will be again a better personification of the idea that professional wrestling is like the circus. As much as Andre desired not to be put in the same category as a three-eyed monster or the half-horse, half-man, watching him grapple with another human being - even of comparably gargantuan size - was not meant to be an athletic exhibition. People were paying to see a living, breathing Giant. Vince McMahon, Jr. and Sr., were his promoters and very instrumental to his career. Andre being a "Giant," they recognized that the best way to bill him was as a touring special attraction rather than keep him in one territory all year long.

Andre was an impressive athlete back in the 60s and 70s. He could do dropkicks and get down on the mat to grapple. Many of us that grew up watching wrestling during the WrestleMania Era unfortunately did not get to witness the matches that his peers held in such high regard. He was a worker. Much like Big Show is today, Andre got it done in the ring. He was just too physically broken by the mid-80s to show it anymore. We got to see the legend, but not the performances that helped make him a legend. He was the Babe Ruth of sports entertainment; literally a larger-than-life icon in sports entertainment lore who will always be put on a pedestal. Seeing him wrestle in the 80s was like seeing Ruth play only in his twilight years as a player. You never cared, though, if you had even an ounce of historical perspective. He was too important in making possible what we all were watching. It is a shame if you failed to appreciate getting to witness the Giant do his work.

At the original *WrestleMania* in 1985, Andre was still big at the box office. Though it may have been Hulk Hogan, Mr. T, Roddy Piper, and Cyndi Lauper that were the primary ticket sellers at Madison Square Garden that night, people were still paying to see Andre. The "Body Slam Challenge" between him and Big John Studd was one of the headlining bouts of the card. His victory in that match, similar to his winning the NFL vs. WWE Battle Royal at the following year's *WrestleMania 2*, were exercises in placing him in important positions without asking him to do too much.

WrestleMania III was announced to take place in the Pontiac Silverdome. It was an ambitious move. The expectation was that they were going to, conservatively, put 80,000 plus people in there. It would have been ambitious had the WWE announced the location 6-12 months in advance and put tickets on sale in November of '86 like they would do today, but the fact that they did not have the venue booked until late January

1987 – just two months prior to the event - was radically pushing the limits. To even think that they could sell out the stadium by March, the WWE higher-ups must have been pretty confident in the match that they had chosen for the main-event: Andre the Giant vs. Hulk Hogan.

When Hogan came to the WWE and lit up the mainstream media with his charismatic appearances, Andre took a backseat. The Giant was still the most eye-popping attraction in modern wrestling history, but Hogan did so much to put a different set of eyes on the WWE product that Andre could no longer claim to be, by the mid-80s, the face of the sport. Andre, himself, may have been mainstream before that point, but pro wrestling was not. The industry had to catch up to him.

The WWE coincided the announcement of WrestleMania's location with the most historically significant edition of *Piper's Pit*, in which Hogan was awarded a larger trophy for being the WWE Champion for three years than Andre was given for being undefeated for fifteen years. Andre walked out, noticeably frustrated and, perhaps, legitimately annoyed that Hogan had taken up so much of the spotlight (both that night and in recent years). On the next show, Hogan was as shocked as any to see that Andre had employed Bobby Heenan as his manager. The evil "Weasel" had been a thorn in Hogan's side for years. To align with Heenan was clearly the work of a changed man.

The execution of Andre's heel turn was extremely effective. As an undefeated Giant, he was the perfect opponent for an unbeatable champion. Hogan was the face of the new sports entertainment entity, having built a massive legion of fans hip to his cause. Those people felt betrayed when the previously gentle giant that was universally loved and respected turned his back on the forces of good and challenged the Hulkster to a title match at *WrestleMania III*. 93,173 tickets sold later and we had modern wrestling's first clash between titans of two eras; the king of pro wrestling in the 70s, Andre the Giant, versus the budding icon who was rewriting the history books, Hulk Hogan. The south may have preferred Hulk Hogan vs. Harley Race; the northeast Hogan vs. Bruno Sammartino. Andre vs. Hogan was what the *world* would talk about.

When Andre ripped that crucifix off of Hogan's neck and made him bleed, something special happened. For anyone who has been around over the last decade or so and witnessed the electricity of the events surrounding such matches as Hogan vs. Rock or Rock vs. Cena – matches that, when booked, give you goose bumps – Andre vs. Hogan was what started it all. More importantly, it was a match that made **professional wrestling** the draw for WrestleMania; not a celebrity. WrestleMania was intended to be the Super Bowl of pro wrestling, yet its first two editions had been sold on the involvement of non-wrestlers. Not to take anything away from those foundational events, but can you imagine having Paul Newman and Frank Sinatra as celebrity head coaches to draw interest for the first football Super Bowl?

Andre vs. Hogan was a match that, by itself, drew in unique viewers, earning the largest buyrate (10.2) in wrestling history. It was the event that set the standard for what WrestleMania should be. There are not many documented stories of wrestlers that chose their profession because of any event before *WrestleMania III*. Young kids like John Cena grew up wanting to be WWE Superstars so that they could emulate what they had seen that night and at the Manias that followed it.

You can debate the performance side of the Andre-Hogan match, but to what end? There is a lot more to a match than just the moves performed. It was never going to be about critical acclaim. Andre could barely move. He was well into living on borrowed time. In fact, his doctors had told him many years prior that he was not even going to be alive in 1987. It meant the world to Andre to be given the opportunity to wrestle that match and to be such an integral part in modern wrestling history. Much of his career in the 80s had been about him finding a way to keep doing something that he loved despite it being so hard on his ailing body. When you are a legend, you never want to be riding someone else's coattails. So, what a special thing it must have been for Andre to step up and be the iconic star that he once was for one more night, passing the torch in a more official capacity to Hogan and taking the WWE to the next level.

In 2087, when the WWE is celebrating the 100th Anniversary of Andre vs. Hulk and holding WrestleMania on the moon, I will likely have been dead and gone for at least a decade. If I do, somehow, make it to 103 years old, you can rest assured that I will be watching, in part, to pay tribute to the Giant one last time.

#55: Jeff Jarrett

When I was a young kid, there was a television show put on by the United States Wrestling Association (USWA) that aired after school in the southeast. Their program featured a young Steve Austin, Dr. Tom Pritchard, and a formative grappler named Jeff Jarrett. At that age, Ultimate Warrior was my favorite WWE superstar. Warrior was a bodybuilder with intensity to spare and a colorful, high energy act. Jarrett, conversely, was younger, smaller, faster, and more agile. I was intrigued. Guys that were his size were not the featured talents in WWE. He reminded me of Ric Flair from the NWA, but Jarrett was a fan favorite. I did not yet understand why, but I was drawn to Jarrett's better polished in-ring skills. He was responsible for my transformation from enamored little boy drawn in by the glitz and glam of sports entertainment (via wrestlers like Warrior) to budding admirer of the art of professional wrestling. It was akin to initially liking basketball because you saw the dunk contest, but then learning to appreciate the game because of the passing, the pick and roll, and the fall away jump shot.

There are two things that Jarrett best became known for over the last fifteen years. First, he was the WCW Champion four times. Second, he was responsible for building the new #2 wrestling company after WCW folded. He started NWA-TNA, which evolved to Total Nonstop Action, and was their feature attraction for several years until they got off the ground.

Unfortunately, Jarrett is not celebrated for these accomplishments. They have, in essence, become the basis for the arguments sustained by his detractors. His reigns combined to be just two months in length and "dying days of WCW" has been described as the time when he was their champion; a period when that title got passed around a lot. However, it is a myth that he did not deserve to be champion. He was a very good wrestler. He was a good talker. He was a very good traditional heel. He was very smart. That is a striking combination in the wrestling business. When you combine those attributes in a man with a chip on his shoulder, motivated to show everyone that he could be a major player, then good things are likely headed in that man's direction. Every success story has a certain element of "right place at right time" and Jarrett was no different. He came to WCW in late 1999 because he did not feel that he was being utilized to the fullest extent of his talents in the WWE. He proceeded to do the best work of his career and became one of their most well-rounded talents. When, by the following spring, WCW had finally decided to push some fresh people into the spotlight, Jarrett was a natural choice to be among them.

As for TNA Wrestling, he should be given more credit for establishing another place for professional wrestlers to earn a living. He traveled the world to get that company going, helping them to establish their own weekly cable television show that has been on the air for over a decade and to, at one point, promote several PPVs a year. That is a commendable achievement.

Jarrett has become somewhat of a forgotten man in modern wrestling lore. Despite many accolades, including fourteen major championships in the WWE and WCW, he has often been placed in the category of scoundrels labeled as a "political schemer." In the movie *Gladiator*, soon-to-be Emperor Commodus tells main character, Maximus, that they "must save Rome from the politicians," with the implication that politics would be the end of civilization. Similarly, wrestling fans view "backstage politics" as one of the worst things in the business. Jarrett's association with WCW's booker, Vince Russo, in 2000, was said to be the reason why he won the World Championship. "Politics" – rather than obvious talent – got him the title, or so the story goes. I respectfully disagree.

The WrestleMania Era: The Book of Sports Entertainment

I remember when he debuted on the mainstream in the early 90s. I was excited to see Jarrett make it to the WWE. I never much cared for the character that he portrayed for, basically, the rest of his career, but my childhood memories emotionally invested me in his successes. He paid his dues and then got a chance to step up to headlining status, becoming a rival of Bret Hart's and entering into a feud with Razor Ramon for the "Bad Guy's" Intercontinental Championship. Jarrett vs. Razor headlined the 1995 *Royal Rumble*, *WrestleMania XI*, and the first *In Your House* PPV. Going by the name "Double J," Jarrett captured the title at *The Rumble*, where they wrestled a hell of a match to open the show, working at various paces and with numerous styles throughout the near 20-minute duration. They chain wrestled, brawled, and went catch as catch can in an underrated performance for both. Jarrett gave a good example of how to play the weaselly heel that will stoop to crowd unnerving lows to get his way.

Jarrett and Razor played a nice game of cat and mouse over the next few months, with Jarrett continually finding the outs necessary to keep the title. He ran out of ways to remain champion in July, though, losing the strap to Shawn Michaels in perhaps his best match. Double J was portraying a crossover star who was part wrestler, part country music singer. That night, he pretended to perform an "original hit" called "Alone with my baby tonight" (actually sung by Road Dogg), the words of which I can still sing in my head from memory. So, it might also have been the biggest PPV showcase in Jarrett's WWE career. He and Michaels were both showmen on full display at *In Your House 2*. Their classic was arguably 1995's Match of the Year. One would think that those in charge of making Jarrett a WCW headliner a few years later were paying attention.

During his on-again, off-again WWE stints, he amassed the second highest total of Intercontinental Championship reigns in history (6) and earned a run with the Tag Team titles alongside Owen Hart. His legacy was built on the handful of really good matches that he had whenever given the opportunity. Against Diesel in a match for the WWE title on *Raw*, he showed his ability to carry weaker wrestlers in giving Kevin Nash one of the better matches of his career. He also had a *Summerslam* mid-card gem of a Hair vs. Hair match with X-Pac in 1998 that cost him his signature platinum blonde locks in favor of the crew cut that he wore for many years. He even managed a more-than-respectable match out of Chyna at *No Mercy '99*.

Losing to a bodybuilding woman likely made it easy for Jarrett to go to WCW, where he amassed three United States title reigns in addition to his World Championships. At *Starrcade* in December '99, Double J was no more, replaced by a new, self-given moniker, "The Chosen One." In a match second only to the '95 bout with HBK in his career, Jarrett stole the show with Chris Benoit in one of history's most underrated versions of the Ladder match. It was not the degree of difficulty that made it great, but the crispness in execution of the moderately high risks. For instance, Jarrett dropkicked the ladder from off the top rope, but he hit it so perfectly (and Benoit timed his fall from it so well) that it looked like the ladder had been blasted onto its side by a cannon. He used the opportunity on WCW's top show to make a statement that he belonged in WCW's main-event scene.

Sure enough, he was headlining PPVs by February 2000. As the new leader of the rebooted N.W.O. and then the face of the New Blood faction, "The Chosen One" fulfilled his self-proclaimed destiny. At *Spring Stampede* in April, he faced Diamond Dallas Page for the vacant World Championship. The match was a really strong effort from two guys that desperately wanted to be in that position and wanted to perform at a high level. Jarrett won the title and became a mainstay in the WCW upper crust until the company folded a year later.

Jarrett put up with some God-awful booking during his time at the top, first losing the title in a tag match to actor David Arquette in one of the darkest hours in the sport's history. He was then asked to lay down for Hulk Hogan at the infamous *Bash at the Beach 2000*, only for Hogan to be immediately fired afterward in a real life moment for the world to see on PPV.

Though many a fan might choose to remember him as the personification of his signature catchphrase, "Slap Nutz," Jeff Jarrett had one of the 20 best championship resumes of the WrestleMania Era and was one of the most consistently successful talents on the roster, no matter which company owned his contract.

#54: Sgt. Slaughter

Hall of Famer, Sgt. Slaughter, became a star in the early 80s portraying a Marine Corp drill instructor and rose to such popular heights that his likeness (and voice) was a guest on the *G.I. Joe* cartoon. The appearances led to his being immortalized with a *Real American Hero* toy that yours truly once proudly owned, making him one of the most well-known personalities in the wrestling business during a time when it began to peak. Slaughter would go on to become WWE Champion in 1991, main-eventing that year's *WrestleMania*, and is regarded as one of the few men in history to be both the most popular star in the WWE and later its most hated villain.

He began his time in the WWE as the prototypical, mean-spirited, a-hole gunnery sergeant similar to what the world came to think of such military stalwarts with R. Lee Ermey's portrayal in the 1987 classic, *Full Metal Jacket*, yelling at and degrading his opponents, the announcers, and the fans with such derogatory terms as "maggot," "slime," and "puke." His early feuds with the likes of WWWF Champion, Bob Backlund, and the first Intercontinental Champion, Pat Patterson, established his credibility as a man who would happily break you down with his words, but would be just as delighted to beat you up, physically.

The "Alley Fight" at Madison Square Garden between Slaughter and Patterson is famous to this day for brutality rarely seen when it took place in 1981. The match was referenced as one of the respective best in each of their careers when Patterson inducted Sarge into the Hall of Fame in 2004. In an era where the style was traditionally more methodical, the two put together a physically demanding and exhausting battle. Slaughter was busted opened during his signature spot where he would take an Irish Whip toward the corner, only for his momentum to carry him over the top turnbuckle and into the steel ring post. As Vince McMahon, on commentary, aptly put it, he was "gushing with blood." They beat the hell out of each other.

My father was a Marine and once described the gunnery sergeant as someone that you hated in the beginning, but came to understand that his tough love was given only to make you better and stronger; that he was someone that many came to hold in high regard. So, interesting, it was, that when the Sarge's character set his sights on the Iranian Iron Sheik, the fans that had jeered him right into #1 contender status as the lead heel in the WWE began to reverently applaud his efforts in defending America. With the Marine Corp hymn playing him to the ring, he had always been just the right opponent away from becoming wrestling's national hero. Sarge emerged from his previously dark clouds, shined the rocket's red glare, and sent bombs bursting figuratively into Iranian air to guard the WWE against the Persian Gulf foe. They were a match made in sports entertainment Heaven.

Slaughter vs. Sheik was one of the greatest rivalries of the 80s. It was a simpler time then. Today, babyfaces that tote the flag or heels that desecrate it are considered cheap and unimaginative. In the early 80s, with tensions still high from the Cold War and the viable, still relatively new threat of nuclear firefall, it was as simple as breathing to emotionally invest in someone that went against our country and in the man brave enough to fight him. Sarge was over more than anyone in the company but Hogan as of 1984. In physically brutal bouts, Sarge and Sheik captured patriotic imaginations. Their story concluded in the iconic "Boot Camp Match" at MSG, with Slaughter seizing the day.

Unfortunately, at the height of his fame and in his prime as a wrestler, a controversial situation arose that found Sarge out of a job. Different accounts have been told over the years, but the predominant story tells of a dispute over Slaughter's *G.I. Joe* action figure. It has been said that the WWE likes to keep a pretty tight rein on their superstar's non-wrestling endeavors and something apparently occurred back in '84 that the individual and the company could not agree upon. He disappeared to the AWA for several years, not to be seen on WWE television again until 1990.

Slaughter returned during the Persian Gulf War between a United States-led coalition and Iraq. It seemed good for morale to have one of wrestling's greatest symbols of America back in the fold during uncertain times for a new generation like mine. However, to everyone's surprise, Sarge turned heel. In one of the most notorious angles to ever take place in professional wrestling, he sided with Iraqi dictator Saddam Hussein, pledging his allegiance on national television to the leader of the country that we were at war with in real life. "An Iraqi sympathizer" they called him. The notion that any press was good press was put to the test. I cannot imagine that something like that would fly in today's liberal society, especially considering that the WWE is publicly traded. The negative attention would be too damaging. In 1990, though, they were fully committed to getting as much interest – good or bad – as they could.

He was getting such white hot heat that it became far more than just a wrestling storyline for him and his family. There were numerous reports of death threats against him. I am unsure if we should applaud him and the WWE's wherewithal in sticking with the angle when it was reaching a point that he had to travel with a bulletproof vest or roll our eyes at the nature of the business. The '91 *Royal Rumble*, at which Sarge received a WWE Championship shot against Ultimate Warrior, took place two days after the official start of Operation: Desert Storm. Due to heavy interference, Slaughter won the title and built the fervor of the storyline to a fever pitch. There was no turning back. *WrestleMania VII* was going to be sold on the turncoat getting his comeuppance.

I have briefly met the Sarge and, in person and out of character, he seems like a very laid back guy. That is probably a good thing. Given what he had to endure as the WWE Champion, I can only imagine that his stress level must have been sky high during the few months that he was at the top of the business again. *Mania VII* was **his** show. The TV programming was built on his character. WrestleMania was originally supposed to be held at the Los Angeles Coliseum, but due to poor ticket sales, they moved it to the L.A. Sports Arena. There were conflicting reports about what actually led to the move, as one suggested that people were afraid to show up because of all the threats of blowing up the larger, outdoor venue (due to Slaughter's off-putting stance on the war) and another was that people had lost interest in wrestling. Add that pressure on top of death threats and the Sarge could have easily been mentally shaken to the core.

As an interesting layer of back story to the *Mania VII* main-event featuring Slaughter defending the title against Hogan, it had been the Hulkster catching on as the media darling and face of the brand in the mid-80s that had made the Sarge be possibly viewed as expendable when he was going through the events that led to his departure. The greatest heels of all-time have been the ones that, much like Slaughter did in 1990, turn to the dark side after becoming beacons of light. Had he stuck around, a strong case could be made that he would have revisited his evil ways during the height of WrestleMania's early success, made a lot more money, and been a much bigger star. Instead, Slaughter missed the 80s boom and came back right after it ended. Meanwhile Hulkamania, as of 1991, had nearly run its course until he assumed the "Savior of America" role. So, you wonder if Sarge took any pride in breathing life into Hogan for a little bit longer, buying him extra time at the top in a role that the Sarge, himself, had popularized.

The work that he did in the months leading up to *WrestleMania VII* was the finest of his career. It showcased his range as both a personality and performer. He was old school in his approach to the controversial persona, keeping it basic and finely walking the line between pushing just the right buttons and pushing the character over the limit. His interviews were quite effective. In the ring, he was an underrated bump taker and seller for his opponents. Slaughter's two month reign as WWE Champion ended in the final match of the biggest show of the year, his comeback complete and his potential reached.

He is a legend and one of the all-time greats. You should remember him as such. "And THAT'S…an ORDER!"

#53: Scott Steiner

When you think of the World Champions who got their starts as part of popular tag teams, you typically think of Bret Hart, Shawn Michaels, Edge, Booker T, and Jeff Hardy. An elite member of that club that is often forgotten - for similar "WCW" reasons as Jeff Jarrett - is Scott Steiner.

Given that we live in a "what have you done for me lately" society, maybe that is understandable. Steiner made a lasting impression for the wrong reason during his last run in the WWE in 2003. It was really bad. In the ring, it was atrocious. Steiner vs. Triple H at the 2003 *Royal Rumble* was one of the worst title matches I have seen in my life. Expectations were high and the production was so, so low.

Of course, he was always awful on the microphone, but I seriously struggle to see how you can hold that against him considering how funny his promos were; he has to be wrestling's king of unintentionally comical verbal snafus. Here is the Top 5 from WCW, WWE, and TNA combined:

#5 - "Throughout my career, I've wrestled a lot of countries."

#4 - "Big Poppa Punk Oyiggup! And the next Heavyweight Championship of the world!"

#3 - "But I far ehk...at Mayhem...I'm gonna give you...at Mayhem...Yur....no match for man with the largest erms in the world...and I'm gonna look at the whole world and say, 'Venny, Viddi, Vuchi.'"

#2 - "And they know that they don't have to wait for the Earth to rotate on a 47 degree axis so the stars can touch the sky and create an equilax so they can see the Big Dipper."

#1 - "You take your 33 1/3 chance, minus my 25 percent chance, and you got an 8 1/3 chance of winnin' at Sacrifice! But then you take my 75 perchance chance at winnin', if we was to go one-on-one, and to add 66 2/3 ch… percents, I got a 141 2/3 chance of winnin' at Sacrifice! See, McJoe; the numbers don't lie, and they spell disaster for you at Sacrifice!"

I just spent the last ten minutes crying because I was laughing so hard watching the videos from those promos. My life is better because of Scott Steiner's communication skills and though my life is not better from having watched the nightmarish second WWE part of his career, neither should be what defines him as a professional wrestler considering that, for over a decade, he was one of the most talented performers in the industry, first as the better half of one of the greatest tag teams in history (The Steiner Brothers) and then as "Big Poppa Pump," the genetically (or otherwise) enhanced freak of a competitor that rose the ranks in WCW en route to becoming their last, pre-WWE World Heavyweight Champion.

Both he and his brother, Rick, had been amateur standouts at the University of Michigan before turning pro in the late 80s. They made their debut as a team in 1989 and became so good so quickly that, within two years, they had developed such a great reputation that they were already thought of as one of the best tag teams in history. Scott, in particular, showed amazing athleticism and a combination of strength and agility without rival until Brock Lesnar debuted. He and his brother would both use Greco-Roman throws of all sorts, which drew my attention, especially, because I enjoy the superstars who utilize various suplexes. The most impressive move in the Steiner playbook was Scott's Frankensteiner. It is not every day that you see a 250 pound guy doing a hurricanrana usually reserved for the cruiserweights.

Being brothers, they had natural chemistry as partners and staked their claim to be the featured duo in WCW with matches against various tag team legends such as The Fabulous Freebirds, The Andersons, Doom, The Midnight Express, and The Road Warriors. Their superlative match was a title defense against Sting and Lex Luger at the inaugural *Super Brawl*; an awesome performance in the hunt for best tag team match of the decade. WWE has had a bad habit of trying to build its tag team division around thrown-together, high profile individual talents that largely overshadow the usual suspects. Back in 1991, it was a borderline dream match to see the best tag team against two top singles competitors.

The Steiners moved onto the WWE in 1992 and had a decent run against Money, Inc. (IRS and The Million Dollar Man), but their tenure was largely forgettable. They were given neither the same chances nor caliber of opponents that they had in WCW. Their best match, against Bret and Owen Hart, was not even televised. Other than winning the Tag Team titles, their claim to WWE fame was being on the first episode of *Raw*. They went back to WCW in 1996, facing the likes of Harlem Heat and The New World Order's Outsiders.

As in every great tag team, natural conjecture arose as to which Steiner could make it as a singles star. Rick had moderate success as a World Television Champion, but it always seemed as if Scott would be the one to eventually break out on his own. He had shown prowess as an individual performer back in the early 90s when he wrestled Bobby Eaton and Ric Flair in very well thought of TV matches. By the end of 1997, The Steiner Brothers had run their course. Coming up on nine years as a team, it was time to see if Scotty had the chops to make it on his own.

"Big Poppa Pump" was born as an homage to "Superstar" Billy Graham. Scott had put on considerable mass in the previous year. I remember watching The Steiners vs. Harlem Heat at the *'97 Great American Bash*, seeing Scott, and wondering aloud about how huge he had become. It was not all muscle, yet. Rather, it was like a video game "Create a Wrestler" where you can make the player wider without increasing their fat content. By '98, he had turned all that mass into muscle. Of course, "Freakzilla" spawned a lot of talk about steroid use with his angry, loud, and obnoxious heel character, but none of it was ever confirmed.

The late 90s proved a perfect fit for his character. I am not sure what it was about Steiner that made him such a strange talker. He graduated from a very good college, so he could not have been lacking intelligence. Thankfully, during the Attitude Era a wrestler could make up for his microphone misgivings by saying random things laced with profanity and it worked. Steiner utilized the old school inflective approach of half yelling everything that he said.

There was a lot to like about him. He had an established name, but he was a fresh headlining act. Despite all the extra mass that had given him muscles in places that most people do not have places, he had maintained his ability in between the ropes and was having good matches in the upper mid-card for the United States and TV Championships.

He was given his chance to be the top heel in the late summer of 2000. After two years as "Big Poppa Pump," the timing was right to give him the ball and see if he could run with it. At *Fall Brawl 2000*, he defeated Goldberg in the biggest singles match of his career. It was a hell of a match. Steiner was Goldberg's best opponent, as their combinations of power and agility made for some eye-popping counters. The year 2000 was a much better year for quality wrestling in the WCW main-event scene after having become well-known during the height of The N.W.O. for appalling workrate. Steiner vs. Goldberg was their best main-event match in years.

Perhaps all that Steiner needed was a little show of faith from the higher-ups, letting him know that they believed in his talents. Having the ref stop his match against Goldberg so that Steiner could do no further damage to the top star in WCW was a nice way to show it. He went on a tear from then until WCW was bought out by WWE, becoming one of the few bright spots during their dying days. Once WCW finally decided to make an effort toward pushing someone who had not made his name before 1990, it opened the door for several talented guys to break through the glass ceiling, giving Steiner motivated competition at the top like Booker T, the WCW Champion when Steiner became #1 contender. Steiner won the title at *Mayhem* in a match that continued to build back the credibility of the WCW title.

Steiner went onto to reign as champion for longer than anyone since Goldberg in 1998, putting together a more than admirable performance record against the likes of Sid, Kevin Nash, and Jeff Jarrett, and saving his best for last when he defeated DDP in a great Falls Count Anywhere match at the final WCW PPV, *Greed*, in March 2001. I wish that the WWE could have signed Steiner right away in 2001. He was on fire and could have been the backbone of the Invasion storyline. If Booker, DDP, *and* Steiner had been there, then I think they could have done much better with it. Steiner was a hell of a wrestler, so I do not think there would have been much transitioning for him. He showed against DDP that he could work the popular WWE main-event style.

It is a shame that he became World Heavyweight Champion during the time when WCW was on the brink of extinction. Business was so bad that his run as champ hardly registers on the historical scale (perhaps another reason why he is not often mentioned in the same breath as others to transition from Tag-to-World title). In three of five statistical categories, Steiner was Top 10 among his Second-Tier peers. Safe to say that his career was a mixed bag. Holla if ya hear me!

#52: Bam Bam Bigelow

I became an instant fan of Bam Bam Bigelow while playing the old Nintendo (NES) video game: *WrestleMania*. As a little kid, the fact that Bigelow's big move was a cartwheel caught my youthfully exuberant attention. My first vivid memory of his actual work was his match against Bret Hart in the 1993 King of the Ring tournament final. Bam Bam was tremendously athletic for his size. A giant of a legitimate tough guy covered in flames from head-to-toe, he did all of the things that traditional big men could do, but he could also throw dropkicks and fly off the top rope. He was quite the combination of size and agility.

The WWE has a history of teaching its big men not to sell (much) for their opponents in order to make them look more dominant. Because Bam Bam had spent a considerable amount of time in Japan, where the emphasis on a big man selling is more important, he sold *and* looked dominant and had better matches than 99% of the big men produced by North American wrestling promotions in the last thirty years.

Two months prior to *King of the Ring '93*, at a live event in Spain, Bam Bam and Bret had an incredible match worked without the limitations of selling previous tournament bouts. I did not see it until years later, but it was one of the greatest David vs. Goliath matches in history. Randy Savage (on commentary) referred to it as one of the finest matches that he had ever seen and, even though he was often prone to hyerbolizing, I agreed with him in this case. It was a prime example of the quality that Bigelow was capable of producing in the ring.

Despite his talent, however, the WWE often seemed reluctant to push him. He had a great run in '93, but he drifted off to obscurity for the year after. To his credit, he kept at it, displaying his considerable skills no matter the setting and the hard work paid off. At the '95 *Royal Rumble* PPV, Bigelow was involved in the finals of a Tag Team Championship tournament as a member of The Million Dollar Corporation (Ted DiBiase's stable). It was far lengthier than most Tag Title matches of that period, allowing Bam Bam to fully showcase what he could do. Equal parts dominant and nimble, Bigelow looked like a star, but lost the match due to his partner's gaffe. After getting pinned by the much smaller 1-2-3 Kid, people were laughing at him, among them former New York Giants Linebacker and NFL Hall of Famer, Lawrence Taylor.

Unbeknownst to the audience, LT had signed a contract to compete at *WrestleMania XI*. Bigelow walked up to Taylor, sitting at ringside in the front row with a small entourage, and questioned why he was laughing. LT tried to let it go with a handshake, but Bigelow pushed him hard enough to send him stumbling back a few rows. Coming across as organic and without pre-planning, the scene lit a fuse and garnered mainstream attention.

The character work that Bam Bam performed in the subsequent build-up to Mania was the best of his career. He was not known for his interviews, but he more than adequately handled the load in hyping the main-event for the biggest show of the year; and that was a tough year for WWE so they needed that angle to succeed in a major way. It was a testament to his talent that the WWE felt comfortable putting him in that situation (ahead of Bret, Shawn Michaels, and Kevin Nash). A year earlier, he was wrestling a filler match at Mania against a guy dressed like a clown. To be in the main-event at *Mania XI* was akin to going from worst to first.

It is a team effort to ensure that a match involving a non-wrestler is successful, but the guy steering the ship at *Mania XI* was Bam Bam. He carried it, unleashing his arsenal (including a headbutt and a modified moonsault off the top rope along with an enziguiri) to keep the bout entertaining. It was a sight to see someone that size doing any of those moves. Looking back at WrestleMania history, Bigelow's work in that match should be recognized as one of the all-time most impressive individual performances.

Sadly, the awesome display at *Mania* did not turn Bigelow into one of the biggest stars of the era as it could have. Instead, he left the company at the end of that year, with the rumor being that backstage political maneuvering drove Bigelow out of the WWE. Put that into perspective for a moment. Imagine if Shaquille O'Neal had left the Los Angeles Lakers after winning his first NBA title in 2000. It would have been a case of getting to the top of the mountain with the premiere franchise in the sport, only to move on prematurely. Without three more trips to the NBA Finals and two more championships, his legacy would have been considerably tarnished and would have been rendered a relative "What if" story. Bigelow leaving the WWE after having just been in the pinnacle spot in the sport was very similar; a lot of "What ifs." Vader's signing was right around the corner; imagine what WWE could have done with a Bam Bam vs. Vader feud. What might have Bigelow vs. Undertaker or Kane looked like? And that is just the big man match-ups. He left a lot of potential accomplishments on the table.

Leaving WWE in 1995 was the continuation of a major trend in his career started back in the NWA circa December 1988. He had a great match with Barry Windham for the US title at *Starrcade '88*, but he left before he could ever capitalize on it. He went to ECW and continued building his legacy, but that was like Shaq leaving the Lakers to continue his career with the Clippers; like it or not, it was a huge step down.

All "What ifs" aside, Bam Bam had a great run in ECW. Vince McMahon might not have always known what to do with Bigelow, but Paul Heyman had a way accentuating a wrestler's strengths. Heyman realized that, in Bam Bam, he had one of the most talented super heavyweights of all-time; one that could work with men of all sizes. So, he simply unleashed the "Beast from the East" in the ring and let the man do his thing. Bigelow had memorable matches with The Sandman and Rob Van Dam, as well as an impressive string of violent bouts with Shane Douglas over the ECW World Championship.

His time in ECW was highlighted by his feud with Taz, who was one of ECW's most well-known original talents. Taz was the World TV Champion heading into a title defense against Bigelow at the ECW *Living Dangerously* PPV in Bam Bam's hometown of Asbury Park, New Jersey. It was a classic ECW style match that makes you look back and wonder how many months or years were taken off their lives, as they put their bodies through hell to ensure that the encounter was successful. One particular moment saw Taz suplex Bigelow from the elevated ramp (that was as tall as the ring) into the rows of steel chairs meant for seating the audience. It was not the typical spot where Joey Styles (the ECW TV/PPV commentator) would yell "Oh MY GOD." Styles did utter those words, but more under his breath in such a way that opined, "OK, that was awesome and I appreciate you doing it, but was it really necessary?" The traditional Styles, "OMG" moment came at the finish, when Bam Bam was locked in the Tazmission (a rear-naked choke). Taz was hanging from Bigelow's back and, to escape, Bam Bam jumped backward with all his weight. When the two of them hit the mat, they went straight through the ring and disappeared! It was an iconic happening that will be replayed from now until they stop showing clips of ECW.

The rematch took place five months later at the *Heat Wave* PPV in 1998. The match was worked much like the previous bout, with brawling through the crowd before coming back to ringside for the bulk of the climax. They beat the hell out of each other before heading up the ramp leading toward the entrance set. Bigelow appeared to be thinking about slamming Taz off the ramp (elevated again to the height of the ring), but Taz countered in mid-move and connected with a DDT that sent them both *through* the ramp! OH MY GOD! Such moves contributed to his untimely death in my professional opinion.

Conclusively reflecting on Bigelow's career brings up one undeniable fact: Bam Bam is in the short conversation for best super heavyweight wrestler of all-time. The only one that may have been better was Vader and that is arguably because he got more chances rather than having more talent. For my money, Vader may have had better matches, won more titles, and been in more main-events, but Bam Bam was the most talented 350+ pound wrestler that I ever saw.

#51: Owen Hart

For the first decade that I lived with my step dad, the closest I saw him come to cooking was pouring himself a bowl of cereal. Then, one night during my senior year of high school, he said he was going to make dinner. Needless to say I was skeptical. I went somewhere and came back in time to eat with my parents and, low and behold, it was a helluva meal; bacon-wrapped filet mignon with grilled asparagus! I looked over at my mom with this bewildered, "where the heck did this come from" expression and she shot me a knowing glance.

Leading into the spring of '94, Owen Hart had been around for a while and I rather liked him. I even remember jumping in the pool yelling "Rocket!" in reference to his nickname back in 1992/1993. Yet, when he was positioned for a headlining match at *WrestleMania X*, I was admittedly a little doubting. In my defense, nothing we had seen from baggy windbreaker pants-wearing Owen suggested he was all that special. Yet, right before the Brother vs. Brother match got underway, an audible, deep-voiced "Yeah, Owen!" came emphatically booming from the ringside area; Bret even acknowledged it. Like that knowing glance from my mom about my step dad's culinary abilities, it was as if the fan knew something that the rest of us did not. Twenty brilliant minutes later, we all knew...Owen Hart was incredible.

Today, Owen's metamorphosis from fan-favorite into the jealous younger sibling to his more popular brother, Bret, is regarded as one of the greatest storyline achievements of the WrestleMania Era. During the ensuing five year stretch, the Rocket was one of the best in the business, a two-time Intercontinental Champion, a four-time Tag Team Champion, a Top 5 draw in 1994, a Top 10-caliber wrestler from 1995-1998, and one of the five best in-ring performers of his era.

Owen had an exceptional year in '94. In addition to the all-time classic with Bret at *Mania X*, he won the King of the Ring tournament a few months later, affording him the opportunity to challenge Bret for the WWE Championship in a Steel Cage match at *Summerslam*. The stars aligned at the right time in the right era and against the right opponent to give Owen (and Bret) the canvas on which to paint a masterpiece on the mat. Owen being in the co-main-event of the second biggest event of the year was significant enough, but the fact that he and Bret had arguably the best Cage match in history ups the historical ante.

If you want to see a Cage match with guys nearly killing each other, then Owen vs. Bret was not the one for you, but if you want to see a Cage match focused on the premise of winning the most coveted prize in the industry at the expense of a hated rival, then it does not get any better than Owen vs. Bret. In modern Cage matches, it might take all of two-minutes (if that) for the wrestlers involved to slam each other's faces into the steel. With Owen vs. Bret, it took 17-minutes. They spent almost the entire match up on the walls of the cage or near the door of the cage trying to escape; because, you know, that is how you win! Tossing each other into the cage was a last ditch effort instead of the first option. They intelligently maneuvered to wear each other down to make it easier to escape, one never quite outfoxing the other. There were plenty of moves off the cage, including the iconic image of Bret giving Owen a sky high superplex off the top, but they were performed logically and with plenty of purpose.

Owen did not win the match – he got his foot hung up in one of the steel squares of the cage allowing Bret to retain the title – but you would be hard-pressed to separate it from his victory at *WrestleMania* in the conversation of which was the best match of his career. The pair of excellent contests with Bret were the springboard to the rest of his life; the affirmation that he could make it as a professional wrestler in the #1 company in the sport. Take them away from the equation and Owen does not make this list (much less the Second-Tier).

His combination of grappling, submission, and high flying made him one of the most gifted in-ring performers to ever – and I mean ever – step foot in a WWE ring. Beyond 1994, Owen's finest work came against fellow New Generation stalwarts, The British Bulldog and Shawn Michaels. On the first *Raw* of March '97, Owen and Bulldog had one of the best matches in the program's history. In the finals of the tournament to crown the first-ever European Champion, they put on a thrilling performance full of twists, turns, and all that you could desire from a classic pro wrestling encounter. It made me clap by myself in front of my television screen; a match like that on television happens but once every few years.

Outside of his foray into the WWE title scene against Bret, the most significant storyline of Owen's career was being the guy that stood in the way of Shawn Michaels' quest to go to WrestleMania and win the WWE Championship. During a match in November 1995 on *Raw*, Owen connected with a perfectly placed enziguiri that, in story, gave Michaels a concussion that put his career in jeopardy. For Hart, it was the first time that he had been involved in a major angle since *Summerslam '94*, as he had largely been asked to carry the floundering tag team ranks. That one kick to the back of the head put him right back in the spotlight where most felt he had earned his rightful place a year earlier. It was a classic *Raw* moment, as the announcers quit talking as the medics tended to Shawn, making it seem more realistic that HBK was legitimately hurt.

When Michaels returned to win the '96 Royal Rumble match, Owen was waiting to block the "Boyhood Dream." They wrestled at the February *In Your House* PPV with HBK's Mania title shot on the line. Michaels is highly regarded as one of the best athletes in WWE history, but he found a near athletic equal in Owen, whose own athleticism was underrated. I have often wondered if it ever surprised HBK that Owen could do just about everything that he could do, physically. Owen did not look like a superiorly skilled wrestler; he looked like the template that you start out with when creating a character on a WWE video game. He was, though, an incredibly gifted athlete.

His final two years in the WWE and, sadly, the final two years of his life, were a story of triumph and tragedy. Following his classic Euro title bout with Bulldog in March '97, Owen would win the IC title and reconcile with Bret. The brothers reformed The Hart Foundation and took on the United States in a rare instance of a group being heels domestically and heroes everywhere else, especially to their fellow Canadians. As a focal point of the group, Owen engaged in a rivalry with Steve Austin during a time when Stone Cold was becoming white hot. He was again put in the "set-up" position, this time putting Austin over for the IC title. He was having a great match with him at *Summerslam '97* when he made a big mistake, forgetting to do a Tombstone piledriver that would have had his knees protect Austin's upside-down head and neck and instead performed a sit out version that spiked Austin right into the mat. It could have, but luckily did not paralyze Austin. Stone Cold made a recovery and became one of the biggest drawing stars of all-time, but it definitely cut his career short due to all the residual effects. It was a match that represents the highs and lows of the Hart family in the late 1990s.

Owen was the only member of the Hart family to stick around in the WWE after Bret left, post-Screwjob. To his credit, he had a great year in 1998, helping to further establish the up-and-coming Triple H and a young Edge, joining The Nation of Domination stable, and having a unique series of matches with former MMA star, Ken Shamrock, that not just anyone could piece together as he did.

In 1999, Owen began performing as the masked "Blue Blazer." Tragically, a stunt that would have seen him descend from the rafters into the ring went horribly wrong. He fell to his death in front of thousands of fans in St. Louis, redefining the lowest point for the Hart family. Ironically, it was Owen's work as the Blazer at *WrestleMania V*, ten years earlier against Mr. Perfect, which had introduced him to the mainstream pro wrestling audience. Life sometimes has a strange way of coming full circle.

RIP Owen.

#50: Arn Anderson

Professional sports have had several tandems that personify "The Dynamic Duo" - Batman and Robin - of comic book lore. In these situations, one athlete possesses an "extra something" that his side kick does not, but superiority complexes are put aside for the sake of accomplishing a goal that one cannot achieve without the other. Perhaps the most famous was the Chicago Bulls tandem of Michael Jordan and Scottie Pippen that won six NBA Championships in the 1990s. They were at their definitive best when teaming together, despite there never being any question that Jordan was the better player.

The NWA/WCW version was Ric Flair and Arn Anderson. Flair was similar to His Airness, while Anderson was perhaps the greatest sidekick of all-time. Together, they formed the core of wrestling's preeminent faction: The Four Horsemen. They were the only two members of each incarnation of the group, both in the 80s and 90s. Their friendship was the foundation for every bit of the stable's success. Along with Tully Blanchard, they traveled the United States, drinking, gambling, and chasing women. They lived a lifestyle of excellence in every avenue. The persona of a Horseman, be it in interviews, in the ring, in their fashion sense, or in the amount of alcohol that they consumed, reflected that they were the best. Their peers could neither keep up with their night life nor their work as professional wrestlers. They prided themselves on being able to go out all night, get to the next town, hit the gym the next morning, wrestle the best matches on every show, and then turn around and do it all again the next day. All the while, Anderson and Flair were shouldering the responsibility of anchoring a group that was keeping their promotion (NWA) in contention with a much larger conglomerate (WWE).

They say that "you are who you hang out with." Anderson and Flair complimented one another. Flair was a flashier presence that gave Arn more exposure by association, while Arn was a good-natured guy and confidant for Flair to keep The Nature Boy's somewhat fragile (real life) self-confidence at a high level. They pushed each other to be better. When you put people together that have similar goals and interests, it often patterns those individuals to work harder. Prior to joining forces, they were each accomplished wrestlers – Anderson as a highly successful tag team specialist as a member of the Minnesota Wrecking Crew with storyline uncle, Ole Anderson, and Flair as NWA World Champion. Both could talk, both could sell, both could grapple, both could brawl, and both could garner a big reaction from the audience. Yet, once they were officially a unit, it raised the stakes and prompted them to take their respective games to new levels.

On the microphone, Flair became arguably the greatest talker in the history of the business, while Arn cut some of the most memorable promos ever, including the interview that officially dubbed their group "The Four Horsemen." In the ring, Anderson's matches put the onus on Flair to step up and perform a classic in the main-event. Flair became known as the "60-Minute Man" for his hour-long matches that often tore the house down, but one of Anderson's matches earlier in the show usually set the tone. Anderson had to share the credit for most of his matches because he was predominantly a tag team wrestler, but to ensure that his match got its due credit, he worked as hard as or harder than anyone on the roster and occasionally stole the show from his Horsemen stablemates. As with any set of competitive friends, they had going a continuous game of one-upmanship.

Just as Pippen was with Jordan, Anderson was often overshadowed by Flair, but their association significantly enhanced Arn's career (and vice versa to a lesser extent). "The Enforcer," as he was known, Anderson was one of the best all-around talents of the 1980s. He was what wrestling in the southeastern United States was all about. A tremendous bump taker, he exaggerated things just enough to make others look good without overdoing it. Despite the intimidating nickname, he dropped the façade of the mean, relentless son of a gun in order to ensure that the crowd got their money's worth in seeing him get beat up. The Georgia-native was a six-time Tag Team Champion and a multi-time Television Champion. He was, perhaps, the greatest tag team wrestler to have ever lived, coming from an era in which tag team matches could be advertised in the main-event and sell out a venue. Arn was the focal point of the Tag Team Championship picture just as Flair was with the World title. His teams with Ole and Tully were headlining acts on some of the biggest NWA cards of all-time.

Arn and Ole were a dominant tag team that peaked during the first year that The Horsemen were together. At *Starrcade '86*, they had a Steel Cage match with The Rock 'N Roll Express, eliciting a response from the Greensboro Coliseum faithful equal to any main-event of the WrestleMania Era. They made you want to see them lose so badly that you were practically begging for them to get their comeuppance.

After Ole was replaced in The Horsemen, Blanchard stepped in to team with Arn to form a stylistically different pairing from the Wrecking Crew. Arn, with Ole, was like a dominant football team that blew everyone out, making you watch to see when a team would come along and shock the world. Arn, with Tully, was more like a team that squeaked out victories, annoying you to the point that you wanted to see someone smack them in the mouth.

One of the few teams to win both the NWA and WWE Tag Team titles, Anderson and Blanchard were one of the truly great pairings. Their natural chemistry was the catalyst to some of the most memorable matches of that era in both the NWA/WCW and the WWE. Pick a team from the late 80s or early 90s in either promotion and odds are that Arn and Tully had an awesome match with them, be it as members of The

Horsemen or Bobby the Brain's "Heenan Family" (as The Brain Busters). The Rockers vs. The Brain Busters in 1989, for instance, was a "how to" guide for aspiring wrestlers learning the tag craft. Tag team wrestling is different from singles wrestling and has a few important nuances that are critical to its success, one of which is the timing of the "hot" tag – the moment when a babyface escapes the opposition after several minutes of isolation so that he can reach his partner. The best tag matches are the ones that draw out a lot of emotion from the fans, building anticipation to that "hot" tag. The Brain Busters vs. The Rockers was a perfect illustration of how to build to that moment.

Anderson's status in wrestling history escalated to legendary during the final years before his retirement. He earned such a place of respect with the fans in WCW – who had watched him come up through the ranks the decade prior - that he was treated, deservedly, as a representation of wrestling tradition in the south. That admiration helped elevate the Dangerous Alliance when it was tasked with replacing the Horsemen as the dominant WCW faction in the early 90s and later earned him a nice singles run where he, among other high profile situations, challenged for the NWA title in a losing effort to former partner, Barry Windham.

As his retirement neared in the mid-90s, Arn and Naitch formed an off-again, on-again team that had some outstanding matches, including one particularly entertaining bout with Steve Austin and Vader that went off the air as they were still wrestling. They wound up facing each other at *Fall Brawl '95* in one of those strange, but interesting occurrences when you want to see if Robin can step out from behind the shadow of Batman. The match was a showcase of old school, technical wrestling with a focus on selling and psychology that few can equal, historically. It was weird, though, watching them wrestle as foes. Much more fitting, it was, when Anderson reformed The Horsemen for a final time in 1998 and reintroduced Flair, who had been on a lengthy hiatus from WCW. The two had a tearful embrace in one of wrestling's special TV moments. They stood side-by-side on TV for a final time at WWE's 2012 Hall of Fame ceremony, where The Horsemen became the only faction to ever be inducted as a group. Arn Anderson will go down in history as one of the most respected individuals in the sport.

#49: The British Bulldog

Wrestling has always had an international flavor to it and the WWE's global movement has prompted some of the world's best to try their hand in North America's top promotions. There is a rich history of foreign-born superstars in the WWE. In the late 1980s through much of the 1990s, one of the most prominent pros from abroad was "The British Bulldog" Davey Boy Smith. Coming from Manchester, England, Smith found early success in a high profile tag team and later climbed the ladder to singles success. He was eventually figured into the main-event scenes of both WWE and WCW.

By the early 90s, the WWE had successfully expanded its television product to Europe and beyond, allowing the market to open up for guys like Bulldog to become bigger stars. After developing a huge following in the United Kingdom after several international tours, Davey Boy was given increased opportunities, none bigger than the chance to challenge his brother-in-law, Bret Hart, for the Intercontinental Championship in the main-event of *Summerslam '92* in his home country. London's Wembley Stadium packed in over 80,000 people as it played host to the WWE's second biggest event of the year. You would have thought it was the English national team taking the field. Chants usually reserved for football matches were hurled toward the ring, as the country came together in support of their wrestling hero.

As someone who enjoys the psychology of sport, I would have liked to have been inside of Bulldog's mind on his way to the ring that night. Lennox Lewis, who was still just a European Champion at the time and not the boxing icon that he would later become, accompanied him as "Rue Britannia" blasted over the massive loudspeakers, helping to provide a musical theme to an incredible scene. How amazing it must have been for the relative mid-carder to receive a huge bump up to the last match on the show in front so many countrymen.

Watching the match numerous times over the years, it has always been impressive how well he handled the pressure of the situation. His winning the Intercontinental title under such special circumstances has given Davey Boy's career a Hall of Fame caliber moment. It was monumental for both he and all other international superstars that followed.

His lone Intercontinental title reign was his highest championship honor. He was also a two-time Tag Team Champion and the first WWE European Champion (defeating brother-in-law, Owen Hart, in a classic to win it). Yet, despite all the accolades, he seems to be a forgotten man in discussions about great talents and future Hall of Famers from his era. Every year, the WWE holds its Hall of Fame ceremony prior to WrestleMania and, with each Mania season, comes the talk of who deserves to be inducted. There are some that suggest Davey Boy will be forever snubbed; I sincerely hope not.

The most definitive knock on his resume is the lack of a World title reign in an era when both major promotions were electing new champions more frequently. He had numerous shots at both the WWE and WCW World Heavyweight Championships, but he was never seen as fit to be more than a challenger. Nevertheless, he was an excellent contender with a handful of matches that would hold up against the best of about 90% of the wrestlers written about in this book. His rematch with Bret for the WWE title at December 1995's *In Your House: Season's Beatings* was brilliant. Though lacking the atmosphere of Wembley Stadium, the December '95 match might well be the best of Bulldog's career. While his bouts with Bret and Owen were tremendous, his match with Shawn Michaels at the 1996 *King of the Ring* was just as good. That match was like watching a soccer game from the English Premier League in which the momentum swings back and forth quickly in the early going, followed by long stretches of one team attacking in the other team's defensive half before quick bursts of counter attacks lead eventually to the climactic final minutes of a nil-nil tie broken by a late goal from a resourceful winner. HBK was the WWE's best athlete in those days and Bulldog was easily in the top 5.

During a nine month stretch between September '95 and June '96, Davey Boy main-evented five PPVs with the WWE title on the line against champions Diesel, Bret Hart, and Shawn Michaels, respectively. It was the most important period of his career. He even had an *In Your House* PPV named after him (May '96's *Beware of Dog*), making him only one of six WWE wrestlers to have either their name or catchphrase highlighted in a PPV name. He was also a headliner for WCW in 1993 World title matches with Vader.

There is a misconception that he was not a very good wrestler, which would have you believe that when he was in The British Bulldogs tag team, it was his partner, The Dynamite Kid, that was the great worker and Davey that road his coattails. Later, when he faced his brother-in-law, Bret Hart, in memorable main-events, it was The Hitman doing the biggest carry jobs of his career, so the narrative has been written. The issue I take with this idea is that it makes wrestling seem like something other than the team sport that it is. One man cannot win a championship in basketball, baseball, or football and one man cannot have a 4-5 star match by himself. In my studies of pro wrestling, I have come to the conclusion that a great wrestler needs, at least, a good opponent to have a great match, with very rare exceptions. Davey Boy may not have been a great wrestler, but he was good enough to be a part of some incredible matches (Top 5 in the Performance Factor among his Second-Tier peers, which is what propelled him to the Top 50). Bret is often one of the guys proliferating the "not that good" label for Bulldog. During a match between Davey and Greg Valentine from 1986, Bulldog got creative and locked on the Sharpshooter – the submission hold that somebody had to teach Bret backstage a few years later in preparation to make it his finishing move. I have always found that to be amusing.

The fact of the matter is that Davey Boy was always good. Dating back to his tag team days with Dynamite, he more than held up his end of the bargain. That is why they were such a world-renowned duo. If you got The British Bulldogs working for your promotion, then your tag division would get a big boost from the skills brought to the table by both Dynamite *and* Davey Boy. That is why the pinnacle moment for The Bulldogs came in arguably the highest profile position of any WrestleMania for a tag team. The Tag Team titles have only been a headlining championship at four WrestleManias and The Bulldogs lone Tag Title win happened in one of them (a ringing endorsement). At *Mania 2*, they defeated The Dream Team in the main-event of the Chicago portion of the three-venue extravaganza. It was critically acclaimed as one of the best tag team matches of the WWE's golden age of tag wrestling and one of the better matches of the early WrestleManias. One respected writer rated it as the 6th best match of the first ten Manias.

While some labels for Bulldog are unfair and unwarranted, it would be a fair and confirmed criticism to state that Davey Boy was easily influenced and that some of the more negatively influential people in his life kept him off the straight and narrow path when it came to steroids and pain killers. As the history of sports shows, bad decisions trump talent. It also shows that such things are swept under the rug by the rival league or promotion when two such entities exist in the same sport. The current NBA and NFL are mergers of two professional associations. Each was quick to poach a top star from the other if the opportunity knocked. When Smith was released from WWE due to steroid use, it took little time for WCW to swoop in and sign him. Coming off his main-event at *Summerslam*, it was a no-brainer for WCW to try and capitalize on his growing name value. They wasted little time inserting him into their main-event scene and, by May 1993's *Slamboree*, Bulldog was going on last for the WCW World Heavyweight Championship against Vader. The competition enabled Davey's poor choices. Sadly, another questionable decision prompted WCW to let him go. He was released from each of the top wrestling companies in less than one year.

The British Bulldog is one of wrestling's many tragedies. He died at age 39 after years of chemical abuse. He is, however, Hall of Fame worthy. He did enough quality work in his World Championship matches to overcome the fact that he never became a World Champion.

#48: Barry Windham

Barry Windham is, simply put, one of the most underrated wrestlers of the last thirty years. How his name does not pop up more frequently in conversations concerning some of the best all-around performers in the NWA/WCW in the late 80s and early 90s is simply because he achieved only marginal success in the WWE. I do not accept that; cases like Windham's were among the reasons why this book needed to be written.

During the near thirty years that I have watched professional wrestling, I have seen few men who were as naturally gifted inside the squared circle as Windham; only Angle, Lesnar, and Orton come to mind. He was 6'6," weighed over 260 pounds, and moved around the ring like he was six inches shorter and fifty pounds lighter. He was put on this earth to be a pro wrestler. Never was that more apparent than in his two amazing matches with Ric Flair in 1986 and 1987. The first was a classic 45-minute marathon, but it was the second that has often garnered 5-star caliber praise. The pacing in the second match was ridiculously fast, packing non-stop action into 25-minutes. What *made* those matches was watching Windham, who towered over Flair, match Naitch's skills. Windham had Flair's athleticism and John "Bradshaw" Layfield's body. He was a prototype for the modern wrestler, with a Wrestler Score bettered by just seven superstars in the WrestleMania Era.

After the Flair matches, the NWA had to figure out what to do with Windham. His work had made him very popular with fans and critics alike. He started a tag team with fellow fan-favorite, Lex Luger, for a World Tag Team Championship match against the titleholders, Arn Anderson and Tully Blanchard, at the very first *Clash of the Champions*. That night was another showcase for Windham. He took quite the hero's beating, kicking out of both Arn and Tully's finishing moves prior to making the tag that led to the decisive, championship-winning pinfall. The two young studs had beaten one of the great teams of that generation.

Yet, just like that, Windham turned on Luger during the rematch the following month and joined The Four Horsemen as their newest member. The Horsemen were enemy #1 in the NWA. Windham had just helped take them down a peg, only to join them. The idea was to put Windham in a position where he could shine. The Horsemen were "it" in that era, so he was getting the chance to be one of the featured performers on every major card rather than wait around until he got another chance at Flair. To set him up for a big run, Windham won the United States Championship.

His first big test as a heel came against the incomparable Dusty Rhodes. They were billed as former friends, with Rhodes mentoring Windham up until Barry turned. Rhodes had battled The Horsemen for years, so it was only natural for the former allies to square off. Their US title match took place at the '88 *Great American Bash* in the summer. While the matches with Flair had been a platform for Windham to show off his athletic ability, the match with Dusty gave him the opportunity to exhibit his in-ring intelligence. He was a smart performer and his knowledge of the psychological component of wrestling, especially when working as a heel, helped set him apart. Windham began using the claw submission hold as an homage to his father, Hall of Famer Blackjack Mulligan. Against Rhodes, Windham locked on the claw for a lengthy stretch. They made a basic move look so dramatic. It was simple, but an example of Windham's command of the moment.

Windham spent the rest of the year defending the US title and gaining traction as a major player. He had a really strong performance against Bam Bam Bigelow, one of the few opponents in his career that was considerably larger, at

Starrcade '88. He always bumped around really well (particularly for a guy his size), but he took a beating like I had never seen him take. He had this thing that he would do where he would get knocked over the top rope, overact (in a good way) the fall to the ground and then stumble head first into the guardrail at ringside. He employed this little move continuously throughout his career and it always made his opponent look all the better for it. Against Bigelow, he continued to show great ability as a heel, stalling and taking timeouts during the match. He also put his strength on display, suplexing and body slamming the mammoth.

His reign as United States Champion came to an end in early '89 when he dropped the title to Lex Luger. This was the turning point in his career that I feel has always held him back. His contract with WCW expired after the match with Luger and, rather than re-sign and continue his ascent, he left for the WWE. Sure, the WWE was still hot and WCW was still not, but the WWE likely saw Windham as nothing more than the Tag Team Champion that he had been in 1985 - he and his partner lost the titles at the first *WrestleMania* - rather than the budding star behind only The Nature Boy on the heel ladder. So, he wasted a year. The WWE did not know what to do with him. He came back to WCW in 1990.

When he returned, he was mainly used as a tag team wrestler. Others had passed him by while he was gone, so he had to work his way back up. He took everything in stride, though, and climbed back toward the top. He rejoined The Horsemen and teamed with Arn for a stretch that saw them have a nice feud with Doom, culminating in a very good match at *Starrcade '90*. Later, he would team with both Dustin Rhodes and Brian Pillman, forming credible duos that had some great matches. The best of the lot was at *Starrcade '92* when he and Pillman faced Ricky Steamboat and Shane Douglas for the Tag Team titles.

Windham and Steamboat went on to have a heated feud that ultimately led Barry back to one of his two remaining chances to be a top star. The first chance was supposed to come in the summer of '91. Windham was a great heel and they needed to transition away from Flair, who was being forced out of WCW. Flair was expected to, as the story goes, drop the title to Windham before leaving. However, Flair got fired. WCW decision-makers decided to put the title up in a Cage match between Windham and Luger at the '91 *Great American Bash*. It was a hell of a back and forth match, but they were doomed from the start by loud chants of "We Want Flair." To their credit, they worked a match full of counters that made the crowd pay attention to them, but the choice was made to turn Luger into the top heel by aligning him with Harley Race. Windham was pushed to the backburner and would not sniff the main-event again until early '93, during which time he made himself so invaluable as a heel in the singles ranks that they really had no other option but to throw "The Lone Wolf" (as he was known by that time) a bone.

With such a valuable asset at their disposal, WCW made the call to give him the NWA World Championship at *Super Brawl III*. Unfortunately, the NWA title, by that point, had taken a backseat to the WCW Championship (after the NWA name was dropped). While still a tremendous honor and a stamp of headliner approval, the NWA title was secondary - much like the World Heavyweight title was in WWE during the Del Rio years.

Windham won the title from The Great Muta and was treated like a big deal. The WCW and NWA titles were heading for unification and he was in prime position to be involved in that momentous occasion. Although it never came to be and it was Flair that was given the honor, Windham had a fine reign as champion. He had two successful title defenses that stick out in my mind. One was against Arn at *Slamboree* in a match where he performed like a man who was thrilled to be holding the NWA title that had eluded him for the best part of his career.

He wanted to show that he had the chops to be "The Man." The other was at *The Clash of the Champions* against Too Cold Scorpio, a talented high flying wrestler that entertained me like few others during my youth. Windham carried himself like a main-event player and dominated throughout, but also had people believing that Scorpio could win – a true sign of a great wrestler. Soon after, he dropped the title to Flair, book-ending the best stretch of his career.

The rest of his career was forgettable, but from '87-'93, few on the planet were as good as Barry Windham. He became a WWE Hall of Famer, as a part of The Horsemen, in 2012.

#47: The Road Warriors

Tag team wrestling has had its fair share of ups and downs over the years, but even at its modern best, there has been just **one** tag team in the last thirty years so extraordinary that it could be positioned at the top of a major card for either the WWE or WCW: The Road Warriors.

Hawk and Animal, along with Paul Ellering, came about in the early 1980s and took not just the tag team scene, but sports entertainment itself by storm. Also known as The Legion of Doom, the duo came to the ring wearing spiked football pads and had their faces painted with intense patterns. They had one of the all-time, "Woah! Look at that" looks in wrestling along with Andre, Big Show, Undertaker, Hogan, and Ultimate Warrior. Everything about them screamed "intensity." Their promos were loud and in your face, complimenting their look and attire. They knocked the hell out of people; the style of their matches was all power. They looked so intimidating, but at the same time they were easy to like.

Wrestling fans are drawn to cheering for something different; and L.O.D. was wildly different. Modern fans are quite accustomed to the body-builder look that has basically became a prerequisite to being a WWE Superstar for 30 years. Back in the early 80s, that look was rare. When Hawk and Animal walked into the AWA with their massive physiques and close-cropped mohawks, they had unmatched presence. They quickly became one of the biggest draws in the AWA, then in the NWA, and finally in the WWE.

People flocked to see them. Once you got a look at Hawk and Animal on TV, you wanted to see them in action live. You wanted to be there and feel the energy when they made their way to the ring, especially with their well-crafted WWE theme song that began with Hawk's classic, gravelly voiced "Oh, what a rush!" I was in attendance for their induction into the

WWE Hall of Fame in 2011 and, even then – well over ten years since their last significant in-ring moment - their entrance brought the fans to their feet. Sadly, Hawk was only there in spirit (and in action figure form), as he tragically died some eight years prior. One would have to think he was smiling from the Heavens.

For every wrestler discussed in this book, there are numerous personal memories that help sculpt each of their chapters. If we were to play a wrestling version of word association and I was asked to describe my overall historical impression of Hawk and Animal in just a single adjective, the one that I would choose is "memorable." The wrestling fan base fluctuates. It is a cyclical business not just in its superstars but in the audience that watches it. There are some talents, though, that transcend the viewership shift - the most iconic stars of all-time. That group consists of the Hogans, Rocks, Austins, Flairs, Foleys, etc. The Legion of Doom is a member of that exclusive club. Once you saw them wrestle just one time in their heyday, you could not possibly forget them.

The first time that I saw them wrestle on TV, I recall seeing their entrance, hearing their music, and watching Hawk valiantly take punishment until shrugging off his attacker long enough to tag in Animal. From there, The Road Warriors mercilessly destroyed their opponents until Animal put two thumbs up over outstretched arms raised above his head. The crowd went wild, as Hawk simultaneously began climbing to the top rope. I could feel the energy of the audience through the airwaves. Animal hoisted a member of the opposition onto his shoulders and then Hawk came flying in for a diving clothesline to complete the awesomeness of their finishing move known as the Doomsday Device. The opponent literally looked like he had been killed – and, frankly, it had to have been one of the most dangerous moves to perform outside of the piledriver, given how Animal just shoved the guy backwards off his shoulders. It was quite a sight to see and it left you wanting to see them do it again.

It was in the WWE that L.O.D. was put together in the perfect production value to fully enhance their aura, but they were one of the rare characters that came into the WWE both in their primes and with an already celebrated reputation. Though their legacy was enhanced through their *WrestleMania 13*-headlining Chicago Street Fight and their *Summerslam '91* Tag Title victory that made them the only team in history to become Tag Champions in the AWA, NWA, and WWE, they were legends before they had ever set foot in Vince McMahon's office.

In the AWA, taking on innovative tag teams like The Fabulous Ones and The Freebirds helped spark The Legion of Doom's own groundbreaking style. They became so popular that the AWA was really banking on them to put butts in the seats once Hulk Hogan left for the WWE. Yet, they also outgrew the AWA relatively quickly. The logical next step for them was to go to the NWA.

The NWA was where The Road Warriors truly became iconic. They are historically underappreciated in how they helped keep the NWA in the game against the WWE when Vince was taking over the business. Their smash mouth wrestling was probably a better fit for the 10-minute match-happy WWE, but The Road Warriors were placed atop the NWA hierarchy and were an integral part in ensuring that the NWA product remained must-see outside of The Four Horsemen and Dusty Rhodes. In their first *Starrcade* appearance in 1986, The Road Warriors were counted on to arguably be the main draw for the show. *Starrcade '86* was dubbed, "The Night of the Sky Walkers," as L.O.D. took on The Midnight Express in a Scaffold Match. They were not given the main-event slot over Ric Flair's NWA title match, but if you go back and look at the VHS tape of the show, it is Road Warriors vs. Midnight Express on the cover.

Hawk and Animal's feud with The Midnight Express instantly made The Road Warriors a force to be reckoned with. The Scaffold match is something that any fan of professional wrestling history must see and study. It defies all conventional match rating to try and review it on a usual scale. The Road Warriors won by knocking both Dennis Condrey and Bobby Eaton off the scaffold as they were dangling from underneath it and attempting to monkey bar across it from one side to another. Try and appreciate the danger of the situation at a time when nobody did things like that. The L.O.D. had other really good matches with The Midnight Express, but none were ever quite so spectacular.

A team of L.O.D.'s stature in the NWA ultimately had to go through The Four Horsemen. After their headlining performance at *Starrcade '86*, they moved onto helping Dusty Rhodes fend off the faction of the 80s. The first ever War Games match – 4v4 or 5v5 teams in two rings surrounded by a giant cage - took place on *The Great American Bash* tour in 1987 and featured The Road Warriors teaming with Dusty and Nikita Koloff to take on the Horsemen. It was another incredible performance for L.O.D. and it afforded them the opportunity for another major *Starrcade* match, where they challenged the NWA Tag Champions, Tully Blanchard and Arn Anderson. Hawk and Animal looked dominant and unstoppable, but The Horsemen retained by disqualification in a finish typical of an L.O.D. loss. One consistent characteristic of a headlining wrestler is that they rarely lose without protection. It is not fair and square when they lose. Only the elite get that kind of preferential treatment. In wrestling, that says all that you need to know about how their promoters felt about them. There was not a more highly regarded team, in terms of what they meant to the monetary bottom line.

The WWE gave Hawk and Animal some new challenges. Seeing them face off against The Hart Foundation and The

Rockers was particularly thrilling for me. I could watch those matches any day of the week. Ellering, who was their long-time manager, had always provided eloquent context to their, at times, odd and disjointed interviews. He did not initially come with L.O.D. to the WWE, though. So, his absence forced Hawk and Animal to branch out with their promos and find a new gear. They did quite well and, by the time Ellering rejoined them in 1992, they had become admirably engaging mic men. Of course, it was their incomparable presence that continued to win them legions of fans. They lasted just two years in the WWE, but it was career-stamping. Their run coincided with the final months of the tag team division as those of us that grew up watching wrestling in the 80s had known it. Soon after, it faded into irrelevance and has only rarely made comebacks.

On the tag team Mount Rushmore, The Legion of Doom is the first team etched in stone. The Second-Tier was the highest that any tag team climbed in the rankings and they were the only ones to make the Top 40 overall in two categories (drawing power and headlining). If I am standing around the water cooler and someone asks, "All things considered, who's the greatest tag team," there is no doubt I take The Road Warriors.

#46: Rob Van Dam

June 2001 was the month in which former ECW and WCW stars began "invading" the WWE. I had just returned from a two year WWE fan hiatus and was hooked by the mere idea of WWE vs. WCW. I made the *Invasion* PPV my first purchase since *WrestleMania XV*. It was a fairly lousy show until, a few matches before the main-event, Jeff Hardy walked out to defend his Hardcore title against a newcomer that had been one of the top talents in ECW. His name was Rob Van Dam, who once held ECW's TV Championship for 700 days. Twenty minutes and the Mid-Card Match of the Year later, after I saw him unleash his full arsenal of dazzling moves, I was out of my chair. I eagerly anticipated every RVD match for the next several years.

RVD vs. Hardy became one of my favorites. I will pop it up online every year or two and just marvel at it. In 2004, when I purchased the WWE's DVD compilation for Van Dam, *One of a Kind*, and got to study the work that had made him such a favorite in ECW, I saw that the match with Jeff was about as close as it came in the WWE to RVD recreating the magic that he had with his greatest opponent from the 90s, Jerry Lynn. The greatest ECW match of all-time, in my opinion, was RVD vs. Jerry Lynn at the *Living Dangerously* PPV in 1999. For my tastes, the hardcore genre was at its best when the competitors used the weapons at their disposal to enhance what they could already do, rather than rely on furniture to be the basis for their matches. Van Dam and Lynn, an Eddie Guerrero-esque wrestler, each had a knack for intricately weaving weapons, be it a chair in hand or a table set up at ringside, into highly risky and dangerous, yet also impeccably executed sequences.

To see RVD vs. Lynn was to witness something you could not see from anyone else. ECW had an amazing list of gifted grapplers come through Philadelphia from Benoit to Malenko to Austin to Jericho to Mysterio to Guerrero, but none of them could do quite what Van Dam and Lynn could do. That is the greatest compliment that I can pay their matches. I have watched the most critically acclaimed work from the WWE, NWA/WCW, AWA, and ECW and I have never seen another match like the incredibly distinct work of RVD vs. Lynn. I have also never seen a crowd ask for "5 more minutes" of action after a draw. RVD vs. Jerry Lynn is, thus, at the top of my list for that genre of the grappling arts; RVD vs. Jeff Hardy comes in at #2.

With Paul Heyman on commentary for his early work on WWE's *Raw* and PPVs, it did not take long for Van Dam's nicknames from ECW to catch on with the mainstream. Within a month of his debut, the audience was chanting along as he pointed his thumbs at himself thrice to the tune of "Rob-Van-Dam" and "R-V-D." He was an instant hit, quickly becoming one of the most popular stars in the company. A bright spot of the lackluster Invasion, RVD lived up to his billing as "Mr. Monday Night" and "Mr. Pay-Per-View" with a run of consecutive four-star efforts. He had a Ladder match at *Summerslam* with Hardy that was one better-timed spot away from stealing the show, followed by a Hardcore title defense against Chris Jericho. RVD and Y2J were two creative minds that put their heads together to create some of the most exciting bouts of that era. One of the things that made Van Dam special was the pace of his counter sequences. Against someone like Jericho with the athleticism and genius to creatively counter his vast array of martial arts kicks, numerous quick (and quite aesthetically pleasing) spots were connected with precision.

Van Dam became such a fan favorite that he was inserted into the WWE Championship storyline between Kurt Angle and Steve Austin. *No Mercy '01* was a milestone for him, as his World title opportunities were few and far between during his six year WWE run. He always fit right into the main-event, both with what he could do and the reactions that he received. A strong case could be made that he deserved to stay at or near the top of the card from that point forward, but the common knock against him was that he could not do interviews well enough to be a consistent headliner. Later in his career, he would prove the doubters wrong with one of the most emotionally charged promos in WWE history at the *ECW One Night Stand* – a heavily promoted ECW reunion concept that he created - in 2005. In between, he just kept plugging away with matches that nobody else could have.

It is a shame that the Hardcore title had been so devalued by the time RVD came to the WWE that they retired it. That division was a perfect place for him to put his unique skills on display, a statement that unfortunately feeds into the misnomer that RVD had to be able to bend the rules to succeed in the ring. Let us put that one to bed because it is just not true. One of my favorite RVD matches was against Chris Benoit at *Summerslam '02*. It embodied that he could intelligently work in his flashy spots in a great, physical match that was well within the framework of the standard rules if given the right amount of time with the right opponent. William Regal was another ring general with whom Van Dam thrived in regular bouts. Such matches earned him a World Heavyweight Championship match with Triple H at *Unforgiven '02*.

He became the top babyface of the Intercontinental (6-time champ) and Tag Team title (3-time champ) divisions. During that stretch, he won a Ladder match for the IC title against Christian in Chicago that was particularly noteworthy. The Ladder match provided RVD with an environment where he could thrive in a manner similar to how he did in ECW. Chicago is one of the measuring stick cities for WWE Superstars and it was kind to Van Dam on that night and others. He had two of the biggest victories in his mainstream career at the All State Arena, both of which occurred in Ladder matches. He and Christian worked very well together. There were only a handful of his WWE matches that were better.

As over as he was throughout the country and in their key markets, the WWE kept RVD on the backburner. I think that the WWE liked the extraordinary qualities that RVD brought to the table, but I do not think they fully understood what they had in him. Though men with respected opinions like Jim Ross were calling him one of the most unique athletes never to win a World Championship, the WWE seemed content with having him work just outside of headlining status, while selling a lot of merchandise and keeping the mid-card relevant. It was their loss. Van Dam was a fascinating star. His varied offensive repertoire with all the fancy coinciding names - the Rolling Thunder, the Van Daminator, the Split-Legged Moonsault, the Van Terminator, the "educated" feet, the Five-Star Frog Splash, etc. – was thrilling to watch.

The WWE, historically, has tunnel vision in the wrestling industry, focusing just on what someone does for them and not placing enough emphasis on what they have done elsewhere. If you took one look at the aforementioned Van Dam DVD produced by the WWE's Home Video department, you would know the full capabilities of what RVD could do for a promotion. His matches with Sabu were so well thought of that people once waited hours for officials to fix a broken ECW ring so that they could see them go at it; and when the ring broke just minutes in, the people still gave all their energy as RVD and Sabu adapted and gave everything that they had.

Van Dam came back from a severe knee injury at the '06 *Royal Rumble* and won the Money in the Bank Ladder match at *WrestleMania 22*, setting him up for the biggest night of his professional life when he won the WWE Championship from John Cena at *One Night Stand 2006*, boosting his Title stats to Top 40 all-time and inching his overall ranking ahead of Windham and The Road Warriors.

#45: Dusty Rhodes

Dusty Rhodes was a flamboyant son of a plumber who took on the role of the working man and parlayed his ensuing success into one of the top acts in the National Wrestling Alliance. The Muhammad Ali of professional wrestling in the 1970s, Rhodes did everything with a certain panache and style that nobody else in the sport quite could match. It was not just an elbow smash for him – it was an elbow smash preceded by a swivel of the hips or a pucker of the lips. He would dance and jive around the ring like Ali with his patented shuffle. It made him an immensely popular draw against the great antagonists of the era like Harley Race in the Midwest and "Superstar" Billy Graham up north.

Had his work before 1983 been factored into the system used to rank the wrestlers in this book, then there would be no questioning his place amongst the very best of all-time. Alas, this is a book about the WrestleMania Era, so Dusty misses the cut to be included amongst the First-Tier. Heavy value was placed on his importance to building the *Starrcade* brand, but I placed a lot of weight toward what the wrestlers were able to do in the WWE and, unfortunately, Dusty did not have much success there. To solely base Dusty's placement on his NWA track record would be like trying to take only Doctor J's ABA days into account in ranking basketball's best, especially since the NWA got its rear so royally handed to it by WWE in Dusty's heyday (read *Starrcade vs. WrestleMania: The Prelude To The Monday Night Wars* for more on that story).

With that being stated, Dusty was an innovator and one of the main reasons why the NWA was able to stay in competition with the WWE in the 1980s. He came up with the concept of *Starrcade* and was the booker during a very good time for the NWA. Of course, it was his lengthy feud with Ric Flair that allowed him to make his most significant contribution to the NWA as the top babyface opposite Naitch's top heel character. Watching those two go at it was a thing of beauty. Back in the 70s when Rhodes was showing that he had more charisma in his bionic elbow than most guys had in their whole bodies, there was nobody that could match him. When Flair rose to prominence and took the NWA Championship from Rhodes in 1981, "The American Dream" met his charismatic equal. They were perfect foils for one another, making Dusty's quest to regain the gold as compelling a storyline as there has ever been in the sport. Their promo battles prompted many to suggest that they were #1 and #2 all-time on the list of the best talkers in the industry (though somehow that failed to translate to the commentary booth, where his unique way of speaking wore thin after the first 20-minutes of a broadcast; he has to be one of the two worst wrestler-turned announcers ever along with Booker T).

After the success of *Starrcade '83*, which pitted Flair against the best heel of the 1970s, it was a no-brainer to try to follow it with a card headlined by Flair taking on Rhodes, the best babyface of the 1970s. The NWA World title and a $1 million check were at stake in the main-event of *Starrcade '84*, which featured celebrities as guest referees and judges in the precursor to the first *WrestleMania* that took place just a few months later. Dusty controlled much of the match, but a cut above his right eye forced special referee, Joe Frazier, to stop the match and award the victory to Flair. Rhodes chased the title for a year, having to go through Flair's new associates, The Four Horsemen, to get back to The Nature Boy.

The American Dream was essential to the success of The Horsemen, for as entertaining as they were with all their talk of wheeling and dealing, they had to have a protagonist that the fans cared about to beat up. Without a hero such as Rhodes, The Horsemen would not have been nearly the villains that they were. The dastardly group had a common enemy in Rhodes and they all benefitted from it, especially Flair, Tully Blanchard, and Barry Windham. Blanchard faced Rhodes in the main-event of the first *Great American Bash* in the summer of 1985. People often reminisce about how everyone that Flair wrestled with in the 80s turned into big stars, but the same can also be said of Rhodes. It was the matches with Rhodes that put Blanchard and Windham at the top of the card.

Arn and Ole Anderson did Flair a favor in the fall of '85, taking out Dusty's knee in a vicious assault that set the stage for the next *Starrcade*, again set to feature Flair vs. Rhodes as the main-event with the NWA Championship up for grabs. Some of the best interviews of both their careers came in the months leading to that match, which subsequently turned out to be the most critically acclaimed that they had against each other. The attention to detail in a rematch of this magnitude is often what makes it special. Modern fans may remember the small touches in the Undertaker vs. Shawn Michaels or Triple H matches in back-to-back WrestleManias. In Rhodes vs. Flair, the cut above Dusty's eye that led to Frazier stopping the match was used to add heat when Flair got opened up above his eye in the rematch. Rhodes got payback for the attack on his leg by going after Flair's, creating for a submission heavy bout. The climax featured run-ins from The Andersons, but Rhodes was able to fend them off and catch Flair with a roll-up to seemingly become the new champion. On that night, anyway, Rhodes looked to have become a three-time NWA titleholder.

Soon after *Starrcade '85*, the decision that crowned Dusty the new champ was changed by the referee, who had been knocked out a few times during the match. He ruled that Flair had been disqualified, which meant he kept the title. It was the first and, perhaps, the most famous use of the "Dusty finish" for which Rhodes became quite illustrious during his time as a lead booker. Though it became an overused ending to big matches, it did create added drama for feuds leading toward grander payoffs. Rhodes and Flair had one final showdown at the '86 *Great American Bash*. In a bloody Steel Cage match, Rhodes and Flair put on a fitting conclusion to their five year rivalry. It was another classic, with Dusty getting the win that made the record books and earned him his third and final NWA Championship.

Rhodes went onto reignite his storyline with Blanchard, leading to a First Blood match at *Starrcade '86*, which he lost, and a Barbed Wire Ladder match at the multi-event *Great American Bash '87* tour, which he won to end their feud. They were involved in another match at the *Bash* that year, which became quite famous. Rhodes introduced his idea for a new gimmick: the first-ever War Games. It was one of the greatest gimmick concepts ever created and lead to some of the best matches of the 90s.

It seemed that no matter which new member was recruited by The Horsemen, it was somewhat of a rite of passage for them to engage in battle with Rhodes. Lex Luger replaced Ole Anderson in 1987 and, by year-end, Luger was facing off against Rhodes in a Steel Cage match for the U.S. title at *Starrcade*. In 1988, when Luger was ousted from the group in favor of Barry Windham, it was again Rhodes that was called upon to establish the newest member as the evil doer that the NWA needed him to be. At the 1988 *Great American Bash*, Rhodes put Windham over for the US title. It was his last match against a member of The Horsemen on a major event. The rivalry that had defined the NWA for most of the decade had come to an end. One could make the argument that the NWA was never the same after that. New heroes emerged to challenge The Horsemen, but the originality that made the stable so initially excellent always involved Rhodes being the main force of good standing in their way.

Unfortunately, the trend in pro wrestling is for the best to go out on somebody else's terms and rarely their own. Dusty was fired after *Starrcade '88*. I think that people have a tendency to forget that Dusty was such a huge star in the 80s for the NWA because of his comedic tenure in the WWE. He may have done his best work, arguably, during his younger years in the 70s when he was the two-time champion, but he did so much in the 80s as a great performer, a brilliant mind for the business, and an innovator that allowed the NWA to stay in the game a lot longer against WWE than they may have otherwise.

    History smiles on "The American Dream" Dusty Rhodes…

#44: Diamond Dallas Page

In the months of preparation before starting to write this book, I had a few historical events to brush up on. One of the main things was the WCW half of the Monday Night Wars. I was not, generally, one of those fans that switched back and forth every Monday. In reviewing WCW's side of that era, I began noticing a name pop up in well thought of matches from the height of The N.W.O. right up until Vince bought the company. After watching many of those matches, I gained a completely new appreciation for what this man brought to the table. In all honesty, it is through writing this book that I can state that I am a late blooming fan of Diamond Dallas Page.

My earliest memory of Page was when he drove his pink Cadillac down the massive entrance ramp at *WrestleMania VI* in Toronto, carrying Rhythm and Blues with Jimmy Hart. My lasting impression of DDP – until I started researching for this book – had been watching him in the horrible movie, *Ready to Rumble*. I also recalled his being demolished at the hands of Undertaker and Kane when he made a brief splash on WWE's *Raw* during the Invasion in 2001 and thought fondly of his *WrestleMania X-8* match with Christian for the European Championship.

I knew, though, that there had to be much more to DDP than I had seen. He was, after all, a 3-time WCW World Heavyweight Champion during a very important period in the business. He was also given the responsibility of helping to carry celebrity angles in 1998 with Karl Malone and Jay Leno as tag team partners that gave WCW much needed momentum against the surging WWE Attitude Era. The higher ups in WCW clearly thought well of him. His reputation on the internet seemed to be fairly strong, too. So, I sought out some of his better star-rated matches. I decided on, first, watching his WCW Championship bout with Goldberg from 1998's *Halloween Havoc*. The match was <u>infamous</u> for being blacked out because the PPV ran too long, but it should be famous for how impressive a performance it was. Goldberg was not thought to be a very good wrestler, but DDP led the way to one of the finer matches of both their careers. I was blown away watching some of the things that Page could do. He was a pretty big guy, so if you had told me that he could pull off a flying head scissor, I would have called you a liar, Mean Gene.

What I found most impressive was the ingenuity of his counter wrestling. Counters create nuance and nuance is part of the art of wrestling. Page may not have been among the best ever at it, but he was definitely one of the best of the rest ever at it. Creative counters became a recurring theme in all the matches that I watched featuring DDP from 1997 onward. His reversal of Goldberg's Jackhammer into the Diamond Cutter, for example, was awesome. Up he went into vertical suplex position, but he slid off to Goldberg's rear, right into a reversed DDT position. Goldberg turned to counter, but straight into the Diamond Cutter. "BANG!" He also got down on the mat and unexpectedly grappled back and forth with Goldberg, doing chain wrestling that you did not often see from "Da Man." My hat goes off and back in time to him for that night in October 1998.

Then, I watched his series of matches with Macho Man. DDP may never have become a main-event star if it were not for his lengthy feud with Randy Savage in 1997. He had turned on The N.W.O.'s Outsiders at *Souled Out '97*, igniting his feud with the faction and ultimately leading to the storyline with Savage (one of the group's most prominent members). Page being involved as a key WCW mainstay stepping up to battle arguably the greatest stable ever assembled helped him step up from the mid-card. The three PPV matches against Macho Man - at April's *Spring Stampede*, July's *Great American Bash*, and October's *Halloween Havoc* - really put DDP on the map. I jotted down the following note after watching the match at *The Bash* while researching Page a few summers ago: "DDP showed surprising athleticism and in-ring awareness. I think he's a bit underrated, historically." After viewing the payoff match, I wrote that "the more I see of DDP, the more highly I think of his work." *Spring Stampede '97* was Page's first PPV main-event. He won the match to give WCW a rare victory over an N.W.O. member in a spotlight situation. Though he lost the next two matches, the quality could not be denied nor could the fact that he had arrived as a major player.

Coming off of the bouts with Macho Man, DDP was no longer just a former manager that looked like a guy you would see walking to the gas station to buy another carton of cigarettes before heading back to the trailer park to re-bleach his mangy hair and lay out in the sun all day until his skin turns leathery. Instead, Page was a force to be reckoned with. He won the United States title and had a strong run in that division battling the likes of Curt Hennig, Raven, and Chris Benoit. Next up on my DDP viewer's guide was his three-way Falls Count Anywhere match at *Uncensored* with Benoit and Raven that was one of the first triple threat matches on a mainstream wrestling event in the U.S. They started off with a very unique triple lock-up and later busted out a triple sleeper hold and a triple German suplex, each attractive spots in the match that reiterated the earlier claim of DDP's creativity.

It was the battles against Raven that got him so over that WCW pushed him into the aforementioned celebrity angles in the summer of 1998. Teaming with Malone and Leno put him opposite the top heel in the entire business in Hulk Hogan and set up his October championship match with Goldberg. Though, as mentioned, the title bout did not air for many PPV buyers, its replay on *Nitro* the following night was the last ratings victory for WCW in the Monday Night Wars. Proof of his being a draw eventually earned him the WCW Championship at the following *Spring Stampede* in 1999. Page was somewhat of a "Mr. Spring Stampede" looking back. Some of his best and biggest matches came at the event – a four year run that included his 1st main-event, one of his best matches, his first WCW title victory, and an underrated title bout against Jeff Jarrett.

His first and second runs with the World title came about two hours apart. He lost the title to Sting in the first hour of the April 26, 1999 *Nitro*, only to regain the title at the end of the show in a Fatal 4-way. It was a silly night of hotshot booking, but Page was the center of attention. The match with Sting was arguably the finest of Page's career. No "self high five" necessary, DDP. I will give you one for that performance.

After losing the title to Kevin Nash, he created an alliance with Bam Bam Bigelow and Kanyon, called "The Jersey Triad," which led to Tag Team Championship gold. It was later partially revisited in the WWE's Invasion angle when DDP and Kanyon battled Undertaker and Kane at *Summerslam '01*. The remainder of his WCW career consisted of him getting back into the title picture. He regained the belt, but then was involved in one of the most controversial (and stupid) angles in wrestling history when David Arquette (actor) won the title in a tag match. DDP remained a focal point, despite never regaining the championship, eventually tagging with Kevin Nash to win the WCW Tag Team titles and then getting back into the main-event picture one last time in a losing effort to Scott Steiner on the final WCW PPV, *Greed*. The match against Steiner was another top notch effort from DDP. Steiner had been on a roll and Page was built as the last guy that could conceivably take the title off of him. The night belonged to Big Poppa Pump, but Page left one more lasting impression in another really good match.

Well-deserved was DDP's time at the top of the card from 1997 until WCW shut down its operations in March 2001. To think that he had started out as a manager, but worked his tail off to make it as a successful, main-event wrestler is pretty amazing. He represents an example of how hard work can pay off in a big way, even in an industry as often politically based as pro wrestling. Injuries (that led to retirement) kept him from repeating his WCW glory in WWE.

I must say that DDP has enhanced my life. I started doing his version of yoga in 2015 and I feel the best I have felt in years. Long clinic hours and a busy family life made finding time for exercise a lot harder, so I do DDP Yoga every morning and night; it is awesome and I highly recommend it. In recent years, DDP also offered me great new wrestling memories, even if they were a decade or more behind the times.

#43: "Mr. Perfect" Curt Hennig

In order for professional wrestling to maintain the suspension of disbelief for its fan base, the wrestlers must make the in-ring product look as real as possible. Even though it is a performance, it has to maintain some semblance of an authentic fight and, as such, the men doing battle must sell the effects of their opponents' blows. It is as fundamental a premise to wrestling success as running the football is to gridiron greatness.

About once a generation, a superstar comes along that goes above and beyond "normal" selling and overdramatizes a punch or a clothesline or a dropkick to make it seem like he got bludgeoned by a battering ram. Not everyone appreciates it since it is a bit over-the-top, but it is the ability to take something so basic and make it flashy that sets that superstar apart. Like Deion Sanders high stepping in mid-sprint – a completely unnecessary but wildly entertaining antic – men like "Mr. Perfect" Curt Hennig would bump all around the ring making their opponents look Herculean in the process. He was every bit the *wrestler* that were the greatest of his era and he could talk a big game to boot, but he added style with how well he sold for the guy he was working with. Everyone wanted to work with him as a result and he became one of the most respected men in the history of the business.

Personally, it was just a single match that has shaped my entire opinion of his career. I remember my dad renting the Coliseum Video of *Summerslam '91*. The second match on the card was Mr. Perfect defending the Intercontinental Championship against Bret Hart. Though he lost the match, Perfect put on such a fantastic show that, even as a kid, I walked away from it knowing that he was equal parts excellent wrestler and showman. That one match forever etched Perfect as a legend in the business. From that point forward, if someone mentioned "Curt Hennig" or "Mr. Perfect," I thought of *Summerslam '91* and images of brilliance danced in my head.

Interestingly, as I would later find out, Perfect wrestled that match with bulging discs in his back. If you have seen the iconic displays of fortitude by Shawn Michaels and Kurt Angle at WrestleManias *XIV* and *XIX*, respectively, then you ought to give Perfect credit by throwing his name onto that esteemed list of tough guys when talking about the 1991 version of the Summer Classic.

Bret Hart was easily Hennig's greatest opponent. You could make a case for his inclusion in the top 50 on their matches alone. Famous were their *Summerslam '91* and *King of the Ring '93* matches, with the latter being arguably as good as the former. If you are a fan of a blistering pace and crisp technical prowess mixed with a few high risks all packed into less than 20-minutes, then *KOTR '93* was for you. It was rated by well-known experts as their finest, though I would give the '91 match higher marks (just by a quarter of a star). The Summerslam match was truly one of the top 5 matches of the WrestleMania Era's first ten years and remains one of the best in WWE history. All-time greats like Edge would use it as inspiration for the in-ring approach that they eventually employed once they broke into the business and it surely fueled men like Chris Jericho, a six-time World Champion, to refer to Perfect as the greatest wrestler to have never won a World title.

There are six predominantly singles wrestlers in my top 50 that never won either the WWE or NWA/WCW World Heavyweight Championship. Hennig was the only one of them to have actually been a major promotion's World Champion. He was the last hope for Verne Gagne's American Wrestling Association. Gagne looked at Hennig, son of long-time AWA wrestler Larry "The Axe," as his long-term answer and he might very well have been had the WWE not been such a financial juggernaut by the time Hennig's star was shining brightest. It was a no-brainer to hitch the AWA wagon to him and see what he could do, but it was too late. The WWE was making its stars the kind of money that wrestlers could once only dream of, so Perfect left for greener pastures.

"Mr. Perfect" was Hennig's WWE moniker, born out of his ability to do so many athletic events far better than average. He could bowl, throw darts, shoot poll, knock down half-court basketball shots, sink 50-foot birdie putts, and play horseshoes with the best of them. He debuted with an undefeated streak the length of which rivaled Bill Goldberg's from a decade later. For over a year, he never lost a match, staying "perfect" every step of the way before suffering his first loss at *WrestleMania VI*. Success did not stop with a single "L" in the loss column. The Intercontinental title was vacated after WrestleMania in 1990 and a tournament was held to crown the next champion. Perfect won the belt in dazzling fashion, last defeating Tito Santana in one of the leading candidates for WWE Match of the Year.

Winning the Intercontinental Championship took his game to a new level. You have to admire a guy that names himself "Perfect." Inherently, it gave Hennig a higher standard to live up to. His Intercontinental Championship reigns were arguably the best ever, in terms of the consistent performance level that he was reaching. Against a wide variety of opponents, he was having the best matches across the country. He made larger athletes like The Big Bossman and less talented bodybuilder types like Kerry Von Erich look like future World Champions, flipping all around the ring and taking a physical beating like nobody else could.

Often, it has been said that the title does not make the man, but that the man makes the title. Others had made the Intercontinental title prestigious. Yet, Perfect not only upheld the value of the belt, he also turned it into a prize that several superstars built their hopes and dreams around winning.

Shawn Michaels (and later Jericho) once saw the IC title work done by Hennig (and, afterward, Bret Hart) and viewed the belt as the "top worker in the company" championship. Therefore, he thought, winning the IC title would be the highest honor that he could achieve in his career. You can see a lot of Mr. Perfect's influence in HBK. If Shawn is the Michael Jordan of wrestling, then Perfect is the Elgin Baylor, an athletic specimen for his time who eventually saw his style imitated and improved upon by someone who took it all to the next highest level.

Perfect and Michaels crossed paths a few times in their careers. They had a high profile match for the IC title at 1993's *Summerslam*, but I would take their March 1991 bout from a week before *WrestleMania VII* over about 80% of the matches from Hennig's career. It was a stunning sample from the two greatest over-the-top bumpers of all-time. They were each so cocky, too; Perfect in his persona and Michaels, in general. Perfect did his usual shtick where he would spit his gum out and effortlessly slap it away (did he ever miss?). He threw his towel at Michaels, who proceeded to pull a card out of the Perfect deck and toss the towel behind his back with one hand and catch it with the other.

Hennig spent most of his career in the WWE, but had a brief run in WCW during the Monday Night Wars. He briefly became a member of The Four Horsemen. It was a shame that Perfect's path did not cross with Ric Flair and The Four Horsemen during the stable's heyday. Perfect and Flair had incredible on-screen chemistry, prominently displayed in 1992 while Flair was plying his trade in the WWE for the first time. Hennig was The Nature Boy's right-hand man and the two of them, along with Bobby Heenan, were a trio that rivaled any faction in history, in terms of entertainment value. Perfect and Flair wrestled one of the better matches in *Raw* history in January of 1993, overshadowed by the '93 WWE MOTY in HBK vs. Marty Jannetty from a few months later. In a Loser Leaves the WWE match, Perfect defeated Flair in dramatic fashion, overcoming interference from Heenan and the first blood spilled on WWE's new cable program.

Mr. Perfect narrowly edged DDP in the rankings, his stats pretty even across the board at Top 10-15 in all but the Headlining Factor among the Second-Tier wrestlers. When he was inducted into the WWE Hall of Fame, posthumously, in 2007, his family stood proud at the podium as his wife, Leonice, said the closing words that now, along with the *Summerslam '91* match, always resonate in my mind when I think about Curt Hennig. "He was what he says he was…Absolutely PERFECT."

#42: Terry Funk

Inevitably, someone will read this book and wonder why Terry Funk, of all the legends that did the bulk of their work in the 1970s and early 1980s (remembering that this book specifically details the period from late '83 to the present), managed to be the only one that cracked the Second-Tier. There are two reasons:

#1 – He was more influential to the modern product.

Funk, at *WrestleMania 2*, was slammed through a table by the Junkyard Dog. That was in 1986, when something like that was unheard of. Three years later, he went back to the NWA, in the territories of which he had been the NWA World Heavyweight Champion for over a year in the mid-70s. He brought with him an aggressive style, attacking and piledriving the reigning NWA Champion, Ric Flair, onto a table at *Wrestle War '89*. In the 1990s, he lent his renowned name to ECW, where he wrestled into his fifties and helped popularize "hardcore" to the point that it became one of the cornerstones of the most celebrated era in sports entertainment history. By 1998, his lasting influence brought him back to the WWE, where he and Mick Foley initiated the mainstream to the borderline sadistic work that they had done together in ECW and Japan. What would have previously been thought of as excessive violence and putting the body through unimaginable pain, subsequently, became commonplace.

In the mid-90s, Terry had reached age 50. There is a scene in the movie, *The Wrestler*, starring Mickey Rourke, where Randy "The Ram" does an independent show for a small promotion built around extreme wrestling. If you have seen that film, then that would give you an idea of what it was like to see this aging, legendary former World titleholder get into a ring with the ropes replaced by barbed wire or get into garbage brawls using weapons ranging from ladders to thumbtacks to chairs. There is a part of me that wishes that I could forget that stage of Funk's career. I can see him in my mind's eye, wearing that "Funk U" t-shirt covered in blood and nearly unconscious after landing awkwardly on an exploding table full of barbed wire, as he did in the *King of the Death Match* tournament finals in Japan against Mick Foley in 1995. I can picture him and Sabu being cut out of the barbed wire "ropes" in ECW...and then finishing the match.

It is weird. I have this strange respect for everything that ECW brought to the table and for Funk, who made it possible for them to emerge as the #3 wrestling company of the 1990s (he was the focal point of the first-ever ECW PPV, *Barely Legal*, on April 13, 1997). At the same time, though, I cannot help but cringe at the lengths that Funk went to ensure that he remained a relevant force in the business back in those days. He was not the only one advocating hardcore wrestling, but he was the guy with the biggest name doing it, which gave that body-punishing style a stamp of approval. Careers were shortened and ended because of that style, which taught the younger guys that it was alright to put themselves at enormous risk. Superstars such as Austin, Foley, and Edge wound up retiring in their thirties because of it. It is certainly an interesting topic that can be debated with strong arguments on either side.

I wish not, though, to condemn but to celebrate Terry Funk. He reinvented himself in ECW, which might make him the most universally loved superstar of all-time. Not only did he succeed in the big league promotions during both of the wrestling boom periods, but he also ushered in an era of extreme. After ECW, he went to work for both WWE and WCW one last time each. His stint in the WWE was particularly memorable for a few of his matches. As Chainsaw Charlie, he teamed with Cactus Jack to win the WWE Tag Team Championships from The New Age Outlaws in a Dumpster match – an entertaining time specific scrap - at *WrestleMania*

XIV. In May 1998, he wrestled Foley in a Falls Count Anywhere match on *Raw* in what was considered an Attitude Era classic and was named in 2013 as the #37 match on the WWE's list of the "Top 50" bouts in *RAW* history.

#2 – He had one of the truly transcendent years of the last three decades in 1989.

When Funk came back to the NWA after a WWE stint in the mid-80s and targeted Ric Flair, the matches that he had from the summer to November of '89 were memorable enough that he joins the likes of Cena ('07), Rock (late '01 to spring '02), Michaels (numerous), Austin ('01), Orton ('11), Angle ('02), and a few others on a very short list of wrestlers that have given us the most consistent excellence over a six month to one year period in the WrestleMania Era.

If you are scratching your head because you cannot readily recall what Funk accomplished in '89, it might be because Flair and Ricky Steamboat beat him out on most lists for Wrestler of the Year. They, too, had unbelievable 1989s. Flair had a record-setting four matches rated by one respected publication as "5-star." Steamboat was the second half of three of them and Funk was the opponent in the other. Unfortunately for Funk, he has gotten historically overshadowed by the other two, despite the fact that he had excellent, 4-star matches with Steamboat and Flair in the summer, participated in a unique concept called the Thunderdome Cage that was a predecessor to the Hell in a Cell, and capped it off with a famous "I Quit" match against The Nature Boy. 1989 was an absolutely awesome year for the NWA thanks to those three men's collective efforts at the top of the card and a slew of talented youngsters covered in this book. Naitch gets my vote for '89 WOTY, but it was Funk who helped him get the nod over the Steamer.

Funk's match with Steamboat flies under the radar. Had it taken place a year earlier, it would have been on the short list for Match of the Year. As such, it was surrounded by so many other great matches. It was still better than anything produced in the WWE in '89.

Of the two championship bouts between Funk and Flair, the "I Quit" match from the November *Clash of the Champions* was the most critically celebrated. I, however, preferred *The Great American Bash* match. Flair was coming back from the "neck injury" suffered at the hands of Funk's piledriver. I never thought that Naitch played a particularly convincing "tough guy" babyface, but thanks to the excellent antagonistic work by the Funker, he was believable in the role at that time. Their match told a great story and the heat from the crowd jumped off the TV screen. They built the match around Funk trying to connect with the piledriver again, with J.R. on commentary suggesting that it could end The Nature Boy's career. Funk seemed equal parts obsessed with taking out Flair and hungry to regain the title. When it became apparent that he was not going to be able to easily pin him, he turned his attention toward making Flair give up, which was the catalyst for their match later in the year.

The two most difficult matches for wrestlers to keep a crowd involved are the "I Quit" and the Last Man Standing. Perhaps that is why I have often pegged Funk and Flair's vaunted Nov. '89 bout as "overrated." Inherently, the gimmick strips away the drama of the near pinfall, making false finishes much harder to achieve. My main gripe is that the action just stops dead in its tracks so that the referee can start his ten count or ask if one of the men wants to quit. So, while Funk vs. Flair "I Quit" was a great psychological battle, with the Funker ultimately getting his comeuppance, I will take their *Bash* title bout any day of the week.

As a Hall of Famer, a former NWA Champion, two-time US Champion, and Tag Team Champion, Funk's place in overall wrestling history is more than secure. Yet, combined with his magnificent 1989 and his significant role in the stylistic shift of the 1990s, he jumps his contemporaries and many of the better known stars on the pantheon of WrestleMania Era wrestlers. Jerry Lawler, Harley Race, and Bob Backlund all made their presence felt when they threw their hat into the modern game, but none of them did as much as Terry Funk to change the culture of the business. To completely redo your image for one generation and still be fondly remembered by another, as did Funk, is quite an accomplishment. Lawler and Backlund may have redefined themselves, to a degree, but their most significant moments in the business came before their mainstream involvement.

#41: Christian

In most cases throughout the history of tag team wrestling, one of the team members has been far more talented and had a lot greater potential to be a singles star than his partner. Yet, that was **never** the case was with Christian and Edge, storyline brothers and real life best friends since childhood who initially made their names as a dynastic duo in the Attitude Era. They captured the World Tag Team titles on seven different occasions and, once they broke off into singles competition, each displayed a striking amount of individual skill.

Chances to shine back in those days were hard to come by, as there were two hours of television per week to make your case for more airtime. When Christian and Edge started teaming as part of "The Brood" (which had incredibly bad ass entrance music), they only got a tiny piece of a very large spotlight. Their Tag Team Ladder match with the Hardy Boys that stole the show at *No Mercy '99* changed that significantly. That was their coming out party. Though they lost, they earned the respect of their peers, the fans, and the higher ups in the WWE.

Six months later, after *WrestleMania 2000's* Triangle ladder match redefined what was expected from a mainstream wrestling promotion's stunt brawl, a new tag team "Golden Age" had spawned with Christian and Edge leading the way as the champions. There were three Tables, Ladders, and Chairs matches at the two biggest PPVs of the year in 2000 and 2001 between E&C, the Hardys, and the Dudley Boyz, each of which put the Tag Team titles into a headlining spotlight. The fact that Edge and Christian won all three of them should tell you everything you need to know about their standing atop the tag team division.

What separated them from even the glory days of WWE tag wrestling and made them comparable to the NWA's classic tag scene of the late 1980s was that, because they were blossoming into entertaining characters that could handle their business on the microphone just as well as a lot of the main-eventers, they were talking in lengthy segments. Thus, they were a legitimate draw as a team that people wanted to see get beaten. The Dudleys, who were great heels, had to be turned into babyfaces because Christian and Edge were *so* good as bad guys that they needed all the other top teams to be protagonists.

From the 5-second poses "for those with the benefit of flash photography" to the amusing antics of Team ECK (with Kurt Angle), Christian and Edge were arguably the most entertaining aspect of each show. Christian using the kazoo to play another wrestler's entrance music and Edge coming up with lyrics to the instrumentals was side-splittingly hilarious, for example. They could also be serious when the time came to lace up the boots and get it done in the ring, complimenting their slapstick comedy to make them a well-rounded, important part of the product. They were not merely pawns, but more like bishops or rooks behind kings Steve Austin, The Rock, and Triple H.

Tag teams, though, are not where the men destined for the Hall of Fame end their careers anymore; it is a starting point and a launching pad, nothing more. In 2001, it came time for Edge and Christian to part ways.

Edge won the 2001 King of the Ring tournament. An earlier round match that same night against Angle showed Christian, despite a loss, to be a singles star on the rise, as well. To truly distance themselves from one another, Christian slowly turned on Edge and ultimately feuded with him over the Intercontinental title, which Christian won from Edge at *Unforgiven* before dropping it back the next month (in a Ladder match) at *No Mercy*.

As his new (and awesome) theme song stated, Christian was, at last, on his own. Unfortunately, he did not receive quite as strong a push as Edge. While he did have his moments, such as an underrated match with DDP at *WrestleMania X-8* and an underappreciated run as a key member of the Un-Americans stable in 2002, Christian struggled to find his way up the card and out of the shadow of his tag team days. A somewhat random foray back into the tag ranks with Chris Jericho, however, ended up being his saving grace, as it gave him both a chance to stay relevant and an opponent against whom he would eventually have a breakout singles performance down the road.

It did not hit me how good Christian really was until *WrestleMania XX*. On that night, he wrestled Jericho in a match culminating a well-told, simple tale of a best friend jealous of his buddy's girlfriend. As far as mid-card matches at Mania go, you will not find many better in its near-thirty year history than Christian vs. Jericho. Christian performed like a main-event player. That entire year, Christian was lights out in the ring and on the mic no matter the opponent.

At the 2005 *Royal Rumble*, Christian had a battle rap backstage that kick started a rivalry to be revisited later in the year with John Cena. On numerous occasions, Christian verbally accosted Cena, much to the delight of the growing number of "Peeps" (his name for his fans) who were hip to his act. He had begun calling himself "Captain Charisma" and earning the praise of the announce team week in and week out. It seemed like everyone was getting on-board with Christian making it to the top, but then an audible was inexplicably called that prevented him from having a full-fledged feud with Cena. Subsequently, he did not renew his WWE contract and ended up excelling in TNA for several years. Admittedly, while not a TNA fan, I ordered their February 2006 PPV just to see Christian win their version of the World title.

When Christian came back to the WWE, I was really excited. Rumors spread quickly of a major angle leading to a headlining match. However, he re-debuted on the ECW brand in February '09. It was not exactly the triumphant return that his Peeps had hoped for, but he did a commendable job in his role as the C-show's top star. Numerous young talents got the chance to show off what they could do in lengthy matches against Christian. Yoshi Tatsu, Zack Ryder, Ezekiel Jackson, and Jack Swagger were just a few of the beneficiaries of Christian's in-ring performance capabilities.

Anyone that thinks of Christian's second run in the WWE is likely to find themselves reminiscing about the summer of 2011. Edge had to abruptly retire as World Heavyweight Champion after *WrestleMania XXVII*, leaving the title vacant. At the time, Alberto Del Rio was rising in the ranks as the likely successor. Christian and Del Rio were placed into a Ladder match for the vacant title at *Extreme Rules '11*. As expected, people rallied behind the 17-year veteran and championed his effort to become the titleholder. I remember thinking that Christian was not going to win, but damn sure rooting for him. In one of the better Ladder matches of the last half decade, Christian's creativity was put on display as he led the way to a memorable 4-star (+) encounter. Christian won the title and embraced Edge in a touching moment to those of us that grew up watching them.

Boom! The title reign ended 5 days later...

On the night Christian should have been celebrating his greatest professional achievement that put the World Championship stamp of approval on his Hall of Fame-worthy career, he lost the title to Randy Orton in an outstanding match between two guys that had incredible, innate chemistry in the ring. In the four consecutive PPVs that followed, Christian and Orton told a multi-chapter story. In the third chapter, he won back the title by nefarious means, setting up the biggest match of his singles career in the semi-main-event at *Summerslam*. It turned out to also be one of his best matches. He and Orton had a match that, on any given random day, I could pull out from my DVD library, sit back, and enjoy it like I was watching for the first time. The best feuds often take the most important pieces of the puzzle from each of their previous matches and insert them into the payoff that ends the story. At *Summerslam*, Christian and Orton included several spots that had made their series so outstanding and a finish that played off their first two matches with Orton winning via RKO out of nowhere.

The loss at *Summerslam '11* essentially ended his run as a headliner, but he proved to everyone on that night and in those four months leading up to it that he deserved the opportunity to be a World Champion and belonged, even for just a little while, at the top of the mountain.

#40: Vader

Vader was the greatest superheavyweight wrestler of all-time. There have been other mammoth athletes tipping the scales at around four hundred plus pounds that have been very good. One even ranks higher than him because of overall contributions. Yet, none could top what Vader could do in the ring. As a performer, he could do things that no other man his size has ever been able to do in North American wrestling. He took his experience as an offensive lineman, with the combination of quickness and power that it required, and went to Japan, where he became a huge star while being taught of an artistry to big man wrestling not often seen in the WWE. When he came back to the States in the early 1990s, he was simply in a class by himself amongst super heavyweights.

The typical style for a super heavyweight, popularized by the WWE in the modern era, was to have the larger man dominate and his smaller opponent work in short bursts of offense. Though it made sense, it was a take on the "David vs. Goliath" match that was, by and large, pretty boring. Vader's time in Japan taught him a different style. He did not use (or let promoters use) his gargantuan size as an excuse to no-sell for his opponents. Vader understood that he was telling a story, but that he was also expected to be entertaining. Coming from the gridiron, he knew that blowouts made many fans leave the stadium and viewers turn off the television. The more competitive, the more exciting.

As first evidenced in his matches with Sting in WCW, he was more than willing to give as much as he dished out (within reason). Legitimately, he beat the hell out of every guy he got in the ring with - his punches and forearm shots perfectly exemplified the term "clubbing blows" - yet, when it came time for his oppositions' comebacks, Vader bumped around the ring like no other 400+ pounder could. He made Sting, for instance, look like one of the strongest men on the planet, allowing himself to be tossed around to the tune of German suplexes, back suplexes, over the rope suplexes, and powerslams. Subsequently, he has as many critically acclaimed matches as the rest of the super heavyweights combined.

When writing this book, I had a lot of fun going back and watching many of the old NWA/WCW matches that I had not seen in many years. The highlight of my NWA/WCW rewind was the Vader vs. Sting series. I was blown away by it. They had some special matches. Wrestling is all about making money, but the quality of the performance can make a one-time viewer into a lifetime fan. David vs. Goliath is merely a story of the underdog. One man seemingly cannot be beaten; the other is the one attempting the impossible. It is a simple formula for making money at the PPV and ticket box offices. What made Vader exceptional was that he was a super heavyweight that could give you success, financially, while also providing the dramatic, Match of the Year candidate that both sells out the arenas *and* sends the crowds that fill them home happy and wanting to see more. There have not been a lot of guys his size that could do that.

Vader and Sting had three PPV matches. The first earned Vader his first World Heavyweight Championship at the '92 *Great American Bash*. Given the physically taxing and exciting nature of their initial encounter, the Vader vs. Sting rematch to determine the "King of Cable" at *Starrcade '92* was a must-see affair. In the period between Ric Flair's departure in 1991 and Hulk Hogan's arrival in 1994, Vader and Sting were the top heel and babyface in WCW. Jim Ross referenced on commentary that their Starrcade match reminded him of the Ali-Foreman "Thrilla in Manila." I'd call it the 1992 WCW Match of the Year. The last of their classic PPV trifecta was a Non-Sanctioned Strap match at *Super Brawl III*. Most critics would likely award WCW's 1993 Match of the Year to either Vader vs. Cactus Jack at *Halloween Havoc* or Vader vs. Ric Flair at *Starrcade*, but I would give it to the Strap match.

1993 was Vader's year. He was World Champion for nine months of the calendar, during which time he had some incredible matches with a variety of opponents. In Sting, Foley, and Flair, he had three different styles to work against and had matches that were critically received as four-stars or better against them all. His title defenses against British Bulldog were also quite good, albeit nowhere near as heralded.

The biggest match of his life was the *Starrcade '93* Title vs. Career match with Flair. Because of the stipulation that Flair had to retire if he lost, the match was very dramatic. The potential last match of an all-time great during a period when rumors spread slowly evoked a lot of emotions from the fans. I think most of the credit should go to Vader for this being regarded as the best match in Starrcade history by WWE. The drama had to carry it, as the wrestling on Flair's end was below the standard that he had set in the past. For all intents and purposes, it was a "Vader" match. The big man did most of the work and Flair simply bumped for him. I loved watching Vader brawl. His opponents, especially an all-time best bump taker like Flair, looked like they were legitimately getting their heads knocked off. Vader lost the title that night by a roll-up, but his performance was the talking point coming out of the match. He dominated the entirety and, in what was perhaps his most athletic display, he missed a top rope moonsault. The visual of Vader performing a moonsault is something that has to be seen to be believed.

If you asked the casual fan to pick between Vader's top 1993 matches, the most common answer might be the Texas Death match with Cactus Jack. *Halloween Havoc* was the setting, but the stage had been set months prior when two brutal matches left Foley with a wicked concussion and in need of two dozen stitches. Remember that ECW, which popularized hardcore brawls, had not gained traction as of '93, so the Vader-Cactus bouts were eye opening in that "I've never seen this before" type of way. Foley was such an innovator, in general, but I think he found the perfect dance partner in Vader, with whom he could play his sadistic game. Put yourself in the 1993 mindset of a fan that had not seen a match quite that hardcore. This was a fight that broke new ground; that entered uncharted territory, in terms of violence, in North America's mainstream wrestling scene.

The remainder of Vader's career paled in comparison to what he accomplished in his first two years, with perhaps the biggest knock against him (and the primary reason why he was demoted to the second tier for the *WM Era, 2nd edition*) being that he never became a force to be reckoned with at the box office. He spent the latter part of his WCW tenure continuing to have very good matches – do yourself a favor and watch him work with Big Bossman - but being slowly demoted down the card. Once he took on the role of "Hogan fodder" in late 1994/early 1995, he was essentially finished as a major player. To his credit, Vader combined with the Hulkster to give Hogan some of his best matches in WCW. He would have made an ideal Hogan opponent in Hulkamania's heyday.

Vader saw the writing on the wall. He had lost to WCW's top act, booked in such a way that rematches seemed unlikely. So, in 1996, he left for the WWE, debuting at *The Royal Rumble* and making a huge splash the following night on *Raw* when he unleashed a full out assault on everyone that dared cross his path, including WWE legend, Hall of Famer, and then-storyline-WWE President Gorilla Monsoon. Just as in WCW, he was pushed straight to the top and, by *Summerslam*, he was main-eventing and wrestling for the WWE Championship against Shawn Michaels. Given their respective resumes – HBK was the master of David vs. Goliath and Vader was the greatest super heavyweight in history - it made for quite the exciting affair to see Vader vs. Michaels on a major PPV.

Unfortunately, Vader never fully clicked in the WWE. I saw a noticeable difference in his WCW vs. WWE matches. One thing that WCW did right with Vader is that they allowed him to be the worker that he had been overseas. They did not ask Vader to conform to their standards. To me, it seemed as though WWE failed to give Vader the same courtesy and got a lesser version of "The Mastodon" as a result. Vader's WWE tenure could have been so much more. I believe that he should have been the one to win the WWE Championship leading to *WrestleMania 13*, where he could have dropped the title to the Undertaker, as scheduled, in place of the far less talented Sid. He had not lost clean in previous title bouts and had defeated Taker at *The Royal Rumble*, so he had the credibility to step in.

Vader will be best remembered for what he accomplished in WCW. His run as the top heel in the early nineties was the highlight of his career. He provided several classic matches en route to winning the WCW Championship 3-times.

#39: "Ravishing" Rick Rude

What I would like to have right now is for all you fat, out of shape Readerland sweat hogs to keep your thoughts focused while I tell you how a real man from Minnesota became one of the greatest of his generation (insert swiveling of the hips, here)...

Rick Rude was one of the top stars of the late 1980s and early 1990s. Both in the WWE and WCW, he was a headlining heel, blessed with the ability to make you love to hate him. Yet, he reminds me of one of those teams in sport that hangs around at the top and is always in the conversation when it comes to the playoffs or the big tournaments, but never ascended to the ultimate heights. You could look at him like the Netherlands national soccer team. For decades, they have been in the mix. Each World Cup comes with a lot of hype surrounding their squad and every now and again they even make it to the semi-finals or finals, but each World Cup goes without them hoisting the trophy. Rude was that way. He was always near the main-event, often facing second tier babyfaces like Jake Roberts or Ricky Steamboat. He went so far as to wrestle for the World title on a couple of PPVs. Never did he, though, actually capture a top promotion's preeminent championship.

It was a different era. During Rude's heyday, a World Champion could hold the title for years at a time. There is an argument to be made that Rude would have been a multi-time World Champion if he had come about in the late 90s on, when the title was passed around more frequently. He was a natural heel capable of drawing tremendous heat, especially with his brief, area specific, taunting interviews before his matches. He often used the general stigma surrounding most wrestling fans as his hook (fat, out of shape, sweat hogs). The ones that fit that bill hated him for pointing it out and everyone else hated him for lumping them into that category. Either way, by the time his opponent was in the ring, the fans were ready to see Rude get his head ripped off. One time, when the WWE visited Madison Square Garden during his feud with Roddy Piper in 1989, "Ravishing" Rick could not even get past "What I'd like to have right now" because the audience was so eager to boo him out of the building. It is conceivable that his act would have worked in the Attitude Era or later to the tune of multiple World title reigns. He is one of the greats to have never achieved that honor.

It is surprising that he did not achieve the WWE title, even as a transitional champion. After merely his first feud (with Jake Roberts), he was white hot. Bobby Heenan was Rude's manager and would pick out a girl in the crowd for him to kiss, playing up to his moniker as a ladies' man. When Heenan picked Jake's wife, it did not go over so well. "Ravishing" Rick vs. Jake "The Snake" was a battle of psychological wrestling experts, made even better by Rude's awesome airbrushed tights with a nice picture of Mrs. Roberts on the front. Their heated brawls were the stuff of 80s wrestling legend and earned Rude a step up the card to semi-main-event status at *WrestleMania V* for the most high profile feud of his entire career against The Ultimate Warrior.

The Warrior, at that time, was the Intercontinental Champion and a name on the rise, but he was not much of a performer. One could say that he was all sizzle and no steak. Rude was an accomplished worker who tried his absolute hardest to help Warrior to a satisfying performance. The results were mixed, as the bout was a bit sloppy. I shudder to think what today's audience would do to a main-event player as careless as Warrior tended to be. Rude did well, though, and the match was actually pretty good (despite the occasional error), ending with "The Ravishing One" winning the IC strap with help from Heenan. Their rematch at *Summerslam* was the perfect example of why Rude, in my opinion, should have been WWE Champion. While the *Mania* match was a tad off and only lasted 6-minutes, the *Summerslam* match was executed with excellent precision and accuracy on each sequence, lasting 15-minutes. Mark it down as one of the finest performances of Rude's career, as it was no small feat to carry Warrior to a match of that caliber.

A year later, the two would continue their rivalry at *Summerslam '90*, only it would be for the WWE Championship and it would be contested within the confines of a Steel Cage. One had to think that Rude, by then sporting an intimidating Patrick Bergin in *Sleeping with the Enemy* look, legitimately disliked Warrior. After working so hard to help Warrior, the far less talented of the two, achieve Intercontinental glory, it seemed as though Rude had earned himself a potential run at the top with the big belt. Yet, that honor went to Warrior and Rude fell to the backburner until the new champion needed an opponent that management knew could work well with him and put him over. Much respect to Rude for doing his job and doing it well. It was another awesome performance from Ravishing Rick, as the match uncharacteristically began at the top of the cage and worked its way back to the ring. Rude scaled and leaped off the cage twice in the 10-minute contest, putting his body on the line like few in that era would have.

After the feud with Warrior concluded, he left to go to WCW, who treated him like the big deal that he was, immediately putting him into a feud with Sting and building a new stable of wrestlers around him known as The Dangerous Alliance (Rude, Arn Anderson, Steve Austin, Bobby Eaton, Madusa, and Larry Zbyszko under the management of Paul "E. Dangerously" Heyman). The Dangerous Alliance was placed right alongside Vader as the top heel act in WCW for the next several months and Rude was at center stage. The faction's peak came at the *Wrestle War '92* PPV featuring what is often viewed as the best War Games match of all-time. Rude had a standout performance. Some of the notable moments in which he was involved included the execution of the first double

Boston Crab that I had ever seen, getting pressed into the air and subsequently into to the top of the cage by Sting, and being wedged between the two rings while two wrestlers yanked his legs in opposite directions. He took a good looking beating. Rude managed to escape direct involvement in his team's loss, with most of his focus in the match being on his budding rivalry with Ricky "The Dragon" Steamboat, previewing a classic match to come that turned out to be arguably the finest of Rude's career.

For all his talent, Rude was rarely given the chance to have those unbelievable, 4-5 star matches. Yet, there was one match where opportunity knocked loud. It came at *Beach Blast '92* in an Ironman Challenge against Steamboat where the most falls earned in 30-minutes would crown a victor. Theirs might not have been the most aesthetically pleasing Ironman match in terms of the moves performed, but the story told was amazing. It had the drama of watching a football game since it was similarly structured; an excellent piece of work by two of the best in squared circle history.

Rude did not have a very long career, thanks to injury. In 1992, he was in the twilight of his in-ring career. His last year in the mainstream, 1993, was significant for him, though. In the late summer, he had a best Two-out-of-Three series with Dustin Rhodes for the US title, which he had previously held for 14 months (2nd longest reign of all-time). He lost the series thanks to interference in the third match from Ric Flair, Rude's last major North American opponent. They battled for Flair's NWA World Championship at *Fall Brawl '93*. Rude won the gold. As it was soon renamed the WCW International Heavyweight Championship after the NWA withdrew from WCW, Rude's victory to capture the World title – similar to Barry Windham's - was a big deal, but not quite as big as it could have been since the major championship in the promotion by then was the WCW title.

Though his career was cut short soon after and though he departed for the Heavens far too early in his life, I remember him as an all-time great, both for his signature pre-match promos and for his in-ring acumen that only a handful of wrestlers could match.

#38: Jeff Hardy

In the 1990s, there was a superstar that we will discuss in greater detail a bit later that became an icon for his willingness to put his body on the line, helping him overcome his physique – which could best be described as "not ideal" - en route to a Hall of Fame career full of championships and accolades. At the tail end of that man's career, a young wrestler from North Carolina named Jeff Hardy began endearing himself to the audience by following a similar, daredevil style. His mindset that he would do to his body what nobody else would helped him ascend to great heights despite his own imperfect stature, ultimately becoming a multi-time World Champion and one of the most popular superstars of the WrestleMania Era.

Debuting alongside his real life brother, Matt, as The Hardy Boys, he rose to prominence with his role in the Tag Team Ladder match at *No Mercy '99*. It is fascinating to go back and watch that match today. The crowd is dead silent when the opening bell rings. All things considered, The Hardys, Edge, and Christian were relative nobodies in the business. Slowly, but surely throughout the match, the crowd came alive. With each high risk taken, the buzz in the arena grew. It was Jeff that most noticeably brought the audience to their feet. His "devil may care" attitude and fundamental need to do the one thing that people would most remember garnered him the loudest reactions of any member of the teams. The match was so innovative that it ushered in another "Golden Age" of tag team wrestling, taking the division to body-punishing places it had never been before.

The Hardys, E&C, and also The Dudleys did some amazing work together, but after the *No Mercy* match, a pattern emerged where the collective breaths of the fans seemed to be drawn into gasps whenever Jeff, in particular, started climbing a structure of any unusual height. It was not long before his Swanton Bomb off the entrance stage in the

Tables match at *Royal Rumble 2000* or the Swanton off the giant ladder and through the table at *WrestleMania 2000* became legendary moments. Throw in his being speared by Edge (from a huge ladder) while dangling from a title-holding hook at *WrestleMania X-Seven* and Jeff was an international wrestling sensation before his 24th birthday.

He became wrestling's version of a teen heartthrob with young women. At the same time, the excitement that The Hardys brought to their matches earned him the respect of the male audience. Everything about them was high energy, from their in-ring style to their excellent theme song - a simple rock tune with a cool guitar riffing sequence that has been on my workout playlist for the last ten years and counting. It was hard not to like the Hardys.

It was a magical two year run, but through all the tables, ladders, and chairs, Jeff emerged with high expectations to be a star on his own. His name was mentioned in the same breath as all-time greats who also started in popular tag teams like Shawn Michaels and Bret Hart.

Jeff's anticipated run as a singles wrestler kicked off shortly after the TLC tag team era unofficially ended in the spring of 2001. He got off to a great start by winning the Intercontinental Championship in dramatic fashion, followed by the Light Heavyweight and Hardcore titles. He had a great series of matches for the Hardcore title with RVD, a similarly gifted master of the extreme grappling arts, that were our first real taste of what Jeff might be able to accomplish as a featured singles performer. All the usual stunts were there from Hardy, just without him having to share the spotlight.

The summer of '01 was an individual test that Jeff passed with flying colors, but he did not maintain his momentum and it seemed like he was heading nowhere fast. Rumors would circulate that such was his own doing. One thing that certainly seemed to be lacking was his motivation. In what was, perhaps, a last ditch effort to get Jeff to realize how big a star he could be, the WWE put him against Undertaker with The Deadman's Undisputed WWE Championship on the line in the summer of 2002. It is one thing to have a great Ladder match with a fellow stunt machine like RVD, but quite another to have one with a legend who has never been in one. Hardy vs. Taker told a tremendous underdog tale, with Jeff being physically dissected but still managing to fight back and put himself in position to win the title. Though he lost, the match itself and the post-match show of respect given to him by Undertaker told everyone watching that Hardy could be a major player if he decided he wanted it.

Unfortunately, Jeff was the Thoreau of the wrestling business. When he wanted to consume himself with other interests, he ventured to a place of solitude and did what he wanted. The time came, however, when his creativity needed its sports entertainment outlet again. Jeff returned to the WWE in the late summer of 2006 after a three year absence. It did not take long before Hardy was back to being as over as any babyface in the company, making you wonder just when – not really if, anymore – they would try him out as a headliner. He had been back about 15 months when he beat HHH to become #1 contender for Randy Orton's WWE Championship at the 2008 *Royal Rumble*. There were 6 weeks between earning the title shot and *The Rumble* and, honest-to-God, it may have been the greatest six week build-up that any wrestler has ever received. Hardy was at his death-defying best and the momentum he built was truly something to behold. He lost, but it would not be his only shot.

Triple H was instrumental to Jeff's career in the singles ranks. It was he who Hardy defeated for the IC title in the spring of '01 and after Hardy had been back in the WWE for a year, it was Triple H who put him over at *Armageddon '07* and gave Jeff his big break as a main-event player. I think Trips simply realized that, as over as Hardy was, there was money to be made in his ascension to the top. So, he took it upon himself to help make it happen. When it still had not happened, as of the fall of 2008, Triple H faced Jeff in a match at No Mercy with The Game's WWE title on the line. It was the first and the best match in a three bout series to go along with two triple threat matches seemingly designed for the specific purpose of making sure that Jeff would never again compete for any title lower than the World or WWE Championship. Jeff would ultimately capture the title in a triple threat also involving Edge at *Armageddon '08*.

    The key aspect that made his run in the main-event a success was that he had the lightning strike capability of winning at any moment, while maintaining a sense of utter unpredictability because the same gambles capable of earning him victories could also lead to his defeats.

    Three championship programs highlighted Hardy's run at the top for about a one year period. The first was the aforementioned matches with Trips. The second featured three PPV bouts against Edge. The summer of '09 brought with it, at the beginning, the definitive conclusion to his longtime rivalry with Edge and, by its end, the finish to his storied WWE tenure. Though Jeff would leave in the midst of the greatest singles run of his career, he did save his best for last. Immediately following what was supposed to have been a feel good moment for fans that had clamored to see Hardy regain the World title from Edge at *Extreme Rules*, CM Punk cashed in his Money in the Bank contract and became the second new champion in a matter of minutes.

    Hardy vs. Punk was some of the better storytelling that you will see in wrestling, with Jeff eventually winning the title back in July. *Summerslam '09*, the sight of the rubber match with his World title on the line, would be the biggest night of Hardy's career. In the main-event, Hardy would once again face

Punk, this time in a gimmick that he had helped pioneer some nine years prior: the TLC match. What was interesting to witness was that the same adrenaline junky, daredevil spirit was there. Jeff put his body on the line as much as he ever had before, particularly with a Swanton Bomb off the top of a 20 foot ladder through the announce table. Yet, the youthful exuberance from the early part of the decade was replaced by a battle tested, psychologically hardened veteran instinct that aided in making the finish dramatic not because of the next spot he might attempt, but because he had quietly become a sports entertainment raconteur, physically narrating his quest to hang onto the World title.

     He lost to Punk and, soon after, rode off into the sunset never to be seen in the WWE again. Why should we have expected anything else from the enigma?

#37: Rey Mysterio

The great Rey Mysterio made his debut at the 1996 *Great American Bash*, bringing with him a stellar reputation from Mexico and a lot of what I call "quiet hype" (when you have people with knowledge of independent or international wrestling companies championing the efforts of a new wrestler that the masses are largely unfamiliar with). Dean Malenko was the WCW Cruiserweight Champion and Mysterio's opponent that night at *The Bash*. Malenko being more of a ground-based grappler and Mysterio known for his aerial tactics, they were an interesting mix in styles. It was an impressive outing and the first of several great matches with Malenko that provided Mysterio an outlet to showcase the full extent of his capabilities to the American audience. He quickly went from relatively unknown to one of the world's most popular superstars.

In WCW, Eric Bischoff did a fantastic job with the Cruiserweight division, bringing in world-renowned talents; on the merits of the Malenko matches, Mysterio was positioned as one of its centerpieces and rattled several of that era's most profilic matches in rapid succession. A month after *The Bash*, Mysterio wrestled Psicosis in a match heralded by one major publication as amongst the best of all-time. Then there was arguably the greatest in his series of matches with Malenko at *Halloween Havoc*, followed quickly by a pair of really strong efforts against Ultimo Dragon at *World War 3* (amazingly high degree of difficulty in the counters) and Jushin "Thunder" Liger at *Starrcade*.

Mysterio was one of the highlights for WCW during the Monday Night Wars and, for a fanbase that was becoming increasingly appreciative of innovative in-ring performance, his role (and that of the Cruiserweight division overall) has been understated. His match with Eddie Guerrero at *Halloween Havoc '97* was a thing of wrestling beauty. It was 1997's WCW Match of the Year. I also enjoyed Rey's work in WCW with

Chavo Guerrero and Billy Kidman, with whom he had one of the two best matches of under ten-minutes in length that I have ever seen.

In 2002, he made his WWE debut. On *Smackdown*, he beat Chavo in a great match and then scaled the walls of a Steel Cage later in the night, launching himself off the top onto a group called "The Un-Americans." It was one of the most memorable introductions of the 2000s.

His first feud was with Kurt Angle, who to this day remains my favorite of Mysterio's opponents. They brought out the best in each other. The mix of their styles, on the surface, seemed a bit of a clash (similar to Malenko), but they had unbelievable chemistry. Mysterio forced whomever he was in the ring with to pick up their pace. Angle had the stamina to turn right around and challenge Rey to keep up with *his* pace. What they pulled off in their matches was extremely complex, but they executed at a 100% clip. Mysterio vs. Angle from *Summerslam '02* is the other of the two best matches of under 10-minutes ever. Opening matches of PPVs are responsible for setting the tone for everyone else to follow, so I do not think it a coincidence that *Summerslam '02* is one of the best PPVs ever when you note that Mysterio-Angle was its first match.

We got to see a lot of Mysterio vs. Angle during the Paul Heyman-booked period in *Smackdown* history affectionately known as the era of "The Smackdown Six." Every week, The Six would square off in various combos to have excellent matches. Mysterio formed a tag team with Edge, Angle paired up with Benoit, and then you had Los Guerreros. So, there were a lot of stellar tag team matches too. They even developed a new Tag Team Championship to keep those guys occupied. Mysterio was a phenomenal partner because, not only did he understand the psychology of tag wrestling, but he also was adept at using his frame to allow his partner to launch him into the air for assaults with a little extra zest. Edge and Mysterio vs. Angle and

Benoit to crown the first WWE Tag Team Champions, exclusive to *Smackdown*, was arguably the greatest tag team match of all-time.

Mysterio's flashy offense and variety of masks made him one of the top babyfaces in the WWE. His reactions were, by the middle of the decade, behind only John Cena, Eddie Guerrero, Shawn Michaels, and Batista. The WWE had put him in positions to headline against larger stars in the past, but he had gone right back to the Cruiser or Tag divisions afterward. At the conclusion of his lengthy saga with Eddie that stretched across the first eight months of 2005, however, Mysterio's career soared to heights no one thought possible.

With a greater push comes greater responsibilities. When Eddie turned heel on him in May, Mysterio had to respond both verbally and physically to meet the demands of the angle. As the drama escalated to Eddie playing mind games revolving around Mysterio's son, Dominic, Rey had to be both dejected and angry, without the assistance of being fully able to facially express it. I do not think people truly appreciated how difficult that must have been. Another thing that stood out to me back then was that Rey was smart enough to adapt his style. When he got to the main-event, his body was already wearing down. He shifted gears to a safer style, picking and choosing when to use his signature high flying spots. The crispness was still there, but the pace was a little bit slower.

I was fortunate enough to be there when Mysterio won the World Heavyweight Championship in Chicago at *WrestleMania 22*. That was a great moment. He deservedly became the smallest heavyweight champion ever. People have often cited Eddie's death as the reason for Mysterio's ascension to Mania headliner. I think you would be remiss to dismiss it entirely, but those people were not paying attention if they think that was the only (or even the primary) reason. Mysterio was being positioned for a run in the main-event for the entirety of 2005. By 2006, it was not a matter of "if," but "when."

It may not have been the most impressive title reign, but the mere fact that he won the World Championship, along with the headlining matches and boosted stature that came with it, propelled him to the First-Tier originally (and I would like to forever refer to him as "First-Tier-caliber"). He became a perennial contender for years and absolutely belonged as a consistent headliner from 2006-2011. Nobody ever did more with less stature.

Mysterio had some injury plagued years following his first World title run, a by-product of his body more rapidly deteriorating after grappling with guys twice his size. It was not until 2009 that he finally got rolling again. His performance in that year's Royal Rumble match remains special for me because it was the first wrestling PPV that my wife (then my fiancée) watched with me. As we sat there amongst my friends, many of the them picking my brain about various WWE topics, I think it finally sunk in for her just how big a fan that I was. Mysterio was the first entrant in the Rumble, which is annually one of the most entertaining WWE matches. He lasted close to fifty-minutes, dazzling my wife with all of his incredible moves. Five months later when we got married, she gave me "vouchers" for future WrestleMania tickets. Thanks, Rey. I am not sure that happens without you, buddy.

At the *25th Anniversary of WrestleMania*, Rey won the Intercontinental Championship and retired JBL in the process. Two months later, he engaged in one of the year's most awesome rivalries when he wrestled Chris Jericho several times within the span of May to July. They had three excellent PPV bouts for the IC title. If Angle was my favorite of Mysterio's opponents, then Jericho was unquestionably a close second. Sometimes the greatest opponent for a guy with atypical offense is the one that can find the most interesting ways to counter it. For Mysterio, nobody was better at that than Angle or Jericho. In terms of the sheer entertainment value, I would put the series between Mysterio and Jericho up against just about any other in history.

From there, Mysterio kept on going for another two years. He bridged the gap between 2009 and 2010 working with Batista, in whom Rey had helped bring out a thoroughly enjoyable evil side. That feud led him to a World Heavyweight Championship match with Undertaker at *Royal Rumble '10*. A forgotten gem in both their careers, they told as enjoyable a big man vs. cruiserweight story as I can recall. All of Rey's spots were realistic and all of Taker's counters were well executed. It was the blueprint for how a big man should work with a cruiserweight.

Mysterio is a first ballot Hall of Famer. He will be remembered as the #1 guy on the list of stars whose matches you would most readily seek out if you could only watch wrestling for ten minutes. He also has quite the legacy with three World titles, two IC titles, seven Tag Team titles, eight Cruiserweight titles, and the 2006 Royal Rumble victory. I was there for his career moment; I would not mind being there for his Hall of Fame enshrinement.

#36: Seth Rollins

As we return our focus to the competition for who will lead the next generation of superstars into the future, we again find a former Shield member at the center of the discussion.

Seth Rollins put together a resume full of remarkable achievements in his first few years in WWE: member of the decade's greatest faction, Tag Team Champion, Mr. Money in the Bank, WrestleMania main-event, headliner of every major PPV, United States Champion, and WWE World Heavyweight Champion. It is quite impressive, already one of the 30-40 best statistical track records in modern history. A lot of wrestlers from the late 2000s on also racked up accolades that looked great on paper, but what separates Rollins is the context of his many achievements. Here are five examples:

<u>1) As WWE Tag Team Champion, he sparked a resurgence for the division, ending years of creative inconsistency.</u>

So many of his 21st century peers can list "Tag Team titleholder" on their respective WWE CVs and, to be honest, it hardly matters. After the Smackdown Six era ended in 2003, the tag team division as a whole lost considerable steam, slowly at first and then in an unbelievable hurry. By 2005, it had hit its lowest point of the WrestleMania Era in WWE, becoming an island for misfit gimmicks and headliners for whom creative had nothing else to offer.

Ever since Rollins won the championships with Roman Reigns after WrestleMania in 2013, the division has been consistently healthier. They brought with them momentum from The Shield's rousing first six months on the roster, but unlike many fellow high profile tag champions from the previous decade, they sported an attitude that never failed to translate to 110% effort in the ring; Rollins, in particular, was relentless in his pursuit of being considered one of the world's best wrestlers. Consequently, he and Roman's tag team matches had a tendency to exceed the reputation of the division's 2005-2012 run of mediocrity.

There is a certain irony to this conversation. Rollins and Reigns fell victim to the same shoddy booking that had hallmarked the Tag Team Championships for a decade; as soon as they won the titles, they began their descent into relative obscurity. With matches the caliber of the one they wrestled against The Usos on the *Money in the Bank 2013* pre-show, they kept showcasing their considerable talents, but the downward spiral continued until they regained their footing in the fall with two of the most emotionally engaging matches in WWE's entire tag team wrestling library against Cody Rhodes and Goldust, captivating performances that put to shame 99% of the genre's body of work since 2003. By their force of will, they survived and wound up becoming the champions that pulled the division up by its bootstraps, giving tag team wrestling a solid foundation that it has continued to build on to present day. Even after losing the titles and leaving the tag ranks after a mere six months, the imprint Rollins left is still visible.

2) Shield or Authority, whichever faction you believe to be the best of this decade, Rollins was the workhorse that shaped your belief.

Both in storyline and behind the scenes, Seth Rollins was the glue that held The Shield together. He was referred to as its "Architect." He was the brains of the operation and their most dynamic performer, the heart and soul of what proved to be the foundational trio of WWE's next generation. A passionately influential personality often incapable of taking "No" for an answer, he could be polarizing, but he believed in himself and his group.

That they ascended all the way to pay-per-view main-event status by their final match together, a dominant elimination-style (3-0) thrashing of the foremost stable of the 2000s, Evolution, seems to suggest that Rollins was akin to a basketball star who lifts his teammates to reach their potential; and The Shield unquestionably reached its full potential. Aside from Daniel Bryan, no debuting act this decade has been more impactful to the product; and through all their classic matches, revolutionizing of the Six-Man tag genre, and elevation to a group worthy by itself of inclusion among the Top 90 of the WrestleMania Era, Rollins was the workhorse.

When he shocked the wrestling world and joined The Authority, he instantly became their workhorse too. The Architect and Authority marriage proved highly productive. Triple H and Stephanie McMahon needed a new go-to guy to bring their regime out of the past and Rollins needed to be pushed (on screen and off) to continue growing as a superstar. He was a revelation as a primary antagonist, surely eclipsing even the greatest expectations that enthusiasts and WWE higher-ups alike could have had for him. After CM Punk quit, Rollins became the most utilized member of the roster and thrived.

<u>3) He was the only wrestler other than Edge to fully maximize the gimmick of being "Mr. Money in the Bank."</u>

The lesson we learned from Edge during his run as the inaugural Money in the Bank contract holder was that carrying that briefcase *could* afford a star on the cusp of something special an opportunity to grow into the role of perennial headliner while fans were continually made aware of his status as the de-facto #1 contender for the World Championship; if he made the most of that chance, it could be the catalyst for grooming him into a credible titleholder, nudging him ever closer to the precipice, building anticipation for his cash-in, and allowing him to burst onto the main-event scene.

After nearly a decade of experimentation with the Money in the Bank model beyond the 101 teachings of the Rated R Superstar, Seth Rollins won the briefcase in 2014 and spent the next nine months re-educating the audience of the gimmick's potential; if the man makes the title and holding that briefcase is similarly prestigious as being a champion, then the man also makes Money in the Bank. Rollins's overall growth as a performer coincided with his time holding the contract; it helped him begin his ascent as a singles wrestler beyond the scope of The Shield.

As he also proved in several gimmick matches, standards are made to be redefined and the Architect redesigned the blueprint for what Mr. Money in the Bank can achieve, cashing in to win the WWE Championship during the main-event of *WrestleMania 31*, arguably even eclipsing Edge in MITB lore, and re-writing the concept's textbook to render the original version outdated.

<u>4) With one notable injury exception, he has displayed remarkable consistency as a PPV headliner during what may prove to be an all-time great era in WWE.</u>

The internal competition between Rollins, Reigns, and Ambrose has had a very positive overall effect on the entire WWE product. One could say that they are wrestling's most recent embodiment of the expression "rising tides lift all ships." Since they embarked on their singles careers after headlining PPVs as a unit routinely from late 2013 to mid-2014, they have all three been Top 5 stars, kick-starting a new era developed largely around their talents. Given the success of the WWE Network during the same period, it makes the so-termed Reality Era led by Punk and Bryan seem like a segue from the Cena-Orton-Batista days to a potential 5-10 year run of dominance led by the former Shield-mates like the New Generation once transitioned Hulkamania to Attitude.

Rollins, as of mid-2016, had been the most consistent of his contemporaries. Armed with his Money in the Bank briefcase and his relationship with The Authority in 2014, Rollins grew so quickly into his role as the lead heel that it was hard to keep him out of the spotlight. Within four months of going solo, he had already main-evented a PPV; within a year, he had headlined PPVs with Cena, Lesnar, and Orton. He carried WWE from mid-2014 until he blew out his knee in November 2015, holding the WWE Championship for 7 ½ months (3rd longest reign in a decade).

<u>5) Seth Rollins is the evolutionary Shawn Michaels.</u>

Can you bestow higher praise on a wrestler than that? If HBK was the Michael Jordan of pro wrestling, Rollins legitimately begs the question, "Can someone in WWE be better than the best ever?" That is an arguably insurmountable challenge for the Architect, but I believe he is the one guy who could eclipse Michaels. He is young enough, he definitely has the determination, and he has already raised the bar athletically. He has also developed a Michaels-like balance of psychological nuance and high risk, meaning his matches are both smart and aesthetically superlative.

The proof is in the pudding: nobody has a better body of work since 2013 than Rollins; borrowing from an HBK nickname, nobody has "stolen more shows." I would be very surprised if he was not pushing for a Top 20 spot within five years or less and, if he can live up to the lofty expectation I have set for him as the guy who will surpass HBK, then the sky is the limit for what he can achieve historically.

#35: Scott Hall

May 27, 1996 is one of the most famous days in wrestling history. If the events of that night's WCW *Monday Nitro* had not happened, then we may never have seen WCW rise to the forefront of the cable television universe or the WWE's famed Attitude Era that developed in response to it. Scott Hall, who had for years competed as a high profile upper card character named Razor Ramon in the WWE, showed up unannounced in WCW, coming from the crowd and jumping the guardrail before cutting a promo that made you think that he was specifically coming from the WWE. "You know who I am," he said, "but you don't...know why...I'm here." He was joined soon after by his good friend, Kevin Nash, and the two "Outsiders" embarked on a mission to "take over" WCW.

The fascinating, dream scenario for any wrestling fan back in the day was to see WWE vs. WCW. Each had national profiles via television contracts that aired their weekly shows in most markets across the map. There was a very real rivalry; between the two companies, between old school pro wrestling and the sports entertainment genre, and between WCW owner Ted Turner (plus WCW VP Eric Bischoff) and WWE owner Vince McMahon. To see the best of each company clash would be the ultimate fan experience, so when "Razor" showed up on *Nitro*, basically said he was coming from the competition, and inferred a hostile takeover without actually saying it verbatim, it was the kind of awesome occurrence that prompted young men like myself to call other young men and talk on the phone like gossiping girls. Having been a long-time WWE enthusiast, by that point, I was strongly rooting for The Outsiders to succeed in their conquest, as if it were the WWE doing the invading.

I was the target market for WCW. They wanted to take all the wrestling fans that grew up on the WWE in the 1980s and present a product to them that better fit their teen-age. Hall showing up on *Nitro* in "Razor" character created the illusion that he was legitimately still a WWE roster member. I knew nothing of dirtsheets (insider wrestling newsletters) back in those days. I was just a kid who flipped to WCW one day and saw Razor Ramon and Diesel in street clothes being called by their real names. What made it work was that it felt real. If everyone had known – like they probably would have today with the internet – that Hall and Nash were already under contract with WCW, then it would not have worked.

WCW provided such a stark contrast to what had become such a cartoonish WWE in the years prior, with its colorful outfits and silly gimmicks. *Nitro* was reality TV before it became popular, with guys like Hall and Nash coming through the crowd and creating anarchy. WCW played it off well, as they seemed legitimately threatened by just these two guys and their warning of a third. Both were fresh faces in the industry coming into a WCW that featured quite literally zero new, homegrown top talents. Most of their biggest names had been on top since the 80s. So, part of the intrigue regarding Hall and Nash's arrivals was also that they were just plain fresh. We were getting WWE vs. WCW *AND* past vs. present all at the same time.

When Hulk Hogan was revealed as the third man, forming The New World Order, it was the start of a magical run for WCW. The face of the original wrestling boom in the WWE, Hogan, was flanked by two of the top guys that had been tasked with replacing him. The key was that both Hall and Nash had been top stars independent of Hogan, unlike the Savages and DiBiases of the world that had arguably ridden shotgun to Hulkamania. They were viewed as equals, even if Hogan's heel turn was the talk of the wrestling world. It started back with Hall and Nash's runs in WWE, which made their WCW impact unique.

Hall hit the pro wrestling mainstream in 1992 when he debuted as a takeoff of Al Pacino's character in *Scarface*. As "Da

Bad Guy," he moved up the card quickly. He performed well and showed a lot of potential in a loss to Bret Hart in a WWE Championship match at the 1993 *Royal Rumble*, but it turned out to be his only one-on-one PPV World title match in WWE. Fans have often called him the greatest wrestler to have never won a World Championship. He was certainly the most influential star of the 1990s not to earn that elusive top spot.

His lack of a World title notwithstanding, Razor moved up the food chain after his match with Hart. It was another year or so before he reached his potential in his all-time classic 1994 Ladder match at *WrestleMania X* with Shawn Michaels. He was the reigning Intercontinental Champion when HBK came back claiming that he was the rightful champion since he never lost the title (which was true). Both belts were hung above the ring for the first PPV Ladder match and Hall and Michaels proceeded to tear the house down in what to this day is called one of the best matches of all-time. If Michaels was the unquestioned critical star of the first Ladder match, then Razor was the star of the second at *Summerslam '95*. In another all-time classic affair, Hall's psychologically sound smarts outshined HBK's acrobatics. While not denying HBK's aerial brilliance, Razor worked the match like a cunning technician. Personally, I think *Summerslam '95* was the best performance of Hall's career.

His biggest singles match in WCW also ended up being a Ladder match. He was the man responsible for ending Goldberg's famed undefeated streak, using a stun gun to help Nash win the WCW Championship at *Starrcade '98*. The main-event of *NWO/WCW Souled Out '99* saw a stun gun hung from a cable as the prize to retrieve by climbing a ladder. The winner was the one to actually use the stun gun on his opponent first. Though Goldberg won the match, it was Hall that carried the way. WCW often talked up Hall as the inventor of the Ladder match, rightfully giving him props for what he contributed to the gimmick's history.

The Ladder matches with Michaels helped Hall become a focal point of the WWE's programming for a solid two years. He was the face of the Intercontinental Championship division at a time when that position in the company still mattered. The WWE was in full swing with their "New Generation" movement and he was certainly one of the stars. At two consecutive WrestleManias, Royal Rumbles, and Summerslams, he was duking it out for the IC gold as an established headliner. He won the title a then-record four times. In WCW, he won the Tag Team Championship seven times and the US title twice, to go along with one run as the Television champ.

Business in the WWE was down during Hall's heyday as Razor Ramon, but he still built a name for himself that resonated throughout the professional wrestling industry and, when WCW had a chance to sign him to a lucrative contract, they did so without reservation. They put a fat contract on the table full of guaranteed money, which the WWE was not offering at the time, and Hall signed on the dotted line to kick start the biggest boom period in wrestling history. Make no mistake about it: Scott Hall was a very good wrestler and a charismatic personality. It was one of the most engaging moments in the history of wrestling when he showed up on *Nitro*. The entire cutting edge story played out beautifully on TV. In wrestling, we often get accustomed to Murphy's Law – whatever can go wrong, will go wrong. Not The N.W.O., though. The debuts of Hall and Nash and the heel turn of Hulk Hogan were handled to near perfection.

The last significant contribution that Hall made to mainstream wrestling was when he returned to the WWE to reform The N.W.O. for *WrestleMania X-8*. He added another huge match to his resume, having the honor to dance with the lights on bright one last time against Steve Austin. Only one other man can say that he headlined WrestleManias against both HBK and Stone Cold (and that is Bret Hart). The N.W.O.'s return was one of the things that locked me back into wrestling for the long haul, with Hall's role playing no small part in it.

Sadly, Hall had a longstanding addictive personality that led him to abuse drugs and alcohol. Could he have found that extra motivational gear to reach a higher peak if he had stayed sober? He had a great peak, as it was, being the third wheel in the most revolutionary group in wrestling's on-screen history and one of the founding members of its most notoriously influential backstage "Kliq." He could have realistically been a World Champion, but Hall is still an all-time great.

#34: Booker T

In a sport featuring doctor's sons, the children of military Generals, second and third generation wrestlers, former professional football players, national collegiate champions, Ivy League graduates, and even an Olympic Gold Medalist, it is great that there are also stories of redemption like that of Booker T. When he was a young man, he was involved in a series of armed robberies, pleaded guilty, and spent nearly two years in prison. Less than five years after he was released, the hard work and dedication that he put in to changing his life landed him a contract with World Championship Wrestling. He would go on to become one of the most decorated wrestlers of all-time. I consider him to be more of a role model for young people than most of his professional athletic peers because he was not blessed with the talent to overcome his difficult upbringing and he fell into the same traps that so many urban youths do, but even though he hit rock bottom, he found something that he was passionate about and found a way to distance himself from his past without allowing it to define him.

As a performer whose accolades yielded a 2013 Hall of Fame induction, Booker got his start in the tag team ranks and followed in the footsteps of Bret Hart and Shawn Michaels to break out on his own and become a six-time World Heavyweight Champion. His first five years in the industry's mainstream were spent alongside his real-life brother, Stevie Ray, together forming one of the classic duos of the 1990s. When you think of the best teams of that decade, Harlem Heat – a record ten-time WCW Tag Team Championship combination – are right at the top of the list with The Hart Foundation, Legion of Doom, and The Steiner Brothers.

Harlem Heat debuted and made an immediate impact, wrestling in the 1993 War Games match and never looked back, capturing their first Tag Title on December 8th of the following year. In their six years of teaming together, their list of championship-winning victories include defeats of The Nasty Boys, Sting and Lex Luger, The Steiners, Public Enemy, The Jersey Triad, The Windhams, and The Outsiders.

Booker also found team success in the WWE, winning the titles twice with Test and once each with Goldust and Rob Van Dam. His partnership with Goldust turned out to be a major highlight in his career. They were highly entertaining, performing comedic skits backstage that displayed a variety of additional character traits that many fans did not know that he possessed. Subsequently, he got over very well as a babyface. There was a moment during "Book Dust's" Tag Title opportunity at *Summerslam 2002* when the New York crowd started a massive "Booker T" chant that helped show not only to the fans watching at home that he was someone to keep an eye on, but also to Vince McMahon, who is well known for putting a ton of stock into what the New York market thinks.

Where he initially found singles success was when Stevie Ray got injured in late 1997, putting Booker in position to move into WCW's Television Championship division. He won the title for the first of six times in December and began working with some of the best wrestlers in the world. In those matches with the likes of Eddie Guerrero and Chris Benoit, he began to round into form as a solo performer.

His "Best of Seven Series" with Benoit was what put him on the map. He had a penchant for imaginative counters that was put to the test in having to vary them in what actually turned out to be eight matches in the span of a few weeks. Physically, Book always had the chops. I was struck, in watching all eight matches in a row while researching this chapter, with his athleticism. I love that move of his out of the corner when he rope-assisted leaps over his onrushing opponent, turns in mid-air, and catches him in a sunset flip. A "Best of," though, is a mental chess game. It is the little things, improved upon during the spring of '98 such as his facial expressions and palpable sense of urgency, that took him to the next level. Booker won 4-3 after the 7th match was tossed out due to a DQ, winning the 8th match at *The Great American Bash* in an exhibition in how to close out a series by teasing the various spots and finishes of the other matches.

    Book's big break came at *Bash of the Beach 2000*, a night infamous for WCW (Vince Russo fired Hulk Hogan live on the air) but incredible for him. He defeated Jeff Jarrett to win the World Championship and was pushed as the #1 babyface in the company until an injury sidelined him for most of WCW's dying days. It was the first of several short title reigns during the middle-to-late part of that year. His matches were bright spots in a sea of WCW darkness. He came back just in time to win the US title on the last WCW PPV and win back the World title on the last WCW *Monday Nitro*, taking the big gold belt with him to WWE as the focal point of the Invasion storyline.

    When WCW was bought by the WWE, Vince made no bones about his desire to see the legacy of his former competition tarnished, creatively. The Invasion of the former WCW stars into WWE was poorly handled and led to WCW looking weak. Booker T was the exception. The higher-ups clearly saw something in him worth protecting. He was the model on how to successfully make the transition to the WWE. Book could not have started any higher, as the WWE put a lot of faith in him early on. He main-evented *Summerslam '01*, defending the WCW Championship against The Rock. I think they felt comfortable with him because, frankly, despite his coming up as a top guy during WCW's worst stretch, Book always seemed extremely comfortable in his own skin. He treated the WWE like a destination and, once he got there, he was all business from his first major singles main-event in the summer of '01 to his biggest singles headlining match at *WrestleMania XIX* to winning the King of the Ring and World title in 2006 and every month and year in between.

Against Triple H at *Mania* with the World Championship up for grabs, Book had one of his best matches. It is not as fondly remembered as other matches on the card, but it told a hell of a story. The racial undertones were prominent. They certainly pushed the envelope in building a personal narrative for their rivalry - one that provoked a lot of controversy - but Booker came out of it looking like a legitimate threat to the #1 guy on the company's #1 show. Booker was involved in the top *Raw* brand title match for that year at an event often considered the greatest PPV of all-time. Persevere to win, he may have not, but he fought through tons of interference, cheating, and a "leg injury" to prove himself worthy of his spot. It was quite possibly the finest act of his career. I never saw him sell better. I never saw him pull off his move set with as much psychology. I never saw him get closer to being one of the all-time elite performers than he did during that match.

When he was not wrestling for the World title, Booker would play all sorts of roles. He was the Intercontinental Champion. He was the United States Champion three times. He had various feuds with all and sundry from Undertaker to Boogeyman, never too far from title contention. About every eighteen months, he would get a crack at the WWE or World Champion to remind everyone that he was still a gamer - October 2001 to March 2003; March 2003 to November 2004; December 2004 to July of 2006.

At *The Great American Bash* on July 23, 2006, Booker could finally stop calling himself the "5-time WCW Champion," as he won the WWE World Heavyweight title from Rey Mysterio. That was his best year, by my estimation. He was the top heel on the *Smackdown* brand and he was downright hilarious as "King Booker." He spoke in a faux British accent and would do this royal cape waving routine on the entrance ramp prior to his matches that ended with him holding his pinkie in the air, as if to signify something incredible about himself. It was so intentionally ridiculous. He went all in with the imperial gimmick and got a lot of traction out of it, holding the title for longer than he ever had before (four months), headlining two Summerslams, and main-eventing Survivor Series (at a time when it was rare for a *Smackdown* title match to go on last at a PPV).

During his career, Booker T won more titles in WCW than any other star in history and had a decorated six year run in the WWE, giving him the 7th most successful championship resume of the WrestleMania Era and a Top 25 all-time Headlining track record. Dig that, sucka…

#33: Daniel Bryan

When WWE bought WCW in 2001, it was both good and bad for the industry. On the plus side, it cleared the path for WWE to join other sport and entertainment conglomerates as the undisputed #1 wrestling brand on earth and put a company with a horrible product out of its misery. On the other hand, it also put a lot of talented people out of a job and monopolized the business, stripping professional wrestling of a strong second organization where aspiring wrestlers could more readily make their living. Plus, in the past, a disgruntled employee of WCW could leave and come to WWE, often bringing with him a name that had already been seen on national TV. Without competition, there was no longer a main source from which to draw new talent. Foley, Austin, Flair, The Road Warriors, Triple H, etc. had all come from WCW. Perhaps the greatest question coming out of WWE's takeover was, "Where were the fresh faces going to come from?"

Several smaller promotions started popping up on the independent scene. TNA grew into the #2 company, while others such as Ring of Honor (ROH) became primary feeders into the WWE. It took a long while, though, for WWE to recognize that places like ROH were producing the most TV-ready wrestlers and, instead, tried to continually find a needle in a haystack of bodybuilder types. In Ring of Honor, Daniel Bryan - formerly Bryan Danielson on the independent scene - developed a reputation as the best technical wrestler in the world and had a lot of quiet hype from a small but vocal fanbase from the internet championing him as an incredible in-ring performer that could bring back what had been missing since Eddie Guerrero and Chris Benoit died. Yet, he went unsigned by WWE (despite being trained by all-time great, Shawn Michaels). Meanwhile, men who could not talk or wrestle were being brought in and failing.

Like another ROH graduate that we will highlight in the First-Tier, Bryan eventually made it to and excelled in WWE. Surprisingly, it was his work as a character that left me most impressed. Though he was the best technical wrestler in the WWE until his retirement, he understood that he had to do more in WWE if he wanted to succeed. He set out to be more entertaining than anyone ever thought he could be. Even his hardcore fans from his indie days were surprised by the persona that he put on display after winning the Money in the Bank Ladder match in 2011 and cashing in to become the World Heavyweight Champion. Who would have thought that he could carry lengthy talking segments or stand toe-to-toe and not look out of place while verbally engaging The Rock, as he did in the summer of 2012 at *Raw 1,000*. He reminded me a lot of Guerrero, in that his personality was far bigger than his physical stature, while his submission and aerial prowess allowed him to remain credible against larger opponents.

One of the finest compliments that I can give Bryan is that he seemed to be the least egotistical of a breed of late 2000s, early 2010s wrestlers that perhaps, in a reflection of society, came into WWE acting like the world owed them something. Bryan, despite his excellent pre-WWE reputation, went down to WWE's developmental territory and sharpened his skills, even though he was set to immediately join the main roster. Subsequently, when he did make his TV debut, he was polished and established an instant connection with the audience.

From 2010 until 2014, he was one of WWE's most consistent all-around performers, wowing people in the mid-card ranks in matches against the likes of Dolph Ziggler, The Miz, and Ted DiBiase, Jr. after he won the United States title and ascending to main-event status by the end of 2011. His four month reign as World Champion ended at *WrestleMania XXVIII* in just 18-seconds, but the reaction to the loss put him in position to become one of the most popular men on the roster.

The entire Miami crowd was chanting his catchphrase, "Yes!" The next night on Raw, the entire Miami crowd was again chanting "Yes!" even though he was not on the show. In thirty years as a fan, I have not seen a single word catch on like that. Only a handful of occasions in the WrestleMania Era have witnessed a star gain more from a loss, such as Steve Austin passing out in Bret Hart's Sharpshooter at *WrestleMania 13*.

In arenas around the country, the reaction to Bryan became so strong that he spent the next several months feuding with CM Punk over the WWE Championship, producing some of the best matches of the year. I had the privilege of seeing one of them live in Raleigh, NC at *Over the Limit 2012*. I was blown away not just by the quality of that match – put it on a bigger stage and it would have been legendary – but also by the lasting feeling that Bryan had staying power at the top of the card. WWE scaled back his place on the card as the calendar progressed from the spring of 2012 through the spring of 2013, but his television time remained consistent. A Tag Team title run with Kane only grew support for what became known as the "Yes! Movement."

Summerslam 2013 was the night that changed the course of Daniel Bryan's history. He defeated John Cena for the WWE Championship, clean in the middle of the ring, to thunderous applause. It was a perfect moment. Right before he delivered the running knee to the face that earned him the victory, the Los Angeles crowd erupted into a massive "Yes!" chant. However, Triple H, acting as guest referee, promptly turned heel, giving Bryan the Pedigree. Randy Orton, owner of the Money in the Bank contract, also turned heel, cashing in to become the new champion. Together with Stephanie McMahon, Trips and Orton formed "The Authority," a modern take on the Attitude Era's "Corporation" with a distinct flair for riling up the most diehard members of the WWE Universe.

With each passing month, Bryan moved further away from title contention. It seemed that it had been WWE's intention to use Bryan's popularity to create a new dominant antagonist. It accomplished its goal very well. What they may not have expected was that, in creating such a hated faction using Bryan as the vehicle to build its heat, WWE simultaneously hit a nerve with virtually the entire fanbase. The people voiced their opinions loud and proud that Daniel Bryan was the guy that they had chosen to be the next WWE Champion and that they would not take anything but "Yes!" as a response from the powers that be. The debate raged amongst enthusiasts as to whether or not WWE was purposefully trying to hold Bryan back. Some felt that it was merely a storyline and that Bryan would, ultimately, win in the end. Others insisted that WWE had their heads stuck where the sun does not shine.

I have seen every major WWE moment that there is to see, so I was on the side that assumed that WWE knew what they had in Bryan and were just waiting until WrestleMania to anoint him as one of their top stars via winning back the title. Yet, the logical moments to ensuring that such a story would take place continually came and went without him being positioned accordingly, testing my patience. I, subsequently, got wrapped up in the Bryan saga more than any story in my adult life. When Batista won the Royal Rumble, while the entire arena was chanting for "Daniel Bryan," I was one of the many who unleashed a scathing review, unabashedly tearing WWE apart for their shortsightedness. Some months later, Bryan seemed to confirm on Chris Jericho's podcast that the original plan was not to give him the title at Mania. So, perhaps it was *The Royal Rumble* that changed WWE's mind.

It was an emotional roller coaster. Frankly, it was amazing. The end result was that Bryan "hijacked" WWE's flagship show in a segment called "Occupy Raw," a play on the political rallies that "Occupied" several cities. Accompanied by hundreds of fans, Bryan forced The Authority's hand and made them listen to the people. Bryan went on to defeat Triple H in one of the greatest opening matches in WWE history at *WrestleMania XXX* and, then, made Batista tap out in a fantastic triple threat match to win Orton's WWE Championship in the main-event. 75,000 people in New Orleans chanted "Yes!" A then-record number of people, combining pay-per-view buys and subscribers to the newly debuted WWE Network, joined in on the fun at home. "Yes," it was one of the most memorable, organic stories ever told in a WWE ring.

No other wrestler has ever quite achieved what Bryan did in a single night. Bret Hart's *WrestleMania X* performance is famous. He too opened the show in dazzling fashion and closed it holding the title. Bryan took it to the next level, though. WrestleMania is a different animal today than it was twenty years ago. To accomplish what Bryan did in modern times forges the former indie star a legacy that fans will be talking about for decades to come and that may have a far-reaching influence on WWE's future; guys like Seth Rollins, Kevin Owens, Sami Zayn, and Finn Balor had to have seen Bryan's moment as a game-changer that kicked the door open for them.

It would be easy for me to sit here and say that it was unfortunate that Bryan was unable to capitalize on his New Orleans success and that I wish he had not been forced into retirement in 2016 after two long years mostly spent on the injury list, but I am never going to forget that stretch from August 2013 to April 2014; absolutely not ever. I will tell my kids about it. In his retirement speech – the single greatest retirement speech in sports history – Bryan said the word that best described how he felt was "grateful." That is exactly how I feel about his WWE run; I am truly grateful that I got to see it. Bryan will go down in history as one of the true legends of sports entertainment.

#32: Kane

One of the most impactful debuts of all-time took place at October 1997's *Badd Blood* PPV during the climax of the first Hell in a Cell match. The Undertaker had victory close at hand over Shawn Michaels when, after weeks of hype from The Deadman's former manager turned enemy, Paul Bearer, "The Big Red Machine" Kane showed up amidst ominous red lighting with an eerie entrance theme and ripped the door right off the cage. Coming face-to-face with his "brother," Kane was taller and larger than Taker. He brought his arms into the air before slamming them down by his sides as fire burst out of the ring posts. Momentarily stunned, Undertaker fell victim to his own Tombstone piledriver at the hands of a massive masked man that became one of the greatest rivals of his career. Kane walked away looking like the next big thing in the WWE.

That is how Glen Jacobs finally found a permanent home in wrestling history. After failed attempts to be a wrestling dentist (Isaac Yankem, DDS) and a faux Diesel (after original portrayer, Kevin Nash, bolted for WCW), the WWE came up with something for him that worked. Jacobs had simply been too talented a big man - in an era where guys like Bam Bam Bigelow and Undertaker changed the game to make agility in a larger athlete more of a prerequisite - to become a story of never was. He has been a major player for the last twenty years thanks to the Kane character giving him the outlet he needed to express his abilities. One of the things that I have always admired about Kane has been his resiliency and his knack for tweaking his persona to stay relevant. He would not have made it this long otherwise.

Lord knows that he has been given more than his fair share of ridiculous storylines to overcome throughout his run. He has had to endure strange on-screen relationships with various women, being committed to an insane asylum, the abomination known as "Katie Vick," setting Jim Ross on fire, "killing" Undertaker, coercing/impregnating/marrying Lita, "May 19, 2006," and putting Undertaker in a "vegetative state." So, Kane has inadvertently become the model citizen for the WWE, putting up with a lot of lousy creative team writing.

His decorated resume includes a WWE Championship, a World Heavyweight Championship, the ECW Championship, 12 reigns as a Tag Team Champion, Money in the Bank, and two runs as Intercontinental Champion. And, though he lacks much success during the WWE's "playoff" time of year (January-April), he does hold a few distinctions like being the man with the most overall appearances and consecutive appearances in the Royal Rumble match, holding the record for eliminations (eleven) in a single Rumble for thirteen years, and owning the victory (over Chavo Guerrero to capture the ECW title) in the shortest match in WrestleMania history.

Kane is one of the rare superstars whose first big storyline was also his most historically significant. He never won a title match against Taker, but their feud in 1998 was as noteworthy as it got in his career. The story of Kane being Taker's long-lost brother, burned and scarred during a fire set at their childhood home that Bearer claimed was started by The Deadman, himself, was at times over the top, but always entertaining. Stripped of the theatrics, it was an excellent and balanced tale. Kane wanted revenge, but Taker would not fight him, at first. So, they became allies. It turned out that the alliance was made only to persuade Taker into a more personal situation. When Taker thought that he and Kane had turned the corner and embraced their brotherhood, The Big Red Machine turned on him again, leaving Taker with little choice but to retaliate. Their *WrestleMania XIV* match was a larger-than-life account of two titanic siblings, one attempting to destroy and the other reluctantly fighting for victory. Kane dominated The Deadman like no one ever had before. Even in suffering an "L" in the loss column, he was presented as the unspoken victor.

In April, just a month after *Mania XIV*, he battled The Deadman in a rematch at the *Unforgiven* PPV just down the road from me in Greensboro. It was the first Inferno Match, in which the ring was surrounded by fire. What a sight! I would put the Inferno match right up there, and perhaps ahead of, the Scaffold Match as the most dangerous *looking* gimmick in mainstream wrestling history. They had another knockdown, drag out brawl even better than the original all while just feet from shooting flames. When either of them would hit the mat, the flames would rise up as high as the ring ropes. What a spectacle it was...

The Taker saga put Kane in the position to be involved in a lot of "firsts" before he had completed a year as a character. He was an integral part of the finish to the inaugural Hell in a Cell match and then took part in both the first Inferno Match and the initial WWE First Blood Match, which took place at *King of the Ring '98* and gave Kane his first shot at the WWE Championship. Steve Austin was the titleholder, at the time, and it would eventually be revealed that Taker and Kane were working together to get the title off of Stone Cold so that they could add the championship to their own story. Kane won the WWE title and held it for approximately one day – he would not hold another World title for twelve years.

Undertaker has always remained his greatest opponent. The matches against his storyline brother were the only ones in Kane's career to have headlined WrestleMania (*XIV* and *XX*, respectively). The pair also has proven to be formidable as a tag team. Dubbed "The Brothers of Destruction," they have main-evented several PPVs together as a unit, most notably at *Backlash 2001* when the Tag Team Championships, WWE Championship, and Intercontinental Championship were all up for grabs against "The Two-Man Power Trip" (Steve Austin and Triple H).

Triple H would likely be voted #2 on Kane's list of adversaries. The Game was involved in several key moments in The Big Red Machine's career. In addition to their 2001 feud that extended from the Bros. of Destruction vs. Power Trip angle (which included Kane defeating Trips for the IC title at *Judgment Day* a month after *Backlash*), they also faced each other at *WrestleMania XV*, in the main-event at 2000's *King of the Ring* (when he teamed with Rock and Taker to help The Great One take the WWE Championship away from Hunter in a six-man tag), and then in two memorable battles that were turning points for Kane. In the late summer of 2002, Kane returned from an injury with a ton of momentum. With there being two brands, it seemed more likely than ever that he might get a longer run with a World title than just 24 hours. Unfortunately, his return and title shot against then-World Heavyweight Champion, Triple H, at *No Mercy* in October came at the same time that the WWE was trying to firmly establish Trips as their go-to guy. Kane failed to become the champion, Katie Vick happened, and his momentum sputtered in a major way. He even failed to make the card at *WrestleMania XIX* six months later.

With his future up in the air approaching the summer of '03, Kane faced Triple H in a Title vs. Mask match on *Raw* emanating from Madison Square Garden. Once again, The Game emerged victorious, forcing Kane to take off his mask and, in doing so, drastically changing his character. He became a psychopath that terrorized families, announcers, and wrestlers alike for a couple of years. The execution of the unmasking was criticized, at the time, but it did turn out to be rejuvenating for Kane. In general, losing the mask set the tone for the next lengthy phase of his career.

Despite the up-and-down nature of his pushes, one of the enduring things about Kane has been his aptitude for the two key aspects in wrestling necessary for critical success: interviews and in-ring performance. He is a very well versed talker. Especially remarkable was the work that he did as the World Heavyweight Champion in 2010. He spent five months as champion doing lengthy promos on a weekly basis, keeping rehashed feuds against Undertaker and Edge interesting with his words. As a performer, he has worked exemplary matches against a wide variety of sizes and styles, using his rare athleticism for a man of his stature to full advantage. Whether it be a high flyer like Rey Mysterio, a catch-as-catch-can connoisseur like HBK, a technical genius like Benoit, a fellow big man like Taker, a brawler like Finlay, or a more traditional WWE main-event style expert like Triple H or Edge, Kane has proven to be more than capable of adjusting to the various methods of wrestling and producing in big situations.

    Kane is one of the top five big men in modern history, eclipsed only by Undertaker and Big Show. His Top 5 stature among his Second-Tier peers in three statistical categories made him a fringe First-Tier selection.

#31: John "Bradshaw" Layfield

There have been several tag team specialists that have become World Champion singles wrestlers. Only one of them – Bret Hart - held the World title longer than John "Bradshaw" Layfield. As Bradshaw, JBL (as he was best known) was a valuable member of the WWE roster during the Attitude Era and was involved in some memorable moments alongside Ron Simmons, then known as Farooq; himself a Tag titleholder turned WCW Champion. In 2004, Layfield made the leap from The Acolyte Protection Agency (APA) to the top of the card and won the WWE Championship in June, holding it until the following year's *WrestleMania 21*.

The APA was not on the level that were the teams that produced the other breakout stars. I would put them in the category of The Powers of Pain (Warlord and Barbarian) that won the Tag Team Titles during a time when the division was comparably stacked in the late 80s. The APA were champions and important, but you would need a *Franklin and Bash* caliber law firm to make the argument that they were even in the top 5 for their era. So, Layfield's metamorphosis from beer drinking, card playing West Texan into the financially successful Manhattan dweller was a huge surprise. If you ever watched the classic TV show, *Dallas*, then ponder what it would have been like to see J.R. Ewing become the Texas oil tycoon on the episode after he had been a ranch hand.

I went back and watched the promo that debuted the "JBL" character. John Layfield walked out to the ring on *Smackdown* shortly after *WrestleMania XX* in 2004 - the brand's roster having been decimated by injury, the WWE Draft Lottery, and Brock Lesnar's departure - and was suddenly this smooth talking, Wall Street, *Fox News* analyst who had written a best-selling fiscal advice book (all true). And he was captivating. Even my daughter, all of three weeks old at the time, turned her head in his direction and stared at my computer screen. That promo was the birth of one of the best talkers in the industry over the last decade.

There was a lot of fan criticism over a long-time mid-carder, more famous for his backstage skits than his in-ring work, getting a boost into the main-event. It was too dramatic an alteration in character to go over well. To go from Lesnar and Kurt Angle as the top heels on *Smackdown* to *BRADSHAW* seemed like such a massive step down. He had a lot to prove to everyone and not many of the fans that ran in my circle gave him much of a chance. Eddie Guerrero, a hero to wrestling purists, was the WWE Champion and the immediate target of Layfield's new persona. When JBL began challenging him for the championship in May, the mere thought of him dethroning Eddie brought the previous day's dinner back to the surface.

Unfortunately in wrestling, unlike with football and basketball, there are not media members solely dedicated to helping put matches, title reigns, and breakout stars into proper historical context. I have often referred to websites like LOP as the wrestling equivalent of the sports media. Without perspective, there was a bias against JBL being proliferated throughout much of the internet. I started reviewing *Smackdown* for LOP at the height of their feud, which saw JBL win the title in controversial fashion in a Texas Bullrope match at *The Great American Bash*. The ensuing internet backlash lasted several months.

Despite the fact that, week in and week out, he was becoming the most entertaining personality on either brand, the internet crowd (myself included) did not wish to give him any credit. The *Judgment Day 2004* JBL vs. Guerrero match was excellent; maybe the most underrated of the last *thirty* years (it was <u>that</u> good). Yet, very few seemed to praise it as such until years later (again, myself included). One prominent writer, who makes his living on wrestling news, referred to it as "hardly main-event worthy," giving the match a rating of [**3/4 out of five]. Pedaling of such absurdity was commonplace. One could argue that the failure to notice Layfield's improvements may also have been due to Guerrero's immense popularity or that JBL was just an outstanding heel, but without multiple voices to balance the easily influenced opinions, the general consensus was that Bradshaw stunk.

JBL and Guerrero had a three match series (2004's cumulative best) that also included an outstanding Cage match on *Smackdown* in July. It took some time for it sink in, but Layfield won over a lot of critics. Once the disappointment in Eddie losing the title wore off, it allowed people to sit back and appreciate just how historic a run that they were seeing from JBL. Some referred to him as a modern day "Million Dollar Man"; I would call that claim and raise you that he was the characterization of many of the controversial parts of conservative America amidst an increasingly liberal society. The "Wrestling God," as he called himself, took on issues like border patrol and the financial sector, veering toward the views that would aggravate the left wing. In one skit, for example, he caught people trying to crossover the Mexico-USA border and kicked them back to "where they came from."

Through consistency in the ring and on the microphone, he solidified himself as a bonafide star. After dispatching of Guerrero, JBL next faced Undertaker. Their match at *Summerslam '04* was another example of preconceived notions clouding the judgment of hardcore fans. People were so blinded by their acquired hatred for JBL that they refused to acknowledge that his performance was commendable. Amusingly, the prominent gripe against the match back then was that it was "just a big man match." In reality, they purposefully stayed away from a traditional WWE "big man" match, working in some grappling and technical wrestling to go along with the offense befitting of their respective sizes (like the classic simultaneous big boot spot).

Time has given perspective, which was lacking in 2004, to Layfield's rise. If you rewind the clock, you can see why the WWE gave him a chance. He was a driving force behind *The Tribute to the Troops* that the WWE has done for the US military mostly abroad and lately in the States (one of the classier events on the WWE calendar). Combined with his successful book and his *Fox News* spot as a financial analyst, it was a smart public relations move to get someone who was in a spotlight outside of the WWE into the inner circle of headlining talents.

WrestleMania 21 was the biggest night of Layfield's career. He was in the co-main-event, defending the WWE Championship against John Cena. He took a legitimate critical jab when the match stunk out the Staples Center. It appeared to have gotten shortchanged on its allotted time due to other matches running over their limits earlier in the show, but Layfield bore the brunt of the criticism. To his credit, he rebounded well in an "I Quit" match against Cena at *Judgment Day* – one of the better matches during a year full of classics and, other than the bouts with Eddie, the best of his career. JBL spent 2005 helping to build the next two big stars in the industry, dropping the belt to Cena and then doing the honors for Batista throughout the summer in unsuccessful attempts to win the World Heavyweight title.

His run was cut short in 2006, when a bad back forced him into retirement. He was able to walk right into a commentating gig, offering quick witted insight that made him one of the best color commentators since mid-90s Jerry Lawler (I just dodged a bolt of lightning, prompting me to come back and emphasize that he was great in 2007 and has been borderline atrocious since returning to that role in 2013). He returned to the ring a year and a half later for fifteen months that definitively stamped his career as Hall of Fame-worthy. He was able to get back to the top of the card amidst stiff competition from numerous well developed antagonists, such as Edge and Randy Orton. From his January '08 comeback to his official retirement from the ring at the *25th Anniversary of WrestleMania,* Layfield worked with a star-studded cast of characters that included Chris Jericho, Mr. McMahon, John Cena, CM Punk, Shawn Michaels, and Rey Mysterio. He also challenged for the WWE or World Heavyweight Championship on five occasions.

JBL was involved in main-events for just a shade over three years. During that time, though, he was memorable, changing the perception of him from "mid-carder for life" to one of the most pleasant surprises in modern wrestling lore. Few could rival his interviews. He was lights out on the microphone, building interest in his title defenses almost solely through his verbal brilliance. In evaluating his "Wrestler Score," I gave him a 10 (out of 10) in that category. He delivered in the ring, as well. He was kind of a poor man's Barry Windham, which I am certain that he would take as the compliment that it is meant to be. If that is not enough to silence any remaining critics, then the longest WWE Championship reign in the history of the *Smackdown* brand should. For 280 days, JBL held the title with dignity, class, and skill.

Appendix B
The Bret Hart Wrestler Score

#	Wrestler	Look	Mic	In-ring	Total
31	Rick Rude	10	8	8	26
32	Barry Windham	8	8	9	25
33	JBL	7	10	7	24
34	Terry Funk	7	9	8	24
34	Kane	9	8	7	24
34	Mr. Perfect	7	8	9	24
34	Seth Rollins	7	8	9	24
38	Jake Roberts	4	10	9	23
39	Bam Bam	8	6	9	23
39	Scott Hall	9	6	8	23
41	Booker T	8	8	7	23
42	Arn Anderson	5	9	8	22
42	Christian	5	8	9	22
42	Vader	7	6	9	22
45	The Koloffs	8	6	8	22
46	Road Warriors	9	5	7	21
47	DDP	6	7	8	21
47	Jeff Jarrett	6	7	8	21
49	New Age Outlaws	7	7	7	21
50	Owen Hart	5	6	9	20
51	The Dudley Boyz	4	8	8	20
52	British Bulldog	8	5	7	20
53	Daniel Bryan	3	7	10	20
54	Sgt. Slaughter	6	7	7	20
55	Dusty Rhodes	2	10	7	19
56	Rob Van Dam	5	5	8	18
57	Rey Mysterio	2	5	10	17
58	Andre the Giant	9	2	6	17
59	Scott Steiner	7	2	8	17
60	Jeff Hardy	4	4	8	16

The Performance Factor

#	Wrestler	Total Score
31	Daniel Bryan	22
32	Seth Rollins	21.75
33	Rey Mysterio	21.5
34	Jeff Hardy	21.5
35	Owen Hart	21.25
36	Christian	21.25
37	British Bulldog	21
38	Vader	20.25
39	Rob Van Dam	20
40	Mr. Perfect	19.75
41	Terry Funk	19.25
42	JBL	19.25
43	Scott Steiner	18.75
44	Barry Windham	18.5
45	Arn Anderson	18.5
46	Bam Bam	18.25
47	Scott Hall	18
48	Rick Rude	18
49	DDP	18
50	Kane	17.75
51	Road Warriors	17.5
52	Dudley Boyz	17
53	Booker T	16.75
54	Jeff Jarrett	16.5
55	Jake Roberts	16
56	Dusty Rhodes	16
57	Sgt. Slaughter	16
58	The Koloffs	15
59	New Age Outlaws	14.75
60	Andre the Giant	12

(Total score is based on the top 5 star-rated matches of each wrestler's career)

The WrestleMania Era: The Book of Sports Entertainment

The Business Factor

#	Wrestler	Comment
31	Andre the Giant	For all the obvious reasons…
32	Sgt. Slaughter	GI Joe + WrestleMania VII
33	Daniel Bryan	WMXXX Network + PPV
34	Dusty Rhodes	The top babyface in NWA for years
35	The Road Warriors	Huge drawing stars for their time
36	Rick Rude	Secondary headlining heel
37	John "Bradshaw" Layfield	Rough start, but strong career finish
38	Booker T	Horrible WCW stats; solid for WWE
39	Terry Funk	1989 was the reason for his rank
40	Diamond Dallas Page	Important contributor to WCW Nitro
41	Mr. Perfect	Rarely showcased to full potential
42	Scott Hall	Tertiary player throughout career
43	Rey Mysterio	Major merchandise seller for years
44	Kane	Important, yet limited role
45	Jake "The Snake" Roberts	Major player, but always mid-card
46	Bam Bam Bigelow	Case aided by WrestleMania XI
47	Jeff Hardy	Impressive all-around numbers
48	Seth Rollins	Huge star in the Network Era
49	Arn Anderson	NWA's version of Jake, economically
50	Barry Windham	See comments for Arn Anderson
51	The Koloffs	Era-specifically huge as foreign heels
52	The British Bulldog	Secondary draw of weak fiscal era
53	Vader	Dominant during weaker fiscal era
54	New Age Outlaws	Contributed heavily in merchandise
55	The Dudley Boyz	Added depth to vaunted "Attitude"
56	Rob Van Dam	Tertiary draw during a down period
57	Jeff Jarrett	One of the top draws during bad time
58	Owen Hart	See comments on RVD
59	Christian	Rarely more than a 4th tier draw
60	Scott Steiner	#1 heel in dying days of WCW

(Ranking is based on best buyrates, buy numbers, and TV ratings)

The Main-Event/Headlining Factor

#	Wrestler	Total Score
31	Kane	61
32	Booker T	38
33	Rey Mysterio	36
33	Jeff Hardy	36
35	JBL	33
36	Scott Hall	28
37	Daniel Bryan	27
38	Seth Rollins	26
39	Road Warriors	24
40	Christian	23
40	Vader	23
42	Dusty Rhodes	19
42	Rob Van Dam	19
42	Scott Steiner	19
42	DDP	19
46	Andre the Giant	18
46	British Bulldog	18
48	Owen Hart	16
48	The Dudley Boyz	16
50	Rick Rude	15
51	Bam Bam Bigelow	14
51	Arn Anderson	14
53	New Age Outlaws	13
54	Sgt. Slaughter	11
54	Jake Roberts	11
56	Barry Windham	9
56	Jeff Jarrett	9
58	Mr. Perfect	8
58	Terry Funk	8
60	The Koloffs	7

(Total is based on cumulatively weighted score)

The Championship Factor

#	Wrestler	Score
31	Booker T	51
32	Jeff Jarrett	31
33	Kane	27
34	Jeff Hardy	26
35	Scott Hall	25
36	New Age Outlaws	24
37	Christian	23
38	Scott Steiner	21
39	Rey Mysterio	20
40	Daniel Bryan	19
41	RVD	18
42	Vader	17
42	Diamond Dallas Page	16
42	Dusty Rhodes	16
42	The Koloffs	16
46	JBL	16
46	Rick Rude	13
46	Sgt. Slaughter	13
46	Terry Funk	13
50	Mr. Perfect	13
50	Seth Rollins	10
52	Barry Windham	10
53	Owen Hart	10
54	The Dudley Boyz	9
55	British Bulldog	8
56	Arn Anderson	7
57	Andre the Giant	4
57	The Road Warriors	3
59	Bam Bam Bigelow	2
60	Jake Roberts	-

(Total score based on "Title Formula")

The First-Tier

#30: Chris Benoit

This was the most difficult chapter to write in this book.

Based purely on the numbers, Chris Benoit was in the top 20. Unfortunately, he is also one of the most justly vilified wrestlers of all-time because of how his life ended. I choose to ignore neither that he was, arguably, the greatest technical wrestler of all-time nor the fact that he murdered his wife and child before committing suicide. Since his death in 2007, the WWE has erased his name from the history books while some fans have clung to their vivid memories. For me, that is too black and white. There are shades of grey that blend Benoit the murderer and Benoit the classic performer. While there was no excuse for the heinous actions of his final hours, there is a clinical theory that I have about cases of repeated head trauma in wrestling that provides greater context to a relatively mysterious situation. In the midst of reflecting on Benoit's career, I will detail my thoughts on his murder-suicide being more than just the result of "roid rage."

Any discussion of Chris Benoit, the man, begins with his crimes, but any discussion of Chris Benoit, the wrestler, begins with his uncanny abilities in the squared circle. He was in the top 15 in the Performance Rankings and one of just eleven wrestlers to receive a "10" on the in-ring skill portion of his Wrestler Score. If you can imagine a football team so diverse that they could interchangeably switch offensive styles from the power running game to the spread passing attack, then you can imagine what kind of wrestler he was. He could do it all. He was psychologically sound, he was extremely strong for his size, he could technically engage the best of the best in the mat game, he could brawl around the arena, and he could fly through the air with the greatest of ease. It would be a shame for history to forget Chris Benoit's elite performance level.

He was literally a 4-star match waiting to happen. He had a match with Eddie Guerrero on *WCW Nitro* back in November 1995 that was one of the best matches in the history of that program. They were both at their athletic peaks and every hold, every counter hold, and every high risk was made to look effortless. The pace was ridiculously fast, as they flowed from one sequence to the next. They performed high flying maneuvers, they tried to make each other tap out, they went hold for hold, they showcased their stamina, and they executed punishing power moves. It was the perfect example of Benoit's all around skills and, even in 1995 – long before he ever really made it big and had his career stamping moment – he was making his case for being the best in the industry.

Yet, the end to that bout provided an appropriate example of an unnecessary, self-inflicted head trauma that could be seen in almost every one of Benoit's matches. Both men went to the top rope. Benoit brought Guerrero crashing down hard to the mat with a cringe-inducing sky high superplex. They hit the mat awkwardly, with Benoit landing on the upper part of his back right where the shoulders intersect with the lower neck. The match ended (as planned) when neither man responded to a ten count. Benoit walked away from the match without any immediately lingering symptoms, but he did legitimately hurt himself. When the body absorbs trauma, the effects are often not seen until much later. Unfortunately, the American health system teaches us to solely concern ourselves with noticeable, subjective complaints like pain or headaches or numbness. If a child falls out of a tree, for instance, parents want to know only if he/she is bleeding, conscious, or needs to go to the hospital. If four years later, the kid is suffering from Migraines, the connection to the past trauma is not made by most doctors. Benoit fell backward off of a five foot high rope support onto his neck and shoulders (on purpose). He was once involved in an incident in ECW that led to a wrestler named Sabu breaking his neck. That trauma produced immediately noticeable effects. Benoit's superplex spot with Eddie did not cause something pronounced right afterward. It quietly took its toll.

In a match against Dean Malenko at *WCW Hog Wild* in August '96, Benoit performed a more aesthetically pleasing, less awkward version of the superplex used in the Guerrero match. He performed the move regularly, up to several days per week. Landing flat on the back is how everyone else does it, in order to avoid further risk of serious injury. Benoit, however, would hit the mat high and tight and then immediately bounce onto his belly, which admittedly looked great, but it was like adding 20mph to a car accident – it did nothing but legitimate long-term harm. Also in the match against Malenko, he used the most awesome diving headbutt off the top turnbuckle this side of Manchester, England (home of the Dynamite Kid, who popularized the move during the 80s). Doing a belly flop onto a thin piece of wood covered by an even thinner piece of matting also has consequences.

Benoit's career was like a double-edged sword. The problem was that, while he was taking risks, he was also excelling. The match with Malenko was 30-minutes of outstanding wrestling for a promotion that historically gave that kind of time only to guys that were expected to be main-eventers. Benoit routinely provided a match on the short list for the best of the year. He showed why he would one day be involved in major matches with some of the top stars in WWE, but in *foreshadowing* future headlining programs, there was also some *forewarning*. Accompanying him to the ring that night in '96 was Woman, aka Nancy Benoit (Chris's wife). An unhealthy person can be driven to heinous, unthinkable acts. I fully believe that the repetitive trauma that Benoit purposefully endured – which were the same things that made him so special as a performer – led his body to neurologically breakdown rapidly and his mental stability to decrease accordingly. Whatever medications, legal or otherwise, that he was taking at the time of the murder-suicide were, in my professional opinion, **due** to his mental state. Taking pills was the result of his condition; not the cause.

     Professional football is going through a major controversy right now in regards to the long-standing damage brought about by the physical nature of the sport. Professional wrestling is just as bad or worse, but the oversight has been slower to reach the WWE. I believe that it will and the sport will be better for it. It begins with an understanding of what is going on underneath the surface, inside the body of the athletes as the traumas accumulate. A guy like Benoit allowed himself to get thrown down a flight of arena stairs during a match against Kevin Sullivan in 1996 that, professionally, highlighted his skill set beyond the 20X20 canvas and made him ready-made for the hardcore turn that the business, in general, would take in the late 90s. In terms of his health, though, the match contributed to his having neck surgery five years later.

     Despite his style creating a higher risk of long-term degenerative conditions, he was remarkably durable and his star continued to rise. In 1999, Benoit had the opportunity to wrestle Bret Hart in a tribute to the Hitman's brother, Owen. Bret, because of his high profile status in the WWE throughout the 90s, was considered the best technical wrestler in the business (by many). Benoit had taken that title from him by the time they faced off on *Nitro*, but it was a match that surely caught the attention of scouts in the WWE. He was a member of the WWE roster three months later.

     WCW was so desperate to keep him that they had him win the World Heavyweight Championship even though he had made his intentions clear that he was leaving. That should go to show how much the industry valued Benoit. At the heart of the Monday Night War, WCW put their title on a guy who was halfway out the door.

Once in the WWE, Benoit wasted little time validating their investment. Within six months, he was main-eventing a PPV against The Rock in an excellent match that often gets lost in the discussion for 2000's best. Within the course of a year, Benoit proved that he could work stellar matches with all three of the era's biggest names. There was the aforementioned Rock match, plus a 4-star effort against Triple H at *No Mercy 2000* and one of the top TV matches in WWE history against Steve Austin on *Smackdown* in May of 2001.

Two of Benoit's most exhilarating matches also did substantial damage to Benoit's neck, leading up to a summer 2001 neurosurgery. During the match with Austin, Benoit unleashed ten consecutive rolling German suplexes. The move involves landing on your back with your head turned while also absorbing the weight of, in Austin's case, about 250 pounds, putting a tremendous amount of pressure on the upper neck (where the most vital neurologic structure in the body resides – the lower brainstem).

Eleven days later, he concluded the second chapter in his incredible rivalry with Kurt Angle, started back in early 2000 and including bouts at consecutive WrestleManias. On *Monday Night Raw*, Benoit and Angle were locked inside a Steel Cage. There were many moments to "wow" about, including Benoit giving Angle a German suplex off the top rope and, most famously, the two trading ridiculous high risks. Angle performed a moonsault (a backflip into a belly flop) off the top of the 15 foot high cage and Benoit countered, minutes after, with a diving headbutt off the top of the cage. Then, the climax saw Benoit getting his head slammed with the cage door by Austin. Ironically, Stone Cold had just come back from spinal fusion. Two months later, it was Benoit going under the knife for surgery to repair a ruptured disc. A sky high superplex, ironically, at *King of the Ring '01* was the straw that broke the camel's back. Those ten German suplexes and the cage stunts weakened the camel's back, first. Angle had neck surgery 18 months after Benoit.

Sadly, these world-renowned surgeons are trained only to identify and fix the damage once it has already been done. There is very little education in American healthcare about the causes that lead to the effects. In my clinic, we place a heavy emphasis on cause and effect, educating patients to understand how various conditions develop. In the case of a disc rupture, you have to be susceptible before it can happen. Each of us are born with a structural support system in our body to help carry the weight of the head on top of the neck and the rest of the body from the shoulders down. The supports are the natural spinal curvatures and the discs in between the vertebrae. Foundationally, the area where the head and neck meet must be balanced or else the rest of the body compensates in adaptation. As with any other structure, the body shifts when the foundation moves. When foundational stability is lost, the structural support curve in the neck is lost, bearing the brunt of the weight from the head down on the discs. The added pressure causes the discs to break down and/or reach a point where the added weight becomes too great; when it arrives at the point of no return, it will bulge then herniate and, eventually, it may rupture if nothing is done to address the causal process.

Clinically speaking, any athlete that has a fusion surgery should retire immediately. It is not about *IF* they can return and perform at or better than they did before; it is about whether or not they *should*. Fusion accelerates a process referred to as degeneration, commonly called osteoarthritis. Peyton Manning will find that out one day, as did Austin, Angle, and Edge (all had fusion surgery and all have major problems). Benoit proved when he came back in the summer of 2002 that wrestlers can thrive after a year of healing, but I firmly believe that his physical break down a year earlier was a sign that, as have others, he ignored. The focus for the rest of his life should have been to ensure that the break down stopped and that his body healed in the long-run. Instead, his body continued to deteriorate, structurally and functionally. Look at Christopher Reeve – he represents an extreme example of what happens when the body goes through major physical trauma. Reeve damaged his brainstem by jamming his upper neck underneath the skull. The brainstem is the control center of the body, regulating internal organ function; it rests partly in the skull and partly in the ring of the top vertebra in the spine. When Reeve fell off his horse and landed on his head, he so severely compromised his brainstem that his reproductive, respiratory, digestive, and genitourinary systems shut down to the point where he needed machines to keep them going. Benoit did not fall into Reeve's category, but the one just below it and just above NFL players.

The focus was on saving his career instead of his life. Look at all of the mental health issues that former football players are having and the suicide rate. That has little to do with steroids. Because it was professional wrestling, the media jumped all over the fact that Benoit was taking prescription steroids as the cause of the murder-suicide. I believe that was a rushed, shortsighted conclusion. Benoit was a sick man whose body was ravaged by years of physical abuse. Chris Jericho described in his second book that Benoit had kind of a strange personality in his later years. The reason was because his body and mind were declining in unison. Taking steroids did not cause his mental state – his mental state caused him to take steroids. In my opinion, the media drew biased conclusions based on an industry standard that changed 15 years ago.

It is sad to reflect on it and study the ramifications of the extreme physicality of the sport, now, but it was captivating to watch Benoit make his comeback then. When he returned, I saw him win the Intercontinental title from Rob Van Dam in Greensboro and he looked better than ever. The fact that he was a better conditioned athlete than 99.9% of his peers helped his cause.

The renewal, third, and final chapter in the Angle saga transitioned him from injury return to the next level of superstardom. Angle was Benoit's athletic superior, molding his style after Benoit's, in many ways. They renewed their series (on PPV) at *Unforgiven '02*, providing the hidden gem of their multi-year chronicle. Watching Benoit wrestle Angle was similar to watching his matches with Guerrero and Malenko. The formers might have looked more authentic, at times, but they could not touch the athleticism of Benoit vs. Angle. They temporarily formed a WWE Tag Team Championship-winning duo in the fledgling division on *Smackdown* and were almost as good as a pair as they were as rivals. Angle became the WWE Champion by the New Year, though, leading to their final PPV match at the 2003 *Royal Rumble*. It was the first and only World title bout in their history. There are not enough good words that can be written about that match. It was one of the best of all-time.

Benoit received a standing ovation from the Boston crowd that night. It was his springboard to the main-event. A year later, he won the 2004 Royal Rumble match, going the distance from 1st entrant and outlasting 29 other stars. At *WrestleMania XX*, one of the most important Manias ever, he made Triple H tap out to win the World Heavyweight Championship in a Triple Threat match also involving Shawn Michaels. He shared the ring with two of the top ten stars in history and was the one left standing in the middle of the ring as the show went off the air, famously embracing his long-time friend and then-WWE Champion, Guerrero. He averaged well over 4-stars per title defense in the ensuing five month reign.

2004 was the peak of his career; like Dirk Nowitzki getting a ring in the twilight of his best years in the NBA. He made it all the way to the top and showed he belonged. He kept contributing for the rest of his career/life, putting on outstanding mid-card matches with the likes of JBL, Finlay, William Regal, and MVP, all the while maintaining his high impact, body-punishing combinations of German suplexes and diving headbutts.

    I believe that Chris Benoit represents that professional wrestling is the most dangerous sport on earth. NFL players talk of how their four quarters are like experiencing a car accident thirty or more times in one game. WWE superstars experience at least that and they do it without the figurative help of airbags or safety measures as do football stars with their helmets and shoulder pads. Benoit should be used as an example instead of a pariah. He is a modern sports tragedy of the highest order; a man whose body was breaking down for all to see with plenty of signs to warn his colleagues and his doctors that serious action needed to be taken. His moods and his use of drugs and his neurosurgery were all the result of his body structurally and neurologically deteriorating at a rate faster than 999 out of a thousand people. Nobody knew to associate those signs with the causes leading to them. They were taught from early on in the business that those things were normal. They are *COMMON*. Not *NORMAL*. There is a huge difference. Junior Seau committed suicide and the media praises the man and talks of his body being donated to research. Benoit's act was far more horrendous and nothing written here is meant to excuse it, but the media focus was all about steroids when it could have been about research, too. The WWE chose to distance itself from the negative media attention, missing the chance to dig deeper into what is, perhaps, the common denominator of most untimely wrestler deaths.

#29: Roman Reigns

When discussing Roman Reigns as of halfway through 2016, there is a lot that needs to be talked about. As someone who has become known as somewhat of an apologist for Double R, I personally think you have to start the discussion about him with his back-to-back WrestleMania main-events; only nine other wrestlers have ever done that, eight of whom are Top 10 all-time and the ninth a Hall of Famer. To me, that is the primary thing that defines the legacy he is forging, along with his status as a three-time WWE Champion, his underrated body of in-ring work, and his prominent historical position as one third of arguably the decade's greatest faction.

You rarely discuss Roman Reigns, however, without first addressing the controversy surrounding him. He is a lightning rod and the diehard fanbase are storm clouds that settle over every city to where WWE travels. Simply put, a sizeable portion of the audience vacillates somewhere between outright dislike of Reigns himself or abhorrence for what they feel he represents: the WWE machine at work, a hand-picked face of the company without the requisite credentials, a Lex Luger or Diesel of the modern era (talents forced into their roles as leaders instead of organically rising to them).

Every top star throughout history has been placed under a microscope, but the world that we live in now dictates that today's elite wrestlers endure more scrutiny than ever before. As the media continues its descent toward blowing everything out of proportion with each public figure, wrestlers included, the life for someone like Roman Reigns gets infinitely more challenging. John Cena was his forebear, absorbing an exorbitant amount of rage from the wrestling media and hardcore enthusiasts for a decade; Roman's cousin, The Rock, was Cena's forebear in that role.

I am no Nostradamus, but I could see the Reigns controversy coming from a mile away. Rewind the clock to the year between *Survivor Series 2012* and *2013*. This big, good-looking guy in his mid-20s full of intensity, power, and presence shows up with Rollins and Ambrose to introduce The Shield right in the midst of CM Punk's and Daniel Bryan's respective peaks. During a period when the best options to dominate the future of WWE were smaller and faster (and definitely not prototypical), here comes this 6'3," 265-pound former All-ACC football player whose dad is part of a Hall of Fame tag team (The Wild Samoans) – he may as well have been created in a WWE laboratory. Even though he was still very much a prospect at that point, you could see the raw intangibles and educatedly guess, assuming he had the work ethic, "That is Cena's heir apparent."

The problem with that train of thought was always rooted in the contemporary nature of wrestling fans. As the wrestling media has become more critical, so has the fanbase. Small things can become big things in a hurry; for instance, when rumors began circulating that Vince McMahon viewed Reigns as Cena's successor, it skewed many diehard fans toward a negative opinion of The Shield's powerhouse, setting up a barrier for him to break down before he could ever break through as a near-universally beloved protagonist. Consequently, WWE would have theoretically had to have handled Reigns perfectly to avoid considerable backlash just because of the undeniable fact that diehard fans relate more to the scrappy guy who scratches and claws and chases the dream than they do the wrestler who is perceived to have been handed opportunities for reasons they disagree with (like innately good looks and considerable physical size).

Clearly WWE's handling of Reigns was not perfect if the goal was to help him get over positively with most of the audience. If their goal was to set in motion another top babyface as loathed by certain portions of the fanbase as he is loved by others, then mission accomplished.

The tipping point in Roman's relationship with the audience was *Royal Rumble 2014*. He re-set the record for eliminations in the titular battle royal and was the runner-up to Batista. Remember, the most vocal fans wanted Bryan to win that year and it was Batista who was unintentionally set in opposition to the Yes! Movement. When it became apparent that Batista was going to win instead of Bryan, fans were outraged and channeled all of their energy into whoever could stop The Animal. By default, that was Reigns. In my mind's eye, I can see McMahon, already determined that Roman was in contention to be his next big star, sitting backstage with his headset on thinking to himself, "Reigns is our guy," in reaction to the thunderous ovation he received against Batista. Here is the thing, though: I honestly believe that you could have put (insert history's most evil figure here) in Roman's place and he would have been given a hero's reception that night just because he was not Batista.

The next few months made Reigns out to be more on the cusp of becoming a universally-accepted protagonist than he might have actually been. One factor was that he was still growing and learning, quite quickly I might add, but growing and learning nevertheless. Another was that The Shield was so good during their last six months together, creatively peaking as an anti-heroic unit in classic feuds with The Wyatt Family and Evolution, that perhaps it gave the false impression that Reigns was ready to assume a leading role.

The Shield hid a lot of Roman's weaknesses and accentuated many of his strengths while he was still getting his wrestling education teaming and traveling with the already well-developed Ambrose and Rollins, but his association with the Hounds also insulated him from much of the criticism that he might have had to endure from hardcore enthusiasts. When

Rollins struck Reigns in the back with a chair to initiate the break-up of The Shield, he also popped the protective bubble surrounding Roman. WWE's subsequent creative strategy for Double R brought straight to the forefront their imminent desire to push Reigns to the top and, in doing so, put him squarely in the path of fan criticism without his Shield. Within two months, he was being pelted with verbal barbs from enthusiasts worldwide.

    I take serious issue with the modern fan tendency to nitpick the product to the point that enjoyment suffers, but credit need be given where it is due to the energy and passion that even the most over-critical fans pour into their studies of pro wrestling. Many deserve criticism for their negative attitudes toward things that they cannot control and for allowing an outlet and a hobby to become a destructive instead of constructive part of their lives, but there is something to be said for being able to identify that, when Reigns struggled to find his footing as a babyface main-event player in-the-making, fans immediately voiced that they were not interested in WWE trying to fit a square peg into a round hole.

    WWE deserves more credit than it is often given too, but a fair criticism to levy on it is an adherence to product-development ideas that may no longer be functional in changing times. Reigns, for instance, built his protagonistic momentum by being a hard-charging badass. With Cena growing older, WWE obviously needed to start thinking about a successor, but Double R never showed the same caliber of innate charisma that did Cena (or Rock before him) which would allow him to navigate the challenging situation of playing a more straight-laced babyface character and be the face of the WWE brand despite so many fans disapproving of him in that role. WWE was hell bent on Reigns being the top face *their* way instead of his. For several critical months during the early part of Roman's solo career, he looked and sounded forced into a role that did not suit him and the end result was a failure by both superstar and promotion to instill a genuinely affirmative emotional connection to the fans.

By 2015, Roman's strengths were his look and his vastly undervalued (by fans) ability to deliver in big matches. Rather than play to his strengths, WWE played to his weakness – charisma/talking. It does not take much to get the diehard fanbase on-board with an everyman, but it takes a great deal to get it to connect with someone who looks like Reigns. "The Look" is a double-edged sword today. Anyone remotely resembling a prototypical WWE Superstar (movie star-like) who tries to play a heroic role for Vince McMahon's product is as much disadvantaged because of the diehard fan reaction to the implied benefits that his look affords as he is advantaged by a look that might very well prompt Vince McMahon to afford him greater opportunities. If WWE had any notion of avoiding another generation of the top babyface also being the defacto top heel, then it chose the wrong path; by virtue of their booking decisions, they put Reigns out on a limb and handed fans in-the-know a chainsaw.

To his credit, Reigns has responded well during the first two years of his solo run. Despite all the criticism of his babyface character, he has found his comfort zone and has continued to excel in the ring, though not everyone would be willing to concede that point. For reasons that go beyond my scope of complete understanding, even the slightest bit of support for Roman's positive qualities is met with the latest round of disapproval. In his match at *Money in the Bank 2016* with Rollins, for example, he acted like a heel in response to the negativity spewed from the live audience. The reaction from the fans who so often beg for him to be a heel? "He was supposed to be playing the babyface." Or when he is one half of a great match, the detractors never fail to jump in with comments such as "his opponent carried him." He says "yes," fans respond "no." He goes right, fans go left. At times, it is as if some fans will never let him win in any way.

A frequenter of my social media discussions named Alastair Gray once posited an interesting theory that the disproportionate aversion to Reigns is "more of an indie/mainstream thing. Reigns is like wrestling's equivalent of a mainstream band that the fanboys hate. They come up with their 'reasons' but it comes down to the fact that he's successful without their help; meanwhile, [fanboys] pop for guys like [Sami] Zayn and Ambrose who are less likely to achieve the same level of success without massive dedicated fan support."

For what it is worth, I feel as though Reigns has become one of the WWE's best in-ring performers. My personal philosophy on wrestling is that the matches are the most important part of the WWE package (especially in this day and age), so an ability to perform at the highest possible level when the bell rings is that which matters most; I am not so much concerned about the histrionics surrounding the matches themselves (though I obviously cannot deny their incredible importance in the WWE equation) or the thought-processes behind the scheduling decision for said matches. For that primary reason, I quite like Roman Reigns and want to make that abundantly clear. Since 2014, he has produced classic matches as regularly as any peer.

In sports analytics, they have a statistic called Wins Above Replacement Player (WARP) that attempts to define how well a team would perform if a key player were replaced with a marginal one; applying a similar concept to pro wrestling, let us rewind the clock to when Reigns first showed considerable signs of blossoming into "The Guy" in early-to-mid 2014; The Shield's matches with The Wyatt Family and Evolution were excellent and Reigns was an integral part of that. He was not a bit player benefiting from the efforts of superior stars, but a superior talent in and of himself reaping the rewards of the effort he had put into honing his skills. Let us examine how successful those stable battles would have been if we subbed Reigns out for someone else. For this exercise, all intangible things (like chemistry among faction-mates) will be equal.

How about Baron Corbin? For those not currently watching the product regularly, Corbin had a cup of coffee in the NFL and has what would be considered by modern standards a much larger-than-average physical frame, but he is not as athletic as Reigns and does not have the same caliber aura. If we replace Reigns in The Shield with 2016 Corbin, are the matches with The Wyatt Family or Evolution as successful? Consider that Roman's mark on those matches was flares of intensity and power during emotional peaks; he was kind of like a fiery heavyweight boxer, hitting hard and deliberate with an outpouring of ardent fury. Given that Corbin has an ounce of Double R's ability to use body language to sell his passion, I would argue that the success of The Shield's renowned six-man tags would have suffered tremendously from the substitution. If Reigns is like Mike Tyson, putting Corbin in his place would be like replacing Tyson with one of the Klitschkos.

What about Kassius Ohno? Had the man originally tapped for The Shield instead of Reigns, a character played by veteran independent wrestler Chris Hero, been around for the faction clashes, he might have added a more accomplished wrestler to the mix, but with only a fraction of the intrinsic presence that Roman brought to the table, the matches again would have suffered. Rollins and Ambrose brought all the in-ring savvy that the matches required; they needed an ass kicker and Reigns fit the bill perfectly. So, in this exercise of establishing SARW (Success Above Replacement Wrestler), I would propose that Reigns scores incredibly well and that nobody on the roster in early 2014 could have played the role that he did any better; and bear in mind that he was still nearly a year away from his breakout performance.

Do not mistake any of this chapter as an implication that Reigns should be immune to criticism, but I find it ludicrous that – in a performance art like professional wrestling – fans struggle to simultaneously express their dislike of a wrestler *and* acknowledge said wrestler's forte. Basketball pundits were able to find a balance between admonishing Shaq for his free throw woes and celebrating the physical dominance that was his calling card; why should wrestling aficionados not be able to reprimand Reigns for his distinct lack of microphone prowess yet also concede that he is a well-rounded in-ring performer?

Since Reigns wrestled Daniel Bryan at *Fast Lane 2015* in one of the most underrated matches of the decade, he has consistently showcased himself to be as physically gifted in the WWE grappling style, as psychologically sound, and as readily capable of expressing his character's emotions as anyone in the game today. The rise of the Roman Empire to present day heights began when he won the 2015 Royal Rumble match and promptly got booed out of every building in the world. A year after perhaps unduly benefiting from the Yes! Movement, he felt its wrath when he – rather than Batista – won the right to face the champion at Mania instead of Bryan. The ensuing match with Bryan before Mania was an excellent example of art imitating life, with Bryan representing the doubters and Reigns being tasked with overcoming them by way of earning the resident everyman's respect. In his first PPV main-event singles match, with the army of haters standing their ground on the front line to see if he would fail, Roman delivered the kind of performance that I have come to think of as his hallmark contribution to the modern era.

He is incredibly versatile between the ropes. Be it against a smaller talent like Bryan or AJ Styles (I loved their series post-Mania in 2016), a giant like Big Show (highly acclaimed Last Man Standing match post-Mania in 2015), a monster grappler like Brock (his selling made the *Mania 31* main-event a remarkable story even before Rollins cashed in), a cerebrally-focused brawler like Bray Wyatt (very smart, physical tales), or a catch-as-catch-can master like Rollins (my MOTY midway through 2016 was their anticipated showdown at *Money in the Bank*), Reigns is capable of adapting to a variety of stylistically different wrestlers and producing stellar work. It is the main reason why I so mightily struggle to understand the concept held by some fans as gospel that he is not a good wrestler. Earlier, I mentioned that Roman did not have anywhere near the innate charisma of John Cena; well, Cena has nowhere near the instinctive grasp of the in-ring performance that does Roman Reigns. If Double R is *this* good in his early thirties, then how good is going to be in his mid-thirties when the combination of power and youth somewhat gives way to finesse and wisdom?

The sky is the limit for him in the ring. One advantage he may have over the likes of Cena and Orton from the previous decade is that, assuming WWE's talent recruitment maintains the course it has set in recent years, Reigns will constantly have the best prospects in the world pushing him to further excel. I would argue that the current WWE in-ring product is as consistently good as it has ever been; there could be a handful of classic bouts per year coming from Reigns through the rest of the twenty-teens.

His former brothers-in-arms will undoubtedly breathe down his neck for the top spot in the industry for years to come as well. If Reigns is to maintain his slim lead on Rollins and narrowing lead on Ambrose in the WWE hierarchy and if he is to ascend to the Top 10 of the WrestleMania Era in the next several years, his major improvements will have to come in the character department; and a lot of that may hinge on the role WWE asks him to play for them. Through mid-2016, his push as the #1 babyface had taken a page right out of the John Cena playbook, continuing to eschew the traditional way to handle pro wrestling scenarios that see the guy who is supposed to get cheered be jeered (or vice versa) and just letting the fans react however they want. The problem is that heroic characters on WWE TV rarely get to explore the depths that do their heel counterparts, though Reigns was beginning to show as of print time a penchant for transcending the black and white "face-heel" label as a tweener immersed in shades of gray. I do personally think he should turn heel; I think he would be fantastic in that role and I think that it would help him develop his charisma by channeling more authenticity.

If he winds up a controversial career babyface like Cena, then I believe Reigns would be well-served to become WWE's version of Marvel's Wolverine, who may not be the most naturally charismatic persona of the Marvel Universe, but he is a complicated badass with a deeply affecting back story. I am confident that if WWE allowed Reigns to play that kind of role, then he would be more relatable to a larger portion of the audience and thus become more popular over time.

What I would at least like to see is the jaded sect of the fanbase embrace the idea that Reigns is the LeBron James of WWE; that instead of some archetypal product of the WWE machine forced down the throats of the self-respecting enthusiast, Double R is just a polarizing figure that may draw your ire but who is undeniably one of the most gifted wrestlers in the world and the type of athlete who draws in unique viewers through that unmistakable yet ever so difficult to define "it" factor.

#28: Goldberg

He was a man who would military press his opponent straight into the air, hold him up, and then drop and catch him coming down with a ring-shaking spinebuster or powerslam…

He was a man who would run full speed, dive forward, and drive his shoulder into his opponent's mid-section like a Spear…

He was a man who would hoist his opponent into position for a delayed vertical suplex only to bring him crashing to the mat with incredible force in a move affectionately known as "The Jackhammer"…

He was "Da Man."

He was Goldberg.

Bill Goldberg is an utterly fascinating story in wrestling history. Though he had the look of a bigger Steve Austin and the strength of Hulk Hogan, he was one of those rare guys that neither said much nor brought much more to the table, physically, than raw power. Yet, he connected with people on such a level that it put him, as Arn Anderson once said, on the same level as Hogan in the 80s and Austin in the 90s. He had that mysterious, undefined "It" factor, thriving on "It" when "It" was about all that was there. Subsequently, Goldberg was, at his peak, as big a star as the industry had ever seen.

In the beginning, he was just an ex-football player that decided to make wrestling his next career. Debuting in the fall of 1997, he went out to the ring every Monday night as a silent assassin, smashed his opponent in seconds with impressive strength, and went back to the locker room.

The people began to respond.

Eventually, WCW added presentation to the table. His excellent theme music built the anticipation for his stage entrance, which featured sprayed pyrotechnics that he would stand amongst, consuming their fumes and literally exhaling the smoke. If you never saw it, it was as bad ass as it reads.

The people started to chant his name.

By the spring of 1998, Goldberg was the center of an incredible winning streak storyline that ranks second only to Undertaker's at WrestleMania in sports entertainment lore. Within seven months of his debut, he became the United States Champion, demolishing Raven and his Flock in one of *Nitro's* greatest moments. He was billed as being 75-0 by then. More importantly, he was an interesting new character in a company notorious for failing to allow anyone fresh to thrive. In a land of dinosaurs who had earned their fame a decade prior, he was unique. He could not have come at a better time.

With the success of *WrestleMania XIV*, the WWE was making a strong push in the Monday Night War and had begun winning ratings battles for the first time in two years. Just as WWE was getting hot, WCW was becoming painfully stale. Though The New World Order had been WCW's cash cow, interest in the faction was sputtering. The bookers had botched the logical climax for The N.W.O. storyline (Sting defeating Hollywood Hogan) at *Starrcade '97* and everyone from the wrestlers to the fans were becoming frustrated with the stagnant creative direction for their product. Despite WCW kicking butt in the ratings and at the box office from mid-'96 to early-'98, their shows were singularly focused on The N.W.O. and lacked forethought. Only one year, in my opinion, was WCW truly a better product than WWE and that was summer 1996 to summer 1997. That was the one year where the cruiserweights and great technical wrestlers dominated the under-to-mid-card while the heavyweights did their thing with cutting edge storylines. After the 4-star classics started dying off and the main-event, N.W.O. edge had been dulled, WCW was left with little to sustain their success.

Until Goldberg...

Goldberg helped keep WCW alive in the ratings war. Without him, WCW's demise would likely have come about much faster. Fans might have changed the channel a lot quicker and in a lot greater volumes. He created a buzz that halted the downward spiral and kept Steve Austin from shifting all of the momentum in the WWE's direction.

With The N.W.O. floundering, WCW needed someone to finally step up and give the faction its comeuppance. Goldberg did just that on the July 6, 1998 *Nitro* from the Georgia Dome in Atlanta. The Georgia Dome is home to the NFL's Falcons. The WWE hosted *WrestleMania XXVII* in the same venue. WrestleMania is a worldwide phenomenon every year and usually sells about 40-50 thousand tickets over the course of the first few *months* after tickets go on sale in November for the annual April classic. So, the biggest event in wrestling every year and Goldberg's first WCW title match (in his home town, granted) drew about the same number of fans into a domed stadium; only Goldberg did it in a week.

On that night, he defeated Hollywood Hogan to win the WCW Championship. My friends, Sac and Mattberg, often recall the night that they watched it from home. My buddy Dean kept a Goldberg poster on his wall in college, in part, because of it. I watched it, too. At that point, it felt like WCW and WWE were still competing. Goldberg emerged as the top star in WCW at the same time that Austin became the #1 guy in WWE. The rivalry between the companies was neck and neck.

You always knew when the WWE legitimately feared the guys who they, internally, felt could take business away from them by the way that they would try and devalue his character with parodies on their own programming. They infamously did so with the Nacho Man, Huckster, and Billionaire Ted skits after Savage and Hogan were signed by Ted Turner and put head-to-head against *Raw* in 1995. When Goldberg, pretty much the last remaining hope for WCW as of 1998, was at his hottest, the WWE brought in Gillberg to mock him. Gillberg was a fraction of Goldberg's size and had zero percent of Goldberg's presence. He looked like someone that they brought in off the street, by comparison. He was actually quite amusing. Goldberg's signature catchphrase, in keeping with his dominant string of victories without defeat, was "Who's Next?" Gillberg, who lost all the time, countered with "Who's First?" The point was that the WWE knew that Goldberg was dangerous.

Unfortunately, WCW flat out dropped the ball. His World title-winning episode of *Nitro* was his peak. As soon as he rose to the top and made it big, keeping WCW in the game long past when they should have been, the complete incompetence of those in charge got the best of him.

Goldberg could have made them so much more money if they had let him. For example, the 7/6/98 *Nitro* did not make much money because it aired on free TV. It was just another highly rated TV show (and they were doing strong ratings consistently that year) with a larger than usual attendance. Had Goldberg vs. Hogan taken place on PPV, they would have made a killing.

Huge matches with Hogan, Flair, and Sting should have kept Goldberg on fire and WCW in play while Austin got hot in the WWE. It would be well worth your while to read *The Death of WCW* to get the details of the fiscal irresponsibility of WCW's decision-makers. The number of boneheaded choices back then was baffling. The last hour of *Halloween Havoc '98* was perhaps the best representation of all that was wrong with WCW.

Ultimate Warrior was brought back to face Hogan in a match that nobody wanted to see, particularly after they had butchered the storyline. Goldberg was defending the title in an outstanding match against Diamond Dallas Page that showcased how good he could be if he got into the ring with motivated opponents who wanted to steal the thunder from the geezers. Unfortunately, WCW put so much attention on Warrior-Hogan that the PPV feed was cut for the main-event World title match. They ran out of air time, infuriating the people that bought the PPV. Goldberg vs. DDP was shown for free on *Nitro* the next night and WCW was forced to offer refunds.

Despite all the creative shortcomings, Goldberg holding the WCW Championship was a psychological reminder to fans that there was hope. Through all of the old stars from the 80s being brought back to participate in some of the worst matches of all time, at least the people had a champion that well represented the present and gave bright prospects for the future.

Until they had him lose to Kevin Nash at *Starrcade '98*...

Goldberg's first loss in 173 contests happened in a terrible match with a controversial finish that left the fans with a bad taste in their mouths yet again. Sure, the winning streak had to end eventually, but after many instances of seeing bad booking that pandered to stars with huge guaranteed contracts, the fans of WCW needed Goldberg to keep winning. Instead, Nash won the title and proceeded to drop it to Hogan via the infamous "Finger poke of doom" segment on the first *Nitro* of 1999, washing away all of that aforementioned hope. It had nothing to do with Nash. He was a fresh face in the main-event. It was about what he represented. Nash was one of those WWE created guys with a massive contract. It was about what Hogan stood for. It was putting the title back on an old, tired act and going back to a well that had long since dried in The N.W.O.

WCW never recovered from that series of events. While Stone Cold was overcoming the odds to defeat Degeneration X and The Corporation at consecutive WrestleManias, the biggest heroes in WCW were either losing or winning in the worst possible ways at Starrcade. While Hogan and Nash were back in cahoots in The N.W.O., the WWE put their World title on a new star (Mick Foley) that they had been building up for two years. Goldberg was WCW's Luke Skywalker; their chance to bring balance back to the product and prevail in a longstanding war with WWE. In WCW land, the bookers would have had Luke lose to Darth Vader in *Return of the Jedi*.

WCW just could not seem to grasp the concept that Goldberg was not just "Da Man," as they referred to him on TV, but that he needed to be "The Man." Austin was given the ball and was running wild with it in 1998 and 1999. He may not have always been the champion, but if he was not wearing the gold, he was chasing the gold because he was the guy that people were tuning in for. Goldberg was, by far, the biggest star in WCW and, though he had his detractors, he was the right guy to move forward with at the helm. It was not just wrestling fans who understood what he brought to the table. He beat The Rock to Hollywood. Anyone with half a brain could recognize that Goldberg's screen presence alone could sell tickets and merchandise and, with some better television scripting, ratings and PPVs.

As an alternative to having him chase the title, though, WCW restarted the Hogan vs. Ric Flair feud over the World Championship. It was dumbfounding! Goldberg continued to win (two years after his debut, he had only suffered two losses), but he was no longer the focal point. Subsequently, the WWE's ratings lead gained substantially and it was never again close.

I will never understand why Goldberg was de-pushed. The ratings, even though WWE was winning, were still very good until he went off to make a movie. Over a decade of historical review provides perspective on these matters and such was not a luxury at the time, but Goldberg was moving the chains; there was no reason to take the ball out of his hands.

Discussing the legacy of Bill Goldberg has become a fascinating topic over the years. When you talk about the "greatest of," your list simply cannot get very long before you have to enter him into the conversation. Arguments are often based on how quickly he rose to the top and what he did for WCW in such a short time frame. It needs to be emphasized and reiterated that if there was no Goldberg, there is no telling how fast WCW would have met its demise. Alas, as quickly as he rose to prominence, he fell to obscurity. His career was sadly short-lived. His time at the top, combining movies, injuries, and such, was from late 1997 to 2000 - roughly two and a half solid years. Add in his eventual one full year in the WWE and it is less than four years. Yet, here we are with Goldberg in the top 30. He could have realistically been in the top 10 if there were proficient minds as the masters of his wrestling fate.

Part of his legacy was also that his career was mishandled by the two biggest wrestling companies in history.

Vince McMahon purchased World Championship Wrestling in 2001. WCW as we knew it died, but two years later, Goldberg emerged from its ashes. In a great moment at *WrestleMania XIX*, a video promo announced that "Da Man" was coming to the WWE. It was one of the fantasy situations that you never thought would become a reality. I sat in my dorm room and watched Goldberg interrupt The Rock on *Raw* the next night and was in awe. His return energized some of my friends to get back into wrestling like they had not done in years. It was great to see him back...

...for all of about a week or two.

WWE and Goldberg just did not mix. They had a one year marriage destined to end poorly. It did not seem as if either party was on the same page. The WWE was struggling to make the transition out of the Attitude Era. Conceivably, the WWE saw him as an opportunity to squeeze whatever they could out of a name that still carried some weight with fans from the boom period. I think Goldberg was just jaded with the business. The WWE, for him, appeared to be little more than a way of making a little bit more money in wrestling before the mainstream completely lost interest in the genre.

It is hard to blame Goldberg for his WWE experience. His time in WCW likely did a number on his opinion of the professional wrestling business, setting the stage for his WWE run to be forgettable. He rose to the top so quickly in a disorganized company that did not have the infrastructure to sustain an entity that was not already established. Plus, there was the notoriously low morale in a WCW locker room full of men who were disgruntled, overpaid, and power hungry. Having come from the National Football League, he knew the importance of locker room camaraderie; and it was like a nest of angry hornets in WCW. He also endured some of the most terrible, incoherent TV writing that there will ever be. When he went to Hollywood, I am sure he saw a more tightly run entertainment ship and sighed relief to have some time away from wrestling. When all was said and done, I would imagine that he saw sports entertainment as an industry full of sharks.

He unfortunately came to the WWE when they were creatively reeling, having squandered an opportunity to potentially continue the wrestling boom period for at least another year by botching the in-ring conclusion to the dream feud of WWE vs. WCW. I can only imagine what Goldberg's run could have amounted to had it coincided with the returns of Hogan, Hall, Nash, Flair, Steiner, and Booker T. All it would have taken was a little bit of patience to get all of those guys under contract at the same time and the WWE could have presented a fitting end to the Monday Night War. The Invasion, as it came to be known, was instead disgracefully rushed. All of the above parties came to the WWE at some point in the two years that followed the death of WCW, but because no prudence was shown, the wrestling world was stripped of its right to see N.W.O. vs. Degeneration X, Hogan vs. Austin, and, of course, the plethora of guys with whom Goldberg could have wrestled in huge drawing main-events. The WWE decided to rush everything before they had signed any of the major players and proceeded to completely bury WCW, making it look completely inferior rather than the competitive entity that nearly took WWE out of business. It was nothing more than ego putting the Great Wall of China in front of a hundred tractor trailers full of cold, hard cash. It is one of the greatest disappointments in wrestling history. WCW vs. WWE was **THE** biggest dream storyline. And it could have been written better in poop pen and better developed on the side of the road by Joe Shit "The Rag Man."

Goldberg did become World Heavyweight Champion, which some could argue solidified his WWE Hall of Fame induction some day, but it has been difficult to separate what Goldberg *did* while in WWE from what he *could have done*. The WWE failed to get any kind of momentum going for him with their booking, rarely treating him like the monster character that made him such an icon. They could not even manage to get something simple done like organizing his limited number of dates. There were stretches where he would just disappear from television without explanation, most notably during the build-up to *WrestleMania XX*. He had a very interesting feud going with Brock Lesnar, dating back to the 2003 *Survivor Series*. With a month left before *Mania*, Goldberg dropped off the face of the earth, not to be seen again until the Show of Shows. Not surprisingly, the MSG crowd took a big #2 on their match and Goldberg was never seen in a WWE ring again.

It was a dream match scenario that turned into a nightmare. The crowd response, a hallmark moment for the internet's influence on live wrestling audiences, made the match extremely memorable. It was insider information **only** that both Goldberg and Lesnar were on their way out after their Mania match. That is not something that, ten years prior, anyone would have really known about. By bell time, everyone knew that both of them were leaving. The NYC crowd let them have it. To Goldberg's credit, his professionalism allowed them to get through the match (while Lesnar lost his cool).

At some point, I hope that he gets the spotlight one final time, preferably at the Hall of Fame. I think it would be a shame if the last moment of his career was what we saw in 2004. Top 15 all-time draws should be celebrated.

#27: "Rowdy" Roddy Piper

Never have words been more powerful...

Like a guard standing just six feet tall in an NBA full of stars considerably larger, Roddy Piper was a man amongst giants in physical stature while one of the top WWE superstars in the mid-to-late 1980s. Yet, if size were measured by the power of the spoken word, then he would have stood taller than even Andre.

Nobody could talk quite like "Rowdy" Roddy could. When it comes to interviews, there may never have been anyone better. Though he does often get passed over in the "best ever" conversation, that may be because Roddy was not the type to build his promos around catchphrases that made promos more ostentatious (and more memorable). He did not need to; he could just talk. Some people just have that natural ability to converse about anything for hours on end. That was what separated Piper from the others. There has not been a more naturally gifted gabber in wrestling history. He was like a politician in that he could draw in your attention and make it difficult for you to take it away.

"Piper's Pit" was Roddy's avenue to utilize his way with words and to create many a feud, all the while using it to get himself over as one of the cornerstones of the original wrestling boom that saw the WWE go mainstream and change the industry. One of the most quick-witted personalities to ever grace the wrestling business, Piper was a master ad-libber. He needed no bullet points nor much direction nor a list of little sayings. You could give him a jobber that no one had ever heard of and he could take that ball and run with it for twenty minutes, sucking you in and making you care about it. There was an exercise that we would do in public speaking courses where we had to stand up in front of everyone and talk about a random topic pulled out of a hat to get us used to thinking on our feet. With Piper's ability to create magic with his words on the fly, I am sure he could have taught the class. I had a daydream about him doing just that, once upon a time. He was my teacher, I dominated the rest of the class with my own gift of gab, and he told the WWE about me. They gave me my own talk show segment on *Raw*. Surely, you have had the "I became a wrestler" daydream, at some point?

What Piper did with the "Pit" was revolutionary, prompting such future stars as CM Punk to champion Roddy as the WWE's undisputed, all-time maestro of the microphone. With consistency and variety, "Piper's Pit" made for some of the most enduring segments ever seen on WWE TV, perhaps none more famous than the one featuring Jimmy "Superfly" Snuka. In a moment that many modern fans may remember being recreated in the build-up to Jericho vs. The Legends (Piper and Snuka among them) for the *25th Anniversary of WrestleMania*, Piper hauled off and whacked Snuka right across the temple with a coconut. My personal favorite was when he had The Haiti Kid on the show and used the African American midget wrestler to mock Mr. T into next Sunday. The tone of voice he used back in those days was the icing on the cake. I am unsure how to put it into words, but he was definitely channeling his inner mad man.

"Sports Entertainment" was merely a concept before Piper emerged in the WWE to run up against Hulk Hogan. The All-American hero needed a villain with distinct qualities unique to any other heel. The original *WrestleMania* that gave birth to sports entertainment was founded on the connection between celebrities and wrestlers, but it was still up to the wrestlers to be the stars of the show. Piper and Hogan were the chosen ones to make it work. Cyndi Lauper, a pop music singer in the 80s, helped light the proverbial match for wrestling to have its Super Bowl thanks to a chance meeting with WWE manager, Captain Lou Albano. WWE's subsequent relationship with MTV started "Rock 'N Wrestling." There would be no selling out

Madison Square Garden for *WrestleMania*, however, by having wrestlers appear in music videos.

  Piper's quiet understanding that verbal confrontation has the ability to make physical battle so much more profitable put him in a position to ensure that the connection between MTV and WWE yielded professional wrestling a new identity in the world of entertainment. Wrestling has and always will be criticized for being fake, but back then the wrestlers and promoters antagonized the detractors by not letting on to the scripted nature of the events. So, when Piper attacked Albano and then kicked Cyndi Lauper, it called into question a lot of what the media thought about the WWE and created a controversy that took precedent over the validity of the match results. People were confused, outraged, and **entertained**.

  If WrestleMania was created to be wrestling's Super Bowl, then *The War to Settle the Score* was its conference championship game. The special aired on MTV and featured Piper challenging Hogan for the WWE Championship. Hogan was clearly the face of the budding super company. His star was shining brighter than any wrestler's had previously. Vince McMahon hitched his wagon to him and rode him to new heights in the business, but he needed Piper. Hulk came to Lauper's aide when Piper attacked. Piper and Hogan were great foils to one another, each charismatic and blessed with magnetic personas that attracted millions. Their match on the MTV special was a snapshot of everything that Vince's WWE intended to be. It was more spectacle than anything, lasting just a few minutes and featuring mostly fisticuffs. While dramatic, it was a stark contrast to what was being presented by the more traditional professional wrestling-focused NWA. The wrestling was not providing the excitement, but rather the personalities of the wrestlers combined with all the pomp and circumstance of the celebrities like Lauper and Mr. T, who sat at ringside cheering on his co-star (Hogan) in 1982's *Rocky III*.

People have argued for years over who was the guy that actually drew the most attention to the original *WrestleMania*. The majority have claimed it to be Hogan. The hero normally does get the lion's share of the credit, though, does he not? Praising the villain is not the way we do things. Yet, to the bad guy may very well be where the credit deserves to go. It was not just Hogan that fans were paying to see, but rather Hogan beating up Piper. It was not just Mr. T's celebrity status that drew fans to Madison Square Garden for the record gate. Fans had flocked to MSG for the MTV special, which drew a 9.1 cable rating, six weeks prior. They wanted to see Mr. T help Hogan give Piper his comeuppance. You could say that heroes are only as strong as their villains and there is no questioning that Piper was *THE* villain in the WWE when the Rock 'N Wrestling Connection set the wrestling world ablaze with *WrestleMania* in 1985.

WrestleMania was the crowning achievement of Piper's career. He may never have been given the accolades that should accompany such an important piece of wrestling history, but here is the thing – it is not just that *WrestleMania* would not have been a success without Piper; it is that it may not have even happened in the first place if it were not for Piper. You cannot have just any old main-event as your main draw for a show of that magnitude. Vince McMahon risked his own fortune on the success of that one night, betting the farm that it would redefine the national perception of the WWE and transition his company from pro wrestling to "sports entertainment." He would not have made that gamble if he did not have something more than Cyndi Lauper to put butts in the seats. If you were to have replaced Piper with any of the other heels from that era, you would not have gotten the same response. That is not a knock on those guys because some of them were written about in this book, but it is a testament to Piper's ability to connect with people in a way that they could not.

Wrestling is, inherently, about putting together athletic exhibitions where something is at stake that people are invested in. People did not care about the WWE title, yet (at least not on the scale that the WWE needed them to in order to create a Super Bowl for wrestling). So, they went to good vs. evil. Piper was General Zod attacking rock n' roll's Lois Lane. Hogan and Mr. T were the Justice League set up to stop him. He was a special kind of bad guy, was Piper, and everyone reaped the benefits of his dastardly actions.

Piper's run as the top heel in the WWE was memorable and profitable. It helped build the WWE into the superpower that it still is today and was instrumental in getting WrestleMania off the ground. Interestingly, Piper had also been a key player in the promotion of the NWA's *Starrcade '83* a year and a half prior, making him the only superstar heavily promoted as a headliner on both of the original biggest events in pro wrestling.

So, why is he not higher up the rankings? It came down to his lack of a World Championship to his name, a merely decent Wrestler Score and Headlining track record that did not compare favorably to his elite peers and, similar to Andre, the absence of a lengthy resume of classic matches. He was a big draw, but success in one category was not enough to overcome a relative lack of success in the other four (a theme to bear in mind moving forward).

In the ring, Piper was a brawler that was capable of much more than he ultimately accomplished. He suffered from a similar lack of opportunities in the WWE that did Mr. Perfect. You cannot have great matches without the chances. A combination of his outside interests (i.e. "I'm here to chew bubble gum and kick ass...and I'm all out of bubble gum") that prompted hiatuses and retirements from wrestling and the fact that he was pretty banged up by the time he even got to the WWE contributed to those chances being few and far between.

Looking at him from a clinical perspective, he was having major surgeries long before most of his 80s brethren.

There was one body-punishing match right before he joined the WWE that stands out as being excellent but also career-shortening. *Starrcade '83* was a launching point to an all-time great career for Piper, but it came with a long-term price. The "Hot Scot" was coming back from an injury suffered at the hands of Greg Valentine earlier that year. That night, Valentine had taken the United States title away from Piper. Their intensely personal rivalry could not be settled in any normal match. *Starrcade* set the stage, but they needed a gimmick that would put over the rabid nature of the war that they were going to wage. Hence, the Dog Collar match.

It was quite a sight to see two men standing in opposite corners of the ring with a huge chain attaching to the dog collars latched around each of their necks. This was no bull rope or leather strap; it was a rather large steel chain and they liberally used it to beat the hell out of each other. They used it as a whip and they wrapped it around the ring post, the ring ropes, and each other's head, face, and neck. Valentine bled like a stuck pig from the forehead, while Piper got opened up on his ear. When you saw the camera shot that showed the ring from above and all of that blood staining the mat, you could not help but shake your head. I will often watch a match like that and try to gauge how well it would translate in the Attitude Era where so much violence was commonplace. Honestly, as without a doubt one of the most brutal and bloody brawls in modern history, it would fit right in.

Arguably the best of his career, the Dog Collar match cost Piper 50% of his hearing in the injured ear. It was also the start of a trend in his career in the mainstream that saw him deliver his top matches as a babyface character. Perhaps his shortage of in-ring classics was because, as a heel, he was often working with larger wrestlers incapable of performing high quality matches; it was a big man's world back then after all. A quick look at the superlative in-ring work of his prime – vs. Valentine, vs. Adrian Adonis, vs. Rick Rude, and vs. Bret Hart – shows that all of his best matches were worked in the babyface role, even though he was a renowned top draw as the bad guy.

My pick for the finest contest of Piper's career was *WrestleMania VIII's* Intercontinental Championship match between him and Hart. Quite frankly, there may not be a better story told in less than 30-minutes of total screen time in the history of the wrestling business.

A brilliant two-minute backstage interview with Mean Gene Okerlund perfectly set the stage and proved that you do not need four weeks of hype to properly get people interested in a wrestling match. If you have two men with established reputations, then all you have to do is create some sort of small conflict and leave it up to the wrestlers to take it and grow it into a story that builds during the match. The two nearly came to blows in the segment and effectively built the tension to a boiling point before the match began.

Piper's grappling skills were put on display in the early minutes. It was seldom that we were privy to such attributes. Hart was quite the chain wrestler and it was a fun sight to see Piper match him. The trading of momentum was fascinating to watch. They made themselves out to be so evenly matched, which was important for Hart's career since he was still a budding (and not yet super) star. Piper used a cheap shot as an excuse for Bret to execute one of the most effective blade jobs I have seen in thirty years. Well executed and quite meaningful, the blood spilling out of Hart's cut above the eye added an element of importance to the match. It was around the point that Bret began his comeback that Bobby Heenan, on commentary, echoed the thoughts of everyone watching the match. "I knew it was going to be good, but I didn't know it was going to be *THIS* good! This is a helluva match!" Amen, Brain.

The climax saw Piper lose control of his temper. Hart was getting close to putting him down for the count when the referee got knocked down and temporarily out. Piper retrieved the ring bell, but refrained from using it. Instead, he opted for the sleeper hold, but Bret countered in classic fashion. In a move that I once used on the playground to escape the chokehold of a bully in tribute to this match, Bret willed his feet up to the top turnbuckle, pushed off backward, and sent himself tumbling still locked in the sleeper on top of Piper in pinning position. Hart won back the IC title. Piper could not have put Bret over any stronger.

So, was that the best representation of what Piper was capable of in the ring and, if so, why did we not see more of that in his career? That match makes me wonder what Hot Rod's resume might have looked like if he had just been lined up with a hungry new star (like Bret) at WrestleMania every year between 1989 and 1995. Remember, he was at Mania in some capacity every year. It would seem as though a lot of Roddy's potential great matches were left on the drawing board in favor of uninspiring appearances and guest referee gigs. You can rest assured that would not have happened twenty years later.

It will not be wrestling matches that forge Piper's legacy. Instead, it will be his words. The use of digital media and WWE Network will allow aspiring wrestlers to study the promo ability that made him one of the original icons of the WrestleMania Era. They will be better for it.

#26: "The Million Dollar Man" Ted DiBiase

In the Attitude Era of the late 1990s, Vince McMahon stepped out from behind the announce table to become one of the greatest heel characters of all-time. As the CEO of "The Corporation," McMahon was as easy to dislike as anyone the WWE had ever put on television and helped usher in a second business boom for his company. Yet, WWE fans got a preview of McMahon's persona a decade prior, when The Million Dollar Man debuted in 1987 as the characterization of the gimmick Vince had once dreamed up as his wrestling alter ego.

Ted DiBiase, a veteran of Mid South Wrestling and the NWA, was chosen to play the role. The 2010 WWE Hall of Fame class headliner was the right choice for the job. DiBiase was fantastic as The Million Dollar Man. He was every bit as entertaining as any of the other top stars of that period, ranking right alongside Hulk Hogan, Randy Savage, and Roddy Piper as the guys that could best capture your attention with their work on the microphone. At the same time, he was also an accomplished in-ring performer with few peers in the WWE during the Hulkamania era. His combination of skills was rare at the top of the card for that time and would have seemingly been a better fit for the NWA, but he embraced the challenge and parlayed his opportunity to play the obnoxiously rich villain into one of the greatest careers in WWE history.

DiBiase was introduced by a series of classic vignettes, in which he claimed that "Everyone has a price for The Million Dollar Man." In situations sure to draw the ire of every age group, DiBiase – seconded by his bodyguard, Virgil - would use his money to ensure he got what he wanted at the expense of others. A personal favorite saw him pay off the manager to close a kid-filled public swimming pool so that he could use it by himself. A rich man flaunting his millions was a recipe for a despicable antagonist. It did not take long for the audience to love to hate him.

The Million Dollar Man was a character that needed to work and in a big way. It was a high pressure situation, as the WWE was coming off the biggest drawing main-event feud of all-time in Hulk Hogan vs. Andre the Giant and they needed to adequately follow it or risk losing steam. DiBiase was, thus, tasked with debuting, getting an entire fan base to dislike him, and becoming the next top heel all in a matter of a few months. He was up to the task. After months of seeing DiBiase taunt people with his considerable wealth, including the famous scenes of the woman getting down on her hands and knees and barking like a dog and the kid dribbling the basketball 14 times only to have Ted kick it away on what would have been the $500-winning fifteenth consecutive bounce, it came time for The Million Dollar Man to execute a "make it or break it" storyline that meant a great deal to the continued success of the WWE. DiBiase called out Hogan and, with incredible poise for his first major angle on the big stage, delivered the interview that became one of the most iconic sports entertainment moments of the late 80s.

Hogan, at the time, was the long-reigning WWE Champion that had overcome all challengers in a near four-year period. People had begun to wonder, after Andre failed to win the belt at *Mania III*, what scenario could be conjured up to cause Hogan to lose. DiBiase offered to **BUY** the WWE Championship. Is not one of the most anger-inducing themes in sports today an owner of a franchise that opens his checkbook to purchase a championship? The New York Yankees in the no-salary cap Major League (of) Baseball have become infamous over the years for outspending everyone, putting smaller market teams at a fundamental, competitive disadvantage. The mere thought of DiBiase buying the WWE title from the heroic Hulk perfectly pushed the collective buttons of the era's target market.

The Million Dollar Man had proven time and again in his short tenure that everyone did, indeed, have a price. The question was, "Did Hogan?" The answer was, of course, "No." Hogan had no price, but a Giant and an Earl were both willing to do business. An infamous match in February 1988 on *The Main Event* saw Andre controversially defeat Hogan to win the title after senior referee Earl Hebner counted to three despite Hulk's shoulder being up (ironic, given Earl's involvement in the Montreal Screwjob ten years later). The ensuing chaos when Andre "surrendered" the title to DiBiase was brilliant to watch even if you did not see it live. If it were not for the crowd roaring in protest, we might have been able to hear DiBiase do his famous evil and maniacal laugh as he stood in the corner opposite Hogan, taunting him with the championship belt. Considering that this scene took place on the most watched pro wrestling event in modern television history, it deserves to be regarded as one of the most iconic moments ever.

It was also one of the best examples in pro wrestling history of how to hit back-to-back home runs by transitioning smoothly from one great story to the next. And to think that they actually hit back-to-back-to-back home runs with The Mega Powers exploding. The Mega Powers were Hogan and Savage, who joined forces to combat the duo eventually known as The Mega Bucks, DiBiase and Andre. DiBiase was instrumental to the success of The Mega Powers story. Because of the work that he did with Hogan and Savage, there needed to be a Mega Powers; and because there was a need for The Mega Powers, that set the stage for The Mega Powers "to explode" (Hogan vs. Savage) in one of the greatest money making matches of that era.

DiBiase's title purchase did not hold, so the title was vacated and put up for grabs in the *WrestleMania IV*, 14-man title tournament. That night was the biggest of DiBiase's career. He might be better remembered had he kept the title until *Mania* and dropped it back to Hogan in what could have set the standard for future main-events at "The Show of Shows." Instead, he put Savage in position to be the star that he became. In Heaven, Savage should be quietly watching over DiBiase as thanks for ensuring his superstardom. Rivalries invest people in the product. The Red Sox would not be who they are in today's sports lexicon without the Yankees playing the bad guys in the "Curse of the Bambino" story and Savage would not have become the second most recognizable name from the 80s wrestling boom if not for DiBiase.

Of course, it works both ways. Macho Man was the kind of accomplished performer that gave DiBiase a dance partner near his in-ring level. The matches with Savage were our first real glimpse of just how much of a ring general was DiBiase. Most of the bad guys put across the ring from Hogan in those days were either sizeable mammoths or excellent interviews, but few were particularly well known for their wrestling skill. DiBiase was quite the in-ring performer.

Modern fans may not grasp the extent of his prowess between the ropes. They are accustomed to seeing a product that has, since the days of Bret Hart and Shawn Michaels as main-eventers, taken a greater interest in producing all-time great matches on a regular basis. In DiBiase's WWE era, the personality was the focus and the in-ring performance took a substantial backseat. Based on their reputations, a modern fan might assume, DiBiase and Savage should have gone out and had 4-5 star level matches in 20+ minute headlining contests around the world. Instead, their feud featured great character work and 10-15 minute matches that most critics, today, would regard as good but not outstanding. Their workrate was not of the barnburner variety that you would expect from a CM Punk or an HBK. To appreciate the wrestling capabilities of Ted DiBiase, you have to pay closer attention.

The cycle for top heels in the 1980s WWE tended to turn quickly. About once per year, usually leading into

WrestleMania, a new lead antagonist was lined up opposite the top babyface. DiBiase had a lot of success during his year in that role. Once his run was over, he remained a headlining act for several years. He was simply too talented not to be used in a significant way. He captained Survivor Series teams back when that event mattered, he won the '88 King of the Ring tournament, and he set a then-record mark for amount of time spent in the Royal Rumble match (45-minutes). All of those accomplishments paled in comparison, though, to his debut of the Million Dollar Championship – a diamond and gold work of art. Personally, I believe it to be the single most awesome title ever created (the early 90s IC belt brought back in 2011 by Cody Rhodes and the winged-eagle WWE title are next...any belt ever tailored to John Cena is dead last). He claimed that it was worth one million dollars and, at that time, I would not have realistically been able to dispute it.

As the Million Dollar Champion, DiBiase involved himself in the affairs of Jake "The Snake" Roberts, stealing his snake from ringside during Jake's match against Andre the Giant at *WrestleMania V*. He went on to "injure" Roberts a few weeks later after Jake had taken money – DiBiase's money – from Virgil and handed it out to the fans at ringside in a move that fit an underlying theme for their feud. Nobody on the roster could better communicate the general hatred felt toward The Million Dollar Man by the "every man" than Roberts. The small town Georgian knew much about people being down on their luck and became the voice of those that DiBiase had wronged over the years.

There were numerous layers to the DiBiase vs. Roberts story, played out over a year's time. The injury to Roberts explained an absence for him to have surgery. When he returned, he promptly stole the Million Dollar belt, feeling it to be the representation of everything that made DiBiase evil. The Million Dollar Man held his Million Dollar belt in the highest esteem, calling it his most prized possession. To steal it was almost a threat on his livelihood; an apt response given the storyline of DiBiase putting Roberts on the shelf for several months and keeping him from wrestling.

Of the feuds that highlighted each man's career, perhaps none was more personal or as well performed. Jake cut some of the finer promos of his career in discussing DiBiase and his antics. DiBiase responded with a rare vulnerability often missing in his other rivalries where he played the role of aggressor putting other men on their heels. Roberts effectively had DiBiase and Virgil reeling. Not always do wrestling storylines tell complete and balanced tales in the build-up to the payoff match, but with Roberts and DiBiase it was fit for the big screen. The Million Dollar Man dominated the first half of the story, but Jake made the triumphant comeback and took control, leading to their headlining match at *WrestleMania VI* - one of the finer bouts of the early WrestleManias.

Later that year, DiBiase had a WWE title match with Ultimate Warrior on *Saturday Night's Main Event* that was one of the better opportunities for DiBiase to show off his in-ring ability throughout his seven-year wrestling tenure with the WWE. Though he was unquestionably one of the top grapplers of his day, his chances to put those skills on display in main-event situations after 1988 were few and far between. The championship match with Warrior is a forgotten gem, hidden by the fact that it took place on television and not PPV. If the WWE ever put together "Everyone Has a Price: The Best of The Million Dollar Man" collection (still waiting on that!), it should definitely be included.

One of The Million Dollar Man's most memorable rivalries was with his bodyguard. For years, he had mistreated Virgil, but by the winter of 1991, it had reached its peak. It was only a matter of time before Virgil snapped. After all, a man can only take so much. It was a good, relatable story that empowered people to stand up to those who acted above them, leading to a match at *WrestleMania VII* in which the Million Dollar Championship was up for grabs. Virgil failed to win the title at Mania and the chase continued to *Summerslam '91*, where Virgil finally defeated DiBiase to win the title. Though The Million Dollar Man eventually regained his belt, the enduring memory was created from the *Summerslam* match of the mistreated employee giving his boss the comeuppance that he so richly deserved. It helped lay the groundwork for the evil owner/boss/general manager storylines that would become so prominent several years later.

DiBiase did a tremendous job of staying relevant during that time, using Virgil's comeback story to showcase that, no matter where he was placed on the card, he was going to have one of the best matches of the night and that he was determined to maintain his place as a headliner. So many talents fall down the card from the main-event, get frustrated, do not fully commit to their storyline that is, comparatively, of lesser importance, and allow their attitude to be their downfall. DiBiase was not one of those guys. He found a way to make sure that, even in facing a relative nobody like Virgil for almost the entirety of 1991, his match was going to be a featured bout on the card.

For the remainder of his in-ring career (post-Virgil), which officially ended in 1994, DiBiase would join forces with Irwin R. Schyster (I.R.S.). They were known as Money, Inc. and were the focal points of the tag scene during the last days that the division was prominently featured prior to disappearing from consistent significance until October 1999 unofficially started the TLC era. DiBiase retired a three-time Tag Team Champion, the Million Dollar Championship pioneer, and a one-time (sometimes unrecognized) WWE Champion.

For a ten year period between 1987 and 1997, there were few superstars in sports entertainment more important to the industry than Ted DiBiase. Whether it was his final days as a financer of The New World Order in WCW, his role in the precursor to the eventual tide-turning Corporation, his run as the Million Dollar Champion, or his initial boom period-extending heel character for whom everyone had a price, DiBiase's "Million Dollar Man" was always successful. Only Hogan, Savage, and Warrior rank ahead of him amongst the early WrestleMania Era top stars.

Just in case you fail to give him credit where it is due, your check is in the mail. Remember, some might cost a little and some might cost a lot, but he is The Million Dollar Man…and you will be bought…(insert maniacal laugh, here)…

#25: The Ultimate Warrior

The Ultimate Warrior was my first "favorite" wrestler. He was a captivating performer, particularly to a young fan of sports entertainment. When his music hit and he flew down the aisle at full speed, ran around the ring, and violently shook the ring ropes, it drew young minds into the glitz and glam of pro wrestling as the 1980s ended and the 1990s began. At my kindergarten age, his entrance had a "wow" factor. His theme left such a lasting impression that my wife and I used it to introduce our wedding party at our reception. The WWE did a good job during Hulkamania of making sure that professional wrestlers became more colorful. Hulk Hogan's red and yellow attire and Macho Man's flashy robes were good examples, but there was no one more vibrant than Warrior. With his Greek God physique, the multi-colored tassels on his biceps and his boots, and his face intensely painted as a symbolic mask, he looked like the most awesome fighter on the planet.

A former bodybuilder, he was still learning the ropes when he made his debut in 1987. He spent the next eighteen months looking good, physically, but struggling as a performer. There was something about him that allowed the WWE to let him learn as he went, though. He had that x-factor, mowing through the competition en route to a record-setting Intercontinental title win at the inaugural *Summerslam* in 1988 over then-champion, The Honky Tonk Man, in less than thirty-seconds.

His popularity skyrocketing, Warrior needed only to prove that he was capable enough in between the ropes to step up to the next level at the turn of the decade. 1989 was an important year for him. It was during that year that I first saw him wrestle. In one of 1989's best rivalries, Warrior traded the IC title back and forth with the incomparable "Ravishing" Rick Rude at *WrestleMania V* and *Summerslam*. Rude deserves a lot of credit in getting Warrior ready for the main-event. He basically taught him how to work. Their *Summerslam* match was one of the best of 1989. It was arguably the top WWE match that year, which was really saying something for Warrior. In the early 90s, Warrior would frequently step up in big match situations and more than hold up his end. The bouts with Rude were the turning point that eventually allowed him to excel. As mentioned in Ravishing's chapter, you could see a marked improvement just from *Mania* to *Summerslam*. In just five month's time, Warrior went from sloppy and out of control to crisp and psychologically sound. The WWE knew it could not ask much of him yet at *Mania*, hence the barely above five minutes in length. At *Summerslam*, they knew that they had a different level of wrestler on their hands and were able to give him more responsibility. He delivered in spades, with Rude leading the way.

To kids, Warrior was like Achilles in real life, human form; a gift from the wrestling Gods. He was seemingly not of this earth. Nothing that he said or did made him seem like a mere mortal to anyone under the age of eight. When he was given a WWE Championship match at *WrestleMania VI*, it felt as if it was Warrior's destiny to win the title, dethroning Hogan in the process.

Warrior vs. Hogan was the most fascinating match of the early WrestleManias, eclipsing even Hogan vs. Andre. After having conditioned their fanbase for decades to believe that "good" would always win in the end, the WWE pitted two heroes against each other and told us all to pick a side. From Sammartino to Morales to Backlund to Hogan, evil had always been defeated. This time, there was no evil. They each had their fan followings and they each held a well-respected championship. Babyface matches, as they are called, had been done in the past, but never in the WrestleMania Era and never in this high a profile. Mania had truly become wrestling's Super Bowl, by then. Warrior vs. Hogan had the feel of Troy Aikman's

Cowboys reaching their peak just as Joe Montana's 49ers were winding it down.

"The Ultimate Challenge" was the name given to their "Title for Title" showdown, making it known that this was not an event built around Hogan, but on his match with Warrior being the most significant mountain he had ever had to climb. Some suggested that the torch was about to be passed. During the 1990 Royal Rumble match, they had a memorable face-off during the climax. It was an electric confrontation. Dare I say that it was one of the best handled pre-Mania moments.

"Feel the electricity," said Jesse Ventura during the early moments of the Mania match. "You can cut it with a knife," replied Gorilla Monsoon. I do not care if they rehearsed it (unconfirmed rumor). It does not bother me in the least that it was fairly pedestrian in its execution. The fact of the matter was that Warrior and Hogan had the nearly 70,000 people in the palms of their hands. It was presented so very well, with changes in momentum at just the right times and one of the most dramatic final sequences in wrestling's history to that point. It was not an exercise in aesthetic perfection, but it was an absolute masterpiece in how to properly carry out a battle between two protagonists. Warrior won the match and the WWE Championship. Pat Patterson, one of the lead road agents and a Hall of Famer, came into the dressing room to check on him a few hours after the show to find him staring at the title, crying because he was so happy.

Warrior was given the ball, though I am not certain that he was ever really given the "torch." He took the lead as the company's champion and did well in title defenses against the likes of Ted DiBiase and Mr. Perfect. Rude then came back to challenge him for the belt at *Summerslam '90*, concluding their multi-year struggle in a Steel Cage match. Savage attempted to be next in line. The Macho King, having won the King of the Ring crown in 1989, blindsided the champion in a maneuvering effort for a title shot. Sgt. Slaughter, though, had emerged as the top heel in the WWE. Warrior's efforts to defend the USA pushed Savage's request for a title match to the backseat. Macho did not much care for being cast aside (probably no more in real life than in storyline) in favor of a guy that had not been relevant in the WWE for years.

Royal Rumble '91 made it apparent that Warrior's win over Hogan the previous year was not meant to make him Hulkamania's replacement as the face of the organization. He dropped the title to Slaughter due to Macho's (heavy) interference, setting up the turncoat Sarge to get his comeuppance at the Hulkster's mighty hand at *WrestleMania VII*. Wrestling lore has likely told the wrong tale in implying that Warrior "failed at taking up Hogan's helm," for that would suggest that Warrior was given the helm in the first place. Promotions have always had multiple tiers of drawing superstars. Hogan was the face of the company and remained the "The Man" even after Warrior defeated him for the title. Warrior could not possibly duplicate what Hogan did for the WWE. He could headline house shows and PPVs, but to expect that he could be the presence in the media appearances expected of the WWE's #1 star that Hulk was? That would not have been fair. It would be like asking Undertaker to do those things as well as The Rock or John Cena. Hulk, Rock, and Cena are personalities fit for mainstream media appearances, while neither Warrior nor Taker are cut from that mold.

I, personally, look at the situation and see that the WWE was testing the waters with Warrior, rather than outright pushing him into Hogan's spot. Surely the WWE knew that Hulkamania was no longer running wild, but business was still strong. I think Warrior was pegged as "one of" the top draws in the company that they could bank on for years to come, but I do not believe that he was intended to be "The Man." If he had been, he would have been paid the same kind of money as

Hogan was getting. As proven by the Warrior's disputes with Vince McMahon in 1991, that was not the case.

At the top of the secondary tier, behind only the face of the WWE, Warrior would have thrived much the same way that Andre or Savage had before him. The problem is that being given the title, the main-events, and more responsibility grows the ego of a superstar. Warrior is and always was a smart guy. He wanted to be on equal footing with Hulkamania's dollars and cents, but Vince was unwilling. It happens in every sport. Stars that do big things want to be paid like the guys doing the biggest things. Would you not want the same?

WrestleMania VII was an interesting night. Warrior vs. Savage, to the avid viewer, came across as just as important as Hogan vs. Slaughter. Putting their respective careers on the line added a stipulation arguably as vital to the buyrate as the WWE Championship. With the Operation: Desert Storm tie-in, however, Hulk vs. Sarge took most of the fiscal credit. The mainstream media blitz, negative as it may have been, begged the question as to whether or not Hogan-Slaughter would have been fine without the title involved and, subsequently, whether the strap would have enhanced Warrior vs. Savage. It is difficult to say, definitively. One thing that we do know is that Warrior and Savage treated their match like it was the main-event, with Warrior even going so far as to airbrush onto his ring gear that his match "means much more than this," referencing a picture of the title in between the words.

In one of my all-time favorite matches, Warrior put on the performance of his career, defeating Savage to temporarily end his.

A few years ago, WWE Home Video released a DVD documenting the Warrior's career entitled, "The Self Destruction of the Ultimate Warrior." It was somewhat of a tongue-in-cheek production that saw his peers poke fun at his interviews and his performance capacity. I remember, upon seeing those interviews, wondering aloud, "Did these guys not watch *WrestleMania VII*?" Not to come across as too much of a Warrior mark, but I cannot recall many horrible wrestlers having a WWE Match of the Year candidate in four consecutive years. You would be hard pressed to name many WWE matches better in 1989 than Warrior vs. Rude, in 1990 than Warrior vs. Hogan, or in 1991/1992 than Warrior vs. Savage.

Everything that Warrior did in his WrestleMania match with Macho King was spot on. He sold the fact that his career was on the line as well as anyone ever has in a similar gimmick. He ran to the ring, full steam ahead in every one of his WWE matches to my recollection, with the exception of the one where he logically would need to conserve his strength and stamina given what was at stake. At *Mania VII*, he slowly walked to the ring. He proceeded to make each move count, carefully picking his spots. He played mind games in an attempt to psyche Savage out. These were not Warrior trademarks. Normally, he was all power, ridiculously intense, and seemingly had just the fifth gear. Yet, with his (kayfabe) career hanging in the balance, he was amazingly smart.

It was a masterpiece. Not only is it a favorite, but I legitimately believe it to be one of the greatest matches ever when taking into account the crowd reaction, the commentary, the psychology of the story told, and the execution of the moves from each wrestler. The much heralded War Games '91 in WCW had nothing on it. The only thing that Perfect vs. Bret (from that year's *Summerslam*) had on it was better technical wrestling. In every other aspect of what makes a wrestling match great, Warrior vs. Savage was superior. I can only imagine, if the championship had been on the line and it been *Mania VII's* main-event, how history might remember it. I think it is top ten at WrestleMania and top 25 overall, as is.

Warrior and Macho had a rematch, the WWE's second babyface bout in a high profile championship situation, at the '92 *Summerslam*. With another piece of work that has stood the test of time and ranks as one of the best matches in the Summer Classic's past, they solidified the legacy of their feud as one of the greats of the generation.

Unfortunately, financial matters cut short the prime of the Warrior's wrestling career. *Summerslam '92* was his last main-event match until a brief stint in WCW saw him rekindle his 1990 tensions with Hogan at *Halloween Havoc '98*. Against Savage, he had looked so very polished as a performer, but six years away from actively wrestling some of the best talents in the world quite noticeably stripped him of his abilities. The 1998 match with Hulk was one of the absolute worst of all-time. Since then, he has gone off into his own little world, changing his legal name to "Warrior," giving public speeches full of obviously intelligent (but also highly unusual) rhetoric about various topics, failing to accept the WWE's offer to induct him into the Hall of Fame, and making questionable decisions that vary from the strange to the deranged (like a profanity-laced tirade blasting a fan that questioned the price at which he was selling one of his old action figures on eBay).

It was such a treat for me to see him come back to WWE for his induction into the Hall of Fame Class of 2014. I was such a fan of the guy in my youth. I still own my Ultimate Warrior "Wrestling Buddy" made in 1990. I wrote a paper about it as a junior in high school and received "A" marks for my description of its meaning. When my son was born in 2015, my buddy, Tony, gave him his own Ultimate Warrior; we take milestone pictures with him next to it.

It was a shame that he left when he did, as he was set up for a good year or longer with the storylines that they had going between him and both Undertaker and Jake "The Snake" Roberts. With as good, call it carryable if you will, as he had become in the ring, I can only imagine the matches that he and the psychologically brilliant Snake could have put together. They were well on their way to a conflict that would have given both of them another potentially celebrated feather in their caps, but each departed before it could ever take place.

The bout I would love to have seen would have been Warrior vs. Undertaker at *WrestleMania VIII*. The Deadman completely dominated most of his opponents in a manner similar but more aggressive to how Warrior had when he was first coming up through the ranks. They were each known for their no-selling (purposefully, be it in character or otherwise, making another wrestler's offense look weak). It would have been an interesting dichotomy to see whether Taker's "power from the urn" or Warrior's "power from the Gods" would win out. It may have, though, derailed the illustrious "Streak" before it ever got off the ground.

My memories of him will never die. He will live on as a former WWE Champion that carried the title for ten months and a two-time Intercontinental Champion that enhanced the stature of the belt. He had some of the most legendary matches of the early WrestleMania Era, headlining the "Granddaddy of 'em all" three times.

Perhaps his most enduring contribution to the wrestling business, though, was his promos. Tony and I went back and watched a bunch of his old interviews with the power of YouTube several years ago. It probably looked like we were watching the best of Chris Rock's comedy tour to a bystander; Tony's wife referenced this in the card she sent with the Wrestling Buddy. Warrior was an off the wall interview, without question. He was certainly charismatic and highly intelligent. Hilariously random, though. It takes a creative cat to come up with some of that stuff, so all the credit in the world to the guy. I did a list for Steiner; I have to do one for Warrior. Here are the Top 5 Warrior promo quotes...

#5 - "The family that I live for only breathes the air that smells of combat."

#4 - "Load the spaceship with the rocket fuel; load it with the warriors!"

#3 - "Dig your claws into my organs! Scratch into my tendons! Bury your anchors into my bones! For the power of the Warrior will always prevail!"

#2 - "And I came here for one reason: to attack and keep coming. Not to ask but just to give, not to want but just to sing; sing the power of the Warrior…because this freak of nature right here is just beginning to swell, and when I get big enough, brother, there ain't gonna be room for anybody else but me and all the Warriors…floating through the veins…and the power of the Warrior."

#1 – "How should I prepare? Should I jump off the tallest building in the world? Should I lie on the lawn and let them run over me with lawnmowers? Or, should I go to Africa and let them trample me with raging elephants?"

Sadly, he passed away a few days after his Hall of Fame induction. I'll never forget watching him interact with his daughters before and during his speech. There is a special bond between a father and his little girl. It makes my heart ache to think of Warrior's girls growing up without him and drives me to do everything I can to make sure I'm healthy enough to be around for my kids. RIP.

There was only one Ultimate Warrior, ladies and gentlemen.

#24: *Eddie Guerrero*

November 13, 2005.

Every morning, I wake up and go through a routine of internet browsing, with LOP being amongst the favorites. On that Sunday morning several years ago, with my eyes still groggy, I was straining to focus as I zeroed my attention in on the wrestling headlines.

> **Eddie Guerrero found dead**
> **More details on Eddie Guerrero's death**

Line after line, the news was all about the 38 year old, most famous member of the renowned Guerrero wrestling family who had battled racial stereotypes, small stature, addictions, pink slips, and strenuous world career travel to reach the pinnacle of his profession, only to have his heart give out while he was brushing his teeth.

I felt like I had been punched in the stomach. I know wrestlers are, on the surface, just guys that we watch on television and PPV, but any diehard fan of any sport knows that there is far more to it. We invest a lot of time in our lives to our favorite teams and players. Like many, I use that outlet as an escape from the real world and as something to enjoy outside of my own profession. Eddie's death was not just "some guy" dying, to us fans. He was a man that we had literally seen progress through life, overcome highly challenging obstacles, and finally make it as one of the greats of his time. People identified with him on a personal level that went beyond wrestling. It was a sad day when he died.

He left behind an incredible legacy.

It was in ECW that Guerrero firmly established himself as "one to watch" in the United States, but he entered WCW and quickly developed a sterling reputation in a series of matches with fellow ECW alum, Chris Benoit. He had more four-star matches in three months (October-December) than the rest of the roster had combined in 1995, capping off the year with one of the top matches in the history of Starrcade against a Japanese wrestler named Shinjiro Otani. Speaking of Guerrero, "Pound for pound, the greatest wrestler in the world," according to Dusty Rhodes, on commentary.

Throughout 1996 and much of 1997, his work in the ring continued to shine against a variety of opponents (a "Who's Who" in pro wrestling history) over the United States and Cruiserweight Championships. He developed charisma and character to compliment his amazing in-ring ability. His defining WCW moment came when he, as the WCW Cruiserweight Champion, put the title on the line in a Title vs. Mask match against Rey Mysterio at *Halloween Havoc '97*. It was an exhibition between two of the best of all-time, taking place at a time when both were still trying to prove themselves. The general consensus, already, was that Eddie was on his way to bigger and better things. Prior to the match, the commentators were rightfully praising him as one of the best in the entire business. "We're talking about one of the most talented men in our sport...*ever*. I'm talking about Guerrero," commented the great Bobby Heenan. Guerrero-Mysterio was one of the top headlining cruiserweight matches of the great three year run for the division and earned WCW Match of the Year honors.

The upward climb to the main-event seemed to have a glass ceiling for guys like Guerrero, unfortunately. He never did advance in WCW. He was as entertaining as anyone on the roster, one of the most over acts that they had, and was routinely having some of the best matches. Yet, the chance to move up the card never came. He lasted two more years, toiling around the mid-card and perhaps most notably creating The Latino World Order (L.W.O.) spoof of The New World Order (N.W.O.). Then, he and most of the mid-card guys that had carried the wrestling side of WCW decided to take their talents to the WWE.

Joining the WWE as a member of The Radicalz (Guerrero, Benoit, Malenko, and Saturn) should have been the best thing that ever happened to his career, but that part of his life was clouded by bad decisions that were fueled by addictions. The turn of the century coincided with Eddie's debut, his fall from grace, and his resurgent effort to overcome the demons and get his life back on track with help from his family and his renewed faith in God. When he came back to wrestling, he looked motivated, healthy, and ready to achieve new heights.

It was his move to *Smackdown* in the summer of '02 that took him to the next level. There were so many great matches that summer and fall on Thursday nights, but one particularly stands out in my mind. Eddie and Edge were wrapping up a three month feud in what turned out to be an unbelievable No-DQ match. It was one of my favorites from my college days. Sac and I will still occasionally shake our heads to this day when one of us brings up that match. I had a suitemate that said on that night, "We're going out to party and meet some ladies and Chad is in here watching wrestling." Well, yeah. I do not mind having missed a party that I would not have remembered, anyway, in favor of seeing Eddie vs. Edge.

Via matches of that caliber, Eddie started to gain quite a following. People on the net already adored him, but everyone else was starting to catch on. In forming Los Guerreros with nephew Chavo, Eddie started accentuating traits of his wrestling persona that caused his popularity to explode like no one ever could have imagined. They openly admitted to lying, cheating, and stealing as their mantra in life. "If you're not cheating, you're not trying," they would say. Both through vignettes and their actions in the ring, Los Guerreros took a heel tactic as old as the sport and turned it into something to cheer about. For a little over a year, Eddie and Chavo helped usher in a thriving tag team division on *Smackdown*, becoming the champions on multiple occasions. They had excellent tag team matches with Benoit and Kurt Angle, Edge and Mysterio, Charlie Haas and Shelton Benjamin, and the Basham Brothers.

"Eddie" was fast emerging as one of the most popular chants by the WWE audience. It was odd that a man cheating to win could make people cheer, but his undeniable charisma was hard not to like; even when they wanted you to dislike him. When Chavo suffered an injury in the spring of 2003, it gave Eddie a chance to branch out into the new United States Championship division. The final of the US title tournament between him and Benoit was my personal favorite of their multi-year series. Guerrero was reaching his peak. In becoming the WWE's inaugural US Champion, he reminded fans and management that he had all the tools to be a major player, connecting with the audience as a character and wowing everyone with his all-around, in-ring skill set (chain wrestling, high flying, psychology, entertainment, etc.).

Once Chavo came back, subtle seeds were planted for an official break-up of their team. They won the Tag Team titles again, but by the beginning of 2004, tension had boiled over and Chavo had turned on Eddie. It was actually not the first time that they had feuded, as they had a storyline in WCW that led to a memorable Hair vs. Hair match at the 1998 *Bash at the Beach*. The quality of that match was unquestionable, making us believe that we would see something comparable when they squared off at the 2004 *Royal Rumble*. However, the 2004 match was merely a vehicle to get Eddie to the main-event. With a decisive victory set to a soundtrack of thunderous chants for his name, Eddie moved on from Chavo and set his sights on winning something that I am not sure any of us ever thought he would: the WWE Championship.

The people that run the WWE are not stupid. They are going to push the guys to the top that are garnering the greatest response. They will listen to the people if the people tell them what they want long and loud enough. Eddie got his chance at WWE Champion, Brock Lesnar, at *No Way Out '04*, but there was still a palpable sense amongst fans that the WWE might be reluctant to pull the trigger and go all the way with him. For that reason, the Guerrero-Lesnar match was incredibly dramatic. The in-ring tale that night was as well told as you could expect; a classic that saw Brock dominate as a man with six inches and sixty pounds on his opponent should. With a little help and a little lying, cheating, and stealing, Eddie found a way to win the title in one of his best matches.

February 15, 2004 was the night that defined his career. Everything that he had worked for paid off. After all the trials and tribulations, he won the top prize in the business and went on to have the best year of his career, validating those that had championed his efforts for so long and leading to several memorable headlining matches.

None of Eddie's title defenses were bigger or more highly anticipated than his *WrestleMania XX* match against Kurt Angle. There was some "best of all-time chatter" in the months leading up to it. Unfortunately, Angle went into the match having aggravated a chronic neck injury, so he was not at 100%. They still had a great match that ranks near the top 30 matches at wrestling's Super Bowl, but it left you wanting more. Angle took time off and became the General Manager of *Smackdown* in the process, targeting Eddie's title reign. Eventually, Angle was successful in screwing Guerrero out of the championship, but exposed himself as a fraudulent GM in the process. A rematch from *Mania* was made for *Summerslam*, with all the lofty pre-match hype rebuilding to a fever pitch. The second chapter reversed the roles from *Mania*, with Guerrero going into the match with a nagging groin pull that prevented them again from achieving their potential.

I was reviewing *Smackdown* when it came time for their rubber match – a 2/3 Falls match in September. Luckily, both entered with clean bills of health. Finally, we got to see them fire on all cylinders and produce the classic that we had been waiting for. It was far athletically superior to their previous two bouts and was more the mental chess match featuring their witty personalities that we thought we would see when rumors of their rivalry first circulated nine months prior. Eddie had gotten himself over based on his charming, cunning, chicanerous antics, but the serious tone at *Mania* and *Summerslam* took their story in a different direction. The third match refocused on some of the key elements that put each wrestler at their best. Angle pulled Eddie's hair, so Eddie pulled Angle's singlet. The psychological games preceded the physical one-upmanship, which featured the hold-for-hold excellence that few combinations of that era (or any since) could produce.

Eddie classically attempted to lie, cheat, and steal his way to victory. He used to do this bit where he would bring a chair into the ring and toss it to his opponent just as the previously sidetracked referee turned around. He would then fall to the mat like he had just been clocked. It never ceased to amuse me, but it backfired when the ref's distraction with Angle holding the chair led to his associate blindsiding Eddie in the ankle with another chair. Angle pounced with the ankle lock and got the tainted tap out win, but the match was a big success. I rated it at 4 ½ stars in my LOP review of the show. We had waited a long time to see *that* match, ending their series with an underrated MOTY candidate.

No one in their right mind would have thought that Guerrero's matches with Angle would pale in comparison to his matches with John "Bradshaw" Layfield, which took place in between the two halves of the Angle feud. Yet, Eddie and JBL had first-class chemistry and three glorious matches. Their work together was, in my opinion, the superlative work of

Eddie's career. He was phenomenal, carrying the *Smackdown* brand on his shoulders, excelling as a babyface champion, and getting JBL so over as a heel that he went from career tag specialist to one of the most memorable characters of the last decade.

Their first match at *Judgment Day '04* was brutally intense. JBL cracked Eddie right in the forehead with a chair without protection - *zero* protection. Eddie kept his hands down and let himself get walloped in the face. It looked like Eddie cut himself with a bowie knife instead of a tiny strip of razor blade, as blood began to literally pour out of his head. It bordered on being outright disgusting and made you immediately wonder if medical intervention was necessary to prevent him from keeling over and dying. I immediately thought back to that match when I learned of Eddie's premature death 18 months later. The amount of blood that poured out of his head made the ring and the ringside area look like a crime scene. The fact that Eddie was able to withstand all that blood loss and wrestle for another 15-minutes still surprises me to this day.

A month later, JBL beat Eddie in an excellent Texas Bullrope match to win the title. In a Steel Cage rematch on *Smackdown*, they took us on another thrill ride. It did not have the blood from the *Judgment Day* match. It did not have the creative gimmickry of the Bullrope match. What it did have, though, was a tremendous amount of drama brought about simply by the conclusive feel to everything they were doing. Little traces of their previous matches could be seen throughout, interspersed with some impressive spots off the cage. They put their bodies on the line one last time to put over the three months of time that they had put into making their rivalry special.

Eddie had the chance to win the match after knocking JBL off the top rope, giving himself a clear path to victory.

However, he got that cocky, "Latino Heat" grin on his face when he reached the top of the cage. In that moment, you knew you were about to see something special. FROG SPLASH!! Guerrero landed his signature finishing move from the top of the cage and launched the match into an extraordinary class. In my opinion, the greatest Cage matches of all-time have featured one classic moment that lives forever in historical hype videos. Guerrero provided it.

Guerrero's stretch of matches from Chavo to Lesnar to Angle to JBL back to Angle stamped his legacy with a seal of main-event approval. He would not have cracked the First-Tier without it. Viva La Raza!

The following year was an important one for the WWE. They needed some fresh faces at the top to stimulate a stagnant business that was making the final transition away from the Attitude Era. Guerrero was an integral part of building up two of the next headliners. From the start of the year, Eddie set his sights on elevating Mysterio. Rey had been a valuable second-tier commodity in his first few years in the WWE, but he had the popularity and merchandise sales to be on the first string. All he needed was an established name to put him over. That was where Eddie came in. The old rivals put together an eight-month program that initially included a Tag Team title run, a babyface match at *WrestleMania 21*, and several matches on *Smackdown*. In their head-to-head battles, Mysterio beat Guerrero every time. It frustrated Eddie to the point of an outstanding heel turn. Though much of his excellent heel work was still met with booming "Eddie" chants, Mysterio got a massive boost from so many close victories over the former WWE Champion and went on to become a consistent main-event threat.

Batista was the other headliner to get a boost from Guerrero, but in a different way. He was already the World Champion and had been put over huge by Triple H. His confidence was what needed uplifting and, both through working with Eddie in a program and just hanging around him backstage, he got his thoughts organized and his act together. Eddie gave him perspective and it was the best gift that he could have given at the time. I think that goes to show how good of a person that Eddie had become. A lot of people talk about the wrestlers being a "road family," but he was one of the few that took it to heart.

Entering the final year of Eddie's life and career, I started noticing something with increasing frequency. He had always been so cardiovascularly sound, with a pop to his moves that was apparent throughout his matches. There were two instances, in particular, where I commented with friends that he was starting to seem lethargic. One was a match against Mysterio on *Smackdown* and the other during his match with Benoit at the first *ECW One Night Stand*. I did not think much of it; it was more a passing observation. Yet, when news broke of his premature death, that was the first thing that I thought of.

November 13, 2005.

Just a few days prior to what I believe would have been the start of his second run as World Champion, Eddie passed away. It must have taken the better part of a year for the "Eddie" chants to finally die down at live events. He had endeared himself to everyone in the world that had the privilege of watching him or being around him and nobody wanted to let him go. Personally, I am thankful that his highest of wrestling highs came at a time when I was reporting on it. He gave me some great memories. Thank you, Eddie. We miss ya...

#23: Ricky "The Dragon" Steamboat

If I had asked you to name the wrestler that owns the WWE and NWA Match of the Decade for the 1980s, how long would it have taken you to come up with Ricky "The Dragon" Steamboat?

The late 80s was a time when flashy personalities reigned supreme in professional wrestling. Stars like Hulk Hogan, Randy Savage, and Ric Flair were the talk of the industry with characters that helped make them household names. And, yet, there was Steamboat in both the WWE and NWA, having matches that are still regarded as some of the best of all-time.

In my mind's eye, I envision a documentary similar in style to ESPN's "30 for 30" series, during the introduction of which the question is posed: "What if I told you that in 1987, a Dragon stole the show from a Hulk and a Giant, and then two years later went onto to have one of the most dramatic rivalries in sports history?"

Steamboat was always well-regarded in the industry as one its best wrestlers. "The best babyface," said the top heel of that era. Yet, before 1987, he had not stamped his career with a defining moment that would live for the ages. In the NWA, he had been a multi-time United States Champion and Tag Team Champion, in addition to regularly challenging for the Heavyweight title. For two years in the WWE, he had faced high profile opponents such as Don Muraco and Jake "The Snake" Roberts. His wrestling pedigree afforded him the opportunity to have perhaps his most well-known match and earn his status as one of the all-time greats.

At the end of 1986, he got an Intercontinental Championship match against then-champion, "Macho Man" Randy Savage. They set up an injury angle at the conclusion where Savage used the ring bell to "crush Steamboat's larynx."

Doctors were brought in to film report of findings sessions, detailing the results of the imaging taken to verify the diagnosis. To any young fan watching at home, it all looked real. "How dare that Macho Man?" Steamboat returned in time to get another crack at the title, but the rematch would be taking place as the co-headlining match on arguably the single most important PPV in WWE history: *WrestleMania III*. Realize that this was not the IC title that you know of today or even from the early 90s. Back then, it was a championship that put you in the position to headline major events. So, for Steamboat to have second billing for the Intercontinental title made it easily the biggest night of his career.

Steamboat and Savage gave WrestleMania the first true classic in its history. Preceded by two stage-setting backstage interviews, the two took the long ride down to the ring on the Mania cart. Steamboat was right: they had "reached their moment." Savage was spot on: "history beckoned." Their match was a proving ground for them both. Neither had yet established the reputation of being a future World Champion. What they had done was put together a very personal rivalry and set up a match where there would be no excuses – just *mano y mano* and may the best man win (for the most part).

Macho Man lived up to his namesake of being "Savage," as he had a maniacal way about him as a heel that brought out the natural heroic qualities in Steamboat, the consummate babyface who was able to sell wonderfully the offense of his opponent and get the crowd behind him with his mannerisms as purely as anyone I have ever seen. What made this match virtually a unanimous choice for WWE Match of the Decade (and the best until the double classic at *WrestleMania X* in 1994) was the over one dozen legitimate false finishes. Today's product has evolved to where the closest near falls involve the heavy use of finishing moves, but the 80s was a simpler time for performers. The fans of yesteryear were not conditioned to expect so many high spots, so guys like Steamboat and Savage could go out and wow 90,000-plus with roll-ups, cradle combinations, and small packages and have the them all believing that a pin was imminent. Moves with less impact meant a lot more and were able to garner a much larger reaction, so when Steamboat won the match with a small package, it was breathtaking.

The concept of stealing the show was born of that match. The Intercontinental Championship, worn to the ring by Savage but carried away from it by The Dragon, was not the title that 93,000 people packed the Pontiac Silverdome to see defended. Hogan vs. Andre for the WWE Championship deserves all the credit in the world for that unbelievable feat. Three matches prior, though, Steamboat and Savage completely and utterly outshined their more famous counterparts and made *Mania III* as much about their performance as it was about Hulk and the Giant's fiscal drawing power.

Commendable was The Dragon's commitment to his family during a time where so much money was there to be made in the wrestling business that guys were terrified of losing their coveted spots. Steamboat winning the Intercontinental Championship effectively put him on the fast track to a co-headlining status across the country - especially with the reputation quickly being gained by his WrestleMania performance - but it also came at a time where he and his wife were expecting their first child. He wanted to take time off to be with them, interrupting his title reign and forcing the WWE to accommodate him. I can see where Steamboat was coming from.

He dropped the IC title to The Honky Tonk Man, beginning the still record-long reign. Steamboat took his time off and came back to pretty much nothing. Conflicting reports suggest that he was being punished for not being more dedicated to the business, while others state that the higher-ups were angry about he and Savage having the most talked about match at *Mania III* over Hogan's defeat of Andre. Whatever the reasoning, Steamboat took a hiatus from wrestling in 1988 before returning to the NWA in the winter of 1989. In story, he came back for one reason: to get a chance to compete for the World Heavyweight Championship that had always eluded him.

What followed was possibly the greatest series of matches in the history of pro wrestling. The NWA World Heavyweight Championship was held by "Nature Boy" Ric Flair, who has often cited Steamboat as the greatest opponent of his career. By Naitch's count, they wrestled each other thousands of times from the mid-70s to the early 80s to the late 80s to the mid-90s, but none of their matches were as famous as their critically acclaimed series from 1989.

The three match saga began in Chicago at *The Chi-Town Rumble*. The two of them were known in the NWA for their ability to excel in lengthy matches that neared the one-hour time limit. Flair had even become known as the "60-minute Man." This was a match, though, with a faster pace that a lot of the modern fan base would find thrilling. It was a distinctly more WWE-style main-event at closer to 23-minutes. I thought that it was perfect.

The Dragon won the title with a roll-up out of a Figure Four attempt. Becoming the World Heavyweight Champion is an accomplishment in professional wrestling second only to main-eventing WrestleMania. The sport has seen somewhat of a devaluation of the top title as a lack of competition since WCW shut down in 2001 has led to this phenomenon of major stars that stick around one promotion for a really long time becoming "above the title." Nevertheless, it is still a pinnacle achievement. If a superstar wins that championship and makes an impression while holding it, then I have the utmost respect for that wrestler. I think that what Steamboat did was a great blueprint for professional wrestling success. He flat out earned a run with the big gold belt by having the best match on the grandest stage possible. He took a big opportunity, embraced it, and turned it into a future huge opportunity. Subsequently, he ends up in the top 25. Does he make it into the top 1/3 of all WrestleMania Era stars without that championship to his credit? No, he does not.

One of the most flattering things that I can write about Steamboat vs. Flair is that I cannot come up with a proper historical, athletic comparison for the chemistry that they had in the ring. No sport offers up something comparable to what they had. It was the thing that made their rivalry one of a kind. They made it look easy whether it was for 23-minutes or 55-minutes, as was their return match at *Clash of the Champions* in April 1989. With Two-out-of-Three Falls rules, expectations were high from everyone, and Flair and Steamboat went out and wrote another wonderful chapter in their rivalry. Without flaw, they locked horns for nearly an hour, trading the first two falls before Steamboat won the third to retain. Jim Ross and Terry Funk, on commentary, called it the greatest championship match *EVER* in the NWA.

Indeed, it set a new standard and, as my tastes have evolved for what I desire to see from a pro wrestling match, I do believe that the 55-minute rematch was the best of the series and is the 1980s masterpiece for professional wrestling. Few bouts in history can compare to that match. They were so accomplished in their sport and so respected by the fans that the crowd ate up something as simple as a lengthy headlock sequence.

Their endurance shown at *The Clash* was off the charts. I have a wrestling-writing colleague that likes to argue the credentials of the Ironman match at *WrestleMania XII* between Shawn Michaels and Bret Hart. He thinks it still ranks as one of the best matches ever, but in our respectful disagreements, I have frequently pointed him to Steamboat vs. Flair. Five-minutes shorter it was, but there is just no comparing the stamina. You are not looking at the clock the whole time during Steamboat-Flair; you do not care. They rarely stopped moving for an hour. A headlock was not held stationary for a minute or more, nor was a headlock viewed as a rest hold. When a headlock was applied by The Dragon or Nature Boy, the other was desperately trying to escape it with a pinning predicament or else. They showed respect to the hold and made the crowd, in turn, care about it. People were invested in the Superdome in New Orleans for the NWA Championship match ten times more than they were in Anaheim for the WWE Championship Ironman match. It is just no contest which match was better and why one has stood the test of nearly 25 years while the other has bordered on boring without the right setting and mood since the year 2000.

      The '96 Ironman is the most famous representation of an hour long match. The people like me that thought it dragged seemed catered to in each subsequent Ironman match from the WWE (WCW never had another hour match after 1989). Bret vs. Shawn had no falls in one hour, leading to overtime. Rock vs. Triple H, Angle vs. Lesnar, and Benoit vs. Triple H all had numerous falls (upwards of 11). Yet, the standard for how to wrestle for an hour remains the 2/3 Falls match between Steamboat and Flair. Watched within the same month today, the '89 classic was more entertaining, was better technically executed, had a more logical pace, and told a better story than the other three; and it did so while placing a premium on high spots. To keep a crowd engaged for nearly an hour without super kicks and planchas, Rock Bottoms and Pedigrees, top rope Angle Slams or F5s is an accomplishment in and of itself. If wrestling was comparable to the history of music, then Flair vs. Steamboat would be like Beethoven or Bach. It was exceptional work without the pomp and circumstance required to achieve the same result in the modern era.

The third and final match of the famous series over the NWA title took place at *WrestleWar* in May. The two previous bouts had been given the elusive five-star status by top critics, thus cranking up the anticipation to as high a level as there has ever been for a final match of a series. Give a ton of credit to the NWA officials for how they handled the atmosphere for the third match. Since the second match had gone an hour, they gave off the illusion that any amount of time would be possible within an hour time limit and brought in three former NWA Champions - Terry Funk, Pat O'Connor, and Lou Thesz - as judges. Their jobs were to score the match in 15-minute intervals so that, in the event of a 60-minute draw, there would be a winner based on points. It was the type of little touch that helped set the stage.

Using the judge's scale, the match was split into three periods. During the first, Steamboat had the clear advantage, making the score unanimously in The Dragon's favor. By the 30-minute mark, Steamboat was ahead 4-2 after Flair had taken two of the three judges' honors for the second period. Steamboat "injured" his knee late in the match, as his penchant for taking high risks caught up with him. Nevertheless, he was able to regain control and go back to work on Flair's arm.

The psychology of any rematch is always fascinating when you are dealing with two consummate pros, but when you add the element of the third match, there is so much history that they can draw from that, from the fan standpoint, part of the appeal is to see how they blend everything together. When The Dragon made his valiant comeback after withstanding the Figure Four leg lock, it seemed like he was in prime position to walk away with the title and send Flair to the back of the line. When Steamboat locked on the Chicken Wing, The Nature Boy era seemed nearly over. If Flair had lost, it would have been the first time that he had reached the deciding match of a series and failed to emerge with the NWA title. It would have potentially signaled a change in direction for the company. However, right when those thoughts started to creep in….BAM! Steamboat's leg gave out and Flair toppled right into perfect pinning position for the win.

Naitch won his sixth World Championship and moved right into a new feud, while Steamboat was the one that rode off into the sunset, never to see another realistic spot in the championship fold. It was no surprise, given that Flair was the best in the world and the greatest of all-time by the end of this series. The Dragon was solidified as his greatest in-ring rival. Nobody ever pushed Flair to be better like Steamboat; a Bird to his Magic, in essence. Three 5-star matches to a large majority of critics in a three match series is an almost impossible task. To this point in wrestling history, it is arguably been done just that once.

The importance of those unprecedented '87 and '89 classics with Savage and Flair to Steamboat's career cannot be understated, but I do not want to sell short his other great matches. I will praise his work with others by simply listing his opponents: The Briscoe Brothers, Terry Funk, Lex Luger, Jake Roberts, Don Muraco, Rick Rude, Bret Hart, Arn Anderson, Steve Austin, Brian Pillman, Barry Windham, Paul Orndorff, and Vader.

There were many highlights in the career of Ricky "The Dragon" Steamboat. During his 2009 Hall of Fame induction speech, he talked about how his career should be measured by his performance. I wholeheartedly agree. His ranking in the Performance Factor (Top 15) helped him jump bigger draws with more headlining longevity. His NWA and WWE Matches of the Decade punched his Hall of Fame ticket.

#22: Kevin Nash

    Kevin Nash is a mesmerizing personality. You would have to hop in the DeLorean, get it up to 88 MPH, and head back in time to a decade or longer ago to find more than a handful of fans with something good to say about the guy. He has become a magnet for criticism since the most relevant part of his career ended during the first year of the new millennium. Current perceptions shape historical realities and, unfortunately, Nash's legacy has a tendency to be tarnished by all the haters. Hopefully, we can be fair in the next few thousand words to both parts of his career because, truth be told, I root for Kevin Nash. I go out of my way to catch his growing number of often praise-worthy Hollywood film roles. When he does make appearances in pro wrestling, I make sure to see them in some way. I am, for lack of a better word, a "mark" for the guy.

    I think one of the nice things about growing up as a fan during an era where the wrestlers still made it a big deal to keep everyone shut out to the fact that wrestling was a performance art (what those in the business call "kayfabe") is that you could more easily get lost in it like you do traditional sports. Wrestling has become so transparent with the online dirtsheets and the books and the interviews where the superstars blatantly disregard that old tradition. Now, you watch wrestling and it is like watching a movie – you know that none of it is real, but you can still get consumed by the entertainment (and sport) spectacle. I do not believe that I would hold Nash in as a high regard if he and I were ten years younger. If you have been a fan since 1999 or beyond, you probably think of "politics, bad booking decisions, and controversial comments" when you think of Nash. Since I have been a fan since 1986, I think of Nash as a WrestleMania headliner, one of the most important figures in wrestling's modern history, and of his portrayal of the "Diesel" character in the WWE's New Generation that led to one of the longest World title runs since 1990.

Only Hulk Hogan and Steve Austin were more important players in the famed Monday Night War between WWE and WCW than Kevin Nash. Despite a one-year stint as WWE Champion that did marginal business during one of the most difficult stretches in the WWE's creative and financial struggle of the mid-1990s, Nash established a name for himself. In a short time, from bursting onto the scene with a show of dominance in the 1994 Royal Rumble match to winning the Intercontinental title at *Summerslam '94* to winning the WWE Championship at a house show in Madison Square Garden three days after *Survivor Series '94* to then holding that title until the 1995 *Survivor Series*, Nash became a major figure in wrestling. When he jumped to WCW for a boatload of guaranteed money in the spring of 1996 and showed up as an "Outsider," it was – as described by Eric Bischoff, WCW's Executive Producer – like making a loud noise on *Nitro* that made people that were watching *Raw* change the channel.

My experience of it was a little bit different. I had moved to a new city with my parents and we did not get the USA Network (which hosted *Raw*) at the hotel where we stayed until our house was built. All I could see was *WCW Nitro* on TNT. So, imagine my surprise at Nash and Scott Hall being on WCW. Nash's presence, in particular, piqued my interest. Hall had been an upper echelon talent, but Nash was a bonafide main-eventer coming off a title match with Shawn Michaels and a Mania match with Undertaker. For him to switch to WCW without hype and seemingly with the intent to take over was something that redefined what the phrase "big deal" meant in professional wrestling. His was the most significant roster change of the entire ratings war.

It creates for a puzzling case when trying to assess Nash's overall impact on the financial end of the business because he was both one of the worst drawing champions of the 90s AND a major part of the innovative and groundbreaking group that stimulated wrestling's rise to unprecedented heights. He is often criticized, too, for his role in the booking that led to WCW continually making bad creative decisions that stymied any potential forward momentum that they could gain past The N.W.O. angle, ultimately leading to the company tanking and being bought out by the WWE just as quickly as it had skyrocketed to the top and nearly put the WWE out of business. In a way, he was as much the epitome of all that was wrong with WCW when it started spiraling downward as he was one of the main reasons that it reached its peak. He was a huge success in some ways and a colossal failure in others.

Subsequently, if there is one thing to be definitively stated about Nash, it is that he is a polarizing figure. No matter your stance on his place in history, the important thing to remember is that he was a huge part of wrestling's rise to national prominence on cable television in the 90s and his role with The Outsiders and The New World Order made the Monday Night War perhaps the most famous time period that wrestling will ever see. Having been a fan through that era, I have a hard time imagining that the sheer number of people that got hooked on the WWE and/or WCW products will ever be duplicated. Wrestling made a lot of people rich (or richer) in those days. Nash was one of them, leveraging his way to a multi-millionaire end game by the time the "War" ended. I think we would be remiss not to credit Nash for his role in making pro wrestling one of the top TV cash cows of its era.

Fans can argue Nash's drawing power, but you cannot argue his headlining status. He was involved in a lot of main-events from 1994-2000. During those years, he headlined over fifty PPVs in WWE and WCW, including two WrestleManias and three Starrcades. He was one of only three wrestlers (Hogan and Bret Hart being the others) to ever win or retain the World Heavyweight Championship on the grandest stages of both promotions, retaining the WWE title against Shawn Michaels at *WrestleMania XI* and defeating Goldberg for the WCW title at

Starrcade '98. He was a six-time World Champion, overall. His championship statistics tie him for ninth, all-time, with Stone Cold and his headliner ranking ties him at 20th with Sting. He was in the top 25 on the business list, as well.

His look and his mic skills also earned him strong marks. There should be no questioning his verbal abilities, though his WWE comebacks in the last decade or so would suggest to fans unfamiliar with his 90s work that he was vastly overrated in that department. Nash could definitely talk back in the day. He was never a great wrestler, but he had the gift on the microphone. It was more of a natural talent, so he thrived in an era where you did not get a sheet of paper with talking points before doing an interview. The more "off the cuff," the better for Nash.

He was at his best when playing the role of the heel – or at least showing heelish tendencies as a tweener. "A Dude with Attitude," as he was known when tagging with Shawn Michaels, Nash's Diesel character was laying the foundation for the success of the anti-heroes (like Austin and DX) around the time that he left for WCW. The glass breaking that Stone Cold made famous was something that the WWE had going for Diesel years prior. It was cool, edgy, and out of the ordinary; the type of little touch that made you want to root for a guy, even if they otherwise presented him as someone you should not.

Where Nash suffers most, historically, are his in-ring performances. Unless he was in the squared circle with an elite wrestler, then Nash just was not up to the task. WCW did not provide him an environment that made him work hard and it led to some stinkers, but in the WWE he had the greatest performer in history to motivate him. Nash was brought to the WWE at the request of Michaels, who had seen him on WCW TV and thought he would make a great bodyguard. That is how "Diesel" was born and how the friendship between Nash and HBK allowed "Big Sexy" to get his foot firmly wedged in the door. In the WWE, Nash could watch top talents like Michaels and Bret Hart and understand the need to at least attempt to be near their level. Not surprisingly, my two favorite Diesel feuds were against Bret and HBK. Their work with Nash produced some of the better matches of the New Generation between '94 and '96. When the Hulkamania spotlight burned out, it was Diesel, Bret, and HBK, along with Undertaker, that were carrying the load for the WWE. It was a time when two elite workers were at the helm, elevating everyone else around them. The focus was on the performance, for a change, and not necessarily the personality. I think it brought out the best in Nash, as a worker.

Diesel and Bret gave us three matches that I view as the best technical wrestling versus pure power clashes of the 90s. The two styles do not always mix, but Nash and Hart had good chemistry. It was those matches that make me dislike it when people say that Nash was a bad worker. I do not believe that bad workers can have great matches, but Nash had several great matches by working with exceptional workers that challenged him to step up his game. If anything, Nash was an uninspired worker for 80% of his career, but as long as he had someone in the opposite corner that would push him, then he could work.

The 1994 *King of the Ring* match with Bret was his proving ground. He was still such a pro wrestling novice, in terms of being a top tier guy, that his being thrust into the main-event spotlight forced him to show what he was capable of. He answered the call. You do not have to be a good worker to be a World Champion, as has been proven numerous times in the last thirty years. What you do have to be able to do is be competent. I cannot imagine an incompetent guy earning the trust of the promoters to the point of being World Champ. Diesel won the World title, so he was good enough to have the belt put on him and see if his look and personality could carry the WWE to a more profitable place.

The 1995 *Royal Rumble* title match with Bret was his validation. There was a unique dynamic in that match for the time, as it was a situation in which Nash was still trying to get over as a babyface and Bret was basically the good guy he had to supplant to shore up his spot. Bret kindly worked as the heel to help him out. I thought they did well to get Nash a good amount of support, even though a lot of people were still going to be naturally inclined to side with Bret after all his years as one of the top babyfaces.

The 1995 *Survivor Series* No-Disqualification match with Bret was his triumph. Nash got saddled with a lot of mediocre opponents outside of Bret and HBK. It takes two to tango and the Diesel character was not exactly given a great line-up of heels to combat while he was responsible for getting over, carrying the company as champion, and expanding the WWE PPV market to include a new series of extra shows called *In Your House*. Yet, when he stepped back in the ring for his third match with Bret in November, you could tell he was up to the challenge. It was the night that his yearlong title reign ended, but he put on arguably the best performance of his career in defeat. It was another babyface match, only this time it was Diesel playing the heel. The entire presentation was innovative. Diesel sending Bret crash landing through the Spanish announce table was one of the first table spots done in a WWE main-event.

Coming out of his WWE run as a top star and transitioning to WCW, there were a few things that you could say about him. One was that he knew how to get what he wanted and learned the political game that goes with the territory of being a major superstar. Such skills served him well through his entire career. Another was that he could be counted on to work hard as long as you gave him a reason. Guaranteeing him money did not turn out so well in WCW because they took away his incentive to be better. I think the most underrated thing about him was that he could work; he might not have been easy for his peers to work with, but you cannot tell me that his major rivals such as Bret, HBK, and Taker did not all come out of their feuds with Diesel better off than they were before. It makes me wonder, all else being equal, what kind of legacy Nash would have if he had spent the back end of his prime in WWE instead of WCW. Would be looking at Top 15 for him instead of Top 25?

Imagine back to your high school days, if you will. Whether you were this person or knew this person, inevitably there was that guy in high school that was athletic and charismatic. While some people despised him for being those two things, he found a way to make the majority of his classmates fond of him. He was the guy that, if he played to his strengths, would always find a way to be successful in life, more based on the charming personality attached to the athletic frame than the penchant for sports. Kevin Nash has always been that type. He played basketball in college and caught the eye of pro wrestling promoters because of his size, but he always had that second part of the combo with his charisma. In the modern era, he was a perfect fit for the wrestling industry. One of the things that I still like about him is that he had success in the business, saved his money well, and does well in those aforementioned acting roles that ultimately reflect well on wrestling. I appreciate his contributions on the positive side of history.

#21: CM Punk

The "Pipe Bomb" was dropped on June 27, 2011. On *Monday Night Raw,* CM Punk was given a live microphone and told that he could use the final segment of the night to air his grievances with the WWE. What ensued was the most famous promo since "Austin 3:16." Punk - a Chicago Made (CM), heavily-tattooed antithesis to the prototypical WWE Superstar – had a lot of things to get off of his chest. His pent-up frustration was unleashed in a five-minute rant that was probably (loosely) intended to cater to the internet crowd, but wound up attracting quite a bit of mainstream attention. Even my favorite sports radio host, Colin Cowherd – who abhors pro wrestling – made mention of it on his show. I wrote the following in "The Doctor's Orders" a day later:

> In a wrestling world where the storylines can only be so interesting because the material can only push the limit ever so much, rarely do we get to see a cutting edge promo that makes us remember why we spend 52 weeks a year watching WWE programming. It's about as rare as once per decade that we get to watch a man deliver so much pent up (truthful) frustration that it instantly resonates and has us finding things in our own lives (past or present) that can relate to it. From a purely wrestling perspective and regardless of what real life parallels I can draw from the guy that feels underappreciated despite his considerable efforts to show how good he is, Punk addressed – in his multi-minute diatribe - about 90% of what the (internet) regularly gripes about. The promo was just brilliant in every conceivable way. What more could you want from an interview other than for it to simply be allowed to reach its natural conclusion. I want to hear more of that. I can't quite picture it all, Punk. I need the rest of it to complete the puzzle that you've created in my mind and make all the remaining pieces fit. In the

meantime, I'll just be sitting back here marveling at your ascension to one of the greatest talkers in the businesses' history. Don't worry; at that point when I decide to write a book about the best in the history of the WWE similar to the Bill Simmons masterpiece *The Book of Basketball*, I will make sure to dedicate an entire chapter to your unheralded and underappreciated excellence. Seriously...how awesome was that promo?

Punk was not contracted with the WWE past *Money in the Bank 2011*, which took place less than three weeks after the "Pipe Bomb" (the nickname for the promo). He had become so jaded with the company that he was going to walk away. Placing him in the main-event of the PPV that just so happened to be in his hometown on the final night of his contract was not viewed as a last ditch attempt to resign him, but rather as a way to make a little bit of money off of his departure. He had been in the WWE for five years and had proven his worth as a top-tier wrestler and personality. Having more than paid his dues, he was upset that the WWE had not called his number to become one of the elite members of the roster after several key departures. Talents with less experience and inferior skills were pushed ahead of him. He legitimately thought himself to be "The Best in the World," but his opportunities to show it were few and far between. Thus, he was prepared to leave.

It was hard to argue with his thought process. Since his first few months in the WWE as a part of the *ECW* brand, he had consistently received one of the strongest reactions from audiences around the country. He had a natural connection with people. His stellar reputation amongst critics who had seen him shine as one of the best wrestlers on the independent circuit, particularly Ring of Honor, translated very quickly to the big league audience. At the 2006 *Survivor Series*, his growing popularity overshadowed that of The Hardy Boys and Degeneration X. Yet, the WWE clearly did not realize what they had in Punk. During the pre-match DX routine, Triple H - recognizing that he was not as over as the young upstart known backstage as the "King of the Indies" - referred to Punk as "the future of ECW." Call it a compliment if you will, but many would counter that it was backhanded.

Frankly, I thought that WWE completely misused him from 2006 to 2009. I remember reading the LOP report in 2005 that the WWE was going to sign the "independent wrestling legend known as CM Punk" and thinking of how much I looked forward to seeing what all the hype was about. By the time he debuted, I had read all there was to know and watched many of his classic matches from the independents. Paul Heyman, whose opinion I greatly respect, had gushed about him. I was surprised, though, when they had him start out as a babyface. Straight Edge is both his actual lifestyle and his wrestling gimmick. He does not drink alcohol, smoke cigarettes, or do drugs. While it may seem an admirable philosophy, my experience with straight edge folks was that they were quite obnoxious about their beliefs. If that is not a heel in our society, then I do not know what is.

Wrestling as a babyface helped him gain popularity. He did, after all, have a unique move set and appealed to a vocal minority within the fanbase. Unfortunately, despite a run as ECW Champion, Intercontinental Champion, Tag Team Champion, Mr. Money in the Bank, and even World Heavyweight Champion, 2007 and 2008 went by without Punk showing much (if any) of the excellent character work that had made him so revered. His in-ring performances were legendary on the independents, but it was his skills with a microphone that had people predicting his WWE success. My pals in the forums were almost zealotic in their Punk praise. I grew tired of waiting to see what they had been talking about. I think much of it had to do with Punk's attitude about being miscast as a hero when he had made his name as a villain. Even then, he seemed jaded.

It seemed as if everything might have changed in the summer of 2009. That was when Punk proved to the world that he was one of the best pro wrestlers on the planet. The first WWE "Summer of Punk" got underway when he successfully cashed in his second Money in the Bank contract (won at *Mania 25*) to become the World Heavyweight Champion at *Extreme Rules* in June 2009. He won the title right after Jeff Hardy had beaten Edge to win it in a Ladder match. Money in the Bank gives you a cheap win with rare exception. Having defeated one of the most popular stars in the industry by nefarious means, Punk was jeered. With the negative reaction from the crowd came an attitude change from his character. Suddenly, his promos contained a lot more substance, as he questioned why he was being booed. He began to accentuate some of the more elitist qualities of being straight edge and, in the midst, ridiculed the fans for choosing to cheer a man like Hardy who was celebrated by the people despite a lifestyle unbecoming of a role model. After listening to a summer's worth of great promos, I said to myself, "That's the guy everyone was talking about."

Punk proved to be the most entertaining character in wrestling during the feud with Hardy. That never changed in the years after. There was nobody more entertaining with a live microphone in hand. He also proved that there was not a better in-ring storyteller in the business. If you gave him 20+ minutes of bell-to-bell time and a decent opponent, he would produce a Match-of-the-Year candidate in almost every outing. Punk and Hardy produced some of the most compelling bouts of the last decade. He might not have been the "Best in the World" yet, but Punk's heel persona showed why he thought that he was.

The summer of 2009 should have been his launching pad. Oddly enough, the WWE apparently was not seeing what everyone else was. They had him drop the title, which he had won back from Hardy at *Summerslam*, to Undertaker. He had two short championship matches on PPV with The Deadman and then moved back into the mid-card. I have wondered about the dynamic between those two behind the scenes, with Taker being the WWE's symbol of locker room respect and Punk being so against the grain. Unsubstantiated rumors suggested that the two were at odds back in those days over Punk's failure to dress like a champion. I cannot help but think that his demotion that autumn had a lot to do with his frustrations boiling over in the summer of 2011.

According to his documentary, Punk was given nothing to do after losing to Taker, so he promptly wrote the WWE creative team multiple months of television. He created "The Straight Edge Society," a wildly enjoyable portrayal of Punk as a faux Jesus, converting "addicts" to the pseudo-religion of "Straight Edge." People were coming into the ring and getting their heads shaved to show their signs of loyalty. "One nation, under Punk, indivisible, with integrity and sobriety for all." It earned him plenty of time on the microphone, but it did not lead to main-events. As great as it was, the WWE still saw it as a mid-card gimmick. I think it could have been an incredible main-event character, myself. The WWE was flat out dropping the ball with Punk. He was not the only one annoyed.

WrestleMania XXVII was the straw that broke the camel's back for Punk's mounting frustrations with WWE. Despite excelling against Randy Orton that night, he was extremely peeved to be passed over in favor of The Miz for the main-event match against John Cena. When combined with the fact that they did not unleash his full arsenal of skills until three years after his debut and that they de-pushed him after he had shown how special that he could be in 2009, WWE giving the #1 heel spot on a WrestleMania full of untested bad guys to The Miz pushed Punk over the edge. Hence, the "Pipe Bomb."

The "Pipe Bomb" was the pinnacle moment in Punk's career; the by-product of several years spent fighting for the chance that he believed he deserved. He won the WWE title from John Cena in his hometown because of that promo. Punk vs. Cena inspired one of the most memorable crowds in history, with 15,000 people pouring their emotions into the match. Only the Sky Dome crowd for The Rock vs. Hogan comes to mind as being on that level. The audience was going bananas for over thirty-minutes straight, nearly jumping the guardrail whenever Cena would connect with one of his finishing moves. He represented a change that so many people wanted to see. I was overcome by that passion. After five years of Cena being on top, I personally needed a guy like Punk to come forward and renew my non-WrestleMania season interest.

In hindsight, the Punk-Cena rivalry on-screen reflected the Punk vs. WWE story backstage. It was fitting. The "Pipe Bomb" shoved WWE into what became known as the "Reality Era," in which WWE used rumored real life circumstances with their television characters to craft a product full of blurred lines between what is real and what is scripted. Punk was the anti-Cena and the pair made for incredibly interesting foils. I once wrote a series of short stories linking them to the fantasy comic scenario of Superman vs. Batman. Cena was unquestionably the WWE's "Man of Steel," with Punk playing the role of the "Dark Knight." For years, WWE was a live, sports entertainment version of a Superman comic (some might say it still is). It was almost too bright a world for a gray personality to thrive, but we live in a society that gravitates toward the intricate complexities of characters like Punk. To watch Punk and Cena do battle was, therefore, to witness a microcosm of WWE's desire to be one thing while the most arduous sect of their fanbase wished for them to be something else. Each Punk victory over Cena – the Straight Edge star never lost a title match to WWE's Golden Boy – seemed to take WWE one step closer to the next step in its history, without ever actually crossing the threshold.

The result of Punk vs. Cena was a situation that made the entire product better. They did a great job of challenging each other to be the best that they could be. When they wrestled or cut promos leading up to their matches, everyone else was forced to step up their games, as well. Punk vs. Cena produced some of the best commentary that Michael Cole has ever done, for instance. The WWE title was elevated by their matches too. They challenged some of the all-time great rivalries.

2011's "Pipe Bomb" marked the beginning of what has become known as the second "Summer of Punk." Until he unceremoniously left WWE, he was the best thing on WWE TV. He skyrocketed up the list of WrestleMania Era superstars with his modern day record 434 day WWE Championship reign from *Survivor Series 2011* to *Royal Rumble 2013*. I have seen every title reign of the last twenty-eight years and perhaps only Ric Flair's 1987-1989, Shawn Michaels' 1996, and Cena's 2006-2007 reigns produced matches of the consistent excellence that did Punk's. He had amazing, catch-as-catch-can style matches with Chris Jericho. He had brilliant technically themed matches with Daniel Bryan on TV and on two PPVs. He had very good matches with big men like Mark Henry, Big Show, and Kane. He dragged watchable matches out of the unseasoned powerhouse known as Ryback. He knocked another one out of the park against Cena. Then, he capped it off with a pair of underrated bouts against The Rock.

Be it through his mic work or in between the ropes, there was nobody in the world better between 2011-2013 than CM Punk. Everything that he was involved with clicked, perhaps no more so than his *WrestleMania 29* feud with Undertaker. His fresh take on challenging The Streak was excellent. It was about creating a personal issue that made him a believable threat. I was there in Met Life Stadium that night. Punk and Taker had us all in the palm of their hands as they produced one of the best matches that I have ever seen live. When Punk kicked out of the Tombstone piledriver, I grabbed my buddy, Tony, by his jacket and hollered in disbelief. Punk vs. Taker stole the show.

Punk embodied a quest for change. When the Second City Saint finally did leave WWE after *Royal Rumble 2014*, it became apparent that Punk and WWE were as oil and water a mixture of wrestler and promotion that the modern era, or perhaps any era, had ever seen. For nearly three glorious years, Punk was a top guy, second only to John Cena in the hierarchy, but it was a near constant struggle. As much as he was able to break the glass ceiling, headlining WrestleManias against Chris Jericho and Undertaker, he wanted more. In the minds of many a fan, he should have been given more. What it boiled down to was a tug of war between a new school talent and an old school mentality. Punk was about the furthest thing from a traditional top guy. Should that have mattered? It depends on your perspective. WWE has always been a company that has had to concern itself with more than talent. In the NFL, Russell Wilson may not be the quarterback prototype, but he is a winner that gets the job done. That is enough. In WWE, that is not enough. You have to be more than just an outstanding pro wrestler to be the top WWE Superstar. Punk was never willing to accept that. Such was clear when listening to his late 2014 interviews reflecting on his departure (before signing with UFC). And that's OK. His WWE legacy is intact, regardless. He did, in fact, make change.

There have been a lot of words written about CM Punk since his abrupt retirement; not all of them positive. I can honestly say that my opinion of him never changed. When I reflect on Punk's WWE career, I will think about that promo and the impact that it (and all that followed it) had on my perception of WWE's modern history. I will remember being at Met Life for the match with Taker. I will remember the brilliant stories that he told on the 20'X20' canvas (like his *Summerslam 2013* match with Brock Lesnar). He may not have been my favorite wrestler but, for those two years, he was what my friend, Mattberg, called "my fan anchor." He was the main reason why I watched wrestling on a weekly basis between 2011 and 2013.

#20: Lex Luger

Do not make the mistake of underestimating the contributions that Lex Luger made to the wrestling industry. When talk begins of a former University of Miami football player that made it big in the WrestleMania Era, most people would assume that the topic is Dwayne "The Rock" Johnson and not "The Total Package" Lex Luger. He was one of the key figures of the war between the NWA/WCW and the WWE and a man who, like so many others, found himself on both sides of the front. He ended up on the losing side which, combined with the controversy surrounding his role a decade ago in the beloved Miss Elizabeth's drug overdose, have made efforts to properly remember him a bit more difficult. Time will heal the wounds, though, and he will be in the Hall of Fame someday.

For those of you that grew up watching wrestling after 1990, the Evolution faction spearheaded by Triple H in the early-to-mid 2000s did not invent the storyline that turned Dave Batista from awesomely physiqued specimen into full-fledged superstar. It was The Four Horsemen - bringing in Lex Luger to be their fifth member in 1987 - which prominently came up with that arc. Luger had his run with the group, capturing the United States Championship as Ric Flair's #2. Yet, when the stable's manager, JJ Dillon, cost Luger the US title to Dusty Rhodes at *Starrcade '87*, the seed was planted for Lex to change his allegiance.

The Total Package split off from the group and was the NWA's potential answer to Hulk Hogan. He was more athletic than Hogan, but he had only been a professional wrestler for three years when he got his first crack at the World title at the 1988 *Great American Bash*. His performances showed that he was more than ready. He was actually quite a good in-ring competitor in the late 1980s. The further he got into his career, it seemed that he regressed in many ways, but those early years were full of great matches. His first title match with Flair set the tone for their lengthy, off-again, on-again rivalry. Luger was never able to win the title from The Nature Boy, but he was brilliant in his attempts. At the *'88 Bash*, Flair got lucky. Luger suffered a cut on the forehead, thanks to Flair ramming him into the ring post, and – despite putting Flair in the Torture Rack – the match was subsequently stopped due to the state athletic commission's appointed physician. The crowd, though, thought that Flair had given up and that Luger was the new champion. It was one of those moments that effectively put the heat on Flair for getting by via the skin of his teeth, while also getting the people even more firmly behind Luger as the guy that they wanted to see win the title.

Their rematch at *Starrcade '88* was tremendous. In some ways, it was the Batista vs. Triple H of its era. The difference was that Lex did not win. Luger surely could have and it always surprised me that he did not. It was perfectly set up for him to become "The Man." Unfortunately, Flair was on such a roll that it was simply not deemed the right time for him to pass the torch. It certainly looked like it would be all the way up until Flair blasted Luger's leg with a steel chair and eventually locked on the Figure Four. Flair looked to have had it won. When Luger battled out and put Flair in the Torture Rack, though, it seemed that Luger would prevail and his big moment had arrived. That was not the case, as Luger's leg gave out and Flair fell right on top of him for the 1-2-3. It was, in my opinion, the greatest match in Starrcade history and it was without question the best performance of Luger's career. He worked his tail off and showed wonderful conditioning in working a heated 30-minute contest. Anyone who claims that Luger could not work needs to watch the main-event of *Starrcade '88*...

The competition with Flair was put on hold until 1990, but Luger still became a big star even though he did not win the NWA World title. Luger's feud with The Horsemen continued, as he took the US Championship off of former partner, Barry Windham. Being US Champion back then was a big deal. It was held mostly by men featured in this book, actually, and was defended on blockbuster cards in headlining positions. Luger was arguably the greatest US titleholder of all-time, recording the longest reign of any US champ in history at 523 days. He turned heel during the early stages of his historic run in the division, prompted by a confrontation with Ricky Steamboat. The Dragon had been able to do what Luger could not in defeating The Nature Boy for the World Heavyweight Championship. Luger's jealousy drove him to want to show the world that he was better than Steamboat, segueing to a match at the *'89 Great American Bash*.

Luger did well as a heel. One could argue that his swagger from his gridiron days made him a natural antagonist. His extended work against Flair the year prior seemed to have rubbed off on him a bit. He was never going to be able to match his charisma to his physical gifts, but a guy with a build like Luger did not need to be a master of the microphone to be effective. For instance, he did a simple pre-match promo prior to the showdown at *The Bash* with Steamboat where he demanded that the stipulation of "No DQ" be removed. Had Flair done that, assuredly he would have been overridden, but the advantage of having a top heel with an imposing stature like Luger was that you could conceivably understand why no authority figure would want to mess with him. The stipulation was dropped and they had a nice match. It would be one of many solid performances from Luger during his reign as US Champion.

As the face of the United States title division, Lex became a seasoned pro. In his first four years in the NWA, Luger held the US championship 65% of the time. He subsequently learned what it took to be a leader and used the division to develop an antagonistic character. Though he would occasionally step up to the World Heavyweight title ranks to take on Flair, Luger spent the majority of his time preparing to one day supplant The Nature Boy as the company's top bad guy.

The NWA was known for putting the World title on a heel, so even though guys like Sting were emerging as better babyfaces, Luger's spot was fairly secure as long as he could shore up the role of successor to Flair. Jim Ross pegged him as one of the leading candidates to "rule our sport" in the 1990s.

You can make an argument that it was a shame that the NWA seemed so intent on making Sting the babyface of the company. Throughout Luger's reigns as US Champion from '89-'91, he was routinely cheered. He had to work extra hard to ensure that he earned the jeers. Luger and Flair could have had one of the most legendary NWA title rivalries had Flair not won every match. The people were always looking for excuses to fully get behind Lex. They went bananas when he temporarily turned face in 1990 for title matches with Flair at *Wrestle War* and *Capitol Combat*. Luger and Flair made each other look like a million bucks every time that they wrestled, even though Lex never beat him. Naitch was easily Luger's greatest opponent, portraying him as wrestling's version of *The Terminator*. Lex worked better as a babyface, in my opinion. His best match list has a top five consisting of nothing but matches with him as the protagonist. It is not that he failed to be a good heel. He was a cocky son of a gun. It should have been easy to dislike him, but it was not.

After his second series of matches with Flair, Luger went back to being the biggest fish in the US title pond through the rest of 1990 and into 1991, but a fantastic Tag Team title match where he teamed with Sting to face The Steiner Brothers at the first *Super Brawl* gave him a lot of momentum to get back into the WCW title (NWA split with WCW by then) picture and set up what looked to finally be his championship winning moment. However, before it could happen, Flair left the company and went to the WWE. Luger did win the WCW World title, but it came in a match against old rival, Barry Windham. The vacated title presented an intriguing scenario. Luger was a babyface seemingly set to the win the title, but he was also the best that the company had, with Flair gone, to play the role of top heel. Windham could have certainly done well as the top heel, but he did not have the lengthy build-up to it that did Luger. So, a rare double turn took place at the *'91 Great American Bash* in the main-event for the vacant championship. Harley Race came back as a heel manager and aligned with Luger, who in winning the title also quickly changed allegiances and was given the daunting task of replacing Flair. It was a challenge that Luger was ready for.

Unfortunately, WCW was being run by a bunch of people unfamiliar with the wrestling business. Jim Herd, a former Pizza Hut manager, basically ran Flair out of the company. His mishandling of Luger, the successor to Flair, was equally as stupid a move. I thought Luger was a great heel. In one segment, he managed to get Ron Simmons over as one of the top babyfaces in wrestling. He asked Simmons to be his chauffeur, insinuating that he was not good enough to be anything else, leading to the main-event at *Halloween Havoc '91*. Luger may have incorrectly taken the blame for financial success dropping from the abrupt departure of their long-time top draw (Flair) and, subsequently, they rarely did anything with Luger for the remainder of his 7-month reign as WCW Champion. The focus, rather, switched to the man that had essentially been his competition for becoming the new face of WCW once Flair left: Sting. The Stinger's quest to regain the World title took precedent over Luger's reign as champion, with Sting being the show closing act at *Starrcade '91* at Luger's expense. Sting won the Battle Bowl to become the #1 contender, setting up the showdown with Luger at *Super Brawl II* in February of 1992.

Many would suggest that Flair leaving WCW in 1991 was the end of an era, but I would counter that it was Luger leaving in 1992 that truly ended said era. Flair had groomed Luger and Sting since 1987 to take over for him as the leading men in the company. Naitch handed WCW their next great rivalry on a silver platter and they threw it away. Luger vs. Sting at *Super Brawl II*, for Luger's WCW Championship, drew the highest PPV buyrate that WCW would draw until Hulk Hogan vs. Ric Flair two and a half years later. WCW could have thrived on the Sting-Luger rivalry for a long time. Alas, Luger dropped the belt to Sting and left the company. When Luger left, it was as if much of what Flair had attempted to build was thrown away, too. Sting was left to fend for himself and WCW marched on, but you just could not ask one person to replace a guy like Flair, one of the top 5 stars of all-time. WCW needed Luger.

At *WrestleMania VIII*, Luger surprisingly showed up as a "member" of the WWE's new World Bodybuilding Federation, but it was never in the plans for Luger to become a bodybuilder. Instead, it was just a way for the WWE to have Luger appear without breaching a non-compete clause in his WCW contract. It started a three year run for Lex in the WWE, but before he ever got started on the wrestling side of things he was involved in a motorcycle accident. The injuries that he suffered firmly established a turning point in his career. Sadly, the biggest mainstream wrestling company and its fans never got to see what Luger could do in the ring as a result of his injuries. He returned to wrestle for the WWE, but his in-ring skills had noticeably diminished.

Performance Factor aside, Luger wasted little time becoming a main-event player in the WWE. By mid-1993, he was wrestling for the WWE Championship. *Summerslam '93* was his most significant night with the company, as though he failed to win the title, the PPV was built around his match with Yokozuna. He would also go on to co-win the '94 Royal Rumble match and be involved in a championship rematch with Yoko at *WrestleMania X*. That short, nine month period was the extent of his relevant WWE run, at least compared to what he had been in WCW. The most interesting note of his WWE tenure was that they tried to turn him into Hulk Hogan, similar to how the NWA had once flirted with doing the same. Apropos, the rest of his career, seemingly, would revolve around the Hulkster in some way.

In one of the most famous nights of the Monday Night War, on the very first night that shots were fired with the debut episode of *Monday Nitro*, Luger showed up during the main-event to admonish Hogan. Everyone – even Vince McMahon – thought that Lex was still working with the WWE. Luger had been working a handshake, non-contractually obligated agreement with Vince. Signing and debuting him right out from under WWE created some noise about the WCW show. After losing to Hogan by DQ the following week, Luger embarked on a two year journey to destroy him. He joined The Dungeon of Doom stable to help other Hogan rivals take him down and was one of the key players that spearheaded an agreement between The Dungeon and The Four Horsemen to create the "Alliance to End Hulkamania." Things really got interesting, though, in '96 when Hogan turned heel and formed The New World Order.

Luger will always be remembered as a WCW guy. He, along with Ric Flair, Arn Anderson, and Sting, were the biggest names that WCW had produced in the early WrestleMania Era. Collectively, they were the natural opponents to face an entity that was made up predominantly of wrestlers best known for their time in the WWE. Luger and Sting, though, were the two that legitimately could threaten The N.W.O. – the ones that had the most natural animosity built toward Hogan and to whomever he chose to associate with. Sting had been "The Franchise" of WCW until Hogan stormed in and stole his thunder. Luger had been forced into a "Hogan-esque" role in WWE that was doomed from the start, only to return to WCW and face Hogan numerous times with laughably minimal success. Hogan and a partner had even defeated Luger and *EIGHT* other guys in a Handicap match. Nobody needed to give Hogan some comeuppance more than Luger.

For a year, Lex did his best to give WCW, which was getting owned at every turn in the feud with The N.W.O., some hopeful moments. Luger scored the biggest blow when he defeated Hollywood Hogan for the WCW Championship on the August 4, 1997 edition of *Nitro*. Hogan had been champion for almost a year and WCW had failed numerous times to regain their signature title. Luger only held the belt until the following weekend's PPV, but it was the little victory that WCW needed to bridge the gap between the summer and the height of The N.W.O.'s feud with Sting that would carry WCW to *Starrcade*. I would argue that, of the entire storyline of WCW vs. NWO, Luger's title victory on *Nitro* was the highlight since Sting's victory at Starrcade was so poorly handled. Luger's win was the crowd pleasing, awesomely scripted win for WCW that you would expect in professional wrestling. That night in August '97 was the crescendo for *Nitro* in the Monday Night War, as the booking decisions started going in the wrong direction from then on. The same could be said for Luger, whose career hit its final peak that evening.

The Total Package of the late NWA days is the Lex Luger that I remember. The younger, pre-injury/pre-WWE version was a great young performer with a ton of potential. I liken him to Anfernee "Penny" Hardaway, one of my all-time favorite basketball players who showed a similar potential only to be derailed by an injury. They sure were special before they got hurt. History has virtually forgotten Penny, who I once named a dog after, and not even in *The Book of Basketball* did he get anything but hate. I do not wish for the same to be said of Lex Luger. The former two-time World Champion had as good an in-ring resume as anyone not named Ric Flair, Ricky Steamboat, or Randy Savage from 1987-1991. He was, perhaps, the greatest United States Champion of all-time, as well as a WrestleMania headliner, Royal Rumble winner, and the one guy to defeat Hollywood Hogan clean at the height of The New World Order's power. *That* was Lex Luger.

#19: The Big Show

WWE Champion twice; WCW Heavyweight Champion twice; WWE World Heavyweight Champion twice; only man to hold the WWE, WCW, and ECW World Championships; United States Champion once; Intercontinental Champion once; WWE Tag Team Champion six times; WCW Tag Team Champion three times; top drawing match at two WrestleManias; headlining match at one other WrestleMania; winner of 1996 *World War 3* Battle Royal; the best talker of all the super heavyweights; Top 20 overall in Wrestler Score; #2 ranked in-ring performer of the super heavyweights; Unquestionably the most physically imposing figure in wrestling history (a cross between Steve Austin's intense face and Andre's size).

Big Show has quietly become one of the legends in the sport. Time goes by so fast that it is easy to forget that he has been wrestling for twenty years. Over that span, the career of the "World's Largest Athlete" can be told in three sections:

WCW

WWE cites Randy Orton as the youngest World Heavyweight Champion in history. What they meant was the WWE's history. The youngest World Champion in modern wrestling lore was actually Big Show, then known as "The Giant." He debuted at *Halloween Havoc 1995* at 23 years old and won the WCW Championship from Hulk Hogan, the man responsible for bringing him into the company. A former basketball player at Wichita State, Show was quite agile for his size, drawing comparisons to Andre almost immediately. They even suggested that he was Andre's (storyline) kid. Much like the Frenchman as a young man, this new Giant could do "anything that a man 200 pounds could do," as William Regal once noted.

Being so young, large, and athletic, he was easy to sculpt into one of wrestling's next great stars. Recall that WCW was stocked full of icons from the 80s wrestling boom. Before his 25th birthday, Show had been in main-events with Hogan, Ric Flair, Sting, and Lex Luger (among others). His run at the top in WCW might have proven far more historically relevant had it not been for The New World Order taking over in 1996. He went from the WCW Champ and top heel to taking a huge backseat to Hogan, Hall, and Nash. In another era, he could have had a Yokozuna-in-WWE caliber year, at least.

Youth did not serve him well in that political cesspool. His next two years in WCW were like everyone else's – mired by disorganized booking and poor executive decision making that threatened Show's long-term career and the company's future. Through feuds with a host of the big names in the industry, he was a hot commodity and a big name during wrestling's most popular time period, but he was one of many rebels without cause.

His decision to sign with the WWE was a no-brainer. Vince McMahon, theoretically, knew just how to book him, after years of handling Andre's career.

WWE: Part 1

I was over at my friend Tommy's house watching *St. Valentine's Day Massacre* when Steve Austin looked to have the evil Vince McMahon beaten in a Steel Cage match. Then, out of nowhere, this mammoth of a man busts out from beneath the ring and emerges like the Kraken from *Clash of the Titans*. "That's Paul Wight," yelled Michael Cole. Just like that, Show was a major player in the WWE, heavily involved in the build-up to the WWE Championship match at *WrestleMania XV*.

It did not take long, though, to realize that he was struggling to adapt to the WWE. He floundered for quite a bit after a strong initial push. It was said that the WWE wanted him to stay sculpted, which would have continued to give him one advantage over Andre. However, both Show and Andre were stricken with the same condition – acromegaly – though Show's was relatively under control after a teenage surgery halted the progression. In WCW, Show was in great shape, but the rigors of the WWE road schedule clearly took their toll and he ballooned in size. The more weight on his frame, the less healthy he was and the less effective in the ring. Those early years were mired by his fluctuation from spectacular looking giant to super huge even for a huge guy.

Despite his struggles both with his health and his in-ring performance, he showed a lot of promise as a personality. Perhaps the greatest difference between WWE and WCW was the emphasis that Vince placed on in-depth characters to draw in casual viewers. Show was given the opportunity to express his range of emotions in a storyline that ultimately led to his becoming quite popular with the audience; to the point that he was the last-minute replacement for Austin in the WWE Championship match at the 1999 *Survivor Series*. Much to everyone's surprise, Show won the title. Though a transition champion, he was well-positioned at the top of the card during the stretch leading to one of the most profitable WrestleManias to that point. He lost the title to Triple H but stayed in the hunt to regain it all the way to his first and only Mania main-event, a Fatal Fourway also involving Trips, The Rock, and Mick Foley in 2000.

In sports psychology, there has been much talk about the phenomenon of an athlete being given too much, too soon. I think the fact that Big Show was eliminated in the first six-minutes of the near forty-minute main-event at *Mania 2000* suggested that the WWE had lost faith in him. Was he a victim of too much, too soon? Well, imagine being a guy who felt inherently flawed by a particular attribute. Let us say you had a really awkward voice. You are thinking that your life stinks and that you will never find your place in life, in large part because of your voice. Yet, one day, a hugely successful animated filmmaker hears you talking at a restaurant and gives you a job that ultimately makes you millions of dollars over the course of a fairly short career. Every film that needs a voiceover from "awkward voice guy" goes to you. That was Big Show in wrestling. He found his home in professional wrestling and it was the perfect profession for him. Now, let us say you were in your early twenties, which means that you are an idiot with limited life experience who thinks he knows everything. Some director makes you work hard and expand your range. You get upset and nearly cost yourself the career that you are literally suited perfectly for. Again, that was Show.

To make him appreciate his craft, the WWE sent him from the main-event of *WrestleMania* with 800,000 PPV buyers and TV ratings that averaged 5.88 in the year 2000 to the developmental territory wrestling in front of fifty people. It was a necessary step for him, but an unbelievably drastic change. He never had to go through the wars to get his main roster spot. Within six months of training in WCW, he was called up to become the World Champ. It was the best thing in the world for him to be sent down to developmental, at least in the long run. In the short-term, he got very out of shape, apparently quit trying, and was de-pushed for all of 2001. He missed *WrestleMania* altogether in 2002 just a month after his 30th birthday.

Maybe it was leaving his twenties that woke him up. Something sure did. When he joined *Smackdown* in the fall of '02, he engaged in the feuds that became the two best of his career, first with Undertaker and the other with Brock Lesnar.

If I was prompted to name Show's top career rival, I would likely choose Brock. They had an odd chemistry. Show seemed to suddenly click with the WWE style of performance when he started working with Lesnar and it had a profound effect on the rest of his career. After spending the latter part of the fall working with Brock for the WWE Championship, he had a match with Taker at *No Way Out* in February '03. It was not excellent, as their future battles years later would be, but it was such a stark improvement over his work with other wrestlers.

After becoming a historical footnote as part of the 21 in Taker's vaunted Streak at WrestleMania, Show went back to the Lesnar feud over the title. Paul Heyman, who was very positively influential on Show's career whenever they got to work together, turned on Brock at *Survivor Series '02* and helped Show win the title. Brock cost Show the belt the next month and then beat Show at the *Royal Rumble* to be the final entrant in the '03 Rumble match. When they picked back up in the spring, their title match on *Smackdown* (Lesnar had regained it by then) led to the famous moment where the ring collapsed under the weight of their sky high superplex. It was like seeing Shaq break the backboard with a dunk, only multiplied times a hundred. It was unbelievable.

Though the ring-breaker was their most famous bout, I was there at *Judgment Day 2003* when they had their best match, a Stretcher match that involved the use of a forklift to give Brock the victory. Their feud kept on, with Kurt Angle entering the fray for the main-event at the first-ever *Smackdown*, brand-only PPV, *Vengeance*. That was where the Show-Brock feud concluded, with a final tally of four PPV matches (three of which were for the title and all of which were favorably reviewed), three title changes due to their direct actions against each other, the return of a gimmick that has only been used two other times in the modern era, and one collapsed ring.

His first run in the WWE concluded with a six month stretch on the new *ECW* brand. He became the ECW Champion and was used to get the new version of the formerly extreme company over with a fresh audience. It was the best work of his career, to that point. On a near weekly basis, he was allowed to use the skills that had often been purposefully held in check due to the idea that he should rarely deviate from wrestling like a giant. To be honest, he probably overdid it in ECW, but he needed to find a balance between working like a 7-footer and using his athleticism. I think he had a fundamental desire to show everyone that he could work smaller and faster and put his body on the line just like all the other guys. It certainly endeared him to me, as I was not overly fond of him until then. More importantly, I would imagine that it earned him the everlasting respect of his peers.

WWE: Part 2

My perception of Big Show changed for good when he returned to the WWE in February 2008 to set up a match with Floyd Mayweather at *WrestleMania XXIV*. He had slimmed down considerably since the last time that we had seen him in 2006 and looked to be in the best shape that he had been in since 2000. Mayweather, the top box office draw in boxing for years, was contracted to work *Mania 24* through Shane McMahon. He sat in the front row at *No Way Out*, but hopped the guardrail and got into the ring to confront Show in defense of the injured Rey Mysterio. Show did not appreciate it and tried to punk out the welterweight, going so far as to mock him by getting down on his knees. In one of those rare WWE moments that ended up on *Sportscenter*, Mayweather proceeded to legitimately break Show's nose, inciting The World's Largest Athlete to move faster than he had ever moved before to chase him down. The story was well covered in the mainstream media, with *USA Today* even covering the "official weigh-in" before Mania.

The expectations for the "match" were quite low. Nobody even knew what kind of match that they were going to have before Lillian Garcia announced it just minutes prior to the opening bell. Yet, when they did start, Big Show embraced the spotlight in the biggest match of his career and guided the way to a very pleasant surprise. There is a delicate balance in those situations between making the outsider look good and maintaining the integrity of pro wrestling. The massive size difference between them was a sight to see, but Show had to be spot-on in respectably selling Floyd's offense without giving up too much ground. There is also a tendency for the live crowd to be fairly quiet during matches involving outsiders, but Show did an excellent job of getting the Orlando audience heavily engaged. To Mayweather's credit, he held up his end of the bargain, but it was based largely on Show's merits that they had the best match involving a celebrity that I have seen in my thirty years as a fan.

I am, at heart, a Big Show fan because of his match with Floyd Mayweather. From that point forward, I started openly campaigning, on the internet, for Show to be involved in one of the main-event title matches at the following year's WrestleMania. I thought that he had most definitely earned the right after what he had accomplished with Floyd.

For Show, 2008 was the kind of year that made you revisit 2006 and better appreciate what he had accomplished in ECW before his hiatus. Sometimes in sports, you get so used to seeing mediocrity from a particular player that you come to expect it. Since the WWE often lacks quality commentators who point out small improvements like you would see in football or baseball, it takes a consistent and marked change in a wrestler for the masses to notice. Stuck on the lowest rated WWE TV program in '06, the work that Show was doing went largely unseen. For those of us that did see it, we could look back on it and recognize that he was much better in ECW and it was not a surprise when he rattled off a career year in '08.

If it was not his career defining work against Floyd that earned him the spot that he has held these last several years, then surely it was the aforementioned matches with Taker. In

October 2008, Show earned perhaps the most impressive victory of his entire career when he knocked out The Deadman with the KO Punch, prompting the referee to actually stop the match. Think about that for a moment – the guy undefeated at Mania with a sparkling win/loss record across the board was so incapacitated (kayfabe) that the official did not think he could go on. That was an amazing moment for Show. The match itself was excellent. Taker was Show's WWE mentor; some day, when he retires and does interviews out of character, I hope someone asks him about his 2008 matches with Show just to hear what he says about how far his protégé had come since his early days. They had two more matches that garnered praise from the wrestling media; a Last Man Standing match at *Cyber Sunday* and a Casket match at *Survivor Series*.

He got his much deserved World Heavyweight Championship match at the *25th Anniversary of WrestleMania*, losing to John Cena in a triple threat match also involving Edge. Since then, he has quietly been adding to his resume, crushing it with Chris Jericho as "Jeri-Show" in 2009, wowing audiences in World Heavyweight Championship matches against Mark Henry and Sheamus in 2011 and 2012, respectively, winning the World title from Alberto Del Rio in 2013, having an underrated Last Man Standing match with Roman Reigns in 2015, and turning between babyface and heel a record 1,460 times.

When Big Show finally retires, it will be nearly impossible to replace him. There comes along a giant who can do what he can do but once in a generation or two. I am unsure that there will ever be a better giant.

#18: Mick Foley

Mick Foley accomplished a lot in the wrestling business. He was one of the greatest of all-time, perhaps forgotten for his role in creating the success that the WWE achieved during the vaunted Attitude Era. Yet, it is not his famous 25 foot fall off Hell in a Cell, his WWE Championship victory on *Raw* in January 1999, or willingness to give up his long-term health for our entertainment that makes me most fondly remember him. What set him apart was that he spectacularly put over four of the biggest stars in industry history, who between them have combined for 47 World Championships. In mafia movies, a new member of a crime family is "made," or initiated into the elite. In wrestling, a headliner is "made" when an already established star does the honors for him in a major match (or matches). If it were not for Foley, neither The Rock, Triple H, Randy Orton, nor Edge would have ascended to the heights that they did in their careers – that is 25% of the remaining pages in this book after Foley's chapter.

Edge was on the precipice of something special when Foley got involved with him. The Rated R Superstar was a big win at WrestleMania away from being solidified as the top heel in the company. A Hardcore match on the grand stage was Foley's element and a victory in that environment would take Edge to the next level. Meanwhile, the one thing lacking on Mick's excellent resume in the WWE was a defining match at "The Showcase of the Immortals." He had a signature performance at every other major event in the WWE, but it had always failed to come together for him on the biggest night of WWE's year.

Their match took place at the first WrestleMania that I ever attended. Edge is one of my all-time favorites. The thought of him mixing it up with "The Hardcore Legend" in a gimmick that quite frankly was ready made for both of them - given Edge's not equal, but still well-known propensity for putting his body on the line, ala Foley - made their match the most highly anticipated on the card for me.

Foley was at his in-ring creative best that night. *Mania 22* saw Foley wrap himself in barbed wire under his signature flannel shirt. When Edge speared him early on in the match, Foley was hurt, but it was his opponent that was incapacitated with a lacerated arm. Sadly, the genre of hardcore was watered down in the WWE when they ran the concept into the ground during the Attitude Era. When a Hardcore match is about more than just two guys whacking each other with weapons, then it can be very special. Foley vs. Edge was special. It was not designed to be epic, but it was a great piece of work that accomplished everything that it needed to. Foley put Edge in position to, ultimately, become a first ballot Hall of Famer.

Rewind the clock to 2003 and the WWE was banking on the elevation of Randy Orton to help build the next group that would supplant the holdovers from the Attitude Era. The WWE did everything in their power to put the 23-year old in a position to succeed, placing him in the dominant stable of the era and feeding him stars on a weekly basis to build his reputation as "The Legend Killer." Yet, the look, the push, the faction, and the skills would not have mattered had someone like Foley not stepped up to the plate and given him a rivalry in which he could gain experience as a featured player in a top tier, fiscally important storyline. He allowed Orton to throw him down a flight of steps at MSG, to spit in his face, to punk him out and make him look like a coward, to legitimately punch him to the point of drawing blood and blackening his eye, to beat him at *WrestleMania XX* in his first match in four years, and then to beat him again in his signature match (another Hardcore, Falls Count Anywhere type). Foley actually made Orton look so good at 23-24 years old that nobody ever lived up to that standard. Not another wrestler did the job for Orton that well again.

Their match at *Backlash 2004* was one of the best of the last decade. It was built up for nearly a year, with several twists and turns along the way, mostly designed to favor Orton. It showed a complete lack of ego on Foley's part. No caveats, no excuses, no "looking good in loss"; it was all about him seeing potential in a new star and taking it upon himself to be the one that elevated him. Foley said during the build-up that "Hardcore meant that I cared enough about the fans to put my body through unimaginable pain." They certainly lived up to that definition. They used a bed of barbed wire, a barbed wire bat, and thousands of thumbtacks, among other weapons. The story that they told of Foley earning redemption after all those months of being jumped, embarrassed, and beaten was quite compelling. Somehow, Orton managed to defeat him and came away looking like a million bucks.

Foley was retired for the second time. The first time had come at the hands of Triple H in the year 2000. He and Trips had a long history with one another, dating back to the summer of 1997, when Hunter's matches with "The Three Faces of Foley" - Mankind, Dude Love, and Cactus Jack - put him on the map as "one to watch." They wrestled at three straight PPVs, with Trips winning the King of the Ring Final, the two splitting the July rematch with a no contest, and Mankind picking up the victory in an underrated Steel Cage match at *Summerslam* that allowed Foley to relive his childhood memory of the Superfly Splash off the top of the cage. Two years later on *Raw*, Trips beat him for the WWE title, which Foley had won for a third and final time on the previous night at *Summerslam '99*.

The two hooked up again at the beginning of 2000. He challenged Trips to a WWE title match at *The Royal Rumble*. Foley ditched the tried and true Mankind persona in favor of the more renowned "hardcore" Cactus Jack, building nearly unequaled momentum on television leading up to the Madison Square Garden Street Fight. Few times in history have seen a challenger more primed to defeat a champion, so when Triple H cleanly defeated Jack after a thirty-minute war that doubled as the finest display of "hardcore" gimmickry in the WWE main-event style and the 2000 Match of the Year, "The Game" had arrived at a level that very few wrestlers ever reach in their careers; one where they are more than just main-event talents, but could conceivably be viewed as the clear cut number one or number two guy in the business.

A month later at *No Way Out* (the highest grossing February PPV ever) Foley put his career on the line in the gimmick that had taken his fame to new heights in 1998: Hell in a Cell. For a thirty-four year old wrestler to hang up his boots when he was one of the top five guys in the most profitable era in sports entertainment history seemed far-fetched. Everything was setting up for a Foley title win, adding a wrinkle to *WrestleMania 2000*. Yet, in a microcosm of some of his unforgettable matches, which saw him bleed buckets, light a barbed wire-wrapped 2X4 on fire, fall off the side of the Cell and through a table, and then be backdropped through the top of the Cell down to the ring (breaking it upon impact), Foley lost to Triple H again. There is not a better way to put over another wrestler then to hang your career in the balance as a stipulation, lose, and stay retired. Foley, in an environment full of massive egos that hang on dearly to their spots at the top, was the most unselfish big name in the history of the sport.

Foley did come back for *WrestleMania 2000's* main-event Fatal Fourway Elimination match, putting over Trips one last time on the grand stage and stamping his own legacy to have earned that spot and confirmed his drawing power. With him and Triple H as the focal points of the January and February PPVs and integral parts of Mania, the WWE rattled off the strongest three month span of PPV buyrates in the near twenty year history of monthly PPVs. He walked off into the sunset for four years afterwards, cementing Trips for his top main-event years as "the guy who retired Mick Foley."

On top of his underestimated PPV drawing power, Foley was also a part of wrestling's highest rated cable TV segment, hosting "This is your life, Rock" on *Raw* in the fall of 1999 during the early stages of his iconically ironic partnership with "The Great One." Before the classic duo known as "The Rock and Sock Connection" was established, Foley was concluding a career year in 1998 and had made it to the finals of the WWE Championship tournament at *Survivor Series: A Deadly Game*. The Rock, a budding hero, joined forces with the evil Corporation and became their Corporate Champion, screwing Foley over in the process. The perception of Rock was that he was more "the future" than "the present" at the time, necessitating that he earn some convincing victories over a well-known commodity to maximize the success of his first title reign and to fully prepare him for his *WrestleMania XV* main-event with Steve Austin.

Foley, who had already presented a strong challenge to former champions in the previous two years, seemed eager to do the job spectacularly. He and Rock wrestled on four consecutive PPVs from November '98 to February '99 and in three other memorable television matches. They traded the WWE title back and forth, with Foley memorably winning the title on the January 4, 1999 edition of *Monday Night Raw* opposite of WCW *Nitro's* infamous "finger poke of doom" match between Hulk Hogan and Kevin Nash. Tony Schiavone, WCW's ringside commentator, read the results of the taped WWE program's main-event and mockingly snickered "That'll put a lot of butts in the seats." Six hundred thousand people immediately changed the channel to *Raw*, awarding the WWE the ratings victory. They never lost another head-to-head battle. Mankind named "I Quit" as the stipulation for their title rematch at *The Royal Rumble*. It was the biggest main-event in Foley's career, doubling the buyrate for the previous year's show.

One of the great things about the Attitude Era was the investment that people had in so many of the characters. Mankind was the WWE's version of Rocky Balboa. He was not supposed to be WWE Champion, headlining big shows and bringing in ratings, but fans connected with him. When watching Mankind vs. The Rock, you were seeing two of the most popular stars ever in their respective primes. As far as "I Quit" matches go, theirs was the greatest of all-time that did not also involve a Steel Cage (including the Flair vs. Funk version from ten years prior). The gimmick is set-up to have a lot of down time, with the ref asking the downed wrestler if he wants to give it up. Foley and Rock used it as an opportunity to trash talk each other and further incite the live audience. That was no easy task for the historically docile Arrowhead Pond in Anaheim.

When it came to taking punishment, Foley had a knack for making even something routine for the era look horrifying. For instance, when he ran knees first into the ring steps, he threw himself into them so hard that it looked like someone shot him in the legs. He took a hell of a beating from Rock, taking a DDT on concrete and bumping from 12 feet onto the speakers near the entrance. The Rock proceeded to handcuff Mankind's hands behind his back. Resiliently, Foley fought back, but there was only so much that he could do. Rock used a chair-assisted People's Elbow to knock him silly. What happened then was painful to watch, even playing it back today.

One unprotected chair shot to the head. A second. Mankind's response? "You'll have to kill me!" Three...Four...Five...Six...it was already uncomfortable by that point...Seven...Eight...Nine...Ten unprotected chair shots to the head, with his wife and kids in the crowd watching at ringside with some of the best seats in the house. His wife's reaction was famously caught on film in the documentary, *Beyond the Mat*. With Foley in a heap on the floor, his voice from their video promo, during which he said that Rock's last words would be, "I Quit! I Quit!" were piped in through the arena sound system, awarding the match and the title to The Rock. Most would argue that the 1998 Hell in a Cell with Undertaker was the most brutal on Foley's laundry list of violent matches, but none were more so, in my opinion, than the "I Quit" with Rock.

There is a difference between a great feud and a great rivalry. A great feud can be relatively one-sided in the win/loss column, whereas a great rivalry features each combatant winning his fair share of matches. The Patriots vs. the Colts in the NFL was a great rivalry because Tom Brady and Peyton Manning out-dueled one another on many occasions, whereas Jordan's Bulls dominated Ewing's Knicks to the tune of a great feud. That is how I see it. A rival is a person or a team that can beat you and yours. Foley's work with Edge, Orton, and Trips would all be examples of great feuds. Mankind vs. Rock was an outstanding rivalry.

Mankind regained the title from Rock in an Empty Arena match on *Halftime Heat* - the WWE's MTV special during the midway break of the Super Bowl - but put Rock over again at *St. Valentine's Day Massacre* in a Last Man Standing match. Rock won the final battle in a Ladder match. The drama of the multi-month saga made The Rock out to be one of the most bad ass wrestlers that ever "walked the face of God's green earth," as The Great One might say. Corporate and sharply dressed as he may have been, The People's Champ came out of his storyline with Foley with the reputation for being tough and resourceful. Foley came out of it with two title reigns that elevated him to the level of multi-time WWE Champion.

Nobody in wrestling history ever played the role of the "set-up man" any better than Foley. For four years between 1997 and 2000, he either was the wrestler responsible for better establishing the new champion after WrestleMania, as he did for Undertaker and Steve Austin, or given the task of making a very strong champion in the months leading up to

WrestleMania, as with Rock and Hunter. That should be his legacy.

Foley will unfortunately be best remembered for the Hell in a Cell match he had with Taker. There can be no denying the sheer visual quality of what Foley put himself through in that match. He got thrown, from a standing position, off the top of the Cell. No – correction for emphasis - he basically took a running leap off of it and crashed through the announce table below. It combined to be the most awesome, the dumbest, and the most famous stunt in the history of sports entertainment. No greater bump has ever been taken. And he did it on purpose! Lest we not forget that he also climbed back to the top of the Cell and got thrown *THROUGH* it, crashing in a heap on the ring mat below. He could barely stand up, but he eventually wrestled for several minutes and finished the match with one of his teeth caked to his nose with blood. Absolutely, it was the catalyst for the rest of his storied career. He nearly killed himself for the WWE and they rewarded him for it. Considerately, I would rather define his career by all that he accomplished and helped others accomplish.

Mick Foley, who became a Hall of Famer in 2013, finished his career as a three-time WWE Champion and 8-time Tag Team Champion, as well as the first Hardcore Champion. Along the way, he wrote multiple best-selling books that helped expand the scope of the WWE's public reach. He was also the sport's all-time most unselfish performer. And finally – with all due respect to Steve Austin – he was the world's toughest son of a bitch. God bless Mrs. Foley's baby boy. What a legend...

#17: Batista

Dave Batista has **THE** look of a star. If that was the only element that made for a professional wrestling icon, then he would have been an all-time great from the start. What he lacked in the beginning was the charisma and the skill to accompany his physique. He embarked on his wrestling career at a time (in his early thirties) when he should have been reaching his physical peak, steepening the learning curve and lessening the likelihood that he could put it all together. To his credit, he worked hard and figured it out en route to one of the finest careers in modern WWE history. It sure was a journey...

His look afforded him most of his early opportunities. It caught the attention of Triple H and Ric Flair as they were picking the two guys that would join them in the stable patterned after The Four Horsemen known as Evolution. He was paired with Flair in late 2002 and put into a feud with Kane that led to a match at December's *Armageddon* PPV. In a bout that showed that he was not quite ready to step up as a featured performer, Batista stumbled and bumbled through the climax after showing flashes of potential earlier on. Nevertheless, his power and presence kept him in the plans and Evolution soon materialized.

A year later at *Armageddon '03*, he got the chance to end a short, intense feud with Shawn Michaels. In the build-up, he had come across as improved, yet uncomfortable on the microphone. During the match, he appeared more confidant, but still got rattled after a mid-match gaffe. The finish went well and it was apparent that he seemed willing to put in the work under the tutelage of his Hall of Fame mentors.

Critically, it was easy to pick apart his game. His promos felt forced, as if he were trying too hard to be a fiery beast when it should have come naturally to a guy of his size. It made him forgettable. He was supposed to be the muscle of

Evolution and he did fine in that role, but his size and strength made you expect more. When he failed to give more, people quit caring. He was coming along alright in the ring, but he was still too clunky. He got winded too quickly. Matches with the likes of Chris Jericho and Edge failed to show the kind of progress that would have kept him on par with his 2002 rookie class that also included John Cena, Brock Lesnar, Shelton Benjamin, and fellow Evolution-mate Randy Orton.

Sometimes, though, either the audience or management (or both) do not wait for a wrestler to hone his skills before demanding that he be given the ball. Like a rookie quarterback being thrown into the fire, Batista was about to be thrust into a very important role. Lesnar prematurely quit the WWE and Orton's attempt to split from Evolution to become the new babyface of the company bombed. As of late 2004, someone new had to step up. Nobody thought it would be Batista, but something very important happened right around that time. It was a simple thing that started a chain reaction. Batista, in a backstage segment, stared at Triple H's World Heavyweight Championship with desire in his eyes. That was all it took. The fans immediately reacted and, all of the sudden, there was a ground swell of support for him. How interesting that **A** look from a guy with **THE** look was all it took to get him over.

Oddly enough, it was literally just a week or two earlier that a fan held up a sign during the elimination match that main-evented *Survivor Series*, confirming the opinion that it was highly unlikely to be Batista stepping into a top spot. The sign read, "HA! Batista Can't Get Over!"

Very quickly, Batista went from a disappointment that got a marginal reaction from the crowd to a huge burgeoning superstar that was getting the strongest babyface reaction of the night from audiences around North America. He and Triple H were set on a collision course. It all played out perfectly on television. Everything that the Orton-Trips feud should have been was what we were seeing from Batista-Trips. Many a little backstage moment helped the tension build. Bigger moments on PPV and in TV main-events were well executed in a way that made people flock to Batista's bandwagon. When he won the 2005 Royal Rumble match to earn a title shot in classic fashion, it seemed as if we had one of the top stars of a new era. Interest in the product, in general, seemed to pick up as a result. Batista's announcement that he would challenge Triple H for the World title at *WrestleMania 21* drew a strong TV rating. His victory over Triple H to win the title resulted in one of the strongest PPV buyrates in modern times.

Unfortunately, the main-event at *Mania 21* still required Batista to wrestle and it became apparent that the WWE had done a great job of hiding his shortcomings in the four months leading up to the event. The match highlighted that Batista still had glaring weaknesses as a performer. As a character, Batista was more comfortable and was not trying so hard. In being himself, he was embraced. Yet, his wrestling was still in need of a lot of work. He caught lightning in a bottle to get over like he did, but whether or not he had the talent to sustain his push was still very much in question.

It was a rough run at the top for Batista. He struggled mightily to perform to the main-event level expected of him. Only one match during that entire two year span was a classic worth multiple viewings - a Hell in a Cell match against Triple H at 2005's *Vengeance*. It was an excellent piece of work, but Batista's matches before and after suggested that it was arguably the greatest carry of Triple H's career rather than a statement of what to expect from the man who defeated him.

Despite the struggles, he went into *WrestleMania 23* with a lot of momentum as a character. Since becoming champion, he had not lost. He had to vacate the title due to injury in January '06, so he was undefeated in championship matches. When they put him against Undertaker, he with the illustrious Streak, it created a buzz. Looking at it on paper, you had a guy in Batista that had mowed through just about every top star in the business for two years. Taker was at a point in his career where you legitimately had to wonder if The Streak was in jeopardy. Batista was as poised as anyone ever had been to end it. Yet, given his in-ring woes, you also had to wonder if he was up to the task of capitalizing on what that could mean to his career. All things considered, Batista vs. Taker was a mixed bag of expectations.

My gut feeling was that it had "bust" written all over it. Batista had given little reason to have high hopes. I believe that is why they were not on last that night. I do not think that the WWE higher-ups thought Batista could deliver. What I witnessed that night, though, is something that I will never forget.

On April 1, 2007, Batista turned the corner in his career. Maybe it was the motivation of wanting to show everyone why he deserved to be in the final match on the card or maybe it was something else, but Batista looked like a different wrestler out there. In front of over 80,000 people, he showed a passion for performing that had been missing. For the first time, I really felt like he "got it." That match was outstanding. I have *never* been that pleasantly surprised at the quality of a match in the entirety of my wrestling fandom. To be honest, "pleasantly" does not do it justice. Euphorically surprised.

Though Batista lost the match, his five championship matches from April-November '07 with The Deadman were perception-altering. I became a fan of his at *Mania 23* and looked forward to his matches in big situations from then on.

Across the board, he just kept getting better. He had a two match series with Shawn Michaels in 2008 that, to me, accentuated how far he had come. He had become a smart worker. Having observed his struggles against HBK several years prior, it was great seeing the difference after watching him put the work in to get significantly better. Mick Foley, on commentary that summer, put it best about Big Dave, mentioning that "Batista, along the way, has become a complete package, adding endurance and strategy (to his power)." I will add maturity and a desire to be the best.

My favorite of Batista's rivals was John Cena. His matches with Cena were a notch below his work with Taker, but the historical context of Batista-Cena was fascinating. After *WrestleMania 23*, a once quiet competition between them began to get louder. If you rewound the clock back to *Royal Rumble '05*, Batista and Cena got eliminated, initially, at the same time. Only after a restart did Batista claim the victory. At *Mania 21* three months later, Cena had won the WWE Championship a match prior to Bats becoming World Heavyweight Champion. Batista was on top of the world until Cena was put in his place as the new face of *Raw* in the summer. Nevertheless, it was Big Dave that was given much of the credit for drawing such a strong *Mania 21* buyrate. When *Mania 22* failed to draw as strongly without Batista on the card (due to injury), it seemed to add to The Animal's cause. *Mania 23's* line-up, though, stated definitively that Cena was "The Man." Cena's match with HBK went on last. Batista and Taker may have stolen the show, but Cena and Michaels were, perhaps, unfairly given more of the credit for the then-record number of PPV buys (1.2 million).

Up until *Mania 23*, Batista had hung right there with Cena despite being on *Smackdown*. He had earned his fair share of main-events on co-branded PPVs and his title reigns were nearly as long and numerous. Cena had taken the lead and never looked back after *Mania 23*. Both of them turned the corner as performers in 2007, but Cena took the torch and has been running with it ever since – by himself.

So, when *Summerslam '08* came about and Batista vs. Cena was booked, there was much more to that match than just the on-screen tension building between budding tag team partners (they won the Tag Team titles together). Many were calling for the match to be postponed until the *25th Anniversary of WrestleMania* the next April, but the WWE went forward with the match, perhaps eyeing a rematch at *Mania* playing off their initial encounter. The 2008 match was quite a sight, a helluva piece of work by two pros won by Batista after two powerbombs. The dynamic of seeing the two top stars in the industry go at it for the first time had unmistakable appeal. Unfortunately, if the plan was to use this as a springboard to *Mania 25*, then another Batista injury put it on hold.

Once healthy, Batista made an anticipated turn to the dark side. Character-wise, he was never better than during his 9-month run as a heel in late '09 through the spring of 2010. As soon as he turned, I called for the renewal of the Cena rivalry. I thought it would have been a shame if those two never faced each other at a WrestleMania, considering how important that they had each been in transitioning the WWE out of the Attitude Era. When Batista engaged Cena at the February '10 *Elimination Chamber* PPV, defeating him in an impromptu title bout after Cena had won the WWE Championship in the event's signature match, it was "on" for *Mania XXVI*. Batista gave their match the best hype of any contest scheduled for that year's biggest show. Week after week, he cut excellent promos, memorably recapping the (mostly) unspoken prior history between the two to help put the Mania headliner into proper perspective. Batista had a legitimate bone to pick. Why would he not be peeved by Cena taking the spot that once seemed his? If you had been groomed by the best in the business (HHH) and beaten that man in the main-event at a WrestleMania, you would likely feel that you were "The Man" to whom the torch had been passed. Yet, that was not the case. Batista beat HHH in 2005, but Cena beat HHH the next year. Whoever got the main-event slot at *Mania 23* seemed to be the tiebreaker for the official #1 guy. That was Cena.

Though *Mania 26* was loaded with historically significant matches, the one that I most looked forward to was Batista vs. Cena. It was 5 years in the making and, in essence, began the end of an era that started with their championship victories at *Mania 21*. If Batista vs. Cena at *Summerslam* was a taste of what *could* be, then Batista vs. Cena at *WrestleMania* was everything that a match between the icons **should** be. In 15-minutes, they opened up their playbooks, thought outside the box, and delivered a great match that does not get talked about enough as one of the best of each man's career. There is something about WrestleMania that adds a little extra zest to any match and both Batista and Cena understood that well enough to allow it to fuel their personas forward to a classic contest. What makes a match like it so special is that it does not happen but every so often. I feel lucky that we got Batista-Cena at Mania.

It was not long after Batista hung up his boots in 2010 that I posted in my LOP column that Batista was in the top 20, all-time, amongst WWE superstars and did not hesitate at all in doing so. I caught a lot of heat for it, with people suggesting that he did not do enough. The only knock against The Animal is longevity (as a main-eventer), but I view that only as a reason why he was not ranked higher. He padded his case with a temporary comeback in 2014 that added another Royal Rumble match win and a critically acclaimed main-event at WrestleMania to his resume. He could move up if he ever comes back again to cash in on his celebrity status from the blockbuster, *The Guardians of the Galaxy,* and his role as a James Bond villain.

Frankly, when you look at his WrestleMania track record alone, he deserves to be in the Top 30 of the last 30 years. In six WrestleManias, he was wrestling for a World

Championship four times. That 67% figure would have undoubtedly been increased had he not gotten injured at inopportune times. He had one of those Manias built around his title shot against Triple H and in two others he was positioned as the champion against two of WrestleMania's most historically significant stars in Undertaker and Cena.

Then, there is the sheer volume of PPVs that he headlined, first as the face of the *Smackdown* brand from mid-2005 to late 2007, followed by the remainder of his years as a main-event force on both brands. If healthy, he was almost always in a top match. You can count on one hand the number of times that he was not in a featured bout on a PPV from 2005-2010 and only in 2008 did he have any sort of multi-month stretch where he was not competing for the World or WWE Championship. He won the WWE title twice and the World Heavyweight title four times. His first World title reign was 282 days in length, which ranks amongst the longest in modern history.

He would not be ranked this high without his in-ring improvements, though. If you add up his championships, number of headlining matches, major PPV track record, *and* the classic matches, then I do not think there is any question that he belongs in the Top 20. To me, Batista's hard work at getting better was his enduring legacy. I will always be a Dave Batista fan for that reason.

#16: Sting

March 27, 1988 was the date of the fourth of the twenty-nine WrestleManias in professional wrestling history. It was also the date of the very first NWA *Clash of the Champions*. In an underhanded tactic to gain leverage over television companies, Vince McMahon had told PPV broadcasters that they could not air the NWA's *Starrcade '87* or risk being unable to show *WrestleMania IV*. Coming off the massive success of *Mania III*, that was not a risk worth taking. *Starrcade* bombed at the box office as a result. The NWA had to retaliate. One of their top up-and-coming stars was Sting. So, the NWA decided to air their first *Clash* on free television to run up against WWE's *Mania IV* and feature Ric Flair defending the NWA Championship against The Stinger. Sting was the kind of new star that might convince viewers torn between the companies to choose paying nothing over paying for the WWE PPV. Thus, Sting burst onto the scene.

In his title match with Flair, he was showcased as a student of the game that had the champion well scouted. At every turn, it seemed like he had Flair's routine down to a science, able to counter and overcome. What impressed many about him were his athletic abilities combined with his natural charisma. In an NWA looking for something to help them in their battle with the WWE, he seemed like a blend between Flair, Hulk Hogan, and Randy Savage. By the end of the match, Sting was on his way to big things. It was a 45-minute time limit draw involving a relative unknown commodity against the long-running heavyweight champion of the world. In essence, the NWA had created a new star and stuck it to the WWE all in one great night.

Though 1988 was a breakout year for Sting, the NWA made the decision to hold off on having him face Flair in any major event rematches. He had the classic match with Naitch to establish his name and then spent the rest of the year teaming with some of Flair's all-time greatest opponents to further build him up. He teamed with Dusty Rhodes, Lex Luger, and Nikita Koloff, working against the likes of Flair's Horsemen stablemates, Barry Windham, Arn Anderson, and Tully Blanchard. The important theme for Sting was that he was working with and against some of the best in the business at that time. These were men that could teach him. With consistency, they put him in situations that would slowly build him up for top contender status.

The slow burn for Sting challenging for the World title became a theme in his career that would be revisited nearly ten years later in the biggest match of his life. Some could argue that they turned the figurative burner on simmer when they could have had him boiling, but Flair was still very much "The Man" in the NWA/WCW in the late 1980s and had Sting defeated him right off the bat, then he likely would have dropped the title right back to him and been forced to sit the sidelines until Flair was ready to pass the torch. The decision worked out in the long run.

1988 saw two young challengers emerge to potentially overtake Flair for the top spot in the NWA one day: Sting and Luger. A quiet, cordial rivalry emerged between the two despite their friendship. Sting's first championship was the World's TV title, a belt he most prominently defended against Japanese star, The Great Muta. Their most famous battle for the title came at the 1989 *Great American Bash*, which was arguably one of the greatest PPVs of all-time. Luger was clearly a step ahead back then, defending the US title on the same card, but Sting was not far behind. Sting came out for his match against Muta with something to prove. They had a different style of match than anything else on the card. Luger had a great match with Ricky Steamboat, but it ended up being Sting that pulled ahead in the race.

While Lex did good things with the US title and Sting dropped the TV title to Muta, The Stinger found himself teaming with Flair for the main-event of the first *Halloween Havoc* PPV in a unique concept called the Thunderdome Cage, pulling a bit further ahead. At *Starrcade '89*, it looked like Luger had Sting figuratively beat when he literally defeated him – pinned him – in a match during that year's (non-title) Ironman tournament, but Sting got the last laugh, wrestling some good matches including a rematch of his well-known bout against The Great Muta and the highly anticipated main-event of the night against The Nature Boy. Flair's stature in the NWA had made him popular no matter what role he played at the time, so the crowd's split reaction, perhaps more so for that match than any other that they ever had, suggested that Sting was well on his way to superstardom. Sting countered at the last second with a roll-up, winning the match and the tournament based on cumulative points. Luger never lost a match, but it was Sting closing the NWA's biggest show of the year in victory.

The saga continued when Sting got hurt in the lead-up to *Wrestle War '90* and was replaced by Luger in a match for Flair's NWA Championship. Lex had two great matches with Flair at back-to-back PPVs, but was unable to win the title. That honor belonged to Sting, who finally dethroned Flair at the 1990 *Great American Bash*, beating Luger to the punch and ascending to the peak position in the NWA. Sadly, the match was not the all-time classic that it should have been. It was a good match that the most supportive fans of The Stinger probably recall quite fondly, but it was not the epic encounter that many, like me, thought it should have been. Just 16-minutes for a potential torch-passing match? Nevertheless, Sting won the belt and held it for six months – the longest championship reign by a babyface in modern NWA/WCW history.

Sting's victory was indicative of the respect that he garnered from men like Flair, who were the gatekeepers of the wrestling business based on their old school philosophies of who should be the champion. The industry was changing, but Sting was the guy that they felt best embodied the qualities of the 1990s athlete. He was colorful, talented, and magnetic to the crowds. His first title reign solidified him as the guy that would carry what would soon be officially renamed WCW well into the next decade.

He became the first babyface to consistently one-up The Four Horsemen, who were his primary rivals throughout his title reign. In the past, anyone that had gone up against The Horsemen and won, quickly found themselves right back in the loss column repeatedly. The Stinger was the exception, holding the World title from July '90 to January '91 and defeating the likes Flair and Sid Vicious in PPV main-events. Flair was the one to take the belt off of Sting, who proceeded to embark on a yearlong journey to regain the title.

Sting's next shot at the World title on a major event would not come until February '92's *Super Brawl*, the culmination of the unspoken rivalry between he and Luger. For half a decade, they had jockeyed for position to become the "franchise" of the NWA/WCW once Flair moved on and, through many swings in momentum for each man, it all came down to their lone PPV title match. The story behind the scenes was that Luger was leaving for the WWE; Sting had won the right to be "The Man." The match at *Super Brawl* was merely a televised confirmation of that which had already been decided. Nevertheless, it makes for a far more engaging backdrop to their match than WCW provided. It had been one of the biggest potential matches that WCW had to offer for years and, when you saw them standing face-to-face before the opening bell, it felt like a major happening was at hand. Though it was not a great match, it remains one of my favorites due to its era-specific historical significance.

With the World Championship back around his waist, the real challenge began. There was no security blanket in Flair and there was no other well-groomed, larger than life athlete there to share the load. It was up to The Stinger to be that which they labeled him: The Franchise.

He certainly started out well, as he concluded the feud that had occupied much of his time in 1991 (with Rick Rude) at *Wrestle War '92* in May. As the WCW Champion, he captained a team in a War Games match against the historically underrated faction, The Dangerous Alliance. The match was awarded the rare "5-star" mark by many critics, featuring Sting in a high quality performance. More than anything, it was a consistent string of great matches that Sting needed to best replace Flair. The Nature Boy's hallmark had been in-ring classics, not necessarily the TV ratings and PPV buyrates in comparison to the WWE's top acts. To step into Flair's shadow was to try and have the best match of the night on every show. That is exactly what Sting did in 1992. He shares credit with the rest of the participants in the '92 War Games match, but that was one of the greatest payoff matches in WCW history.

As good as War Games '92 was, the Sting vs. Vader series from April '92 to February '93 produced the best matches of his career. They worked so incredibly well together, as Sting appeared to relish the role of the underdog. Those matches were very important to Sting's legacy. Not only did they give him a signature rival against whom he did the caliber of work necessary to uphold the heritage of those top stars that came before him in the NWA, but he proved that he could work extremely high quality bouts in opposition to a much larger athlete. Vader's style brought something different to the table and it was Sting's ability to adapt to it and thrive against it that earned him so much respect as a wrestler. To have an awesome, athletic showing against a Ric Flair or a Rick Rude is expected given their similar statures, but in the history of professional wrestling, you will not find a finer display of athleticism between a heavyweight and a super heavyweight than Sting vs. Vader.

Hulk Hogan's arrival in 1994 signaled the end of Sting being the top guy in WCW. Sting's relevance decreased as Hogan's increased and he was pushed to the backburner for the next couple of years. It was a difficult time to be a Sting fan, almost akin to seeing your favorite football team win a championship or two and be the country's hottest ticket, only to see them regress to the point of comparative mediocrity despite still being in their prime. Hogan, along with fellow former WWE star Randy Savage, dominated the product. WCW homegrown talents were made secondary (a fact that only intensified once Scott Hall and Kevin Nash signed and The N.W.O. was formed).

The winds of change were blowing in strong for Sting in those days. He was forced to evolve, as a character, because quite frankly his surfer boy shtick had worn out its welcome years prior and made it easier to push him aside. He was the ultimate babyface in WCW, but as WCW was finding out by bringing in the beyond tired (and beyond ultimate) babyface Hulkamania character, the world no longer wished to see that. It actually turned out OK for The Stinger. He did not do much for the next couple of years, but he also did not get overexposed. Hogan had to turn heel to reinvent himself. Sting did not…

In the mid-90s, a movie called *The Crow* - about a rock star that got murdered (along with his wife) only to be resurrected by a crow and seek revenge on the guilty criminals - became a cult classic in the U.S. If you have not seen it, you ought to. Great movie. Apparently, Sting agreed.

In 1996, The New World Order took over the entire business. Storyline-wise, they took over WCW and made everyone on the roster look like idiots, with the exception of one man: Sting. Though it was Flair that truly represented what the NWA/WCW was all about, he was old and lacking in confidence. Sting, however, was the man that was supposed to take the reins and lead WCW into the future. He was still looked at as The Chosen One, of sorts. The second era for Sting came after he ditched the blonde hair and joined the rest of the world on the brink of the 21st century. He started his "Crow" gimmick. He hung out in the rafters with a baseball bat and did not speak. Few things sell better in wrestling than unpredictability. Sting's final words for a year were "the one thing that's for sure about Sting is that nothing's for sure." How much more unpredictable does it get than that?

At the spring of 1997's *Uncensored* PPV, The N.W.O. defeated a WCW team for the umpteenth time, but as they were celebrating with the event going off the air, Sting repelled from the rafters and took out Hall, Nash, Randy Savage, and Hogan. For an entire year, he was the only guy that was able to consistently one-up The N.W.O. The ratings for *Nitro* were a full point higher on the average than *Raw's* and much of that was due Sting vs. The New World Order. The whole point was to build to the biggest match in the company's history: Hogan vs. Sting. It was, quite frankly, one of the few things that the WCW bookers ever got right in the main-event scene (outside of The NWO) during the Monday Night War. Sting vs. Hogan drew *Starrcade '97* the best PPV buyrate in WCW history. From a business perspective, it was an incredible success. Sadly, from a quality and historical perspective, it may have been the first nail in the coffin for WCW. It was a terrible match with a God awful finish that just made everyone with any sense about wrestling roll their eyes and wonder, "I wonder what the WWE is doing?"

Wrestling is rooted in the same qualities that entertainment employs to make movies and TV shows great. In the end, the good guy has to win. Bottom line. Every now and again, the good guy can lose, but at the end of the day, Zack Morris has to end up with Kelly, Batman has to defeat The Joker, and the Titans have to win the Virginia state title and show us that black and white people can coexist. If you deviate from that, then the masses are going to be disappointed. Well, in WCW, Hogan and The New World Order had prevailed almost non-stop for 18 months straight and had no other challengers left. All that was left for WCW was Sting. He was their last chance. He wins and everyone rejoices and they move on to the next storyline with the kind of momentum that might have actually put the WWE out of business. But he did not win in the way that good guys are supposed to. First, he lost. Then, he actually did win after the original loss was wiped out. It took shenanigans for the good guy to win the title.

I have spoken to many fans over the years that stated the way that the *Starrcade* match played out was it for them with WCW. Some quit watching wrestling for years after that. It was the wrestling equivalent of *Star Wars* ending with the Emperor killing Luke Skywalker, only for the Force to bring Luke back to life so that he could prevail. It would have been a stupid way to do it, unnecessarily giving the Dark Side a chance to save face in defeat. The end of the story called for evil to get its butt kicked. The same was true of Sting vs. Hogan/N.W.O.

Had The Stinger defeated Hogan to win the World title that night, then WCW might still be here today. That would entail that at least one person running that company had the foresight to understand that The New World Order storyline had to reach a conclusion and that Sting was the right person to bring it about. If that had happened, then my wife might have taken me to Starrcade as wedding gift instead of WrestleMania.

Sting, overall, is the second best NWA/WCW wrestler of the last thirty years (Flair is #1). That is the way that he should be remembered. When you think of Sting, think of *The Clash of the Champions*, the NWA and WCW Championship chases and reigns, The Franchise of WCW, and the fantastic yearlong storyline that led to the most financially successful night in WCW history. It did not end well, but enough time has passed that Sting should be defined more by what he did than for the foolishness of those that controlled his fate.

#15: Brock Lesnar

I have always said about Brock Lesnar that "I will never forget when he returned to WWE one night after *WrestleMania XXVIII* because I never forgot when he left after *WrestleMania XX*."

Here is what it felt like when Brock ditched the WWE to try out for the National Football League in 2004:

Imagine that Peyton Manning, a man seemingly born to play quarterback in the NFL after an incredible college career, had won the Super Bowl in his first few years as a pro and the media had hyped him up as the face of the League for the next fifteen years, only for him to abruptly quit football to try his hand at an NBA contract despite not playing competitive basketball in ten years.

That was Brock Lesnar leaving the WWE in a nutshell.

He was the ideal professional wrestler. He weighed almost three hundred pounds, yet he was quick as a cat. He was both freakishly strong and ridiculously athletic. There might be a few guys that can throw a log further, but Lesnar would make it look easier. All the physical tools were there. He won the NCAA National Heavyweight Championship at Minnesota. He had a mean streak a mile long after growing up a relatively poor farm kid, from which came the motivation to make a lot of money. It was a no-brainer that Lesnar was going to be a megastar in WWE. I remember watching his debut on the Monday after *WrestleMania X-8* and instantly knowing that I had just witnessed the dawn of a new era. Nobody was surprised when he tore through the roster in his first year, main-eventing the three biggest shows of the next twelve months. When he botched a Shooting Star Press and nearly killed himself at *WrestleMania XIX*, it was expected to be a career highlight of a superstar who had a ceiling of "all-time greatest."

When he left, just four days shy of the two year anniversary of his debut, wrestling fans felt betrayed.

His reason for leaving? He could not handle the travel…

Travel to a pro wrestler is like getting hit in pro football; it is just something that you sign-up for if you want to be in that line of work. So, it was not as if fans were losing Lesnar to Hollywood, i.e. The Rock. Dwayne Johnson had unbridled charisma; when he made his first movie, we all quietly knew he would soon be gone. Lesnar, though, had no other discernible skills. "He was a wrestler; he should have continued wrestling" was the stance of almost every fan.

As fans, we invest in these guys. It was easy to get invested in Brock because he was so good, so fast. In his first main-event match, he had one of the Top 15 matches in Summerslam history, followed it up with double classics in his first two title defenses, and then had an awesome match at his first WrestleMania. He was great for two years; his *first* two years. So, despite feeling deceived for having spent those two years thinking that we were witnessing someone who would be historically mentioned in the same breath as Hogan, Austin, and Rock, some people still rooted for him to succeed in his other endeavors. You share in the success of these guys, whether they like it or not. I was happy to see him excel in mixed martial arts. It turned out that Brock was born to be in a ring; there was just no specification for what kind.

He quickly became UFC's top draw, earned the UFC Heavyweight title, and helped further expand that sport to the point that it is now one of the most popular in the world. I do not know much about MMA, but I assumed that he would do well. His combination of power, size, and speed is and always has been the greatest I have ever seen in any sport, with the exception of Lebron James. Unfortunately for him, his body started failing him. He developed a nasty intestinal condition called diverticulitis, in which the body loses the ability to regulate digestive function, causing pockets of fluid (diverticula) to build-up in the bowels; the body recognizes the pockets as abnormal and attacks them with inflammation (an immune response). Lesnar was ravaged by the condition and retired from MMA.

The WWE and its fans were waiting for him. As an established draw in a sport that had surpassed pro wrestling in box office appeal, Lesnar was an attractive free agent. The WWE offered a lot of money for not a lot of work. As such, the fans who were around ten years prior got one of their guys back and newer fans got a fascinating new star to enjoy. Lesnar returned with a hybrid style that made him must-see in a whole new way.

Lesnar has significantly enhanced his historical stature since returning to WWE. The significant knock on him in the past was that he was not a draw, with his name forever attached to the worst WrestleMania buyrate in modern history in 2003 and a general decline in business from the time he became a headliner (even if that was not entirely fair given the changing landscape). That has clearly changed thanks to his MMA career. Oddly enough, he would not have had the same MMA career had it not been for his time atop the wrestling world and vice versa. Funny how the world works. His ties to the legitimate sporting world helped WWE establish an on-screen relationship with ESPN. I never thought I would see WWE highlights on ESPN. Never. His name value brought a 23% average buyer increase in the two PPVs that he main-evented in 2012. One can assume that his presence at *Mania 29* also assisted the much-maligned Rock-Cena rematch in drawing over a million buys again and there should be no questioning his impact on the WWE Network's prosperity. He is his own brand and he is highly successful.

In the ring, his first match in eight years with John Cena was an utterly breathtaking piece of work. Cena was brutally beaten, bloodied, and embarrassed, making Lesnar look like a killer. It was one of the most compelling matches of the last decade on the first viewing. Critics praised the follow-up two years later at *Summerslam 2014* for the same reasons. The format essentially became his signature in-ring style, which I have nicknamed "Beast Mode." In a glorified squash match, he mauls his opponents, takes them to "Suplex City," and calls it a night. Though I would personally prefer to see him more often wrestle the kind of match he had with CM Punk at *Summerslam 2013* – a modern masterpiece of the David vs. Goliath genre – I can neither deny the appeal of the "Beast Mode" style nor undervalue the aura it has created for Lesnar (which is Undertaker and Andre the Giant-esque). He brings such presence and legitimate ferocity to table; he is riveting to watch.

He already had as many classic matches in his initial run as most guys have in their entire careers, so now his body of work is approaching all-time elite caliber levels. His list of outstanding performances is lengthy and full of examples of his underrated in-ring versatility. The match at *Summerslam '02* with The Rock, in which Brock took from him both the physical belt and the title of youngest WWE Champion in history, was a showcase of athleticism between prototype WWE top stars. Rock was a bigger guy who developed a style of incorporating high impact moves with crowd pleasing antics and could vary up his pace. Brock did not miss a step, made all the more impressive by holding up his end of the bargain in his first feature length, headlining match.

Two months later, he successfully defended the title in a Hell in a Cell match against the Undertaker. It was a brutal battle that showed Brock's ability to brawl, bleed, absorb unusual amounts of physical punishment, and endure in the end. He also had a mat-based clash for the ages with Kurt Angle at *WrestleMania XIX* and an amazing 60-minute Ironman match on *Smackdown* in Raleigh that I had the pleasure of seeing live. Many thought the Ironman was the 2003 Match of the Year (it was awarded that honor by PWI). He capped off the first chapter of his WWE career with a great match against Eddie Guerrero at *No Way Out 2004*, just one month before he abruptly left the company. Eddie's style was a balance of aerial and technical prowess, prompting Brock to once again adapt to a different grappling approach. Since his comeback, he has produced the all-time classic with the well-rounded Punk and the "Beast Mode" series with the likes of Cena, Rollins, Reigns, and Ambrose.

Lesnar's dominant, eight month title reign ahead of *WrestleMania 31* makes him a four-time WWE Champion, with all four of his reigns lasting at least three months. He also won the last PPV King of the Ring tournament and the 2003 Royal Rumble match. He has main-evented two WrestleManias and has now headlined four others. He has an incredible look for a pro wrestler; though that was far more the case when he was 25 rather than 35 years of age and before diverticulitis. He can talk, but only when it is organic and he really believes in what he is saying. Most of the time, in the scripted nature of the business, his voice has been hidden by Paul Heyman's, but it has been a brilliant pairing. Lesnar is one of the greatest ever.

You know what is weird, though? Even with the stacked resume, I struggled not to invoke the subjectivity clause and keep him back a few spots. Why? He reminds me of this kid I went to school with who never studied, partied all the time, breezed right through every test, and then paraded around his ridiculously hot girlfriend who did not even go to our school but was always around; he did it, by the way, with this pompous attitude of "that was so easy." What a douche; what a brilliant, gifted douche. Everyone in my class secretly wanted to put "Colon Blow" in his banana smoothie like they did to the jackass in *Van Wilder* and snicker as he ran out of the room during test time to poop his bowels out in a trashcan. Brock Lesnar is the physically gifted douche who works a tenth of the dates, never has to work harder to get better, makes ten times more money, and gets to go home to a still smoking hot Sable. I am 90% sure that most of the WWE roster feels about Brock like we did about "The Bear" (he was an Animal Steele-like hairy douche).

So, here is another weird thing: in my statistical analysis, I did my best not to be swayed <u>at all</u> by winning and losing because it barely matters in an all-time greatness discussion, but the main reason why I felt comfortable overlooking the fact that Lesnar has such a gigantic inherent stat-advantage over most of his modern peers (only wrestles major shows, always in the main-event) is because of one single victory. Not just any victory, mind you. He beat "The Streak."

The Undertaker was 21-0 at WrestleMania heading into the 30th edition in New Orleans and no one was expecting, by then, that the elusive loss would ever come. My group and I were watching it on a delay (I demand that nothing disrupt my viewing of Mania and anything that does gets met with the pause button). About midway through the Lesnar vs. Taker bout, text messages started flying in. One of our group members looked noticeably distraught, but even when he grimly stated, "I wish I hadn't read that," nobody thought anything of it. I received a text from my buddy, Tony, who had watched with me in New York the previous year as Taker had laid waste to victim #21. It said, "Wow. I didn't see that coming." It never once crossed my mind that The Deadman might have lost. I recall thinking that Sting had probably showed up after the match.

Minutes later, when Brock connected with a third F5 and scored the pin, everyone knew why the texts had been sent. Tony was shocked because the Streak had ended. The other guy in our group was upset because the surprise was spoiled. THE STREAK WAS OVER.

Now, let us back up for a moment. In the two years that Lesnar had been back, WWE had basically stripped Brock of his mystique. He lost that match to Cena in 2012; he lost to Triple H at *Mania 29;* he struggled to beat CM Punk. When he returned, Brock was a God amongst men. By bell time of the Taker match, he was most decidedly mortal. Such is why nobody thought it worth their time to even fathom that a mere mortal like Brock could take down the previously immortal Streak. It was for that reason that the match had garnered almost zero energy from the crowd before the finish. Yet, after those three seconds that handed The Phenom his first WrestleMania defeat, Lesnar was, once again, divine. The mythological status restored, Heyman's nicknames for Brock – "The Conqueror" and "The Beast Incarnate" – were no longer the savvy words of a master orator; they were the truth.

"It was a victory that Brock truly needed," said Paul Heyman later that year on Chris Jericho's podcast. "It once again separate[d] him from everybody else. I can sit there on television and quote his credentials, but it's all hype and hyperbole unless you give (the fans) back up and credence to what I'm saying. So, when he's the one guy in twenty some odd years that has beaten Undertaker at WrestleMania, now it all comes together."

And come together it did. Whoever beats him will be a made-man for having defeated the "1 in 21-1." Most people are hoping that an emergent star gets the honor. Lesnar is one of the two greatest wrestling prodigies of our time and a future Hall of Famer, but he can erase the one remaining knock on his legacy by giving back to the business that made him, putting over the next "Next Big Thing."

#14: Kurt Angle

If the WWE and its fans are lucky, there will come an athlete about once a generation that is such a natural fit for sports entertainment that he will provide us all with memories that live forever. For the NBA and its fans, Lebron James is that type of athlete. He was simply born to play basketball. Kurt Angle was that caliber of athlete for the WWE. He was a freestyle wrestling Olympic Gold Medalist in the 1996 Summer Games in Atlanta. A man with that kind of credential shifting to the professional ranks is rare, but nobody could have imagined that he would make the transition to pro wrestling so seamlessly. Never had the word "prodigy" been more applicable.

Angle began his training to wrestle professionally in the fall of 1998. Even the best of athletes usually take a few years to become good enough to compete at a high level, but Angle debuted as a major character on WWE TV one year later in the fall 1999 and proceeded to have the greatest rookie year in modern wrestling lore.

Imagine if Lebron had, in his rookie season rather than his fourth, taken Cleveland to the Playoffs, gotten past the first and second rounds with ease, defeated the multi-time Eastern Conference Champion Detroit Pistons with historic performances to reach the NBA Finals, and then (for argument's sake) beaten the three-time World Champion San Antonio Spurs to become an NBA Champion…all in his first year. That was the kind of rookie year that Angle had in the WWE. He won the Intercontinental and European Championships, won the King of the Ring tournament, beat Triple H to become #1 contender to the World title, and then became WWE Champion by beating The Rock in a four-star match…all before the one year anniversary of his debut.

Such a rapid rate of progression was astounding. Angle's learning curve was so very small.

It was one thing for him to be given the opportunity to win titles and defeat big names – that happens all the time - but for him to do so in such high quality matches was very unique. When he reached main-event status and became champion, he was still learning his craft, but it took him no time at all to become one of the most consistently brilliant wrestlers in the WWE for years to come. In the (October) *No Mercy 2000* match that saw him win the WWE title, for instance, many shortcuts were taken to ensure that the match was a borderline classic. Subsequent matches with Undertaker and Triple H and a 6-man Hell in a Cell gave him "trial by fire" experience, whereby his rematch with Rock that saw him drop the title at (February) *No Way Out 2001* needed no shenanigans to earn definitive classic status.

Equally important to the in-ring component of pro wrestling is being entertaining when they hand you the microphone, so while Angle's rapid progress between the ropes was a perfect display of his natural athleticism, it was his ability to catch on quickly as a character that ensured his long-term success at the top. He modestly began his career with interviews about his three "I"s (Intensity, Integrity, and Intelligence), depicting himself as a facetious role model, but once they threw him out there with Stephanie McMahon, Triple H, and The Rock, it did not take a critic to notice that there was something special about him. He fit right in with two of the best talkers of all-time. In time, he showcased a wide range of acting from downright hilarious to extremely intense. His comedic timing ranks amongst the best.

The combination of his grappling and interview skills were a smash hit, but one event separates the beginning of his career from the rest. *King of the Ring 2001* took him to a new level. He did not win the tournament as he did the year before, but he came away from that night with a respect from the fans that he did not have before. He wrestled three matches, beating Christian in the semi-finals and losing to Edge in the finals due to interference from his last opponent of the evening: Shane McMahon. Angle vs. Shane was an exceptionally brutal Street Fight and the greatest match of all-time that involved a non-wrestler. Shane had a well-deserved reputation for his willingness to put his body through hell, but Angle was primarily a mat-based wrestler playing off his heralded amateur background. In the Street Fight, Angle blended his penchant for a variety of suplexes with hardcore elements. He suplexed Shane, as an example, into and then through several glass-like set pieces on the stage, causing each of them to bleed buckets from all the ensuing lacerations. He was already a star before that night, but that epic performance - after having wrestled twice already - put him over the top.

Kurt had been a heel for two years, but the *KOTR '01* crowd started turning the audience in his favor; so much so that the WWE felt comfortable putting him against the company's biggest star, Steve Austin, who they were desperately trying to turn into a heel after years of being the top babyface. It was an interesting dynamic for Angle and Austin, feuding over the WWE Championship throughout the summer and early fall while each were attempting to develop new wrinkles in their personas. To their credit, their *Summerslam '01* match gave Angle the sympathy needed to become a successful protagonist and actually got people to jeer Austin (Note – Austin's heel turn was largely considered a business-altering failure). It also helped Angle take another step forward by upping his intensity to the next level. He had largely made his name on being a goofball, but after losing a few pints of blood, kicking out of two Stone Cold Stunners, and nearly beating Austin on several occasions only to be screwed out of the title, Angle walked away a sympathetic bad ass.

The pinnacle moment of the Angle-Austin feud came at *Unforgiven* in September 2001. Taking place just twelve days after the 9/11 terrorist attacks against the United States, the American people needed a distraction. Angle, a legitimate American sports hero, was the WWE's version of that escape. In his hometown of Pittsburg, PA, Angle won the WWE Championship by making Austin tap out to the ankle lock. The crowd chanted "USA" before, during, and after the match. After his victory, Angle, donning tights that paid tribute to the American flag, was hoisted onto the shoulders of his family members, who represented the millions of Americans watching at home.

2001 was a year full of accolades for "Our Olympic Hero" (he also added the WCW title and the US title to his championship list), but 2002 was a year in which he amassed as many great matches with a variety of opponents in a 12-month period as has ever been seen in pro wrestling. Immediately after the brand split, Angle engaged in a rivalry with Edge that was memorable for several reasons. First and foremost, it produced a handful of four-star classics. It also led to the "You Suck" chants in rhythm with his entrance music that came to be a staple for the rest of his WWE tenure and for Angle opting for his signature bald headed look to hide his receding hairline by way of an amazing Hair vs. Hair match at *Judgment Day*. In the matches with Edge, Angle turned yet another corner. It was as if he woke up one morning, looked back on everything he had done since October 2000, and said to himself, "You know what? I'm freakin' good at this...Oh, it's true!" His competitive instinct reached a higher level as he set out on a quest to be remembered as one of the greatest of all-time.

It was a joy to be a fan and get the chance to see him every week, tearing the roof off of every arena with great match after great match. Whether it be against a top star on the rise like Edge or a 50-year old Hulk Hogan or two of the top stars of all-time in Rock and Undertaker or an untested rookie in his first televised match in John Cena, Angle was on fire.

Despite two unquestionably excellent years in 2001 and 2002, Angle did not yet have a defining moment or headlining opportunity on the stage that would matter most to his budding legacy. As *WrestleMania XIX* approached, Angle won the WWE Championship for the third time. Soon after, the WWE built a stable around him - an underrated trait of the best of the best, for it means that the promoters think that you can rub off on and make potential stars out of your stablemates. Team Angle, featuring newcomers Shelton Benjamin and Charlie Haas, was designed to combat the onslaught of a prodigy similar to Angle in Brock Lesnar. Yet, first, Angle had some unfinished business in his most critically acclaimed rivalry with Chris Benoit.

Angle vs. Benoit was an expression of Kurt's swift improvement in pro wrestling. Dating back to *WrestleMania 2000*, when Benoit took the Intercontinental title from Angle, the two embarked on a three year, off and on run that culminated at the 2003 *Royal Rumble*. The *Mania 2000* bout was above average, reflecting where Angle was at that point in his career. As he had gained experience in the year that followed, it came as no surprise that when they squared off again at *WrestleMania X-Seven*, the result was a well-received mat-wrestling match that was once ranked by their peers as one of the top 10 matches in Mania history. The 2001 portion of their saga featured two other very good PPV matches, each of feature length between 25-and-30 minutes, and a classic Steel Cage match that was the true showcase of just how far Angle had come in a year. Neck surgery for Benoit put off their next match until September 2002's *Unforgiven*. In a scintillating display of amateur and pro wrestling combined, Angle and Benoit had their best match to date. The crème de le crème, though, was the WWE Championship match at the 2003 *Rumble*.

2000 was a year where Angle was still learning. 2001 showed that he had progressed to being able to back up his headlining stature. 2002 saw Angle take off to rarefied air amongst the best in the industry. 2003 was when he took that final step and became one of the best ever. The match at the *Rumble* was one of those rare situations where you knew who was winning ahead of time – Angle vs. Lesnar had been obvious for *WrestleMania* since the previous fall. Yet, the near falls in the Angle-Benoit match made you second guess the assumed plan. Angle had developed an uncanny knack for selling a near fall, kicking out at the very last nanosecond of pin attempts and keeping his hand raised inches off the mat when locked in a submission hold to make you think he might well tap out. They worked a brilliant 20-minute match that incorporated everything in their arsenals and more. If a match is good enough that it keeps you guessing from bell to bell, then it is a classic. If the wrestlers can do that despite you being 99.9% sure of the outcome ahead of time, then it becomes an all-time classic. Angle vs. Benoit was an all-time classic and one of two 5-star matches of Angle's career. Angle won the match and retained the title, moving onto face Lesnar at *Mania XIX* and earning 2003's Match of the Year in the process.

Unfortunately, Angle found himself in a situation all too familiar. Back in '96, Angle severely injured his neck during the Olympic trials. He managed to win the gold, but he did so while his neck was still healing from significant damage. Fast forward to '03 and Angle, preparing for the moment every pro wrestler dreams of, hurt his neck again. He opted to go ahead with the match against Lesnar. He was risking his life. In one of the gutsiest performances in history, Angle wrestled Lesnar to an awesome match, dropping the title to him in the main-event of *WrestleMania*. Watching that match and knowing the situation at hand was as nerve racking an experience as I have had during nearly 30 years as a fan. Every bump had me counting the seconds before he got up.

Thanks to an unconventional surgery, Angle was back in action after three months to resume his feud with Lesnar to much fanfare. With the crowd heavily supporting him again, Angle won the title in July, prompting Lesnar to turn heel. They wound up telling a very thorough story of Angle antagonizing Brock, only to have Lesnar earn his respect. They would gain mutual respect for each other that created a friendship until Lesnar became so obsessed with being champion that Kurt regaining the title from him pushed Brock over the edge. Though Angle defeated Brock at *Summerslam* to start one of the first "You Tapped Out" chants, Lesnar won the payoff on *Smackdown* in a classic Ironman match that was, perhaps, the best match that I ever saw live. It was in Raleigh, North Carolina, where I was attending NC State University. Theirs was easily the best hour-long match in WWE history. None of the other WWE Ironman matches featured the combination of athletes that were Angle and Lesnar.

By that point, Angle had become too good for his Mania headliner status to be a one-off. For the next three years, Angle was one of the top stars in the company. After capping off 2003 with a fantastic match with John Cena at *No Mercy* that helped Cena start moving toward his modern day success, Angle entered the next year with the goal to further his legacy and help Eddie Guerrero get established as a main-event player for the final two years of his career/life. 2004 featured an Angle vs. Eddie Guerrero feud that was similar in length to Angle-Lesnar, during the course of which Angle evolved into a more serious character, predominantly shedding the goofy nature from his past. His story with Eddie was based around his belief that reformed drug addicts should not be representing the WWE as its champion. They had a great match at *WrestleMania XX*, with Eddie retaining the WWE Championship. Later in the year, they wrestled at *Summerslam* and numerous times on *Smackdown* once Angle's brief, injury-caused run as the *SD* General Manager came to end.

There were many great programs in Angle's career from 2000-2004, but the 2005 storyline with Shawn Michaels was his all-time best. By November 2004, I was as big a fan of Angle as I was of anyone not named Shawn Michaels. At *Survivor Series '04*, when Angle foreshadowed his series of matches with Michaels by claiming he could make Shawn tap in seconds, I was instantly hyped. The anticipation built through their first actual encounter in the '05 Royal Rumble match and on through to *WrestleMania 21*. I went to the *Raw* roughly one month prior to Mania and held up a sign that reflected my honest feelings about their match. It read, "Angle vs. HBK: The Dream Match at WrestleMania." There probably was not a bigger potential match for me, at that time. My favorite of all-time (HBK) vs. my favorite of that generation (Angle).

It is a rare thing when your expectations are "five-stars" and the actual end result is "five-stars," but that is what Angle and HBK managed at *Mania 21*. Bobby Heenan called it the best match he had ever seen. I remember, going in, I wanted to see Angle do the moonsault and catch HBK with the top rope Angle Slam in one of those incredibly athletic sequences of his where he would run up the ring ropes like stair steps and catch his turnbuckle-sitting opponent with a throw off the top. How often are you able to correctly predict, in a way, two key spots in a match that you had dreamed of seeing? I was enthralled; I never wanted it to end. Angle's victory was probably the most important of his career without a title on the line and without question his most significant WrestleMania victory.

Their rematch at *Vengeance* a few months later was just as aesthetically pleasing as the first match, just without all of the pomp and circumstance of Mania. Some respected, Wrestling Media friends of mine said it was better than the original. HBK won the second match at a great PPV in Las Vegas. I had just turned twenty-one, graduated from college, and was headed to Vegas a few days after the event. It would have been an incredible experience to see HBK vs. Angle live.

Unfortunately, I missed them by a week and their third epic PPV match never came to fruition. To this day, if I wanted to show somebody that was not familiar with pro wrestling what they needed to see to gain an understanding of the art behind it, I would show them HBK vs. Angle. It was the match that I used to introduce my wife to why I love watching wrestling matches.

    A year later, Angle left the WWE and joined TNA, but not before joining an esteemed list of wrestlers to offer up MOTY candidates in six consecutive years (from '01-'06). Angle had long hoped to face Undertaker in a match at WrestleMania. It nearly happened at *Mania 22*, but plans changed and they ended up wrestling at *No Way Out* six weeks prior in a match for Angle's World Heavyweight Championship. They developed an in-ring chemistry over the years that helped make their title match a phenomenal 30-minute contest, yet I cannot help but wonder what it would have been like had the Chicago crowd for *Mania 22* been cheering it on. I was there in Chicago that night and it was one of the truly great honors of my wrestling fandom to have had the chance to see Angle defend the World Heavyweight Championship at the first Mania that I ever attended, but I think Angle-Taker would have been a 5-star (perfect) encounter that might have been enough to convince Angle and the WWE to work out something that would have allowed him to stick around past that summer.

    I have missed watching Kurt these last several years. His prodigious rise to the top in pro wrestling is without parallel, historically. Combine his critically acclaimed in-ring achievements with his numerous World titles, his ability to entertain, and his headlining status at four straight WrestleManias and there is no question that Angle is one of the greatest ever.

#13: Randy Orton

    I may be the only one who looks at a former eleven-time World Champion that has main-evented two WrestleManias and headlined two others and either challenged for or defended a World title at one or more of the WWE's Big 3 PPVs in all but one year from 2004-2015, yet writes about his career being somewhat disappointing. That is, though, how I feel about Randy Orton. He has had a tremendous run over the last decade, but he should have been challenging for the Top 10 by now, not far behind his fellow 2002 rookie classmate, John Cena.

    Orton reminds me of a prodigious athlete in team sports that gets stuck on a lousy team. Through some fault of his own, but primarily the blunders of others, he has not become what he once seemed destined to be when he broke into the WWE as a member of Triple H's Four Horsemen-style stable, Evolution, in 2003. The Game was the leader, with Ric Flair as a wrestling version of JJ Dillon and Batista as the Enforcer-type, but Randy Orton was the undeniable future star. The group basically existed to make Orton and Batista into two of the next great wrestlers. Yet, just as Orton was about to carry out his purpose as the WWE's "Apex Predator," horrible booking decisions figuratively slammed a steel chair on him. It happened again five years later. Subsequently, Orton is not everything he should be.

    It was not supposed to be that way. When Orton was spitting in the faces of Hall of Famers and defeating a laundry list of top guys as a rookie sensation, he looked poised to take the throne from his "King of Kings" mentor and ascend to becoming "The Man." I first took note of him in a match against Rob Van Dam, in which Orton won the Intercontinental Championship at *Armageddon 2003*. For me, it was like that scene in *Top Gun* where the lead air combat instructor -

coincidentally named Viper - is flying against Tom Cruise's Maverick and mutters to himself, "Damn, this kid's good."

Where things really started to come together for Orton was his feud with Mick Foley. Live from Madison Square Garden, Orton tossed Foley down a flight of stairs. He began referring to himself as "The Legend Killer" — a gimmick that would serve him well for the next few years. He seemed as though he was on the fast track to being the next great WWE star and, while not as verbally gifted as the other famous third generation wrestler, he was clearly a gifted in-ring performer. Orton was set like few other 23-year olds in the history of the business. Every effort was being put into him becoming a huge star.

By the time he met Foley at *Backlash 2004*, he had rounded into form and was excellent as the cocky young punk. He was still a little bit rough around the edges, but he had come a long way very quickly. The investment was paying off. The PPV, largely built on the back of the Orton-Foley saga, drew a buyrate that garnered approximately one hundred thousand more orders than the previous year (featuring Goldberg's first WWE match) and over fifty thousand more than the next year (which saw a rematch of Batista vs. Triple H from *Mania 21*).

Orton had his first great match and came away looking legitimately tough. Without that match, there was no way he became the youngest World Heavyweight Champion in history four months later at *Summerslam*. Surely, it was in the plans for him to become champion, but I have serious doubts that they would have made that move without his performance at *Backlash*. He hit one out of the park and looked every bit the star that the WWE was pushing so hard for him to be. He also made some new fans that night. Not long after, he had to up the cockiness in his promos to fend off a growing legion of people that wanted to cheer him.

He was still the Intercontinental Champion, so when the feud with Foley was over, he moved back to defending the title throughout the summer. The belt was in a better place than it had been in a long time because of him. Unequivocally, he looked like a veteran in back-to-back title defenses at the *Badd Blood* and *Vengeance* PPVs, racking up an underrated performance against Shelton Benjamin and one of best IC championship matches in history versus Edge. I cannot help but think ahead to *WrestleMania XXIV* when I watch the playback of Orton vs. Edge. They were my two favorites of that generation. Sitting in the Citrus Bowl watching *Mania* live, I watched them defend their respective WWE and World Heavyweight Championships, the top two heels in the business. Since I never got to see HBK or Bret wrestle for the title at a PPV, Orton and Edge's moments were my moments. I look back on their *Vengeance* match and their short-lived faction, Rated-RKO, and it makes *Mania 24* a very special night - the proudest night of my wrestling fandom.

Orton became #1 contender to Chris Benoit's World Heavyweight Championship for *Summerslam 2004* in Toronto. He once again rose to the occasion, but the interesting thing was that the Toronto faithful, who presumably would have been solidly behind Benoit, actually popped stronger for Orton. The bottom line was that the Legend Killer's talents were impressive. A 23-24 year old wrestler being able to step into the squared circle and excel at that level reminded me of Lebron's first game in the NBA when it was very noticeable that, despite his youth, he was already one of the top players in the league. It was astounding to see Orton be so good.

If only the WWE had not so badly botched the next night's *Raw*...

In a pristine suit with the beautiful gold title on his shoulder, Orton strutted out to the ring on August 16, 2004, cocky as ever. He proceeded to cut the most scathing promo of his young life, ripping the audience, self-aggrandizing like only great heels can, coming across like the biggest jerk on the planet. There have been some bad ideas in pro wrestling. Many of them have occurred in the last thirty years. Honest to God, though, I cannot think of anything so poorly handled than what came next for Randy Orton. At the end of *Raw*, after he had defeated Benoit in a *Summerslam* rematch, the rest of Evolution hit the ring and turned on him. At 9PM, he reaffirmed his status as the world's most pompous S.O.B. At 11PM, the WWE told us to sympathize with him because Triple H kicked him out of Evolution. It was a WrestleMania storyline that needed to be cultivated, but they rushed it and completely botched it right from the outset.

8/16/04 is one of the darkest days in the industry's last decade. If I walked up to you and said, "I hate your guts, you fat buffoon," is there even a remote chance that you like me the following week just because I share a distaste for another person that you dislike? That one night took a guy that was sure to be one of the top draws of the next decade – already showing signs that he could bring in the money – and set the tone for him to flop. I still cannot fathom that someone who made so much money as an iconic promoter like Vince McMahon would give the green light to that creative decision (wait, he signed off on HHH crawling into a casket to pretend to hump a dead girl).

The horrifying thing about it was that their ensuing PPV match actually drew a helluva buyrate, with *Unforgiven* earning the identical number to *Backlash*. That was the era of brand specific PPVs and the only one that outdrew the pair of 2004 events built around Orton's matches was a stacked *Vengeance 2005*. I should be bringing up Orton in the top ten. He would have been if smarter decisions had been made on his behalf. Blame his well-documented childish behavior on the road all that you want, but in a land of adulterers, alcoholics, and drug addicts, a young man learning to deal with the trappings of success and the corresponding pressures yelling at a fan or relieving himself in a woman's travel bag were forgivable offenses. He could have made the WWE a lot more money than he has.

To his credit, Orton was able to eventually bounce back. Pushed aside in the WWE's push to create the two next big stars at *WrestleMania 21* in favor of Batista and Cena, he spent the year 2005 feuding with Undertaker; certainly not a bad consolation prize and one that he made the most of. They wrestled on four PPVs, including *Mania* and *Summerslam*, with a Casket match and a Hell in a Cell as two featured gimmicks in their rivalry. It was important for Orton to get that rub because few people looked at him the same after what happened with his ill-fated babyface run. He did not look the same. As of the matches with Foley, Edge, and Benoit, he looked supremely confident in the ring. After the debacle, you could tell by his performances that he was noticeably shaken. Hell, how would you have felt if you were the golden boy one year at your job, poised for the big promotion, and then you were given the impossible project that logically tanked, were blamed for it, and then ended up getting passed over by two guys that you had owned the year prior? Orton *needed* those matches with The Deadman to get his career back on track.

At *WrestleMania 21*, he came closer to toppling The Deadman's Streak than anyone had in a long time. I give a lot of credit to Taker for essentially rescuing Orton and helping him get through a difficult time in his career. The WWE had to salvage what they had put into him prior to 8/16/04. There was a lot chatter that Orton might end "The Streak." He was the first to actually make a storyline goal out of it, starting a trend that continued for a decade. Because of where he was and the traction that Cena and Batista were gaining as babyfaces, it was thought that, perhaps, Orton beating the Taker would keep him on their heels. It did not happen and you could make the argument that it was a missed opportunity. Orton did beat him at *Summerslam* in a much better match than their somewhat clunky *Mania* bout. He seemed to be pulling it together, by then. By year's end, he had split his PPV series with The Deadman at two wins apiece, giving him the credibility to headline *WrestleMania* for the first time in 2006 in challenging World Heavyweight Champion, Kurt Angle, along with Rey Mysterio in a triple threat. An extended PPV feud with Angle, a *Summerslam '06* match with Hulk Hogan, and a partnership with Edge took him all the way to the spring of 2007, when he finally got the career that he appeared destined for three years prior back on track with a memorable run in the main-event, culminating in the victory over Cena and Trips at *Mania 24*.

He suffered an injury in June of '08 that put him on the shelf for several months and, when he came back, he brought a new and far more intense character with him that would eventually become known as "The Viper." For those of us that thought he had turned the corner in '07-'08, his vicious persona bordering on the mentally unstable blew us away. He won the 2009 Royal Rumble match just days after punting Vince McMahon in the head, appearing to literally make his neck snap. "The Punt" – a well-timed running kick to the side of the head - was an integral part of Orton's game for a few years. It was the beginning of a crusade against wrestling's First Family that saw Orton take out Shane and eventually Stephanie, which brought Triple H back into the fold as the WWE Champion defending his real-life wife's honor (the first time the marriage was directly acknowledged on TV).

It appeared as though Orton was on the brink of fulfilling his considerable promise. Cena had a firm grip on the "face of the company" spot for which it had once seemed that Orton was being positioned, but at no point had Cena found a consistently viable rival. Orton vs. Cena had already given us a classic *Summerslam* main-event (in '07) and two-thirds of a *Mania* headliner. However, there was this sense, even during his 6 month WWE title reign, that Orton had yet to figure it all out, in terms of who he wanted to be and how far he thought he could go after the fall of '04 disaster. When he morphed into The Viper, you could tell that the switch had flipped. He was confident as a personality, sure of himself in all that he was doing be it on the mic or in the ring. Smooth as silk during his matches and spot on with each and every sadistic facial expression, Orton emerged as the clear cut #1 heel in the business to provide Cena a foil. All that he needed was a stamp of approval by way of Triple H putting him over on the grand stage in the main-event, one-on-one contest for the WWE Championship.

But Orton lost at the *25th Anniversary of WrestleMania*...

I could not believe it. If ever there was a time for the heel to come out on top in the last match, it was Orton vs. Trips. In the big picture, The Viper had everything to gain. Considering that the on-screen motive for his plot against the McMahons had been to exact revenge on Hunter for ruining his life five years prior, it would have only been right for Orton to conquer his demons and become the top heel in the WWE for years to come; a legitimate draw as the lead antagonist. Triple H, on the other hand, had nothing to gain and nothing to lose by taking the loss. His status as an all-time great had long since been solidified. I am not a fan of all the "Trips hate" concerning his "not putting others over," but that was the one night where I got really upset with his actions. I was very disappointed. Orton lost and gained nothing in the process; neither did the WWE. Just when he was getting back to where he might have been without 8/16/04, Triple H beat him. As it stands, the best that anyone has ever put him over remains Foley.

Mania 25 was the first of his two main-events at the "Granddaddy" and the third of his four times headlining with a World title on the line. It just could have been more. **He** could have been more. As a big fan of his since the beginning, I wanted more *for* him.

In 2009, he was still the Wrestler of the Year and the brightest spot on *Raw* during an otherwise lousy year for the company. Someone got the bright idea to try and attract new viewers by having celebrities "host" the show each week, which did not have a noticeable effect on the ratings but did produce some of the most discombobulated, terrible television in WWE history. Orton, ever deranged and flanked by his protégés, Cody Rhodes and Ted DiBiase, Jr. (a group known as "The Legacy"), became a reflection of our society, in that he was unpredictable and angry. With all the financial turmoil in the world economy, he was actually relatable in his compulsive and erratic behavior.

The only wrestler in the WrestleMania Era that owned their character quite to the level Orton did in 2009 is Undertaker (for the last 25 years). For that reason, his renewed rivalry with Cena still wound up being the best of his career. They competed against each other for the title at five PPVs in a row, exemplifying the expression "tearing it up" in the last three. Cena won the strap in an "I Quit" match and Orton won it back inside Hell in a Cell. The final battle was billed as an "Anything Goes Iron Man" match. For 60-minutes, they wrestled to see who could score the most falls. It was a truly memorable performance and my pick for the best match of his career. The feud with Cena was the height of Orton's storytelling ability and psychological mastery.

Aside from the matches with Cena, Orton's superlative work came in 2011 against Christian. They wrestled on four straight PPVs, producing the TV Match of the Year (when Orton defeated Christian to win the World title in early May) and a pair of strong candidates for the overall MOTY at *Over the Limit* and *Summerslam*. I wrote this about their Over the Limit PPV match in The Doctor's Orders:

Good GOD what a match! Easily the best pure wrestling match of the year and, dare I say, one of the best pure wrestling matches that I've seen since Shawn Michaels vs. Undertaker at *WrestleMania 25*. Their counters were so crisp; their exchanges so fluid. They intricately worked in spots from their first match and modified them just a bit – which is one of those little things in wrestling that we don't see enough but makes a huge difference in the overall performance because it makes it look far less scripted (they look like they've adapted, which is what real fighters do). Frankly, that was one of the best matches of both their careers. Orton hasn't had a match of that caliber in a very long time.

Though he never reached the heights once thought possible and has slid down the pecking order ever since 2009, his overall resume has become similar to another Randy's. Macho Man peaked during a five year stretch from '87 to '92, was the top guy just once but was almost always a Top 5-10 talent for 15 years who frequently reminded us just how good he was and occasionally got to be the focal point again. Orton peaked during a similar five year stretch from '04 to '09, was the top guy in '09 but has been a Top 5-10 talent for nearly fifteen years who has frequently reminded us just how good he is and has occasionally gotten to be the focal point again. Time will tell if Orton can keep going long enough to crack the Top 10.

#12: Chris Jericho

    The Lionheart. Y2J. "The best in the world at what he does." Simply put, Chris Jericho is one of the most talented all-around wrestlers in the history of professional wrestling. He is one of the best talkers and one of the most dynamic in-ring performers. He has proven to be a great ambassador for pro wrestling through other entertainment avenues such as his successful rock band (Fozzy), his appearance on ABC's *Dancing with the Stars*, and his two best-selling autobiographies. Other than his smallish stature, Jericho is the ideal modern superstar. His overall skills landed him 8th in total Wrestler Score.

    He also ranked 10th in the Championship Factor as the first Undisputed World Champion in modern lore and the owner of more Intercontinental championship reigns (9) than any other superstar. He was one-half of three WrestleMania World title matches to go along with countless other headliner/main-event related accolades, good for 10th in the WrestleMania Era. Though his Performance Factor rank was just 13th, it was in that category where I noticed, perhaps, the greatest part of his legacy. When I sat down to research his chapter, I compiled a list of all of his good-to-great matches. Closer examination of the entire list revealed a staggering number of different names listed on the other side of "versus Chris Jericho." By my count, nobody in the WrestleMania Era has had as many critically acclaimed (3-stars or better) matches with as many different wrestlers. It just goes on and on.

    The following is a list of twenty-five memorable Y2J matches, telling the story of his exemplary career:

25) vs. Lance Storm (*ECW One Night Stand 2005*) – Jericho described his one year stint in Extreme Championship Wrestling, which brought him to the American scene in 1996 after wrestling around the world in the early 1990s, as "fun." When the promotion made its WWE-produced comeback in '05,

Jericho opened the show by sending fellow Canadian, Storm, into retirement. Their fast-paced, non-stop, and crisply executed work was a reminder that ECW was more than just garbage brawls on fire. Much of the wrestling on their shows had been world class and an excellent alternative to the slower WWE style, thanks in no small part to the efforts of grapplers like Jericho.

24) vs. Kurt Angle (*Rebellion 2001*) – It would have been thrilling to see Jericho work a faster, ECW paced match with Kurt Angle. Each had incredible stamina. I always wanted to see them in a feud for a World title when they were in the prime of their careers. They faced each other numerous times when they first came to the WWE, but each was still finding his respective groove. By the fall of 2001, they were both hitting their strides and, though they never had a major, personal rivalry, they did have a very good match at a PPV held in the U.K. with Y2J's WCW Championship on the line.

23) vs. Hulk Hogan (*Smackdown* 2002) – Had Y2J been around during Hulkamania, then he would have brought out the best in the Hulkster, much like he was briefly able to do when Hogan returned to the WWE in 2002. Hogan was very much a routine-oriented wrestler. The key to making Hogan's matches interesting was to break him from his mold. Jericho had a knack for helping his opponents change up the order of their key moves to ensure maximum drama. He wrote in his book about how much he enjoyed working with Hogan.

22) vs. Randy Orton (*Armageddon 2007*) – Jericho has kept himself fresh over the years by taking extended periods away from WWE when he saw fit. It has helped him avoid overexposure. Each time he has returned to much fanfare. In 2007, he re-debuted with a modern take on his 1999 debut, using a series of *Matrix*-like vignettes slowly decoding until he showed up on *Raw* to challenge Randy Orton for the WWE Championship. Their feud never reached a definitive conclusion

or produced a match for the ages, but they always did very good work together. Three years later, a match against Orton was Jericho's last for eighteen months.

21) vs. Ricky Steamboat (*Backlash 2009*) – It was a match for the ages between Ricky Steamboat and Randy Savage that inspired a young Jericho to get into the wrestling business. Jericho and Steamboat put on a thrilling performance at the end of a 3-on-1 match at *25th Anniversary of WrestleMania*. The following month, Steamboat came back for a final one-on-one match. What a show it was. It was like watching a shorter version of a Ric Flair-Steamboat match.

20) vs. Juventud Guerrera (*Super Brawl 1998*) – Jericho is one of the smallest top stars ever. His original body of work came in WCW as a cruiserweight. He was strong despite his lack of size, so when working with someone less than two hundred pounds like Juventud, he was able to do some quick paced, lucha style grappling - learned from his time in Mexico - which strictly WWE fans may never have seen him do. He did great character work as a smarmy, annoying heel champion of the WCW CW division, as well.

19) vs. X-Pac (*No Mercy 2000*) – Transitioning from WCW Cruiserweight to WWE Heavyweight involved an increase in expectations for Y2J. He struggled throughout much of his first year and was still very much in need of consistently strong performances when this Cage match with X-Pac came about nearly a year after his WWE debut. If he could potentially steal the show from the likes of Triple H, Rock, Austin, and Angle, then he could show the WWE that he was ready to be a top tier player. He may not have earned "best match" honors on that night, but he and Pac set the tone for the others to follow. The theme, amusingly, was to see how many times they could crotch each other – on the ropes, on top of the cage, or on the cage door.

18) vs. Evan Bourne (*Fatal 4-Way 2010*) – Though he did eventually become a regular main-event talent, Jericho would occasionally find himself lost in the shuffle for a month or few at a time. The seed of equivalent benefit in that defeat was that he could have a random match on a PPV that stole the show. The match with Bourne was an excellent 12-minute bout that had very little story behind it. You went into it thinking, "Jericho will win a solid encounter against this relative nobody and call it a night." As the match went on, you started thinking Evan was going to look great in defeat. Then, he actually won! Jericho was great at playing the overconfident, headlining heel against the new guy. He reminded me of Flair in similar scenarios from back in the late 80s/early 90s.

17) vs. Batista (*Cyber Sunday 2008*) – Jericho was not often given the opportunity to work with significantly bigger wrestlers, but when he did he pulled out some of his most underrated performances. Jericho's prowess for creative counters was made all the more impressive against a guy of Batista's size. He had to be more cunning in his execution. For instance, he had one of the best counters to the Batista Bomb that I have ever seen, grabbing onto the top rope in the midst of being hoisted into Powerbomb position. With the World title on the line in late 2008, he so nicely worked over Batista's knee that it helped make each false finish from the middle of the match onward seem like a legitimate end.

16) vs. Dean Malenko (*Great American Bash 1998*) – One of the main reasons for the WWE signing Jericho in 1999 had to have been his work in 1998 with Malenko, during which he showed the potential to be more than just an undercard wrestler. Their feud showed flashes of the "Y2J" character that became famous in the early part of last decade. His whiny heel persona put him on the map. They had solid matches together, but the most memorable performance of their storyline was Jericho's promo listing his knowledge of 1,004 holds (four more than Malenko, "The Man of 1,000 Holds").

15) vs. Shelton Benjamin (*Backlash 2005*) – The most undervalued aspect of Jericho's game is his athleticism. He does not look like much, physically. He is the wrestling equivalent of Billy Hoyle from *White Men Can't Jump*. If you saw him and did not know him, you might think "there is no way that he is amongst the top wrestlers of all-time." Playing Sidney to Jericho's Billy in the spring of 2005 was the ultra-athletic heavyweight, Shelton Benjamin. Not many could match Shelton's agility, thus helping to showcase his physical tools, but Jericho was able to have a great match that made Benjamin look like the second coming. The finishing sequence was particularly impressive, as Benjamin countered the Walls of Jericho by "flipping" Y2J over with his legs into a pinning combo. It looked awesome, but it was just as much Jericho getting the timing right as Benjamin having the leg strength to execute it.

14) vs. Rob Van Dam (*King of the Ring 2002*) – RVD was a similar opponent for Jericho as Shelton, in that he brought to the table a unique skill set. He was spot heavy, with a concentration on high flying moves that were aesthetically pleasing but could be viewed as random if he was not being guided by a ring general like Jericho who could help space them out logically throughout the course of a match. These two had several bouts with each other over a two year period, but this was the one with the best format and most superior execution. For a match that involved several moves with a high degree of difficulty, it went off without a hitch.

13) Vs. Eddie Guerrero (*Fall Brawl '97*) – Excelling in matches with RVD and Shelton came from years of working in Japan, Mexico, and the WCW CW division. Occasionally, he would find himself across the canvas from a fellow ring general like Guerrero. One of my favorite of Jericho's CW title defenses was against Eddie in September '97, where he lost the belt to Guerrero. Jericho was not quite as small as a lot of the higher flying cruiserweights, cut more from the Malenko mold of the

wrestler who was capable of top rope maneuvers, but had a more ground-based game. Jericho-Guerrero was two young maestros that cut their teeth in Japan showcasing their submission acumens before transitioning to a more North American pleasing series of high spots.

12) vs. Christian (*WrestleMania XX*) – Christian was another such ring general. The matches between Jericho and Christian are what I would describe as "inappropriately forgotten." Rumor had it that Y2J had a lot of input into the storyline between he, Christian, Trish Stratus, and Lita that led to one of WrestleMania lore's best mid-card matches. Few in the WWE could pull it off, but Y2J transitioned from hated heel to sympathetic babyface in a matter of weeks. Jericho and Christian had great chemistry and had several high caliber matches in 2004. He also had a very entertaining dynamic with Stratus, reminiscent of his work with Stephanie McMahon in 2001 (i.e. "Filthy, dirty, disgusting, brutal, bottom feeding, trash bag hoe!").

11) vs. Edge (*Smackdown* 2002) – Jericho also had a memorable rivalry with Christian's best friend, Edge. While not nearly as high profile as their *WrestleMania XXVI* match for the World title, the Steel Cage match on *SD* from eight years prior was their best match. It was an example of two men in their athletic primes pulling out all of the stops in an era where wrestlers pushed their bodies to the limit like never before and during a year where SD featured a PPV-like competition for match of the night honors on a weekly basis. Matches like this likely kept Jericho motivated to keep giving his all after such a dramatic de-push following his loss of the Undisputed Championship at *WrestleMania X-8*.

10) vs. John Cena (*Summerslam 2005*) – In the summer of 2005, Jericho had a brief chance to work with a newcomer named John Cena. In 2002, Y2J had been one of the first to voice his opinion that Cena had the goods to become an all-time great.

Three years later, Cena was in the midst of his first run as WWE Champion and drew the ire of many fans for his lack of performance quality in championship matches. Jericho helped him temporarily silence those critics at Summerslam. Working with Jericho taught Cena how to up his game to the main-event level. It was refreshing to see Y2J back in the main-event for the first time in three years, but it was also the catalyst for a three year hiatus.

9) vs. Stone Cold Steve Austin (*Vengeance 2001*) – Though I never thought that the matches between Jericho and Austin lived up to the expectations that their combination of talents suggested, there is no denying that the most famous match of Y2J's career came on the night that he defeated Stone Cold just twenty minutes after beating The Rock, becoming the first ever Undisputed World Champion and uniting the two most prestigious titles, the WWE and WCW Championships, into one. Forever and always, Jericho will hold that amazing distinction.

8) vs. Ultimo Dragon (*Bash at the Beach 1997*) – Taking one last look at his WCW days, the best example of Jericho as a cruiserweight wrestler was his work with Ultimo Dragon. They worked a thrilling 15-minute set of intricate catch-as-catch-can sequences in a 1997 title match. The unmistakable quality produced by these men, even though they were missing on a couple of key spots down the stretch, was truly something to behold. Put this near the top of your short list if you are having a lazy day and want to get caught up on WCW cruiserweight history.

7) vs. Chris Benoit (*Royal Rumble 2001*) – To watch some of Jericho's CW title matches in WCW was to see a young, confident wrestler. Much of that confidence was stripped away when Y2J came into the WWE. Luckily, his matches with Benoit in 2000 happened. They helped build Jericho into a reliable WWE-style performer and rebuilt his self-confidence. Jericho and Benoit had several PPV encounters leading up to the blow

off to their feud in early 2001 for the Intercontinental title. It was a Ladder match, but rather than concentrate on high risks off the ladder, they came up with countless ways to use it as a weapon. It was not until the final five minutes that the IC title belt hanging above the ring came into play, for the bottom line was that Jericho's story with Benoit was personal.

6) (w/ Chris Benoit) vs. Triple H and Steve Austin (*Raw* 2001) – Jericho turned right around and teamed with Benoit soon after their feud concluded. He had some great tag team matches in his career, but the one that stood out above all others and truly showcased his skill set was the all-time classic television match that saw he and Benoit capture the Tag titles from Steve Austin and Triple H. It was easily one of the best TV matches of all-time. Austin and Trips brought a lot of credibility to the straps, making it mean a hell of a lot more when Jericho and Benoit knocked them off the mountain top. Famous for seeing Trips gut out the final minutes after tearing his quadriceps, this match stands the test of time while being underrated, in terms of Jericho's performance. It was such a rare thing to see a legitimately awesome tag team match without ladders or tables in the Attitude Era.

5) vs. Triple H (*Fully Loaded 2000*) – The proving ground feud for Y2J was with Triple H in the summer of 2000, leading to a Last Man Standing match at the July PPV. The toughness that he showed and the fight that he put up against the WWE's top heel, even in defeat, made him a legitimate star on the rise and assuredly instilled confidence in the WWE that he could get it done in a headlining match. Last Man Standing matches typically feature quite a bit of standing around while the ref counts toward ten at usually inane times where you know that there is little chance of a finish. It is the rare – and subsequently the best – version of the gimmick where the counts take place at logical moments; such is why Jericho vs. Trips was one of the best LMS bouts of all-time (if not the best). They wasted no

motion and made every move seem like it would count toward the eventual end.

4) vs. CM Punk (*WrestleMania XXVIII*) – Jericho came back to the WWE in 2012 for the specific purpose, it would seem, of putting over a guy that needed someone with a big name to put him over. He could not have picked a better stage than the most financially successful WrestleMania of the PPV era. Y2J is a class act. CM Punk needed a win over a top star to solidify his status and Jericho had the professionalism to realize it. Jericho vs. Punk was reminiscent of Jericho vs. Shawn Michaels from *Mania XIX*. The fact that the WWE Championship was on the line only served to further cement the encounter as one of the best of his career.

3) vs. Rey Mysterio (*The Bash 2009*) – During the late spring/early summer of '09, Jericho engaged in a series of matches with Mysterio that I could sit back and watch all day and not get bored. Sometimes, two guys get in the ring and just make magic happen. Mysterio has worked effortlessly with several wrestlers, but Jericho might have been the best of the lot. Many of the spots that Y2J pulled off with Rey looked so difficult when you play them in slow motion, but in real time were made to look easy. The timing, in this bout, was unreal. There was one sequence where Mysterio did a springboard cross body block back toward the center of the ring and Jericho perfectly connected with the Codebreaker in mid-air; just a thing of beauty. They wrestled two other PPV matches and numerous times on TV, but this was the Title vs. Mask payoff to their story and the best match that they ever had together.

2) vs. The Rock (*No Mercy 2001*) – The Rock was involved in many of Jericho's pinnacle moments. It was Rock who he interrupted when his Millennium Countdown ended to debut his "Y2J" persona in late 1999 and it was their series of matches in 2001/2002 that were the primary reason why Jericho became a consistent top guy from that point forward. If the bout with

Trips in 2000 put Jericho on the map, it was the matches with Rock a year later that put Y2J over the top. In wrestling, emerging stars need established main-eventers to put them over, as otherwise people cannot take the budding headliner seriously as a legitimate threat. Against Rock, Jericho showed that he could be counted upon to bring it in every aspect of the game. The two had great chemistry in the ring just as they did in verbally interacting. At *No Mercy '01*, they had an excellent match that saw Jericho get his first taste of big time victories when it mattered, defeating Rock for the WCW title.

1) vs. Shawn Michaels (*No Mercy 2008*) – Jericho's greatest rival was Shawn Michaels. Y2J and HBK had two fantastic feuds in 2003 and 2008, respectively. *Mania XIX* was the defining performance of Jericho's career and one of the top fifteen matches in "Granddaddy" history, helping him shed the label that he could not live up to the hype on the "grandest stage" after a disappointing main-event at *WrestleMania X-8*. However, I firmly believe that his best performance was the *No Mercy* Ladder match five and a half years later. It was an epic match that stamped the Y2J vs. HBK rivalry as one of the all-time greats. After Jericho won the World title on the same night that he lost an Un-Sanctioned match to HBK, it set the stage for one more clash between the two with the gold on the line. The story was the key. Ladder matches are often all about the ladder and less about the wrestlers climbing/using it. With a downright brilliant plot already in place, Jericho and Michaels used the ladder as a part of the final chapter to the book of HBK vs. Y2J. The finish was amazing and the best closing sequence in the history of the Ladder match. They shared in unhooking the belt and each grabbed one end of it. They proceeded to have a game of tug of war that ended with Jericho retaining the title. It was amazing drama.

At what he did, Chris Jericho was indeed the "Best in the World."

#11: Edge

11-time World Champion, 5-time Intercontinental Champion, 1-time United States Champion, and 14-time Tag Team Champion. The 2001 King of the Ring, the 2005 (and inaugural) winner of the Money in the Bank Ladder match, the 2010 Royal Rumble match winner, and a 2012 (first ballot) inductee into the WWE Hall of Fame.

If you knew nothing of professional wrestling, you could still read the above list of accomplishments and assume that the accomplisher was one of the most heralded in history. Yet, the achiever is actually quite underrated in the all-time sense. I would be willing to bet, in fact, that at least one knowledgeable fan reading this paragraph is bewildered by Edge being placed so high. Well, the numbers do not lie. Edge was awesome.

Perhaps part of what makes Edge fly under the radar, historically, is that he was not the franchise. At no point in his career was he the guy that was expected to carry the load as the top superstar in the WWE. In Major League Baseball, the New York Yankees are the ratings draw. In the WWE, one particular star is usually going to be the Nielsen alpha male comparable to the Yankees. Edge was not the Yankees. He was not even the Boston Red Sox. He was more like the St. Louis Cardinals. The Cards are an excellent, popular franchise that has won numerous World Series Championships in the last decade and has been a consistent force in MLB. They do not have the flash or the country-wide appeal that do the Yankees or Sox, but they are a top flight team with the hardware to back it up. That was Edge in the WWE.

Luckily, historical perspective allows us to take a step back and evaluate. Just as the Cards will be ranked right up there with the top teams of the last thirty years in baseball, so too will Edge be remembered as one of the greats in wrestling.

Unquestionably, what has always set Edge apart has been his passion. Jim Ross called him the most passionate superstar he ever encountered. Edge had such a love for wrestling that it permeated through his work in and out of the ring. Many kids grow up enthused about baseball because of the Yankees or Red Sox. Adam Copeland became Edge, the WWE superstar, because he went to *WrestleMania VI* as a kid and was captivated by it. From that point forward, all that he wanted to do was become a wrestler so that he could perform at WrestleMania. That resonates with wrestling fans. Edge was the epitome of dreams becoming reality.

Edge is one of my personal, all-time favorite wrestlers, in large part because of his passion. Seeing Edge wrestle in big matches, especially when he made it to the big time and started being a featured, headlining act, was a perfect example of how far passion can take you in life. Edge wore his heart on his sleeve and was one of those guys that would break down in tears in front of a live audience even if he was supposed to be portraying a bad ass. That was just who he was – passion personified. When he won the WWE title from John Cena and began noticeably crying during his celebration, he was supposed to be the evil opportunist, but the emotion just came pouring out. Before a main-event against Cena later that same year in his hometown of Toronto, he got so emotional that he broke down again. That same crowd had booed him out of the building two years prior when he was playing the good guy. This time, he was the top heel in the business and they gave him a hero's reception. I love seeing stuff like that.

2006 was the year that Edge became a headliner, but it was back in 2002 that I first took notice of him as a singles wrestler. It was April 21, 2002 at *Backlash*, specifically. The WWE executed one of the most historically significant business decisions that they ever made a few weeks earlier when they split their roster into two separate brands. Edge was one of the guys that most benefitted in the first year of the split, as it gave him the chance to shine against main-event talents and, subsequently, mold himself into a top level star. Up to that point, he had been one of the greatest tag team wrestlers of all-time and a fairly accomplished secondary champion, but he was nowhere close to headlining on his own. *Backlash* was his first big opportunity. Against Kurt Angle, Edge showed that he had the chops to be a future star.

The feud continued with the classic Hair vs. Hair match at *Judgment Day*. There were so many dramatic false finishes, as the style back then was so intense and fast-paced. Angle was the embodiment of that style, but Edge could hang with him. It was one of many Edge matches that made wrestling must-see TV again for me. There was a consistently high match quality from week-to-week in 2002 that has never been matched before or since. Edge and Angle's matches that spring prompted me to call up my best friend, Sac, and proclaim that "Edge is my new favorite wrestler for the future." It is awesome to see a guy that you watched come up through the ranks make it to the top. I remember seeing Heath Ledger's first movie while I was in high school and then seeing him work his way up to that iconically tragic role as The Joker. There is something extra special about that performance for me since I saw him before he was a superstar. I look at Edge's rise the same way. I actually had the privilege of seeing him reach his pinnacle moment when I was live in attendance at *WrestleMania XXIV* for his main-event World Heavyweight Championship defense against The Undertaker.

His string of great matches continued well past the series with Angle. 2002, from the Angle series onward, was an incredible year for Edge as a singles wrestler. He also had very good matches with Chris Jericho, Chris Benoit, and Eddie Guerrero. His No-DQ match with Guerrero in September was particularly memorable. They had not initially seemed to have overwhelming chemistry in their two PPV matches, but they blew me away that night. It was one of the best matches in the history of *Smackdown* and the kind of match that had to have made people backstage look at them as future World Champions. Edge also captured the Tag titles with his childhood hero, Hulk Hogan, that year.

One of the best matches that Edge had in 2002 was actually one that few people know about since it took place at the UK-based *Rebellion* PPV. That night, he wrestled Brock Lesnar and Paul Heyman (in a handicap match) with the WWE Championship on the line and tore the house down. I did not see this match until four years after it happened, but I will never forget sitting there and thinking to myself, "Matches like this are why I pegged Edge as my favorite that year." It was a match that put the stamp on Edge being a guy that they could eventually push to the title. They put him in the main-event, had Brock Lesnar give him every move in his arsenal, and allowed Edge to come back and nearly win the WWE Championship. It was a great test for him and he passed it with flying colors.

Unfortunately, he became one of several wrestlers that went under the knife for spinal surgeries in the early 2000s. The style of wrestling during the late 1990s brought with it a lot of physical consequences. Edge was a casualty of the car crash-throw your body to wolves mentality. He had made a name for himself during the latter half of the Attitude Era in TLC matches with Christian, the Hardys, and the Dudleys, putting his body through hell. Those guys will never be the same and took years off their qualities of life trying to take the next step in their careers. The neck injury came at a time when Edge was at the peak of his athleticism. He was not able to return until the spring of 2004 – over a year after the surgery – and he was never the same caliber of athlete again. I think injuries of that nature teach wrestlers to be smarter, though. He learned to tone it down, but become more effective.

One of the greatest tools in Edge's arsenal was his ability as what I call a "closer." A closer is a wrestler that always finds a way to make the climactic sequences at the end of his matches as thrilling and dramatic as possible. It is akin to a movie director known for putting together intricate twists and turns in the plot toward the end of a film. Edge was one of the best closers in the business. He was very creative. He had numerous moves that he found ways to execute in different orders. If anything, the modifications that he made to his game, post-injury, made him an even better closer.

As a performer, Edge was ready to move up to the next level when he came back in 2004. However, he was not making a strong enough connection with the audience. A real life situation proved to be just the thing he needed to figure it out. In 2005, rumors began circulating that he was having an affair with Lita, whose long-time boyfriend (and Edge's friend), Matt Hardy, had been released from his WWE contract. Edge took a lot of heat for it. The love triangle eventually became a storyline on television after the overwhelming support for Hardy prompted him to be rehired. When Hardy came back in the summer to get as much out of the real life drama as possible, Edge took the last step toward superstar status. It seemed to me that any remorse he may have felt for his actions had been replaced by annoyance in how Hardy had aired the dirty laundry in public. Many critics had cited Edge's lack of fire during his promos as being one of his major on-screen character flaws and said that he lacked that look in his eye that said he "wanted it." I remember there was a promo he did backstage where he basically told his side of the story and you could see that inferno burning through his retinas. He turned the corner right then and there.

As the story unfolded with Hardy, the WWE decided to pair Lita with Edge as his manager, of sorts, to take advantage of the heat. It proved to be a wise move. They were a great duo that only helped to better the heel character that Edge was developing. During the spring of '05, Edge won the inaugural Money in the Bank Ladder match at *WrestleMania 21*. The prize for winning the match was a contract for a World Championship match at any point in the 12 months that followed. It was a concept that went over very well, eventually spawning its own PPV event of the same name. The success of MITB largely depended on Edge. Had he not been successful, MITB may not have been either. Its legacy is linked to Edge's historic rise and the efficacy of his cash in.

    The idea was so fresh that nobody knew what to expect, in terms of when or how Edge would cash in his contract. He won it on April 3, 2005. He had until April 2, 2006's *WrestleMania 22* to have his title match. I think most assumed he would do it at *The 2006 Royal Rumble*. Just days into 2006, though, Edge was in a match with Ric Flair at *New Year's Revolution*. Edge suffered an injury late in 2005 that left him unable to capitalize on the aftermath of the Hardy feud. His match with Flair at *NYR* was the opener and they wrestled for a few minutes before going to a DQ finish. It was a ho-hum night for Edge until Mr. McMahon came out after the Elimination Chamber match for the WWE title (the main-event of the evening) and announced that Edge was cashing in his title opportunity. I was on the edge, pun intended, of my seat! That was one of the most exciting moments of my fandom. Edge cashed in and won the WWE Championship.

    One night later, he had a memorable "Live Sex" celebration on *Raw* that, little did I know, my future wife happened to watch out of sheer curiosity. The segment drew a huge rating (for that time period) – the largest in a very long time. Suddenly, Edge was a huge, ratings grabbing star. The "sex" segment gave him the nickname "The Rated R Superstar," a moniker that will forever be attached to his name. The next week, he had an incredibly entertaining match with Flair – in a TLC match no less – on *Raw* in one of the best performances of his career. Ratings were huge again! He ended up dropping the belt back to Cena at *The Royal Rumble*, but the three week reign turned Edge into a major player and he never looked back. He was put into a match with a returning Mick Foley for *WrestleMania* that year and arguably stole the show when he Speared Foley through a flaming table to earn the victory.

With his main-event character swinging the momentum in his direction, Edge won the WWE title again in July, writing the next chapter of his story with Cena. Theirs was a rivalry that worked wonders for both of them. They were each other's first great main-event feud. I started reviewing PPVs for LOP the month prior to their main-event at *Summerslam*, so their series holds a special place for me. The *Summerslam* match was the one where they began clicking in the ring together, but it was their TLC match at *Unforgiven* a month later that pushed their tale to legendary status. It was my choice for 2006 Match of the Year - an absolutely amazing match that put the finishing touches on one of the better rivalries of the modern era. Some of the bumps that they took in that match no doubt led to Cena's eventual neck surgery and Edge's eventual retirement. The human body just was not made to endure matches like that, but the drama was awesome and I thank them for the memories.

One of the most memorable nights of Edge's career came at the *No Way Out* PPV some three years later in February 2009, in which Edge went in as WWE Champion, lost the title in the *Smackdown* Elimination Chamber to start the show, and then entered the *Raw* Elimination Chamber to end the show, winning the World Heavyweight Championship. Who did he take the World title from? John Cena. It set up the renewal of the Cena-Edge rivalry at the *25th Anniversary of WrestleMania*. Big Show was inserted into the fold, but it was satisfying that such a good rivalry ended up getting featured in at least some way on the grandest of stages. The last great match that they had together came the next month at *Backlash* in a Last Man Standing match. Shawn Michaels vs. Undertaker from *Mania* is highly regarded as one of the great matches in history, but had that match taken place in a different year, then Edge vs. Cena from Backlash might have been named the best of 2009.

Edge had two fitting nicknames in his career. The first was the aforementioned "Rated R Superstar"; the second was "The Ultimate Opportunist." The latter was earned when he goaded the 2007 Money in the Bank winner to put his contract up for grabs. Edge defeated him and then cashed in to win the World title from Undertaker in May 2007 after The Deadman had suffered through a Cage match and a post-match assault. It ignited not only a new moniker, but also his greatest rivalry, leading to the main-event at *WrestleMania XXIV* (the only time that Edge had the honor of going on last at "The Show of Shows"). During the feud with Taker, he joined forces with Eddie Guerrero's widow, Vickie. Edge used her role as the General Manager of *Smackdown* to protect his championship status. Much like the pairing with Lita, the dynamic between Edge and Vickie was a surprise hit.

The matches with Taker were the best of Edge's career. The *Mania* main-event was excellent (and underrated). So, too, was their TLC match in June 2008. What a dramatic match that was. The stipulation attached to the match was that if Taker won, he would win the World title, but if Edge won, Taker would have to retire. Typically, those matches are quite predictable, as the wrestler that could be forced to retire rarely loses. Edge, in a surprising victory, further proved that the TLC match was his money gimmick as a main-eventer. He owned it. Their other big match that year was the main-event at *Summerslam* inside Hell in a Cell. It was a phenomenal effort that made an argument for best HIAC match of all-time amidst stiff competition. At the very least, it was the blueprint for the modern day version of the gimmick, which relies on a taller Cell that no one would be foolish enough to fall off.

There were numerous other memorable matches and rivalries in his career, including high profile feuds with Kane, Batista, Degeneration X, Rey Mysterio, Jeff Hardy, Chris Jericho, Dolph Ziggler, and Alberto Del Rio. Yet, it will be his superior work at WrestleMania and his matches with Cena and Taker that best define his legacy. Edge had a higher understanding of WrestleMania than most. From the moment he arrived on the scene, he always put forth a show stealing effort. I admired that about him. The mentality seemed to be that if he could steal the show there, then he could steal it anywhere. I had the honor of seeing three of his ten Mania matches in person, two of which were his best singles matches (vs. Foley and vs. Taker). Mania meant a lot to him as a wrestler and it means a lot to me as a fan to have seen him perform there.

I will never forget the *Raw* just eight days removed from *WrestleMania 27*. That night, Edge emotionally announced that he had been forced into retirement. I knew of Edge's health history and I had always wondered how long a man who had spinal fusion surgery in his late twenties could continue in the profession of pro wrestling, but I did not think it would come so abruptly. I had been in attendance in Atlanta when Edge had won his World title match (for the only time in four tries at Mania). Little did I know that it would be the last match of his career. On that day, I saw clearly that Edge would be remembered as one of the all-time best.

The Greatest Of The WrestleMania Era

#10: *"Macho Man" Randy Savage*

The best all-around wrestler in the WWE from the first fifteen years of the WrestleMania Era was the "Macho Man" Randy Savage. His interviews were legendary, his personality jumped off the screen, and his matches were epic. With distinctly gifted character traits and a "reckless abandon," intense wrestling style, he was one of the central reasons why the mainstream opened its arms to sports entertainment during the late 80s boom period.

Nobody cut more entertaining promos. With the unusual voice, the rapid changes of inflection, and the signature catchphrases ("Ohhhh Yeaaahhh! Dig it!"), Savage had a style like no other. His Slim Jim commercials used to beg the question, "Need a little excitement?!?!" There was nothing more exciting than two minutes of listening to Macho Man talk. There are video compilations on the internet of the best Macho Man segments with Mean Gene Okerlund and other backstage personalities. If you are having a bad day, they will cheer you right up. Even if but for a moment, like in his cameo appearance in 2002's *Spiderman*, his gravelly tone could hook your interest. My dad and I used to shush surrounding crowds when his one line in that movie came up. "Bone Saw is READY!"

Often lost amidst the madness was Macho Man's intelligence. He had quite the interesting way of getting his point across, granted, so you had to concentrate on what he was saying. Assuming, of course, that you could keep up, his interviews were unusually eloquent. In an industry where 99% of the greatest of all-time have had to be masters of self-promotion, Savage was a man amongst boys.

In the ring, he was a game-changer. Up to that point, only the grapplers that could regularly wrestle for an hour were placed into the conversation for who was the best. The WWE was shifting toward a different target audience, viewing the

"60-minute match" as the wrestling equivalent of baseball. An increasingly "instant gratification" minded society did not have the attention span to remain engaged for that long. So, they decided to become more like football or basketball, whose professional organizations paid much mind to giving the fans the most enjoyable experience possible. Macho Man may not have been the first to pick up the pace inside the squared circle, but he was the one making use of the rapid fire tactical approach to garner the most praiseworthy critical reviews. It was never explicitly stated that the WWE made Savage's method their modus operandi, but he provided the finest example of how to work fast and efficient and still gain the respect of wrestling connoisseurs. The definition of a "5-star" performance changed accordingly.

One of Savage's most important contributions to the wrestling industry was what he did for WrestleMania in its early years. He was as important to building WrestleMania on the performance side as Hulk Hogan was to the business side. His matches, especially those at *WrestleManias III, IV, V, VII, and VIII*, stand the test of time as five of the greatest individual nights in any wrestler's career.

It began at *WrestleMania III*...

The first taste of what Mania would become featured the first true classic in its history. Savage defended his Intercontinental Championship against Ricky Steamboat in what is still regarded by some as WrestleMania's preeminent match. If there was any doubt prior to, then I do not think anyone left with any qualms about Macho Man being a main-event player and a future World Champion. That was the kind of match that takes a career full of promise and turns it into a career full of momentous accomplishment. From that night on, Macho was a headliner for life.

The next year was dedicated toward getting him ready for the next level and, at *WrestleMania IV*, he fulfilled his destiny and won the WWE Championship after four grueling matches in the famous 14-man title tournament, last defeating Hall of Famer, Million Dollar Man, in the finals. For each of his tournament battles, he had a different outfit prepared. Pomp and circumstance was not just the title of his entrance theme, but also an adequate description of his character.

Since Hogan had dominated the top babyface spot for so long, it seemed like a no-brainer that the tourney would be little more than his latest obstacle to overcome. It was somewhat of a shocker upon initially viewing the event to see Savage emerge victorious. However, I think any fan of any age with any knowledge of the business could take a step back and view how great a heel Savage had been, see Hogan standing next to him in the ring as he celebrated his *Mania IV* title triumph, and have the forethought to 1989's *WrestleMania V*, where a fairly obvious Savage vs. Hogan match would take place. When the WWE dubbed them "The Mega Powers" and set them up as teammates throughout 1988, you could not help but watch for the subtle signs of discord. Even as a youngster playing catch up via the magic of Coliseum Home Video, I watched *Summerslam* and *Survivor Series '88* with an eye out for tension. It took until *Survivor Series* in November for the major signs of a break-up to show. The Mega Powers had not "Exploded," yet, but the pressure was building inside their heroic bubble.

The eventual turn came in early 1989 after Savage became resentful of Hogan's friendly relationship with his long-time manager and real life wife, Miss Elizabeth. Macho unleashed a vengeful, spiteful attack on the Hulkster that lit a fuse that traveled all the way to Atlantic City's Trump Plaza for *Mania V*. It was some of Savage's absolute best character work, as he played the crazed and jealous "boyfriend" to a "T."

Some would argue that, for a night to be "yours" in sports, you have to win. I do not think that said standard holds true in professional wrestling. Winning is *very* important, but there are other intangibles to consider in a sport where the outcome is predetermined. Wrestlers may know who is going to win, but they are still competing with each other; trying to take command of a spot at the top that someone else wants. *WrestleMania V* was the biggest night of Savage's career. He may have lost the title to Hogan as expected, but it was an event that still remains near the top ten WrestleManias of all-time, in terms of the business it generated. Imagine if it had been held in a football stadium ala *Manias III and VI*, respectively. Savage did big business as the top heel and established himself as one of the all-time draws in the industry.

My favorite of Macho's classic in-ring performances was against The Ultimate Warrior at *WrestleMania VII* two years later. It should have been for the WWE Championship and I think both of them truly believed it. Their feud had been building since the fall of the previous year, with Macho having won the King of the Ring tournament and dubbed himself "Macho King." He felt that he had earned a title shot, but Warrior would not oblige him with a championship opportunity. To this day, I have no idea if their match at *Mania* was originally intended to be for the title. If it was, then plans changed leading up to *The Royal Rumble*, where Savage cost Warrior the belt to Sgt. Slaughter. The WWE must have looked at Savage-Warrior as the second main-event for Mania, as they did their best to put it on equal footing with the title bout by making it a Career match where the loser would be forced into retirement.

Everything about Savage vs. Warrior, on the night of, made it seem like it was the main-event. The commentating from Gorilla Monsoon and Bobby Heenan was flawless, as they set the stage for what was at stake and put every ounce of their emotion into putting words to Savage and Warrior's physical tale. Heenan took the side of the Macho King, giving perspective to what it meant to Savage to win the match. He said, as Savage was warming up, that Macho did not look like a man who came to lose. Such comments can make a match so much more compelling. Macho King rode to the ring on a throne, alongside the "Sensational" Queen Sherri, as the atmosphere in the Los Angeles Sports Arena rose to the occasion.

The attention to detail was outstanding. From the announcing to the psychology of even the entrances and the outfits, Macho King vs. Warrior was an epic encounter. When the match got underway, you could see on their faces how much it meant to them, making it easy to believe in everything that they were doing. They each displayed the mindset that you would expect from two men fighting for their professional lives. Simultaneously, they gave the expressions and movements that coincided with the personal nature of their rivalry. Warrior kicking out after five flying elbow drops by Savage was one of the great false finishes in wrestling lore; ditto for when, just minutes later, Macho kicked out of the same press slam-body splash combination that had put down everyone from Hogan to Andre to DiBiase to Rude. It was such desperate moments that put their match on a completely different level from anything that had been done before it.

Savage vs. Warrior from *Mania VII* was the birth of the modern day WWE main-event. It raised the bar and made a near fall following (or special counter of a) finishing move almost a prerequisite for a match to be considered a classic. It demanded that every battle between top guys from then on feature several twists and turns in momentum in grand fashion. Simply switching from one headlock sequence to the next would no longer cut it. The Steamboat match from *Mania III* had set a new standard for WWE sports entertainment (not be confused with still traditional pro wrestling NWA/WCW), but the standard was reset once Savage vs. Warrior had concluded.

As if the match itself were not enough, the post-match drama that saw Sherri turn on Savage, only for Miss Elizabeth - who had been sitting at ringside - to hop the guardrail and come to his aid was the most perfectly executed emotional moment of that variety in wrestling history. There were literally hundreds of people in the crowd crying when Savage and Elizabeth embraced. I still, to this day, get tingles up and down my spine when I see that moment replayed.

(Sigh)...Words cannot express how much I love that match...

I have often called Savage the original "Mr. WrestleMania." Shawn Michaels adopted the moniker after years of stealing the "Show of Shows" with amazing performances seemingly every year and there is no denying that the nickname is his and his alone. However, when you take what Macho Man had already done as of 1991 and add 1992's *WrestleMania VIII* match with Ric Flair, in which Savage won the WWE title for the second time, you have the best in-ring Mania resume pre-HBK. Three of Savage's matches crack the top 15-20 in wrestling's Super Bowl history. Some of my fellow wrestling "beat writers" claim that Savage vs. Flair was the best of the three. It is indisputable that it was an exceptional piece of work. It was kind of a dream match in its own right, despite the fact that the world was expecting Flair to face Hogan that year. Flair vs. Hogan would have been the Jean Claude Van Damme vs. Arnold Schwarzenegger of the 80s. Savage vs. Flair was Chuck Norris vs. Van Damme – still a dream scenario, but just not the definitive dream.

The storyline devised was perfect, as Macho's reuniting with Elizabeth in 1991 - culminating in their wedding at *Summerslam* - made the two of them the best couple in wrestling (then and maybe ever). Flair singling out "Liz" as his former lover was a stroke of creative genius, for The Nature Boy knew just how to milk such an angle. Savage had one of the best and most believable babyface acts, in part for how fervently he would come to the defense of his wife. Jake Roberts had made Liz a mark with a venomous wedding gift and Savage's response during their subsequent feud was off the charts, in terms of the acting job. He sold so well that he wanted nothing more in the world but to get his hands on Jake, most notably during the 1992 Royal Rumble match when he blasted out from behind the curtain and ran what might have been clocked as a WWE record for the 40-yard dash to the ring, where Roberts awaited. When the storyline with Jake concluded, Flair picked up where Jake left off, psychologically attacking the spouse in a different way.

Evidence to Macho Man's authenticity as a hero could be seen and heard via the crowd response he earned at *WrestleMania* in the Hoosier Dome. I have watched every Mania a dozen times or more and I would put Savage's pop that night in Indianapolis up against any other. It is quite the compliment that you can pay two wrestlers that, when their match was on, the entire wrestling-watching world seemed onboard with Savage crushing Flair. Crush him, Savage did not, but he defeated and bloodied him before taking the symbol of success that Naitch desired most in the world – the WWE Championship. It was the second straight year where Savage's work had not only garnered "Match of the Night" honors on the most important card of the year, but had also gotten a larger reaction than anyone else including Hogan (whose matches closed both shows).

The temperament of their Mania match was carried over to WCW, where it was Savage's father that was Flair's target instead of his wife. On the night that Randy's dad, Angelo Poffo, was inducted into the WCW Hall of Fame, Flair and Arn Anderson brutally assaulted him. Flair slapped on the Figure Four and away he and Savage went again. The Macho Man was at his best when he was emotionally charged. They traded victories at *The Great American Bash* and *Bash at the*

Beach in 1995. The dichotomy of their feud changed when Macho won the WCW Championship in November. Flair's a 16-time World Champion. Wrestling is The Nature Boy's life - his greatest passion to be the World Champion. When one of his enemies would win the title, it would always seem as if Flair took it personally. With a little help from Anderson, Flair defeated Savage for the title at *Starrcade '95*. Macho won the title back from Flair on *Nitro* in January, having surrounded the ring with several elegantly clad women to mess with Naitch's mind, but Flair got him back (big time) a month later. Miss Elizabeth, despite being divorced from Savage in real life, had come to WCW to be his manager the night after he had won the title. At *Super Brawl '96*, in the midst of a Steel Cage match between Savage and Flair, Elizabeth threw away ten years of being the "First Lady of Wrestling" to align herself with The Nature Boy. Assisting Flair by allowing him to borrow one of her high heel shoes to be used as a weapon against her ex-husband, Elizabeth became a heel and brought the Savage vs. Flair rivalry full circle. Naitch won the championship and ended their story.

Savage's most underrated opponent was Diamond Dallas Page. The New World Order dominated WCW in the second half of 1996, initially making Savage a target. In 1997, however, he became one of their most productive members. DDP was on The N.W.O.'s list of prospective recruits, but was resistant to joining. Savage was the primary Order mercenary to take exception. In reality, Page was a hard worker who needed a break to take the next step in his career. Macho was willing to help build Page and they had some great matches because of it. Savage put him over in the main-event of *Spring Stampede '97*, giving DDP his biggest victory to date. They wrestled two more matches on PPV that year in a storyline that was one publication's choice for "Feud of the Year" for 1997. Their second bout, which took place at *The Great American Bash*, was a Falls Count Anywhere match that I thought was the best match of all The N.W.O. vs. WCW battles. Their feud ended at *Halloween Havoc*. DDP came out of it one of the biggest stars in the business.

Since the first edition of this book was written, a couple of important things have happened that I explicitly requested in my original Macho Man conclusion. Finally, Macho Man made it into the WWE Hall of Fame in 2015. He is no longer the glaring omission and we can stop wondering why he was not in it. Also, WWE did a proper Randy Savage documentary-DVD set. Young fans must learn of the late, great Macho Man.

On the night that Larry Bird retired, Magic Johnson was on hand to commemorate the occasion and he said one thing, in particular, that will live on through the ages. He pointed out that, while there will probably be another Magic Johnson, there will "never, ever be another Larry Bird." Well, as I sit here and look at the top ten of the WrestleMania Era, I can tell you that there will probably be another one of each of the guys ahead of Randy Savage, but that there will never be another "Macho Man" Randy Savage. He was, hands down, the most unique wrestler of all-time.

#9: Bret Hart

Being the child of divorced parents can be difficult, even if the resulting situation turns out to be just fine. In 1992, my folks had been split for about two years. My dad and I remained very close, but the transition to seeing each other every other weekend was not easy. Renting WWE pay-per-views from the video store every two weeks for a year made the transition easier. In those videos, essentially chronicling the WWE's PPV history from 1987-1992, the wrestler who stood out most was Bret "Hitman" Hart. Even though we also witnessed some of the greatest names in wrestling lore – Hogan, Savage, Piper, Flair, and Andre among others – it was Bret who shined brightest.

During his rise through the ranks from Tag Team Champion to Intercontinental Champion to WWE Champion, there were three matches that differentiated him from his peers: vs. Mr. Perfect (*Summerslam '91*), vs. Roddy Piper (*WrestleMania VIII*), and vs. Davey Boy Smith (*Summerslam '92*). The only three matches in WWE history, up to that point, that were anywhere near as good as those three matches were Savage vs. Steamboat from *Mania III,* Savage vs. Warrior from *Mania VII*, and Savage vs. Flair from *WrestleMania VIII*. Bret Hart was an artist. His matches were the difference between a Michael Bay blockbuster full of visual effects and a gritty, Oscar-winning film that told a brilliant story. The wrestling ring was Hart's canvas and, though he painted many a masterpiece, those three Intercontinental Championship matches spanning the year from August '91 to August '92, in particular, taught me that wrestling matches were capable of being more than just spectacles.

Despite lacking the requisite glamorous personality usually required to be the biggest star, Bret rose to the highest levels that pro wrestling had to offer. He was so good in the ring that people were drawn to him not by his words, but by his actions. Once in a generation will sports entertainment produce a top star whose wrestling spoke greater volumes than his promos. Dating back to his lengthy run with Jim "The Anvil" Neidhart (his brother-in-law) as The Hart Foundation, it was Bret's wrestling ability that got them over, which eventually got them to the top of the tag ranks. Their road to becoming one of the finer tag teams of all-time was forged in 1985 and 1986 against teams like The Killer Bees and Fabulous Rougeaus. People may not have known much about them when they got to the arena, but The Hitman and The Anvil would leave an impression. In town after town, the crowd was buzzing by the end of each Hart Foundation match.

"You can't hold down talent" and if you take advantage of your opportunities to show it, then you will eventually get bigger opportunities. At house shows, The Foundation was working with The British Bulldogs in matches to which Vince McMahon was paying close attention. The quality of those matches afforded them the chance to finally get some meaningful TV time, which they parlayed into the first of two runs as WWE Tag Team Champions. Though their 1987 run with the titles was not memorable, they continued to work hard, having the match of the night quite often ahead of guys with bigger names that were given more time to work. It meant a lot to Bret to carry a division. He was in the tag team ranks for seven years and it was important to him to achieve its highest honors. However, he was clearly destined for more, as proven by his August-to-August stretch in '91-'92.

It was because of *Summerslam '92* in England that Bret cracked the top 10 of the WrestleMania Era; it was that important to his career. The victory over Perfect was big. The win over Piper was huge. WWE Championship gold, though, may never have come if it were not for the Intercontinental title match against The British Bulldog at London's Wembley Stadium. Bret was originally scheduled to face Shawn Michaels at the event, but suggested that it would be a big draw if he wrestled Englishman Davey Boy Smith (another brother-in-law). The decision was made to make the change, giving Bret a unique opportunity. Never before had an Intercontinental Championship match been the main-event at a PPV. On the same card, Randy Savage defended the WWE title against Ultimate Warrior in a major rematch from *WrestleMania VII*, so the WWE put a lot of faith in Bret to deliver the goods.

With Vince McMahon doing commentary at ringside, taking in the atmosphere of 80,000 people in attendance for a rare open-air setting, Bret put together one of the finest performances of his career. It was a match that highlighted his mastery at making the little things count. A kick to his opponent's head when they were rushing him in the corner, for instance, was made to look devastating because he was so sharp and on point. He had a knack for the psychology of a wrestling match. Vince got to see Bret steal the show and orchestrate what is largely regarded, to this day, as one of the best matches of all-time in front of the third largest crowd in WWE history. *Summerslam* began as a chance for Bret to show that he could be a top guy, but his work solidified that he was capable of leading the next generation for the company. A month later, he was the WWE Champion.

It was because of Bret's title defense that I made *WrestleMania IX* in 1993 my first ever PPV purchase. After a summer of jumping in the pool onto my dad yelling "Hitman" and putting him in the Sharpshooter (Bret's leg lock submission finisher) in his apartment, I became one of Bret's biggest fans.

After co-winning the Royal Rumble match in 1994, Bret captured the WWE Championship for the second time, getting a second chance to carry the company as the leader of The New Generation. That year, he had a career-enhancing rivalry with his brother, Owen. Their match at *WrestleMania X* was one of the top ten matches in the history of the event. In the pantheon of WrestleMania Era greats, the best of the best all have at least three unquestionable classics on their "grandest stage" resumes. It is the unspoken rule of threes. Bret's matches with Steve Austin and Shawn Michaels get prominently featured as contenders for WrestleMania's definitive best ever, but the bout with Owen often gets left out of that discussion. It should not be. I once wrote that Bret vs. Owen was the blueprint for having a classic wrestling match without all the bells and whistles often used to cut corners away from basic storytelling. Every aspiring young wrestler should be required to watch it. The same could be said for Bret and Owen's heralded rematch inside the old blue-barred Steel Cage at *Summerslam* five months later.

The *Summerslam '94* Cage match gave Bret one-up on everyone else who ever performed at the WWE's second biggest event. If Shawn Michaels is "Mr. WrestleMania," then Bret Hart is unquestionably "Mr. Summerslam."

His work throughout 1995 in classic matches against The British Bulldog, Diesel, 123 Kid, and Hakushi earned him his third WWE title reign, beginning at *Survivor Series* and leading to his most famous title defense at *WrestleMania XII* against Shawn Michaels. Bret, despite all his great matches and people like me that looked up to him all the same as kids once had to Hogan, was never viewed on Hulk's level. The search constantly continued to find a new torchbearer. The WWE decided to give Michaels a go, having him defeat Bret in a historic, one-hour Ironman match where the man with the most falls wins. One could make a strong case for it being the finest match of his career.

But everything changed after that match...

Any thorough historical perspective on Bret has to discuss the events leading up to the infamous "Montreal Screwjob" or risk omitting a major piece of his history. My perspective on it comes from watching it all play out on TV and then studying it over the years through every available written and video avenue. A one sentence recap, before we get to the mixture of how I both saw it and came to understand it: in November '97, Bret was let out of his WWE contract and signed a new deal with WCW, but on the way out of WWE was asked to drop the WWE Championship to Shawn Michaels and refused, prompting Vince McMahon to concoct an elaborate, unscripted ruse that ended with Bret losing the title after the bell abruptly rung to end the match.

When McMahon had Bret put Shawn over for the title at *Mania XII*, he might have made a huge mistake. Michaels was a brash, cocky, and insecure person. A guy in such a poor mental state should not have been made champion and should not have been asked to carry the company. He was not prepared, as I think Bret would have been, to handle the backlash that came with WCW starting to dominate the WWE in the summer of '96. WWE had other problems, including an inability to change with the times as the business was evolving, but Michaels was put in a tough situation and he started to crumble.

WrestleMania XII was the end of The Hitman's career as we knew it. He took a lengthy hiatus and came back for November's *Survivor Series*, whereupon he was set for a match against a budding star named Stone Cold Steve Austin. Much to the dismay of Hitman fans like myself, Austin had made Bret the target of many a hateful promo and seemed to hold a strange grudge against him. He came across like a neighborhood bully and I badly wanted Bret to give him comeuppance. I vividly recall Bret, in an in-ring interview, telling Austin that, "We'll just see who kicks who's ass!" It was the most emotionally invested Bret Hart feud of my fandom. During their match, I sat there biting my nails, hoping and praying that Bret would win. It was an excellent match, in the midst of which I had an epiphany that Stone Cold was quite impressive. I did not want to be impressed. I wanted him to lose and be humbled. Bret ultimately won the match, but it became clear that a growing number of people venerated Austin.

I felt as relieved as Bret looked when he barely escaped with the victory. It seemed like Austin had Bret's number...and he sure did. Though Austin never beat Bret fair and square during the height of their feud, which continued onward until *WrestleMania 13*, he screwed The Hitman numerous times and drove him to his mental breaking point. Austin cost Bret the WWE title the following month. Then, after Bret had technically won the Royal Rumble match in '97, Austin cheated the system to eliminate Bret (after Bret had already eliminated Austin and the refs did not see it). Bret managed to win the title the next month, but Austin clocked him with a chair during a title defense allowing Sid to win the championship.

The Hitman being one of my boyhood heroes, I was as frustrated as could be. Austin was injecting a lot of attitude into the WWE, but it was at Bret's expense. The once whitest knight in all the land was turning into an angry shell of his former self. At *WrestleMania 13*, though, he finally gave Austin that bloody beating that I had been hoping for since the previous fall. He beat Austin within an inch of his life, making him pass out in the Sharpshooter. I remember the emotions of that moment well; feeling elated that Bret won the match, but saddened by his actions afterward (he would not end the beating). That was not the Bret that helped me through some of my darkest hours. He was a changed man that I no longer liked, though I was not ready to admit it.

It took me a long time to realize that the *Mania 13* match was one of the best ever because of what it meant to me, as a fan. Mainly, it was the 13 year old's memory that Austin's crowning achievement that launched a new era coincided with Bret's downfall. As the years have passed, I recognize the sheer brilliance in what Bret and Stone Cold were able to do that night in Chicago. To execute a double turn – in which a babyface becomes a heel and a heel becomes a babyface all in one match – is wrestling's hole-in-one. To fully appreciate that, you have to put yourself in a situation where you make the seemingly impossible a possibility. Bret had been the consummate babyface and Austin had been the definition of heel. They finished off a lengthy drama with an almost equally as rare 5-star match that has often been called the greatest match of all-time and that gave the crowd the green light to completely embrace Stone Cold while turning their collective backs on the New Generation's aging icon.

I think when Bret came back eight months after *Mania XII*, it was like Marty McFly in *Back to the Future II* losing the sports almanac to Biff and time traveling to an alternate 1985 – it was the same year, but so much was different. The heels got cheered like babyfaces and the champion had alienated himself from everyone else. Rather than look at Bret as someone who could help, Michaels viewed Hart as the biggest rival to his newly earned "spot" and their once solid friendship deteriorated in a hurry. His attitude and Bret's mixed like oil and water from then on.

Austin was an unspoken, important piece of the puzzle to the Bret-Shawn situation. Neither of them was counting on the explosion that was Stone Cold. Austin's rise was the cold front moving in from the north that helped make what was happening the "perfect storm." The Austin feud has got to be bittersweet for Bret. Historically, it produced some of his finer matches and showed his range as a character, which I think people sometimes forget about due to all the other stuff going on. Yet, it also took him out of his relished position as the hero. Many of the best of all-time have said that they found it easier to play the villain, but I doubt Bret would agree. He took the responsibility of being a role model seriously and he appreciated that his work was respected vocally via adoring crowds. Austin took that away from him. The business changed and Bret was forced to change with it.

Turning heel was the beginning of the end for him. Critically, Bret Hart's turn was some of the most compelling television of the Attitude Era. It was also very unique, in that no other wrestler had ever turned heel on the United States yet maintained their hero status everywhere else in the world. Bret wrote in his book that he was worried about pushing away his fans by slamming America. I was one of those fans. The whinier he became, the more disenchanted that I became. He was one of my childhood heroes, third only to my dad and Maverick from *Top Gun*. To see him allow the forces of evil to twist and turn him into a maniac was tough to watch. He vented his real life frustrations about the changing business on television and sped along his demise. He was the old guard; the man firmly planted in the way of the WWE going full tilt with a more risqué product.

There were two crowning achievements of his run as the top heel before it all went to hell. The first was *The Canadian Stampede* PPV that saw the reformed Hart Foundation (Bret, Neidhart, Owen, Bulldog, and Brian Pillman), with the Hart family at ringside, win a 5-on-5 main-event in front of Bret's hometown crowd in Calgary. The second came a month later when he defeated Undertaker to win the WWE Championship for the 5th and final time. Bret and Taker had a lot of respect for each other as the locker room leaders through a rough time for the WWE. The *Summerslam* match was the most high profile match that they had together. Adding another element was HBK as the special referee. For modern fans, think of the scenario at *WrestleMania XXVIII* with Taker, Triple H, and HBK and the dynamic of those three personalities blending together. *Summerslam '97* with Bret, Taker, and HBK was the equivalent.

Taker was not a technical wrestler, but he could wrestle technically. Bret brought that side out of him for one of the forgotten matches of their careers. The Hitman was a character that prided himself on being the "Excellence of Execution." Against the likes of Yokozuna, Diesel, and Sid, Bret had shown himself to be very capable of having good matches with big men, but the match with Taker at *Summerslam* may have been his finest. The wrestling was spot on and the situation that played out between that era's three biggest stars was thoroughly engaging.

Bret's character was a shot in the collective arm of the WWE, but WCW continued to win the ratings battle and Bret's contract was simply costing too much. The backstage situation with Shawn got out of hand, so when Bret got a chance to go make a ton of money for less work, he rightfully took advantage. The personal issues between he and Shawn grew so out of control with the combination of Shawn's insecurities and Bret's pride that Hart would not drop the title to Michaels in Montreal like had become tradition for the champion leaving a promotion. The turmoil and animosity came to a head at *Survivor Series '97*. I do not care who you are, there will always come a time in your life when things spiral out of control in some way. When it happens, it is often devastating.

McMahon felt forced to act. The war with WCW made people do things that I do not believe they would have done otherwise. Shawn was the hired gun to make it happen in the ring. During their title match, Shawn put Bret in the Sharpshooter and referee Earl Hebner called for the bell. They pulled a fast one on Bret. Just like that, a man's thirteen year career that had been one of the best stories in wrestling history blew up in smoke. All the things that have been said over the years – they are all partly true. Vince and Shawn screwed Bret *and* Bret screwed Bret. They all screwed each other and somehow it worked out to where the WWE came out more successful for it. They suffered for it, though, behind the scenes. Tragedy befell many of the key players involved in the incident. Shawn broke his back and had to retire for four years, while Earl Hebner suffered a brain aneurysm all within a few months of Montreal. Yet, Bret's life continued to crumble for years. His brother Owen died and so, too, did Davey Boy Smith. The Hitman's professional career ended with a mistimed kick to the head after years of being underutilized in WCW. To top it off, he suffered a stroke.

Everything happens for a reason, though. The stroke led to Bret and Vince mending the fence, which led to DVDs and a Hall of Fame induction to help people remember Bret not for one night in November 1997, but for the career that puts him in the discussion for being the greatest of all-time. It also paved the way for Bret to come back to the WWE in 2010. As a fan, it was an amazing moment to see Bret back in a WWE ring after all of those years. To see him and Shawn bury the hatchet was a lesson to everyone that things can always come full circle. Far too often, wrestling fans are jaded and criticized for liking a misunderstood genre of sport and entertainment. There are stories told in that ring, however, that can leave impressions and teach life lessons. If my kids end up finding a passion for wrestling, then I can use the Bret-Vince-Shawn story to teach them about the ups and downs in life and forgiveness.

Bret Hart is the Tim Duncan of professional wrestling. While there is no questioning his place as among the elite, his relatively quiet, workman-like way of handling his business will cause fans to move guys ahead of him on the all-time list because we are a society enamored by flashier stars. Still, anyone that knows wrestling can look at his body of work and admit that he was one of the best there was and best that ever will be.

#8: "Stone Cold" Steve Austin

Despite owning two of the top five matches in the history of WrestleMania along with numerous other classics; setting PPV buy records that were so fiscally strong that they still top modern standards despite $20 of inflation in the last decade; owning the majority of the most memorable moments in WWE television lore (and the cable TV ratings records); being the tide-turning superstar that sunk WCW to bankruptcy while saving the WWE; owning one of the top ten cumulative championship trophy cases; and being generally thought of by Vince McMahon (along with millions of others) as the greatest ever, "Stone Cold" Steve Austin did not statistically crack the top 5 of all-time. The reasons were simple: he wrestled as a top star for just <u>four</u> full years, missed a WrestleMania in his prime due to injury, and was pushed to the backburner for another WrestleMania. Subsequently, though he ranks in the top ten of every category but Wrestler Score (his fairly plain look knocked him to 12th), he fell behind his elite peers whose lengthier runs afforded them more consistent opportunities to win more titles, headline more PPVs, and compile a larger list of classic matches. Nevertheless, any of the top ten of the WrestleMania Era could make a strong case for the greatest of all-time.

It took "The Texas Rattlesnake" ten years to sniff the top of the wrestling world, but when he did, he set it ablaze, leaving a trail that no one may ever be able to follow. The definition of an anti-hero, in wrestling, is a good guy that acts like a bad guy. Austin was wrestling's greatest anti-hero, gaining international fame and recognition amongst many as the single most popular superstar of all-time. He came of age in a rebellious time period and lit a spark that ignited professional wrestling to ridiculous business heights. On the other hand, not everyone loved him. I could not stand him during the Attitude Era. By conventional terms, anti-hero simply means the opposite of a hero – in essence, a villain. I considered him to be the best heel of all-time for pulling the shades over everyone else's eyes, blinding them from the Stone Cold Truth. Being from the south, Austin was every bit the stereotype from which I attempted to distance myself. The beer swelling redneck from Texas may have been the "every man" to a big portion of the wrestling audience and a beacon for literally several million new people to join the WWE fan base, but I was brought up to appreciate common courtesy and manners and doing things the "right" way to get to the top in life.

    I was too young to understand or appreciate that Austin had busted his rear end for years to finally be given the chance to succeed on his terms. I, now, have all the respect in the world for Stone Cold, but back in my early teenage years, I found him unbearable. After all, he brought about the beginning of the end for two of my all-time favorites in Bret Hart and Shawn Michaels on television. Austin's antics were cutting edge and riveting to watch for a growing portion of the viewership, but I saw it coming at the expense of Bret, who acted like I thought a hero should. Michaels was better suited than Bret to adapt to the changing environment, but my all-time favorite wrestler's first retirement came on the very same night as Austin's coronation at *WrestleMania XIV*. Stone Cold's success was a constant reminder that Bret and Shawn were gone. Subsequently, as new fans were entering the fray in droves to see Austin, I was pinning my hopes to his every challenger. It has often been said that Austin was the type of guy that "you'd want to have a beer with." I would rather have thrown a beer at him, at that stage of my fandom. Someone might light this book on fire for me writing this, but even as he was going toe-to-toe with Vince McMahon in the amazing boss vs. unruly employee angle, I often found myself sympathetic to Vince. If I hired an office manager who wore cut off jean shorts, flipped off my patients, and used foul language answering the phone, then I would surely want her to change her attitude in a hurry or hit the road.

I was not a Vince McMahon supporter, by any means. I certainly was not sitting at home rooting for The Corporation's boss – but I understood some of his basic arguments. I got behind his "corporate" championship hopefuls such as Mick Foley, against whom Austin made his first title defenses. Portraying the Dude Love character, Foley turned on Austin in an attempt to earn the gold. People frequently referred to Stone Cold as an "every man," but I thought that description better fit Foley.

Austin vs. Dude Love at *Over the Edge '98* was one of the most underrated matches of that entire era. To put it into historical context, both men had early career defining moments in the same venue (the MECCA arena in Milwaukee, WI) two years prior at *King of the Ring '96*. That was the night that Austin famously won the tournament to become King of the Ring, launching him into prominence after his crowning ceremony yielded arguably the most significant interview of all-time. He wore no crown, defiantly shunning tradition, and uttered the words (in Jake Roberts' direction), "You sit there and you thump your Bible, and you say your prayers, and it didn't get you anywhere! Talk about your psalms, talk about John 3:16... Austin 3:16 says I just whipped your ass!" A megastar was born. Foley had his first WWE PPV match on the same night, defeating Undertaker. You could have counted Taker's losses on one hand from his first five years with the company and, yet, Foley beat him in his debut. It was a huge night for both of them.

They returned to Milwaukee in May 1998 to main-event the PPV with the WWE Championship on the line. It was a great Attitude Era-style of match that featured lots of shenanigans and work outside of the ring without regard for the long-established rules. Overbooked to delight, it was a dramatic brawl, as were most of Austin's classics from 1998 onward.

The only opponent during the height of the Austin era from March 1998 to October 1999 that I did not favor was Vince. I cheered for Kane when he won the title from Stone Cold at *King of the Ring '98*, I very much hoped that Undertaker would dethrone The Rattlesnake at *Summerslam* in a sloppy, yet to this day thoroughly entertaining clash of historic titans, and I eventually championed Triple H's effort to knock Austin from his perch atop the business. The Rock, though, represented the perfect foil, embodying all of the qualities that I felt Austin lacked and that I simultaneously desired in life. The Austin-Rock rivalry worked so well because they were so different. They shared the desire to be the best, but their personalities, looks, and in-ring styles offered wrestling fans the sports entertainment equivalent of giving a group of wine connoisseurs two exceptional $100 bottles of pinot noir; you could not go wrong with either, depending upon your tastes. For my tastes, The Rock was "The Man."

Oddly enough, The Rock was a heel. I had developed such distaste for Austin while he was a bad guy that the irony in cheering for a bad guy in opposition to him did not dawn on me until years later. Stone Cold changed the game forever, in that regard, blurring the lines between hero and villain and simultaneously making wrestling as "real" as it ever was before. In real life, the dichotomy between good and evil is a palate of fascinating shades of gray. Since we are all different people that come from various backgrounds, what resonates with one person fails to do so with another. Traditional sports have embodied that fact with franchises scattered about countries, creating natural allegiances in the name of city pride. In the Attitude Era, Austin and Rock tore down the long-established wall that had made wrestling so black and white. Austin did things that I hated, so I turned to The Rock; many felt it was the other way around. In essence, the fans were given the green light to openly embrace whoever they felt a connection instead of being steered directly to the clear cut, company-anointed idol.

Austin vs. Rock was the greatest rivalry in the history of professional wrestling. Never before have there been two all-time box office powerhouses in the same company at the same time. It was wrestling's equivalent of Magic Johnson-Larry Bird facing off in the NBA Finals every other year. Austin and Rock main-evented *WrestleMania XV* and *X-Seven*, respectively, with the WWE Championship up for grabs. The latter was a match that will stand the test of time as one of the best ever, destined to remain at the top of fan lists for decades to come. Though it doubled as the end of the Attitude Era and the night that Austin joined forces with Vince in an ill-fated attempt to turn heel, it is considered by most to be the pantheon of all WrestleMania main-events.

As of 2001, leading into *X-Seven*, both were so wildly popular that the WWE did not bother trying to make one of them the top television villain. Yet, back in 1999, Austin was at the climax of his storyline with The Corporation. Rock, their clearly evil Corporate Champion, was quickly coming into his own. Their *Mania XV* clash was a huge financial success that effectively slammed the door shut on the Monday Night War. It was nowhere near the quality of the match from two years later, but it was arguably more important for business given that WCW was not quite yet out of the hunt. WCW had no answer for Austin vs. Rock.

They had a match the month after *Mania XV* at *Backlash '99* that was the forgotten classic in their multi-year series. It was, actually, the best showcase for the differences in their personalities (all Mania matches included), as both characters were hitting their strides and reaching the peaks of their initial popularity. The Rock got on the commentator's headset and talked trash for the world to hear. Austin flipped the double bird on multiple occasions, at one point hilariously giving the world the double middle fingers as Rock was "borrowing" a television camera to, I guess, get a more memorable view of the audience.

    My favorite Austin-Rock match took place at *WrestleMania XIX*, the third and final "Show of Shows" at which the rivals came to blows. It was the match that forever changed my opinion of Stone Cold. I was in college by then and my studies of the wrestling business were expanding by the month. *XIX* turned out to be my favorite Mania, as well. The month or so leading up to it gave us a preview that Austin was likely almost done with wrestling. Creatively, The Rock was the star of that feud. Austin was no longer his character equal, which should have signaled the inevitable. We would not find out until a year later - during a brilliant documentary that I watch every winter called *The Mania of WrestleMania* - that Austin was planning for his match with Rock to be his last. He had worn down too much, physically, and he decided he did not want to risk his long-term quality of life.

    Getting dropped on his head and severely injuring his neck (more in the long-term than the short), the fusion surgery, the knee problems, and the mental exhaustion finally caught up with him the Saturday night before Mania. He took in a mixture of coffee and energy drinks, all designed to chemically induce a boost, but his physical state could no longer handle the letdown that always followed. He was rushed to the emergency room with a panic attack. All the mixed emotions that must have come with the last match in his career, combined with the pressure of performing at a high level on his way out and the state of his broken body created the perfect storm. Spending the night in the hospital was the antithesis of the ideal pre-Mania routine. To have called off the match or improvised would have been horrible for business, but totally understandable for personal reasons.

    And then he had that match on Sunday...

It is funny. In the matches where the majority has praised Austin in victory, I had always praised The Rock in loss. At *Mania XIX*, the masses hailed Rock's victory as one of the top performances of his career, yet it was Stone Cold's loss in my mind that historically took center stage. To be fair, both of them did so well in every match that it is almost asinine to try to claim a better man. Yet, when you take everything into account that Austin went through prior to his final match, which also included a 9-month hiatus due to creative differences that saw The Rattlesnake slither away from the company without warning, what Stone Cold pulled off at *Mania* in 2003 was worthy of being called one of the top 5 gutsiest pieces of work in modern wrestling lore. "The Toughest S.O.B." in the WWE lived up to his nickname that night.

I love that match. I have re-watched it as many times as I have re-watched any other. Rock deserves the heap of praise that he received, but Austin told the story of an embattled warrior making his last stand. He gave an inspired effort that hid his physical condition, made all the more impressive by the beating that he took. Two Rock Bottoms were not enough to put him away, so it took an emphatic, ring-shaking third and a People's Elbow to get Austin's shoulders down on the mat for a three count. After the match, Rock pushed the referee out of the way and, beyond the audio perception of the cameras, paid his respects to Austin for everything that he had helped him accomplish.

At my house in North Carolina, I sat there watching all of this play out, initially, without any knowledge whatsoever of the non-televised back story. Even then, it changed my opinion of Austin. It made me shed the pre-teen bias born out of things beyond Austin's control and see the Stone Cold character for what it was: legendary. In subsequent years, especially after learning of the tumultuous months and one horrible night that preceded the final bout of his career, my respect for Austin grew exponentially. Though I will never be an "Austin" guy for all of the non-HBK and Bret reasons mentioned earlier, there are few wrestlers that I hold in higher esteem than Steve Austin.

After *WrestleMania XIX*, I went back and watched all of the old Austin classics. The *Survivor Series '96* match with Bret is a personal favorite, but what he accomplished with Bret at *WrestleMania 13* was breathtaking. The story that they told had a degree of difficulty beyond any other tale in the last 30 years, but they told it in 5-star fashion. It is not my favorite, but it is the best. Austin screaming in agony, blood pouring down his face as he desperately tried to escape the Sharpshooter, has become arguably wrestling's most enduring image. The saying that a picture is worth a 1,000 words has never been more applicable. Austin became a star in the making at *King of the Ring '96*, but his rise to the WWE's choice for "greatest superstar of all-time" - words echoed by Vince McMahon during The Rattlesnake's 2009 Hall of Fame induction - began at *WrestleMania 13*.

The Austin-McMahon marriage, of sorts, turned out to be just what both of them needed. You could actually go back to Austin's time in WCW as "Stunning" Steve and see the personality waiting to be unleashed by a promoter with the means to bring the best out of his superstars. In a match with Ricky Steamboat at the *'94 Bash at the Beach*, you could see not only Austin's ability in the ring (which nobody ever questioned) but that glare in his eye that he stumbled upon while in the WWE. That icy stare could have scared the urine out of a child; it was just hidden by blonde hair and a lack of television time. Vince was not responsible for Austin's transformation, but he followed Paul Heyman's lead and gave Steve a platform to become Stone Cold. Heyman, who was excellent at harnessing the good qualities of his talents in ECW, had worked with Austin in WCW in the awesome "Dangerous Alliance" stable. He knew that Austin had "it," so when WCW unceremoniously fired Steve, he gave him a job in ECW and let him off the leash. Vince basically repeated the entire WCW-ECW experience for Austin, minus the firing, putting him far down the card and then unleashing him. He just did it on a much grander stage.

On-screen, Austin and McMahon were the subject of roughly half of *Raw's* all-time most memorable moments. Austin getting arrested after giving Vince the Stunner for the first time in September 1997; interrupting the introduction of Mike Tyson to the WWE and nearly coming to blows with him, earning a ton of mainstream press in the process; driving the Zamboni out into the arena and using it as a launching pad to attack Vince in 1998; putting the toy gun to Vince's head and pulling the trigger only for a flag bearing the words "Bang 3:16" to pop out, prompting "McMahon 3:16 to piss his pants"; and, of course, the greatest of them all (and there were a dozen others), with just six days until *WrestleMania XV*, Austin drove a Miller Lite truck to ringside and doused the top members of The Corporation with a beer bath.

At that point, the ratings battle was the key to success. The Monday Night War brought attention back to wrestling for the first time since the late 80s. It made wrestling a hot commodity again. Advertisers were going to flock to who was winning. Even with Mike Tyson being brought in at the beginning of 1998, the WWE was still losing by a full Nielsen point every week leading up to *WrestleMania XIV* on March 29. The night after, on March 30, *Raw* pulled within 0.4 of *Nitro*. The week after, they got their first victory in 84 weeks with a 4.7 to 4.6. It was their highest rating of the Monday Night War, up to that point. After losing the ratings battle for two years, the WWE - with Austin at the helm as its number one star – won 22 weeks to WCW's 15 weeks in 1998. The WWE never lost another ratings battle to WCW after October 26, 1998. Austin provided a huge, momentum changing boost. From *WrestleMania 13* to *WrestleMania XIV* prior to Austin becoming the WWE Champion, *Raw* averaged a 2.8 rating. After Austin became the WWE Champion at *WrestleMania XIV* to *WrestleMania XV*, the average *Raw* rating went up two full points to 4.9!! When 1999 rolled around, *Raw* consistently jumped above the 5.0 mark and quite frequently hit 6.0 or better (on twenty five different occasions in '99, to be exact). May 10, 1999 set the pro-wrestling cable TV ratings record with a staggering 8.1. Ratings that strong allowed the WWE to pick up numerous big name sponsors and let the cash start to pour in.

Stone Cold made the WWE a ton of money. If you look at the PPVs from 1999 alone, Austin was involved in 12 PPVs (including *Survivor Series*, which he was advertised for but was written out of storylines via an injury angle that took place at that event; but not including *Armageddon*, the last event of the year where Austin was not involved). In those twelve PPVs, Austin was in the main-event, advertised as a part of the main-event, or expected to be in the main-event (*Survivor Series*) on every card. Subsequently, for the only time in WWE history, the PPV buyrate average for those cards was 1.45 (which, by the standard definition over the last decade or so, was 566,000 buys per show) and none of them dropped below a 1.05.

Today, Austin is revered, by Vince McMahon just as much as the fan base. Remember, Vince was on the verge of losing everything before Austin caught fire. There is always going to be an argument as to who was the biggest WWE star of all-time when you take inflation into account and Hulk Hogan will win a lot of them; so will Austin. I think what will always separate Austin from Hogan is that Vince is the one that knows the numbers better than anyone. He will readily tell you that Austin re-wrote all of the records and it may not take into account the difference in the dollar from the late 80s to the late 90s, but it will take into account one very important intangible. Hogan helped Vince build his empire when Vince was still a young man. Yet, Vince lost much of that fortune. You take things for granted until you lose them (or have them challenged). Austin rescued Vince from the depths of despair, financially, and he will subsequently be the McMahon family hero until their dying days.

Creatively, the minute that Austin and McMahon became allies, the Stone Cold character spiraled downward, leading to the frustrating exit in 2002 and the eventual retirement in 2003, but his body of work in 2001 was some of the best of his career. He came back strong after having neck surgery in late 1999 and was the WWE's MVP. With Triple H suffering a major injury and Rock spending some time making movies, Austin had to lead the way in forcing a square peg into a round hole in the abomination otherwise known as the WCW Invasion. His workrate was excellent. In February, he had one of the greatest matches of all-time with Triple H in their storied Three Stages of Hell match. In April, he had one of the greatest matches of all-time (and a top 5 WrestleMania match) against The Rock in Houston. In May, he was involved in one of the best tag team matches of all-time on *Raw* and then had one of the best TV matches of all-time against Chris Benoit on *Smackdown*. In August, he had one of the best matches in *Summerslam* history against Kurt Angle. In November, he capped off his incredible year of excellent matches with arguably the best traditional Survivor Series match in history, where he was the last man eliminated in the conclusion of the WWE vs. WCW feud. He spent the year having 4-5 star matches.

Austin's last epic moment was at *WrestleMania XIX*. He had a great match against his greatest in-ring rival at the biggest show of the year. It is rare in sports that stars get to go out on their own terms. Stone Cold was one of the few that truly deserved to have the perfect sendoff.

#7: Hulk Hogan

There may be some of you that, if you have not already thrown this book across the room because of the placement of #8, are getting ready to because of the placement of #7. The Stone Cold truth was explained in Austin's opening paragraph. Before I celebrate the Hulkster, allow me to explain why he is not as high on the list as you, perhaps, thought he should be. Much as with Austin, it was due to a simple, low statistical ranking in one category; in Hogan's case: performance. He was 24th. The rest of the top 10 from here on had smaller holes in their overall resumes. No previous literary work, to my knowledge, has dared to critically review every candidate's complete, modern era body of work and rank accordingly. This one dares. The results surprised me, too.

If Hulk Hogan had not participated in *Rocky III*, then I would not be penning this fan account of wrestling history. Vince McMahon would not have seen an opportunity to take Hogan's small but commanding role and use it to light the match that ignited a mainstream craze for professional wrestling the likes of which had never been seen before. Without Hogan, then there would have been no *WrestleMania*. If there was no *WrestleMania*, I still would have been a wrestling fan as a kid, but the allure of it would have worn off. Without Hogan, whose dynamic personality transcended the typical perception of a pro wrestler, the WWE would not have been able to rebrand itself "sports entertainment." There have been four, true faces of professional wrestling as we know it today and Hogan was the first. He was the George Washington. He was the pioneer.

33 million viewers once watched Hogan wrestle on television; a figure that remains the standard bearer for wrestling to this day. Not even during the famed Attitude Era was greater viewership ever achieved. From the moment that he burst onto the scene in 1983, quickly winning the WWE

Championship for the first time in January 1984, Hulkamania began to run wild. He was "The Man" during one of its most profitable periods, ushering in unprecedented success for wrestling in both network TV and the fledgling pay-per-view market. To this day, his is the name that most people associate with professional wrestling around the country.

There is no mistaking Hogan's impact on the wrestling industry. Yet, conversations about the "all-time biggest star" usually end in comparing him to "Stone Cold" Steve Austin. Despite all that Hogan accomplished, there is a sense that he was manufactured by Vince McMahon. Wrestling puts a premium on wrestlers that invent their own character and get themselves over to the point that a Vince McMahon-type promoter has no choice but to listen to the people and push them to the moon. It is for that reason that I think Austin often gets a leg up from many fans and historians in the argument. Austin was the perfect example of the self-made man. Hogan was signed by McMahon due to a hit cameo appearance as "Thunder Lips" in 1982's fifth highest grossing film. There is a sense that Hogan did not have to scratch and claw his way to the top. The thing people need to remember, though, is that he may have had Vince behind him, pushing him from day one to be his top star, but it was his charisma that made it work. It was Hogan that clicked with the fans, Hogan that worked hard to embrace the chance the WWE was taking on him, and Hogan that morphed himself into a larger-than-life personality that attracted unique viewers to wrestling.

Hogan was never a critical darling like Stone Cold, partly because he was different than the traditional champion of the NWA and WWE to that point. He was a special attraction type performer not known so much for his in-ring talents as for his physique and on-screen presence. Champions of the pre-Hogan period were grapplers; the types that were dedicated to the art of the craft like Harley Race, Ric Flair, and Bob Backlund (and eventually Austin). You could make the argument that, in the

70s and early 80s, Hogan would have made for a great traditional *challenger* to the World title more so than a *champion*. However, McMahon wanted to get away from the sports side of the business and concentrate on the entertainment. Hogan, with his television magnetism, was ideal for Vince's new philosophy. He had such a natural connection with people. He could rally audiences behind him to a greater degree than any wrestler before or since.

McMahon wanted to change the game. He wanted the WWE event to be a destination; a family affair that could draw like any other mainstream sporting event. Hulk gave Vince a spokesperson that could travel the country, lending his time to major media outlets to help build new brand equity in sports entertainment. Much of the growth seen by the wrestling industry in the mid-to-late 80s can be attributed to Hogan's efforts. Vince had the freedom to take substantial risks that altered the landscape of the entire business because of the luxuries afforded him by Hogan's personality.

Just look at the success of the very first *WrestleMania*, marketed as the Super Bowl of pro wrestling. McMahon put all his eggs in that basket and bet the farm that it would work. Surely, there were a lot of key ingredients to making it successful. It was Cyndi Lauper that handed the WWE "The Rock and Wrestling Connection" on MTV. Her involvement as a manager in the build-up to *Mania* on TV was a big selling point, as she was at the height of her musical career in 1985. It was Muhammad Ali, Mr. T (of television and big screen fame), and Liberace that added to the pop culture appeal with their advertised appearances. None of their contributions can be questioned. Yet, it was Hogan, the World Champion at the time for the previous year, doing the national promotional touring on behalf of the WWE. He deserves as much if not more of the credit. He was the glue that bonded everything together. He was particularly instrumental in Mr. T's involvement. Their connection was established in the aforementioned *Rocky* sequel and Hogan used it to create a bond that quite possibly saved *WrestleMania* from being a colossal bust. There were numerous occasions when "T" reportedly wanted to back out of his commitment. Hogan was there to corral him back in and keep him a part of the show.

WrestleMania reportedly grossed $12 million (a huge amount of money back then). They hit a home run that launched their already booming business to even greater heights. A month after *WrestleMania*, Hogan became the only wrestler in modern history to be on the cover of *Sports Illustrated*. A couple of weeks after that, he wrestled in the main-event of the first *Saturday Night's Main Event* – a huge coup for the WWE that gave them network TV in place of *Saturday Night Live* several times per year and made the WWE a cool $450,000 per show (again, major money circa 1985). *Saturday Night's Main Event* was another big success for the WWE and Hogan. The ratings for the first five plus years were tremendous, especially considering the genre. The success led to a Friday night primetime spinoff called *The Main Event* that hit the jackpot in ratings for professional wrestling in 1988 with the *Mania III* rematch of Hulk Hogan vs. Andre the Giant. It drew a WWE (and pro wrestling) record rating of 15.2 (good for 33 million viewers). For all the talk of the ratings success of the Attitude Era, Hogan vs. Andre drew a rating that likely will never be matched.

Hogan vs. Andre at *WrestleMania III* was the pinnacle main-event match in wrestling history, drawing a then-indoor attendance record of 93,173 and the largest PPV buyrate in wrestling history (a 10.2). In 1987, only about 6.5 million homes had access to PPV. The 10.2 buyrate means that over 10% of those people ordered *WrestleMania III* --another incredible and likely untouchable mark. The matches with Andre were iconic for the atmosphere that they provoked and the box office records that they wrote. Their *Mania III* encounter was the Wilt Chamberlain vs. Bill Russell clash of sports entertainment; an unforgettable spectacle. Wrestling peaked with Hulk vs. Andre. That was the match upon which the *WrestleMania* franchise was built.

    The Hulkster went on to several more successful PPV main-events, including three more WrestleManias that drew very well and the invention of three more yearly PPVs (*Survivor Series, Summerslam,* and *The Royal Rumble*). The first-ever *Survivor Series*, set in direct competition with NWA's *Starrcade '87*, earned a 7.0 buyrate. A year later, the overall PPV market began to grow, in large part, due to the success of Hogan-headlined WrestleManias. He was rumored to have made over $10 million per year during the height of Hulkamania. He would not have achieved that kind of success if he had not prepared for it. Hogan busted his rear for years in the AWA, attempting to become their champion. He had spent years working with the top stars in several territories and in Japan. When Vince gave him the ball, he was ready to run with it.

    The WWE did well to nearly match the PPV numbers for *Mania III* when they spent the year between *Mania IV* and *Mania V* building to Hogan vs. "Macho Man" Randy Savage. The Mega Powers "Exploded" at the Trump Plaza in Atlantic City, New Jersey, giving way to one of the most anticipated main-events, past or present. To this day, my buddy Tony and I will email back and forth the video clip of Hogan's backstage interview with Mean Gene prior to challenging Savage for the championship. Hogan was such a talker that he could go on and on, adlibbing all the way to his big points about his "24 inch pythons" and "Hulkamania running wild!" His multi-minute rant recapped their entire situation, hilariously referencing how Donald Trump had figuratively had the foundation of his Towers checked by a "whole team of seismotalogists" to make sure that it did not crack amidst the pressure of The Mega Power collision. That was, hands down, the most memorable interview in the history of wrestling, for me; not the best, mind you, but the one that I remember most. I could recite most of it right now.

Hogan had so many huge main-events. Roddy Piper, Ted DiBiase, Ultimate Warrior, and Sgt. Slaughter added to the historic rivalries with Andre and Savage to give Hogan an unmatched resume of opponents.

Had Hogan left the WWE in 1993 and retired, I might buy an argument that Austin was the bigger star. Just when it seemed as if Hogan's star was burning out in 1994, he received a life line from World Championship Wrestling, was thrown a tickertape parade, and immediately won their World title in his debut – a true dream match against Ric Flair that the WWE famously failed to deliver in 1992. He was the same old Hogan character for the better part of his first two years, trying to squeeze every last drop out of Hulkamania. About a third of his size was gone after kicking steroids, so the man that had once filled the red and yellow trunks was gone. It was like a huge defensive end shrinking to average quarterback weight. The people did not respond to the act anymore. In fact, as of 1996, the people had fully turned on it. The kids that had once cheered him on had grown up, changed their attitude, and demanded edgier material. Nevertheless, Hogan's presence commanded respect and it earned WCW a spot opposite WWE's *Monday Night Raw* with a Hulkster-dominated new program called *Nitro*. The Monday Night Wars began in September 1995.

In July of 1996, he infamously re-invented himself as "Hollywood" Hulk Hogan when he turned heel and created The New World Order with Scott Hall and Kevin Nash. Hogan's turn was several years in the making. It took him almost five years to finally do what the fans had been practically daring him to do. You have to adapt and evolve in wrestling to avoid losing your relevance the same as you do in any other industry, but Hogan had a formula that had worked so very well. He was reluctant to change and the promoters were reluctant to change him.

The WrestleMania Era: The Book of Sports Entertainment

The transition, once made, proved financially fruitful for all involved. The buzz created by Hall and Nash appearing on *Nitro* and threatening to take over was amplified by Hogan's heel turn. 84 subsequent weeks in a row, WCW beat WWE in the Monday Night TV ratings.

Stone Cold eventually came about and set the world on fire to end WCW's winning streak and start a second wrestling boom period. Hogan and Austin, accordingly, are indelibly locked in a battle for biggest star in history based on that time. In support of Austin's argument, the numbers do not lie. Austin reset the record books (without accounting for inflation) and won the Monday Night War. However, consider that Stone Cold may never have made it as big if not for being **the response** to what Hogan was doing in WCW. Hulk was arguably as responsible for the second boom as he had been the first. It was his work in The New World Order that people credit for lighting a creative fire under the WWE's backside, forcing Vince to give Austin the ball and launch the Attitude Era. Every story told about the Monday Night War came about because Hogan turned heel. Plus, you cannot argue with the longevity of his main-event career and the fact that, perhaps up until recently (with The Rock's legitimate Hollywood fame), Hogan was the most recognizable name in the sport.

Of the five categories that rank these all-time greats, the only one in which Austin trumped Hogan was performance level. In all other aspects, Hogan won by a narrow margin. There were not many knocks on Hogan's overall career, but his wrestling ability could rightfully be questioned. He does not have a long list of classic matches. For those modern fans that dislike the formulaic John Cena match, during which he gets beaten down by the heel for most of the contest only to courageously comeback and dominate the climax, that formula was perfected by Hogan. It is not a critically popular formula now and it was not a popular formula then. For the longest time, Hulk vs. Macho Man at *Mania V* was the best "Hogan formula" match (until Shawn Michaels topped it at *Summerslam 2005*). Not that the analytics should take anything away from what was still a memorable battle between the Batman and Robin of the original wrestling boom, but the bout has not maintained overly positive reviews. His work with Savage was some of the greatest of his career, but much like his match with Andre, it was far more heralded for its box office success than its critical reception.

Part of Hogan's problem on the performance side was that he had an aura to uphold. Vince marketed him as a blockbuster attraction and he presented him in the ring accordingly. Following the aforementioned formula, Hulk's matches were stories of good handily triumphing over evil. When green lighted to ditch the formula, Hogan had some awesome matches like his four-star clash against Ultimate Warrior at *WrestleMania VI*. My fondest childhood Hogan memory came from that match. As time has gone on and Mania has become a bigger deal with wrestlers outperforming many of their predecessors, Hogan vs. Warrior in "The Ultimate Challenge" remains one of my favorite matches of all-time and endures as one of the best. Hulk never got much credit for his in-ring talents. Yet, what he lacked in technical skill, he made up for with a near-unmatched relationship with the fans. People's investment in a wrestling match is what matters. You can be the greatest technical wrestler in the world, but you have to be able to draw someone into the story. For six years, Hogan built a legion of Hulkamaniacs, who cried, felt his pain, laughed and rejoiced with him. They turned out to be the great equalizer for him, too. His time in the ring may not have been the most aesthetically pleasing, but it was the most entertaining because of the intangible quality that his fans brought to the table. Looking at his work in a vacuum without 20,000-to-90,000 people in the arena, Hogan was just a basic big guy with better than average athleticism. Insert the energy and passion of the 67,000 people that packed the Skydome in Toronto at *Mania VI* to see him, though, and it was an incredible spectacle.

The WrestleMania Era: The Book of Sports Entertainment

Ask a young Edge, who sat in the crowd rooting for Hogan and, after that night, made the decision to follow his dream to be a wrestler.

Warrior could not have had that match with anyone else but Hulk. I give credit to Warrior for his work, but it was the best performance of Hogan's career (not to be confused with his best match). *Mania VI* was a real notch in the belt of Hogan's legacy.

Hogan's best match came at *WrestleMania X-8* twelve years later (and in the same building) against The Rock. Even the old sign from *WrestleMania VI*, prominently featuring Hogan's blonde mane sporting a red and yellow headband, made an appearance. For as long as I live, I will never forget watching that match. I was a senior in high school and wrestling was not a big priority at the time. I had taken a bit of a hiatus from it for a year or so and come back to more casual viewing. I sat there, though, and watched that Toronto crowd bring Hulkamania back to life. I can admit to never having been the biggest Hulkamaniac, but I knew his routine. I knew all the poses and the facial expressions and the hand gestures. All of those memories from being at my dad's apartment watching old PPVs on VHS tape came flooding back. That entire match was a nostalgic roller coaster. You could not help but get wrapped up in it. The audience was so solidly behind Hogan that it was like a fever sweeping across the airwaves.

At that moment where he "Hulked up" and rallied his fans behind him, I fell in the love with wrestling all over again and I have not stopped watching since. When the big boot and the leg drop connected, he had me fully engaged on a new level. In one of the great "WrestleMania moments" by my recollection, The Rock kicked out and went on to win, but the raw energy that Hogan brought to the table was what made the match. There are better matches in wrestling's rich history, but none are quite as unforgettable.

I hate that his life has fallen apart in recent years. His reputation soured after decades of heavily rumored backstage political maneuvering, for which he was as notorious as anyone had ever been. It perhaps detracts from where he is placed on the all-time pedestal. Time will change that, I hope (though the revelation of his racist comments in 2015 did not help). I think it is difficult to blame a businessman for being shrewd in a business like pro wrestling. Hogan did, indeed, swoop in after the promoted main-event at *WrestleMania IX* to win the title. It did him no favors with an audience clamoring for something different than Hulkamania. He did fail to take a clean loss to Sting when the time was right at *Starrcade '97*. That was a travesty that began the demise of WCW as quickly as it rose to prominence. However, these were instances where the guys in charge felt Hogan should either be given one last night of glory or protected at all costs. Desperate men like Vince or Eric Bischoff do desperate things when tensions are high. Whether or not Hogan directly influenced those decisions is not a debate I can take part in, having not been there. I just do not think it is realistic to think that anyone in Hogan's shoes would have done anything differently if given the chance to regain or maintain the #1 spot. That is up to the promoter.

I have a lot of respect for Hulk Hogan. He might be both the greatest hero <u>and</u> greatest villain of all-time. One thing in my mind is for certain, though: he was bigger than Austin. Hulk Hogan is wrestling history's all-time biggest star.

#6: Shawn Michaels

Shawn Michaels is one of the people in this world that I try to emulate. We all make mistakes and he was no exception. He made some lousy choices in the first half of his WWE career, but he is proof that redemption can be achieved. If we get over ourselves and realize that there is something greater in the universe, just about anything is possible. During the second half of his WWE career, Michaels was the model for how to balance family and work life and has proven since retiring in 2010 that it is possible to find a new purpose, seamlessly moving from one phase of his life to the next. He is my all-time favorite wrestler.

If this were a book based solely on match quality, then there is no doubt that Michaels would rank #1. Sitting atop the performance charts, The Heartbreak Kid made his name on being the best in the business when the lights were on brightest, earning the title of "Mr. WrestleMania" and becoming famous for his innovation as the focal point of the first Ladder, Ironman, Hell in a Cell, and Elimination Chamber matches. Along the way, he became the first WWE Triple Crown winner, having won every title that the company had to offer, including four World Championships, three Intercontinental titles, and five Tag Team titles. He was also one of three men to win consecutive Royal Rumble matches and was the first to do it as the first entrant.

Michaels was the Michael Jordan of professional wrestling. Nobody has ever outperformed him or put together a body of work that includes as many iconic matches, especially when it comes to his efforts at WrestleMania. Just as MJ was untouchable in the NBA Finals, HBK had no peers at WrestleMania. They oddly had similar retirements in the middle of their careers, making their triumphant comebacks and subsequent legacy building second halves all the more special for their fans and for their respective sports, in general.

Many of Jordan's classics earned little taglines. In honor of HBK, I have singled out his finest work and given them each their own heading.

A Show Stopper from the Start

When Shawn Michaels debuted in the WWE alongside Marty Jannetty as one half of "The Rockers" in the late 1980s, he was already an innovator. The Rockers were known for their party habits, their willingness to give up their bodies in order to make their opponents look good, and their taking of moves popularized in singles competition and performing them in tandem. From dropkicks to elbow drops to punches to pressing kicks to kip ups to dives from the top rope, Michaels and Jannetty did them all simultaneously.

Jordan, as a freshman at the University of North Carolina, hit the game winning shot in the 1982 NCAA National Championship game. Michaels made his name by being a part of some of the best matches in the WWE from 1989 to 1991, none better than The Rockers vs. The Orient Express at *Royal Rumble '91*. Both men gave a preview of their unlimited potential. HBK would say some years later that "I will give you a show like you have never seen before. Why? Because I can." By then, it surprised no one when he did.

The Monday Night Shocker

Jannetty had been Shawn's mentor and friend in the early part of their careers. As The Rockers evolved, it became clear that the younger Michaels would easily surpass his older partner. In December 1991, Michaels famously superkicked Jannetty on a talk show segment called *The Barber Shop*. The kick - a signature move of the duo - was a proverbial stab in the back. He then threw Marty head-first through the glass window of the set. As Michaels became "The Heartbreak Kid" and rose the singles ranks to winning the Intercontinental Championship, Jannetty disappeared.

By 1993, HBK had well-established himself as a wrestler on the brink of superstardom. As the IC titleholder for nearly seven months as of May 17th, he had the cocky, Nature Boy-esque character down pat. Expectations were high for Shawn when he broke away from the tag team scene and he needed a critically acclaimed match that blew people away to live up to them. It came on the 5/17/93 *Raw* in an impromptu IC title bout against a returning Jannetty. In his version of Jordan's 63 point game in the '86 Playoffs against the Boston Celtics that earned high praise from Larry Bird, Michaels tore the house down with the best WWE match of fifteen minutes or less since *Mania III's* Savage vs. Steamboat, earning high praise from Macho Man (on commentary). It was voted the PWI Match of the Year for 1993.

The Ladder Match

The reason for the Jordan comparison is simple: Shawn Michaels was the best when it mattered most. In the NBA, a player's legacy is forged by what he does in the Playoffs. In the WWE, a wrestler's legacy is forged by what he does at WrestleMania. HBK's seminal moment came in the first PPV Ladder match against Razor Ramon at *WrestleMania X*. People still talk about that performance. His fans and peers have often stated that he went out "and had a match with a ladder." His leaping splash from the top of the ladder is one of the most frequently replayed clips every year during WrestleMania season, just as Jordan's buzzer beater – famously known as "The Shot" - over Craig Ehlo is when the NBA previews each year's Playoffs.

HBK redefined what it meant to steal the show at WrestleMania, inspiring a generation of superstars to get into the business. He did everything memorable in that contest except for win it. Even then, it was the way that he lost – by so dramatically getting caught up in the ropes after crash landing off the ladder and desperately trying, but failing to prevent Razor from grabbing the belts – that became one of the bout's signature memories. Garnering "5-star" praise from nearly all critics, fans, and colleagues, the Ladder match still ranks as one of the top Mania bouts in history.

"The Boyhood Dream Has Come True for Shawn Michaels"

It is as iconic an image in WrestleMania history as any other, Shawn Michaels gliding down from the rafters toward the sea of people sitting near ringside at the Arrowhead Pond in Anaheim, California.

"There's only one Heartbreak Kid, Shawn Michaels…" – Vince McMahon

It is as iconic an imagine in NBA Finals history as any other, Michael Jordan driving through the center of the lane, leaping up and switching the ball from one hand to the other to lay it in.

"A spectacular move by Michael Jordan!" – Marv Albert

HBK's life changed after *Mania X*. Two years later, he was preparing to wrestle for the WWE Championship for a second straight WrestleMania, only this time he was gearing up to win it and take over as the face of the company. Standing in his way was the greatest work rate rival that he ever encountered in his twenty plus years as a wrestler: Bret "Hitman" Hart. No two more gifted in-ring talents have ever been at the top of a promotion at the same time. Hart was less than two years from the end of his WWE tenure when Michaels challenged him for the title at *WrestleMania XII* and, much like Jordan defeating Magic Johnson did in the 1991 Finals, HBK was taking the proverbial torch.

The "Ironman Match" was a crafty idea. Everyone in the world knew that they were the two best in the business between the ropes and no better concept was ever created for a single match than to put sixty-minutes on the clock and see which man could earn the most falls. It would leave no doubt as to who was the better man. Some have called it the greatest match of all-time. It was once voted as the best in Mania history by their peers. Fans and critics have been mixed in their reaction, but when you have a substantial number of people that consider it historically excellent, then its place in the pantheon of all-time classics is safe. I think that it is a masterpiece for its time. What it meant for Michaels cannot be overstated. The image of him of looking down at the title, on his knees and spent from the longest match of his life, is emblematic of the highest point in the career of arguably the very best performer in the history of sports entertainment.

In Your House: Mind Games

Like Jordan in the Playoffs, most of the matches on the list of HBK's greatest took place at WrestleMania or some other major event. Yet, sometimes, he would give you something incredible that stood up against his more famous showcases. MJ dropped 64 points in a regular season game against my Orlando Magic back in '93. Though not as memorable as his Finals MVP performance a few months later, it was one of the highest scoring outputs of his career. In 1996, Shawn Michaels was the WWE Champion and putting on classic after classic, but while he was athletically taking the catch-as-catch-can approach to the next level, he still had his critics who thought he lacked toughness. At the September PPV against Mankind, HBK was the aggressor for much of the match, taking his usual bumps but also dishing out the kind of punishment that many would have expected to come only from his opponent. Mr. Perfect, doing ringside commentary, remarked, "I've never seen this side of Shawn Michaels before." Few had. It showed a toughness that had been missing from his matches. One of my knocks on Ric Flair, the only consistent threat to the notion that HBK is the best ever, was that he looked out of place trying to play rough. Michaels got over that hump with Mankind.

Is he already the greatest?

For the best of the best, there comes a moment when they know it and everyone else realizes it. In wrestling, it goes with the territory to be vocal about it after proving it. Through Degeneration X, he had been given the green light to push his sophomoric antics on *Raw* that helped spark the eventual victory in the Monday Night War. DX opened the door for the genuinely cocky HBK, who had confirmed himself as "The Man" in 1996, to be open and honest about his feelings of grandeur. Who could blame him? He had become like his idol, The Nature Boy, in not only telling the world that he was the best in the business, but in backing it up time and again. In October 1997, DX was in full swing and HBK was engaged in a feud with Undertaker that led to the first ever Hell in a Cell match at *Badd Blood*. HBK had been heralded on-screen as a giant slayer and behind the scenes as the ideal opponent for any of the larger athletes, citing his matches with Diesel, Vader, and Sid. Expectations for a Michaels vs. Taker match were huge. Add in a new style of Steel Cage with a roof on it and the hopes of an all-time classic increased. It was exactly the type of match that Michaels lived for.

Michaels took cringe-inducing punishment, crashing around to make Taker's offense look superhuman. Their climb to the top of the structure was, at that moment, one of the most stunning visuals in wrestling history. Watching HBK subsequently fall off the side of the Cell and smash through the announce table made the climb seem ordinary. The original Hell in a Cell was one of the greatest matches of the 1990s (arguably of all-time). MJ scored 69 points in a single playoff game; HBK added another 5-star "first" to his name, begging the question as to whether or not he was already the best that the industry had ever seen.

The Career Threatening Back Injury

Having a herniated disc in your lower back is excruciatingly painful. I suffered from it twice. It makes it difficult to walk – to even get out of bed. So, it is astounding to me that Michaels was able to gut it out through a severely herniated disc to wrestle the main-event of *WrestleMania XIV*. It was the gutsiest performance that I have ever seen. He even missed on what was usually his routine flip into the corner turnbuckle spot, sending his back into spasm and making a horribly painful situation that much worse. In the 1997 NBA Finals, Jordan was sick as a dog with the flu. Though it would have caused most to sit out, he played and had one of the greatest games of his career – "The Flu Game." For HBK, *Mania XIV* was the equivalent, only Michaels went into it knowing that he was wrestling his final match long before he was ready to retire. To a competitor of his class, that had to have been weighing on his mind just as heavily as the injury and risk of paralysis. He got through the match and put over Steve Austin for the WWE Championship to kick start the Attitude Era as we knew it. Then, he went home for four years.

The Comeback

Seeing the potential best ever in a sport hang it up in their prime leaves the fans disappointed, wondering what might have been. Jordan and Michaels both retired with strong arguments in favor of them already being the best, but they needed more to solidify their cases. After a two year hiatus, MJ needed just five games to show the world that he was still the best. He dropped 55 points on the New York Knicks in a vintage performance. HBK had more than double the retirement period and a major surgery, thus making his comeback in an

Unsanctioned "fight" with Triple H at *Summerslam 2002* all the more incredible.

Much like with Jordan, fans could not be sure what to expect from HBK's return. Could he possibly be anything close to what he had been after a four year absence? As a huge Michaels fan, I was most concerned with his health. He was cleared to return, but how much his surgically-repaired back could handle was going to be the mental and physical story of the match – it would be on everyone's mind. For me, the fight was not about wins and losses. I wanted him to defeat Trips, who had turned on his old mentor and friend to ignite the feud, but it was more about HBK surviving the night with his health still intact.

HBK's performance was brilliant. He sold so well that I was unable to tell the difference between him being in legitimate agony and him acting the part. It was not until he kipped up, and then jumped up and down, that I knew he was truly alright. Afterwards, it seemed appropriate to sit back and bask in the nostalgia of seeing what shockingly appeared to be the same old Michaels, with maybe just a bit more maturity on his side. It was amazing. At one point, as it became apparent that he absolutely still had the skill, he looked around at the commentators and the audience and said, "Do you remember me now?" Following the best match in Summerslam history, how could we not?

"He's Back"…to Stealing the Show

Once Michaels had wrestled a few more matches after *Summerslam*, anyone that had followed his pre-retirement career could not help but look ahead a few months to *WrestleMania XIX*. A late December rendition of Sweet Chin Music left little doubt as to his opponent. Chris Jericho was the ideal antagonist to harass HBK's developing new persona. All eyes were on the payoff. HBK had not had a standard feature length wrestling match in five years. Was he capable of recapturing the magic on the grandest stage? It took 23-minutes for him to answer and, though it has often been left out of the conversation for being one of the best WrestleMania matches of all-time, you would be hard pressed to ever find a better blend of excitement, pacing, psychology, and finish. The story was what one might expect had we ever saw Kobe Bryant challenge Jordan. It was the young lion hoping to catch up to and surpass the man that motivated his style. Much like Kobe is an MJ-lite, Jericho is an HBK-lite (and I mean that in the most respectful way possible). It was a true joy of my fandom to have watched Michaels vs. Jericho live on PPV. It ages like a fine wine and gets better with each viewing.

To make the comeback was one thing. To steal the show at WrestleMania was completely another. Jordan came back, had some great games, and even won the 1996 NBA title, but it was not until he hit the 20 foot buzzer beater to take Game 1 of the 1997 Finals against a formidable opponent that it really felt like the old MJ was back. HBK stealing the show on the most star studded card in the history of the "Granddaddy of 'em all" - the card featured wrestlers with a combined *eighty* total World Championships - was the moment we knew "The Showstopper" was back.

Good Luck Following THAT

Consecutive show stealing performances at *WrestleManias XIX and XX*, respectively, prompted Michaels to begin calling himself, "Mr. WrestleMania," but the night that he took a definitive hold on the moniker was *WrestleMania 21*. His match with Kurt Angle was so incredible that Bobby Heenan, who had seen every major match for thirty years, called it the best he had *ever* seen. For yours truly, it remains my favorite of all-time.

Michaels had always walked into a match as the superior athlete. There were things that he could easily do that nobody else could if they tried a hundred times. Angle provided the only exception. Even past his prime, HBK still possessed a greater combination of athleticism and guile than each and every one of his opponents, the gold medalist included, but Angle was more physically gifted, overall. The things that Kurt could do blew me away. I get goose bumps writing about their match all these years later. The expectations that I had for it were astronomically high. I had come to favor Angle as the best in the industry until Michaels started connecting with classic after classic. As sports fans, we often pray for a scenario in which the best of the best - #1 and #1A – have a chance to dance with the lights on brightest. We want to see Brady vs. Rodgers, Lebron vs. Kevin Durant, and Nadal vs. Federer. If the stars fail to align, then we feel cheated. Luckily, in pro wrestling, we got Michaels vs. Angle.

I actually had dreams about how the match might play out, as silly as that may read. I basically had the entire match built up in my mind before it happened as the greatest in history. And it arguably was. MJ had a game in the '92 Finals where he hit six 3-pointers en route to 35 points in the first half. After the last of them, he looked over at the broadcast table and shrugged, as if to tell anyone that was watching, "I don't know how I can be this good, but I am." Michaels was notorious for refraining from such things on camera, but once he got backstage in front of his peers, he would yell, "Follow that!" Only HBK, himself, could follow the match with Angle.

The PhD of Professional Wrestling

When a wrestler is coming up through the ranks en route to the main-event, he customarily encounters a variety of top flight superstars along the way that teach him the different skills to hone his craft. In 2007, John Cena was coming along well, having been taught the nuances necessary to become an elite performer by the likes of Angle, Jericho, Triple H, and Edge. Yet, when it comes to performance, there are the equivalent of undergraduate and Master's level professors...and then there is Shawn Michaels.

HBK was the final teacher giving the last lesson that Cena needed to graduate with honors from the school of sports entertainment. Cena had already worked a few classics by then, but he had never worked a non-gimmicked match of longer than 23-minutes. Gimmicks can hide a wrestler's weaknesses. So, on the grandest stage at *WrestleMania 23*, Cena defended his WWE Championship against his PhD professor, HBK. For 28-minutes in a standard match, Michaels taught the young lion what it took to succeed without a ladder or cage and with all normal rules in play. A few weeks later, Michaels and Cena battled again, this time on a *Monday Night Raw* from England. At *WrestleMania*, HBK had clearly been in control, writing the tale as they went. In the rematch, Cena was the one with the pen. He scripted an excellent, back and forth, psychologically sound, intelligently worked television masterpiece that lasted nearly an hour and earned "Match of the Year" according to numerous critics. For Cena, it was the beginning of his time as one of the best in-ring performers in the business. For Michaels, it was another feather in his cap. I once saw Jordan play my home state Charlotte Hornets on a random winter night in 1997 and beat them with a shot at the buzzer. It was a moment, like Michaels vs. Cena from *Raw*, where you took a step back and appreciated that you were lucky enough to be watching "the best" at work.

"I'm sorry...I love you."

At *WrestleMania XXIV* in Orlando, HBK was given perhaps his most difficult challenge to date. He was asked to help his idol, Ric Flair, have the greatest sendoff in professional wrestling history befitting arguably the greatest professional wrestler in history. Flair was nearly sixty years old. Mission:

Impossible? It was like giving Jordan four guys from the NBA retirement home and asking him to win the title. To his credit, Flair was still quite good and could go better than most of the active roster, but still. Put yourself in Shawn's shoes, mentally. It was a very emotional situation. At the Hall of Fame ceremony the night before, the emotions just poured out of Flair as he tried to come to grips with his retirement. Michaels had to keep him engaged in the story they were telling (that if Flair lost, his career was over).

He did all the heavy lifting, unleashing high risks that looked fantastic, but were surely felt for weeks later. The reversals turned out perfectly, the near falls induced the exact reaction hoped for, and the drama of the climax was breathtaking. The closing moment, during which HBK tuned up for Sweet Chin Music and, with Flair crying like a baby knowing that the time had finally come, mouthed "I'm sorry...I love you," was the most poignant finish to a wrestling match that I have ever seen. The presentation was considered wildly successful. Michaels earned heaps of praise and the match was named "Match of the Year" by many. Just as Jordan had done in the '93 Finals when he torched the Phoenix Suns for 55 very efficiently scored points to take firm control of the series, Michaels gave an iconic performance that was impossible to forget.

Painting the Storytelling Masterpiece

Once the HBK-Angle match had ended in 2005, I legitimately thought that we had seen the best Michaels match that we were ever going to see. From that point forward, everything else was just competing for second place. As of my first viewing of the match at the *25th Anniversary of WrestleMania* that pit Undertaker's vaunted "WrestleMania Streak" against "Mr. WrestleMania," I felt justified in my thoughts. Though it was as emotionally invested as I have ever been for any match, I did not share the popular, post-match belief that it was "the greatest of all-time." I could not understand that strong an adoration until I got a hold of the DVD and watched it again. I thought afterwards, "OK that was better than I remember." And then I watched it again. It was like watching *The Dark Knight* repeatedly, in that each viewing revealed another subtly great moment.

I decided to wait a year before watching it again. The next time that I watched it was one week before their rematch a year later, after watching all of HBK's other top Mania matches in chronological order. That was when it hit me that it might have been the best match I had ever seen. It was odd. I had always placed such great emphasis on the first time that I saw a match. I hung onto the idea that HBK vs. Angle was better for another year or so, in part because of my fondness of the first viewing, but I watched them back-to-back in early 2011 and could no longer come up with a reason to hold HBK-Taker down. It took numerous screenings for me to gain the respect and reverence for HBK-Taker that it deserved.

Wrestling has become so much about intricate storytelling. The pre-match hype must excel, the creation of the highlight video for the feud must set the stage moments prior, and the wrestlers cannot miss a cue on their way to the ring. They must sell that seminal moment before a match to grab hold of the audience. Michaels vs. Undertaker was the perfect combination of all the above. Stories now demand definable organization and more layers of drama. A decade ago, twenty-minutes of working fast and smart with a bunch of false finishes during the climax earned MOTY contender-status. HBK-Taker created a new standard. If you look at the best matches since, including their own rematch, each has featured enhanced psychology and more animated and identifiable flashpoints of expression. The near falls all have to be more logical and more attention must be paid to their placement. It is an all-out production. Fans are smarter now than they have ever been before and they are holding the superstars to an incredibly high standard because HBK and Taker made a new blueprint for what defines the perfect match.

I do not hold the "Streak vs. Career" match from *WrestleMania XXVI* in nearly as a high regard, but I admit that it was a wonderful follow-up to the greatest match ever. When Michael Jordan retired in 1998, he did so in the best possible way – sinking the game-winning shot to win the NBA title for a sixth time. Shawn Michaels had the best match of 2010 on the heels of the best match of all-time. There has never been a more perfect end to a career.

#5: The Undertaker

One of the wrestlers that I have truly grown to admire over the last several years has been Undertaker. Though I had seen his entire career, from his 1990 *Survivor Series* debut to being in attendance for his untouchable record 21st victory without a loss at WrestleMania, it was not until the middle of last decade that I could honestly call myself a "Deadman fan." My new-found admiration came from what I have come to affectionately call "The Streak within the Streak" – an unprecedented series of consecutive Match of the Year candidates at WrestleMania that took his already legendary undefeated record at "The Show of Shows" to unparalleled veneration.

In an interview from the early 2000s, Kurt Angle called Taker "the best in the business" and praised him to no end. That was a common narrative written by the Deadman's peers. "Best" to me has always implied performance (as in "best in the ring") and maybe I was in the minority but, as an in-ring performer, I thought Taker was vastly overrated when the calendar turned to 2006. Other than his achievement of the near-impossible with HBK of giving Steve Austin and Bret Hart's Submission match a run for its money for 1997 Match of the Year in the first-ever Hell in a Cell at *In Your House: Badd Blood*, what classic Undertaker match really stood out as of the mid-point of his so-termed second "Decade of Destruction"? Angle himself had as many great matches in 2002 alone as Taker had over a fifteen year span!

Comments like Kurt's are a microcosm of why I felt this book needed to be written; there is a difference between being the best and the greatest or between being the biggest and the most accomplished. The most accomplished wrestler in the business as of the early 2000s? I could have bought that argument for Taker. You could look at his resume and see the unquestionable success as a headliner, as a multi-time WWE

Champion and 7-time Tag Team Champion, and as an innovator in creating gimmicks (Casket, Buried Alive, Hell in a Cell, Inferno). Yet, Angle was regurgitating this commonly held belief among the wrestlers that Undertaker was one of the best *performers*.

I could see his amazing raw athletic ability; he was one of the great physical marvels of our time in *any* sport over the first twenty years of his career. A small handful of near seven-foot, three-hundred pound men on the planet could do what he could. He could have been a great basketball player with his combination of coordination, quickness, and ridiculous vertical leap. Just because you are a transcendent athlete does not necessarily mean, though, that you can be a great wrestler. From 1990-2005, I would have called Undertaker a *good* wrestler with one amazing match (HIAC), two borderline great matches (at *Summerslam '97* vs. Bret Hart and at *WrestleMania X-Seven* vs. HHH), and a long list of good matches; someone with a respectable resume, but the *best*?

But something changed in 2006, fittingly in a match against Angle. In their 30-minute clash for the World Heavyweight Championship at *No Way Out*, Taker appeared more dedicated to excellence than ever before. He had wrestled technically-styled matches in the past, but nothing that could hold a candle to the technical artistry put on display with Angle. Considering that the match was originally supposed to happen at *WrestleMania 22*, I have since come to think of Taker vs. Angle – one of the Top 2 matches of 2006 – as the unofficial beginning of "The Streak within the Streak."

Blessed with a timeless gimmick, the long-time veteran decided to get into the best shape of his life in his early forties and spend his twilight years performing at his highest level. In no other athletic endeavor can someone get that much better fifteen years into his career without the media accusing him of taking performance-enhancing drugs; wrestlers are of a different breed, often getting better with age like actors.

Do you remember when Tom Hanks broke out in the mid-1990s as one of the greatest actors ever? That was Taker from 2006-2013. Hanks made some good movies, many of them (i.e. *Big*) were even highly re-watchable like a lot of Taker's matches, but when he made *Philadelphia*, that was the game-changer; that was when he started to become truly iconic and started winning Oscars. For about eight years, he churned out classic after classic. To go along with *'Philly*, he made *Sleepless in Seattle, Forrest Gump* (knotting him his second Best Actor Oscar in a row), *Apollo 13, Toy Story, Saving Private Ryan, The Green Mile*, and *Cast Away*. Nobody could touch him. *No Way Out '06* was the start of Taker's perception-altering run to me. Seven straight WrestleManias with four-five star matches and a handful of other classics in between? It is not just that nobody during that seven year stretch could touch that, but nobody in history can touch that! Not even HBK!

The legend of The Deadman began growing to its current levels when he won the 2007 Royal Rumble match to earn a shot at Dave Batista's World Championship at *WrestleMania 23*. Batista was coming on strong as one of the WWE's new leading stars and had never lost a title match. Creating an interesting historical backdrop to the match was that it was actually his injury that demoted Taker to a lesser match at *Mania 22*, prompting the aforementioned audible that bumped one of Taker's all-time best matches to a lesser PPV. Imagine where The Streak would be if it had included Taker vs. Angle with the Chicago crowd from *Mania 22* behind it. As it stands, The Deadman's first truly epic match at Mania was postponed a year.

In the most unpredictable match in the modern days of The Streak, Taker dethroned Batista for the World title and stole the show in what many claimed was the 2007 Match of the Year (which would have made it two in a row for the Deadman). It was not an epically long match, but it certainly had an epic feel. Rumor had it that both men expected to be going on last, given that it was Taker's first title shot at Mania in a decade. When they learned that Michaels vs. John Cena would close the show, they were extra motivated and produced one of sports entertainment history's most pleasant surprises. It also sparked a competition between Taker and Michaels for WrestleMania's best match and the Match of the Year that lasted until HBK retired in 2010.

Taker got his chance to main-event WrestleMania again the next year against Edge. If defeating Batista for the World Championship in critically acclaimed fashion laid the foundation for Taker to go on his landmark run of 4-5-star Mania classics, then the night he went 16-0 to capture the title by beating The Rated R Superstar did well to build the first story of the mansion. The match at *WrestleMania XXIV* was easily the most underrated of the entire Streak. While praised as an all-time great, it gets lost in the shuffle. There is no mistaking that Taker-Edge as one of the Top 20 bouts in Mania history. Comparing it to the other Streak matches, it was the one that best showcased Taker's ability to go hold-counter hold with a competitor quite skilled at it. Edge was a genius at creating counters. Both wrestlers had numerous big moves in their arsenals and they put together what seemed a record number of counters for two guys both checking in at over 6'4". The story told, which chronicled each of their encounters dating all the way back to Edge cashing in Money in the Bank on Taker in May 2007, was a rare example of continuity in the era.

On a personal note, my dad and I attended *Mania 24* in Orlando and amongst his lasting memories of the experience was Taker's entrance. I remember sitting in a Denny's having breakfast with him and my then-fiancée during Christmas season that same year. He and I were reminiscing about the event as Sarah was getting her first taste of both my father's personality and our mutual interest in pro wrestling. My dad animatedly summed up Taker's entrance, which was a phenomenal sight at night in an outdoor stadium, by loudly exclaiming, "GONG!!" He also noted that he loved how I playfully chanted back at the kids rooting for "Six-teen and Oh" with "Fif-teen and ONE!"

Edge was one of Taker's best opponents, evidenced as much by the arguable 2008 Match of the Year at *Summerslam* as the Mania bout (three in a row), but if you aim to narrow down his greatest, the short list begins with Michaels. Combining their original Hell in a Cell from '97 with their pair of WrestleMania matches that earned 2009 and 2010 Match of the Year honors (four and five in a row), it is hard to argue against the case for HBK. The *25th Anniversary of WrestleMania* will forever be known as the site for perhaps the greatest match of all-time featuring the most heralded encounter of the two most critically acclaimed WrestleMania superstars. It was Taker's most distinguished performance, made all the more dramatic by the moment in which he nearly killed himself with his over the top rope dive. The son of his very first WrestleMania opponent, Jimmy "Superfly" Snuka, was dressed as a cameraman and was supposed to break Taker's fall, but the junior Snuka was out of place. When he nearly landed on his head, I thought that The Deadman had brought his character into reality; I thought he was dead. It seemed like an eternity before he got up. When he finally did, he and HBK went onto to the have my choice for wrestling history's modern masterpiece. It simply does not get any better than that match, with its "light" vs. "darkness," "Heaven" vs. "Hell" theme.

I do not believe it to be coincidental that Taker's physical struggles have been far more pronounced since his top rope dive gone awry. He battled nagging injuries, had numerous surgeries, and spent the majority of each year recovering from the effects of one match per calendar since 2010. Taker's health seemed to limit his mobility in the "Career vs. Streak" match at *WrestleMania XXVI*. Though it was still a tremendous match that told an incredible tale - the desperation of one man trying to hold onto his career by ending The Streak – there was a notable decline in Taker's athleticism compared to the previous year from that point forward, whereas he had looked as fit as he ever had when the bell tolled at *Mania 25*.

Finding a better two match series would be an unenviable task. Your best bet might be to look ahead to Undertaker vs. Triple H at *WrestleMania XXVII and XXVIII*. "The Streak within the Streak" earned its tag-line after The Deadman nearly equaled the quality of his bouts with Michaels in a larger-than-life clash with Trips in 2011. I had the honor of seeing it live in Atlanta. I honestly was of the mindset that it was not possible for Taker and Trips to have an outstanding match comparable to Taker-HBK. The moment that I realized how wrong I had been was when Taker, after being assaulted for minutes on end, tried to goozle Trips as he had done to so many to start his comebacks over the years. Yet, Triple H shook his head, "No." My wife, who took me to *Mania 27* as a wedding present, was sitting next to me. I leaned over at the 30-minute mark and whispered, "People will be talking about this one for years."

Their story was just the right fit for 2011 and 2012. For The Game, there was not much left to do in his career than give Taker that elusive "Loss" – to be "the one" (as in 18-1). He made that point clear in the hype for *Mania 27*, which included one of the best segments in *Raw* history where neither of them spoke, but each of their actions told the story of two legends preparing to collide in an epic battle. Trips beat the tar out of him. Though he won the match, it became the first time that The Deadman could not leave the ring under his own power.

When Mania season began in 2012, Taker showed up for the first time since *Mania 27* and challenged Trips to a rematch. The stakes were raised when Shawn Michaels was named the special referee and when Triple H demanded that it be a Hell in a Cell match. For as great as the *Mania 27* match truly was, the *Mania 28* match was better. It was a work of art featuring perfect placement of all the pieces of the puzzle. The match featured the single greatest false finish of the entire Streak, in which HBK awoke from a Hell's Gate induced slumber to blast The Deadman with Sweet Chin Music, sending him right into Triple H's Pedigree. Never had The Streak seemed in greater jeopardy. Their multi-year story ended with the iconic image of Taker, Michaels, and Trips standing at the top of the entrance ramp together, post-match. Toward the end of Taker's career, Triple H emerged as another candidate for his greatest rival. Only Rock and Austin had as many matches at WrestleMania together as Taker and Trips.

Year after year, the incredible legacy of "The Streak within the Streak" grew. His match with CM Punk at *WrestleMania 29* was every bit the classic that we had come to expect. Punk had come on strong as a leader in his generation, but did not bring to the table the same historic stature, as of 2013, that did the current and future Hall of Famers that came before him since 2007. The one thing that Taker and Punk had to do in order to put their match on par with The Deadman's previous six was to make the people believe that Punk, who had less chance of winning as any of his recent predecessors, could actually end The Streak at *WrestleMania*. Mission accomplished, en route to another of the greatest matches in *WrestleMania* history. Amidst increasing talk of his imminent retirement, Taker delivered yet another amazing performance on the grandest stage, putting himself one step closer to eclipsing Michaels as the best in Mania lore.

In 2014, both "The Streak" and the streak within it came crashing to a halt, sending him into the countdown to retirement. Think of what "The Streak within the Streak" did for the Undertaker for a moment. Sure, before it started, he was already the most respected man in the business, a locker room figure on Andre's level of reverence. He had accomplished enough to be considered one of the fringe Top 10 of the WrestleMania Era. However, "The Streak within the Streak" put him into the discussion for the definitive greatest of all-time. Eight straight cycles of producing inarguably one of the Top 2 matches every year, all but one of which took place on "The Grandest Stage," drove him to keep adding to his legacy. Taker was pushed by his own success to tack another decade onto his incredible run as a headlining wrestler, giving him the greatest longevity of anyone in the WrestleMania Era. He also now owns the third most impressive performance track record of all-time (behind HBK and Ric Flair) and there is a direct parallel between Taker's "Streak within the Streak" and the all-time heights in popularity that WrestleMania has reached over the last decade.

"Undefeated at WrestleMania" was as impressive as any other pro wrestling accolade and subsequently made Taker as synonymous with "The Showcase of the Immortals" for winning as Hulk Hogan was for main-events or Shawn Michaels was (overall) for performances. "The Streak within the Streak," though, allowed The Deadman to eclipse both of them to find a place not only as perhaps WrestleMania's greatest superstar, but in the Top 5 of the entire WrestleMania Era.

There are certain things that I do not expect to see in wrestling again; one of them is title reigns that last quadruple digit days and the other three belong to Undertaker. We will never again see anyone maintain a gimmick for over twenty years, we will never see a wrestler get anywhere close to being 21-0 at WrestleMania, and we will never see another superstar have seven straight incredible matches at WrestleMania.

#4: Ric Flair

WOOOOO!

One of the most memorable live experiences that I have had as a wrestling fan was at *WrestleMania XXIV* in March of 2008. It was the night that Ric Flair retired from in-ring competition for the WWE. For the previous twenty-five years, Flair had become known as quite possibly the greatest wrestler in history. My dad and I were two of the nearly 75,000 people to pack the Orlando, Florida Citrus Bowl to see Flair's final match. I have been to dozens of wrestling events, including other WrestleManias. I am one of those fans – and if you have been to a live wrestling event prior to 2009, you know the type that I am referencing - to immediately, upon walking into an arena or stadium, belt out Flair's signature catchphrase "WOOOO" as loud as I could. Hundreds to thousands of others would usually chime in. It helped set the mood for the evening. "WOOOO" is, in my opinion, wrestling's most famous catchphrase. I have never heard so many people yell, "WOOOO," in one setting as I did at *Mania 24*. My dad loved it…

Flair was my dad's all-time favorite wrestler. The chosen opponent for Flair's last match was Shawn Michaels, my personal all-time favorite. There was a unique dynamic with my dad and I, separated by a generation, watching Flair and Michaels, also separated by a generation, going toe-to-toe on wrestling's grandest stage. Flair put on a vintage performance that will live through the ages. Despite being fifteen years past his prime at the age of 59 years old, he held up his end of the bargain and produced a match that I will never forget. It was one of the most emotional matches I have seen, as Flair knew that it was the end of the road. When it came time for the climactic finish, Flair had already begun to break down in tears. Michaels, about to connect with his finishing move, took notice of Flair's emotions and told him, "I'm sorry…I love you." All of us in the building could see exactly what Michaels had said on the giant screens hanging above the ring. I nearly teared up, myself. We gave Flair a standing ovation and a fitting send off. He had just given us a performance of a lifetime.

The Nature Boy

If you have had anything more than a passing interest in pro wrestling over the last thirty years, then you would know that there is no need to compare Ric Flair to a figure from another sport. He was a wrestling institution. His thirty year career had a lasting influence on professional wrestling that we still see today and will continue to see for decades to come.

Flair was a perfect wrestler to bridge the gap between what wrestling had been in the past and what wrestling became as the WWE's takeover of the business turned it into sports entertainment. He was all about entertainment. While he could back it up in the ring – people often said that he could have a fantastic match with a broomstick – he was also one of the greatest showmen to ever be handed a microphone. There was not a better talker in the history of the business. The only guy that comes close is The Rock, but what separates Flair from Rock is that The Nature Boy was always geared toward pro wrestling. Rock would get bored and try to challenge himself to be funny and, though he was, it would often take away from the serious tone of the feud he was in. So, I would say Rock had more charisma, but Flair was the better talker because he always had a more focused purpose.

Take, for instance, the *'92 Royal Rumble* victory that earned Flair the WWE Championship. His performance in that match was second-to-none in Rumble history, but it was his post-match interview that resonates most. Nobody could ever put over the importance of the World Championship better than Flair. When he won the Rumble match, he made the championship belt seem as important as any major sports title in the entire world. To Flair, that is exactly what it was. "With a TEAR...in my EYE...this is the greatest moment of my life."

He came from an era where being World Champion was more than just an honor, but a responsibility. He took it upon himself to ensure that everyone around the world firmly understood how he felt about being "The Man." Subsequently, his poignant promos were one of a kind. Nobody understood what it meant to be the best in pro wrestling more than Flair and nobody could better communicate it verbally. There is a reason why virtually all of Flair's best work in his career came with the World title on the line. Every feud involving it invoked serious emotion. Each comment about his suits or his watches or his lifestyle was a reflection of the spoils of being the champion. Being World Champion back then was not like it is today. In the WWE, Vince McMahon decides who should be champion. If ratings go down, then maybe a title change may fix it, in his mind. If PPV buys are lacking, then the belt will get passed on. The National Wrestling Alliance had a committee that appointed who should be champion and that committee consisted of promoters from all around the United States. When Flair won the NWA title, it was because multiple people had decided that their best bet for making money to feed their families was to have him as their World Champion, touring the country to face the top guys in each territory. He took great pride in being given that chance.

When he won the belt in 1981, it was the beginning of an obsession for him to be thought of by the NWA Board and his peers as the greatest. For that reason, I think Flair is easy to relate to for a lot of us. His sense of self was tied up quite a bit in what other people thought of him which, for most of us, is a common theme in at least some stage of our lives. His insecurities were obvious, as was his confidence when things were rolling for him. He wore his emotions on his sleeve and, no matter the situation, it helped us get to know the real Ric Flair. You do not often see that in wrestling from a bunch tough guys. After he won the title from Harley Race at *Starrcade '83* and started his second title run, he broke down in front of the audience and gave a heartfelt, teary speech. He had been champion for over a year with his first title reign, but he took it personally when he lost the title. The second reign seemed to give him assurance that the NWA Board believed in him. Once he felt that belief, it was off to the races.

He wanted to be one of those champions that held onto the title for years on end, like Lou Thesz, Dory Funk, and Harley Race before him. In terms of the number of World titles won in his career, he is by far the greatest. He was #1 in the Championship Factor by a landslide. With his sixteen World titles in fifteen years, his score was approximately thirty-eight points higher than Hogan's, who came in second in that category. Here is an amazing statistic for you: Flair had five World title reigns of nine-months or longer. In that regard, there will never be anyone that comes close to Ric Flair. Times have changed and the ability to hold on to a World title for nearly a year - much less do it five times - is unlikely to happen again.

Thesz was the man that really brought wrestling out of the dark ages and made it more exciting. He was the first NWA Champion and was one of the most watched men on television when TV was in its infancy. He was a sharp dressed, classy gentleman who could entertain. Subsequently, he became to an entire generation of fans an icon, inspiring many to get involved in the sport like Babe Ruth inspired people to want to play baseball. The greatest compliment that I could ever give to Flair would be to say that he was our generation's Lou Thesz. He was the greatest combination of pro wrestling skill that I have ever seen.

The Dirtiest Player in the Game

Flair was not a large athlete, even in his prime. He had to overcome his smaller stature and fairly average body type, as the wrestling business was becoming more about the "look" than the skill. So, he had to develop a style that made him seem a legitimate threat against all challengers. Otherwise, he never would have been able to carry a company on his back like he did. He usually played the role of the heel, but even when working as the hero, Flair used illegal tactics to gain the advantage in his matches. In his *Starrcade '93* World title match with Vader, in which his career was on the line, Flair took every opportunity to cheat. Fans did not care, though. To us, it was just him showing how much the title meant to him.

He would employ the use of low blows, eye gouges, and foreign objects. He would put his feet on the ropes or grab a handful of his opponent's tights to gain leverage when attempting pins. He would plead for mercy and then use the moment of created sympathy to go for a cheap shot. The combination of all of his underhanded tactics made him very difficult to beat. During his lengthy stretches in the 80s as champion, he very rarely lost.

I thought he most deservedly earned the "Dirtiest Player in the Game" nickname against Lex Luger, Flair's former protégé from his famous stable, The Four Horsemen. Luger was a great athlete and seemed like the logical choice to supplant Flair as the champion. The two had natural chemistry and their matches were stellar. At *The Great American Bash '88*, the two locked horns for the World title and did tremendous work. They made you wonder how Naitch was going to escape with the belt. Flair got lucky that night, but he had to face Luger again at *Starrcade*. It was another excellent match. Flair vs. Luger provided an example of how to build to a main-event at the biggest show of the year. It was one of the great Starrcade matches of all-time and it was particularly impressive for Flair given that Luger was still somewhat green. Flair made him look like a million bucks. And how did we win? He pinned him with his feet on the ropes.

Space Mountain

Wrestling has always been known as a party business, as the guys are like a fraternity traveling the roads to some of the biggest cities in the world. You expect a certain amount of debauchery to come from those conditions. Flair, in addition to all his other accolades, is also the greatest partier in wrestling history. I am surprised he is still alive, frankly. He was as well-known for running up outrageous bar tabs as he was playing the part of the champion of the world - he wanted everyone to know that he was on top of it. Flair was the embodiment of a lifestyle and he tried to turn being World Champion into an almost rock star-like position in pop culture. He, Arn Anderson, and Tully Blanchard lived life to the fullest, partying and gambling until the wee hours before getting up and wrestling for an hour the next day. Of course, to the victor go the spoils. One of the spoils happened to be a lot of women. Space Mountain is a ride at Disney World, but it also became Ric Flair's "member" and, as The Nature Boy often said, the line was just as long for the Naitch's version of the ride as the one in Orlando. WOOOO!

I imagine he felt fairly untouchable during those times. He was quickly building a reputation throughout the mid-80s as the best in the world. Despite the all-night partying, he still performed at a level of consistency that no one ever had. Sometimes, he would wrestle for an hour twice in one day. He was having great matches on some of the most famous wrestling events of the era, so why not live it up? From Nikita Koloff to Road Warrior Hawk to Barry Windham, he was wrestling all types of wrestlers and having stellar matches.

Flair started to hit his stride in the mid-1980s.

The matches he had with Windham in early 1986 and 1987 were highly regarded as some of the best work in both their careers. Flair had increased his cardio to astonishing and legendary levels. Other guys had wrestled nightly for an hour in the past, but not with the kind of pace that Flair brought to the table. Windham could step up and match Flair's endurance. So, if you are a fan of near sixty-minute matches, then you should take a look at the early 1986 match between Windham and Flair.

In the last decade, there has been some question as to the strength of Flair's drawing power - his ability to put butts in the seats and draw money. I am unsure why there is an argument against Flair being a draw. In the 80s, he kept the NWA afloat as they searched for answers and made bad business decisions to try and stay in the game with the WWE. Flair and The Four Horsemen were an undeniable draw. They sold out arenas throughout the southeast and midwest with consistency. The NWA was not as flashy as the WWE, but Flair was all the glitz and glamour that they needed to offer the pro wrestling fan. People wanted to be Ric Flair. Hell, my dad was Ric Flair minus the wrestling. People wanted to see Naitch wrestle, to party with him after the show, and to follow him to the next town to do it again the next night.

Limousine ridin', jet flyin', kiss stealin', wheelin' dealin' son of a gun!

The persona of The Nature Boy rounded into form in 1984 and 1985 during his renowned feud with Dusty Rhodes. They were polar opposites in character. The chemistry with Dusty in and out of the ring became about as great a case of fire vs. ice as you could imagine in those days. Dusty, the common man and son of a plumber, against the limousine ridin', jet flyin', kiss stealin', wheelin' dealin' son of a gun. WOOOOO! You could not have asked for a more perfect pairing. Rhodes was Flair's greatest rival.

Flair actually began the World title feud with Rhodes by beating him in '81 to win his first NWA World Championship. The two consecutive *Starrcade* matches in 1984 and 1985, though, were on a whole different level. I particularly enjoyed the match that saw Dusty win the title back at *Starrcade '85*. They had built so wonderfully to that moment for two years, with Flair and The Horsemen making Rhodes their first major target. It was that feud that helped The Horsemen get established as the top faction of the 80s and arguably the greatest of all-time.

The Nature Boy had many great rivals, but the best of them were those that came across as vastly different to his personality. The feud with Rhodes clicked because he was the "every man" to Flair's cocky, "better than you" attitude. On a similar level, that is why Flair's story with Ricky "The Dragon" Steamboat worked so well. Flair, ever the wild man out on the town, measurably contrasted with a man like Steamboat, whose family came first. They had, unquestionably, one of the greatest series of matches – if not THE greatest series of matches – of all-time in 1989. Steamboat defeated Flair for the NWA Heavyweight title in Chicago, which was followed by a draw weeks later before Flair won the title back in the third match. It was a rare case in pro wrestling history where all of the matches in a series were given the elusive 5-star rating. I have never seen fit to disagree with that level of praise. Because of that series, Flair vs. Steamboat in 1994 flies under the radar.

Some five years after the Dragon won the title at *The Chi-Town Rumble*, WCW came back to Chicago for *Spring Stampede '94*. In another thirty-minute classic, Flair and Steamboat tore the house down again. The level of athleticism in pro wrestling had increased by then, Steamboat was about to retire later that year, and Flair was long past his physical prime, so it was interesting to see how they adapted. The key for them was that they had wrestled each other so many times dating back to the 1970s that they never lost their chemistry. They worked a simple match, but they accentuated the little things so masterfully that superior athleticism was no longer required. The *WCW Saturday Night* rematch was arguably even better. The pair of bouts was not as good as their '89 matches, but they were pretty close. Steamboat was Flair's best opponent.

The REAL World's Champion

Flair peaked as a performer when the WWE was at its hottest in the late 80s. In 1991, he got fed up with the business decisions being made by the people in charge of WCW, opening the door for him to go to the WWE. He was still the World Champion and he never dropped the title before leaving WCW, so he paraded around with the big gold belt when he got to the WWE while Bobby Heenan referred to him as the "Real" World's Champion.

The '92 Rumble match was one of a handful of Flair's last great performances and seemed to signal the beginning of the dream feud between Flair and Hogan that would have led to a WrestleMania match. However, Flair was positioned to face Randy Savage instead. The '92 Rumble and the storyline with Savage, combined with his incredibly entertaining faction, of sorts, with Heenan and Mr. Perfect (Naitch's wingman), defined his 1992 stint in the WWE. Miss Elizabeth, according to Flair and Perfect, was one of the many women to have ridden Space Mountain. This enraged Savage and quickly built an intense rivalry that the crowd in Indianapolis for *WrestleMania VIII* ate up with a spoon. The match was one of the top 15 in WrestleMania history. Savage won the title, though he would drop it back to Flair after *Summerslam* later in the year. Flair's run in the WWE was a lot of fun for fans like me that grew up watching him, even if the Hogan feud did not happen as expected.

To Be "The Man"

Without question, Flair was the greatest that the NWA/WCW ever produced. Remember that the Starrcade franchise pre-dated WrestleMania by a year and that said franchise was built on Ric Flair's foundation. Every bankable star that the NWA created in those days to try and compete, sans for Dusty Rhodes, had some sort of tie to Flair. The rivalries with Rhodes, Magnum TA, Windham, Luger, and Sting, leading to the classic matches at Starrcade, The Great American Bash, and The Clash of the Champions; the title reigns, the interviews, and the parties alongside The Four Horsemen - without Flair in 80s, the NWA would have ended up like the AWA. He defined what it meant to be "The Man." He was the top guy in the NWA throughout the 1980s. He was given the World Championship immediately upon joining the WWE. When he came back to the NWA (turned WCW) in 1993, he was again positioned as the #1 star.

1994 was his last truly great year, in which he carried the weight of WCW on his back and provided the caliber of performances on which he had made his name in matches against the likes of Steamboat, Vader, and – finally – Hulk Hogan. Hogan had been "The Man" in the WWE, continually main-eventing WrestleMania. Flair was "The Man" in the NWA, continually main-eventing Starrcade. Mania was dominating, business-wise, but the quality of Flair's main-events were undeniably better. Hogan was drawing money like no one ever had, but the aesthetics of his matches paled in comparison to Flair's. Everyone had always wanted to see Flair vs. Hogan. It was the dream match of that era, pitting its #1 draw against its #1 wrestler.

WCW jumped at the chance to run Flair vs. Hogan as soon as they signed the Hulkster. The first match in the series, at *Bash at the Beach*, was the best. There is just no replacing the feeling that you get when you see two all-time greats lock horns for the first time. Even though they had two other matches in '94 and both were quite good, I never got invested past that first match. I loved the initial encounter, but from then on it was all Hogan. Egos got in the way of better business. It was still great to see it happen, even if it could have been more memorable.

"Slick" Ric

From 1995 until his 2008 retirement, Flair's role in the business changed. He would show us occasional flashes of his once consistent brilliance. He had another series with Savage once Macho Man joined WCW, including the main-event at *Starrcade '95*. Once back in the WWE, he had several notable moments, including the *Mania X-8* bout with Taker, the spring '03 *Raw* main-event with Triple H, his lengthy run as a member of Evolution, his Ladder match on *Raw* with Edge, and his last in-ring masterpiece with Shawn Michaels at *WrestleMania*. These matches allowed an entirely new generation of wrestling fans and aspiring wrestlers to see what all the fuss had been about during the best years of his career.

Flair will likely be buried in a $5,000 suit with a Rolex on his wrist and the old NWA Championship around his waist. On that day, fans around the wrestling world will do one last strut in his honor and yell out one last time…

**ature*Diamonds are Forever; and so is Ric Flair*

#3: John Cena

If you were to put together a list of the qualities necessary to be the face of the WWE, it would ideally feature (in no particular order):

-Good looks
-Well-spoken
-Elite talent (athletic, charisma)
-Ambition
-Healthy ego
-Big financial draw
-Media savvy
-Capable of drawing emotional reactions from people without rival amongst his peers

John Cena, a generational icon for the last decade, spent his first three years in the WWE proving that he could be all of those things. It was no accident that he was given the keys to the kingdom in 2006 considering that he spent 2002 through 2005 working his tail off to put himself in that position. Right from his debut on *Smackdown*, you could tell that he had the intensity, the drive, and the looks. Throughout 2003, his groundbreaking hip hop, freestyle rapping character showed that he had charisma to spare. Though he morphed from a verbal envelope-pushing heel to a silly, poop joke-telling babyface in 2004, he proved capable of appealing to the entire viewing audience. As the last mid-card champion to elevate his title to consistent headlining status (as the United States Champion), he displayed a dominant personality. In 2005, when he became WWE Champion and released an album that made it to #15 on the Billboard charts, he showed that he could both carry the WWE flagship brand and attract mainstream attention, while also exhibiting a knack for well-representing the company in the media.

Yet, a lingering question about his in-ring abilities has unfairly remained over the years amidst a jaded sect of the diehard fanbase that does not appreciate him. Chants of "You Can't Wrestle" still occasionally fill arenas all over the world, despite the fact that he long since debunked the myth of his being anything less than critically admired by anyone that has studied the dynamics of the in-ring performance. He has more four-five star matches in the last ten years than just about anyone in wrestling history.

There was a time when challenging him to step up his game was warranted, but it was all the way back in 2003. Back then, he was awkward. He was the type of athlete that had to learn coordination in between the ropes. As a character, he was firing on all cylinders, becoming so good with his freestyles that the audience was starting to love him. Wrestling fans often get labeled as the morons of society, but as yours truly can vouch for, that is not at all the case. We appreciate greatness and know how to recognize it, especially when it comes in a form we have not seen before (Doc's note – yes, I know that I just stated that jaded fans think Cena sucks when he actually does not, which would suggest the moronic label fits, but I will come back to that). When Cena was ripping people in rhyme, it was cutting edge and the fans loved it. I can think of a handful of his raps right off the top of my head that I would put amongst the most innovative promos that I have ever seen. Naturally, the WWE wanted to make him a good guy and capitalize on his potential to be a financial windfall. He had to pass a test first.

At *No Mercy 2003*, Cena was set to face Kurt Angle, with whom he had shown natural chemistry in his debut match the summer before. Angle was about as automatic a 4-star match as there was in the business at the time, so Cena's performance was expected to be great. Essentially, I have come to view that match as Cena's audition for a future top spot. If he excelled, then "Word Life," it would be basic push-to-the-moon-anomics. If lackluster was all he could muster, then it might not work out for Cena. As the Cena era that raged for a decade suggests, he did not disappoint against Angle. In his first feature length PPV outing, Cena held up his end of a great match. It saw the birth of the dueling chant that became a fixture in his matches, though it was one of the rare times when those cheering in his favor were the vocal minority. Though he lost, he looked polished, turning the corner as a worker. The following month, he became a babyface and has been ever since.

Five WrestleMania main-events later, plus a record-tying eight WWE/World Championship matches at "The Show of Shows" and fifteen WWE/World Championships over a nine year span (including a record thirteen reigns as WWE Champ), and Cena undoubtedly belongs in the discussion for the greatest of all-time. Truth be told, I believe that he will end up owning that moniker before all is said and done if he can stay healthy (with one caveat to be discussed momentarily).

Yet, controversy will likely reign supreme over all his accolades. Such a vocal portion of the fan base – mostly teenage to adult males – made its feelings clear since *WrestleMania 22* as to how they feel about the WWE's "golden boy." They just flat out do not like him. The mixed reactions started in Washington, D.C. for his *Summerslam 2005* match with Chris Jericho, in which the audience was split almost right down the middle despite the face-heel dynamic being crystal clear. The dueling chants were fascinating, quickly spreading across the country. By *Mania 22* in Chicago eight months later, the crowd was decidedly anti-Cena, blasting him with profanity-laced chants. I was live in the All State Arena that night, in awe of what I was seeing and hearing during his match with Triple H. It has been the same ever since. Cena has his fans, but he has just as many haters. Oddly enough, the WWE has never seen fit to change him. Diehards have been crying for a heel turn for several years, but it has never happened (though it almost did in 2011 when Punk got hot).

I have often wondered how it may affect his legacy to have never been the dominant force in the company as the antagonist. If there is one reason why he may never surpass the others in the discussion for "The G.O.A.T," it may be that they all successfully played the #1 good *and* #1 bad guys. In my opinion, it will take him eventually making the turn for him to be considered #1. Cena was an excellent heel early in his career, so there is not much doubt that he can do it. Unfortunately, it is not entirely up to him. The WWE has built WrestleMania into the global phenomenon that they always hoped it could be with Cena as their go-to guy. He sells more merchandise than anyone else, he has amassed a huge social media following amidst the expansion of that outlet, and he is moving up the all-time list of WWE draws with each passing WrestleMania. Business-wise for many years, it was a risk to turn him. Approaching forty years old and with the NXT Generation taking over? I can no longer be sold on the risk being that great. He strikes me as one of the most self-aware and legacy-conscious stars, a true fan of the business, so I would think he would creatively relish the opportunity to play the villain.

One could argue that he is already the top heel in the WWE (in addition to the top babyface) based on his crowd reactions. In that regard, he has changed the game; a fact that might be the most enduring part of his legacy. Before him, every character was clearly defined as a babyface or a heel, sans for the occasional tweener that quickly wound up getting the "good" or "bad" label. When the WWE embraced that Cena was getting booed out of the building all around the world, but was still drawing sellout crowds, his shirts were still flying off the shelves, and the brand was expanding with the endorsement deals and major media spots that he was landing, they basically said "to hell with tradition." When The Rock got booed, they turned him heel. Conversely, when they started cheering him again, they turned him babyface. Austin started to backslide as a babyface, so they turned him heel to freshen up his character. When it did not work, they turned him back. The crowd turned on Cena in his first year on top and he is still playing the same "Hustle, Loyalty, and Respect," modern take on Hulkamania to this day. WWE does not seem to care and neither does Cena.

Subsequently, the face-heel dynamic has shifted more toward that of competitive sports, in which fans choose their loyalty to their favorites and stick with them despite the opinions of other fans whose loyalty lay elsewhere. The general labels still apply, but they no longer mean what they once did. Heels get massively cheered all the time; babyfaces get booed all the time. The traditionalist in me does not like it, but the progressive thinker that wants to see the WWE embrace the sports side of entertainment loves it. Love it or hate it, we can thank Cena for the marked change.

I applaud Cena for being able to endure, staying true to his core values despite all the negativity heaped upon him. Walking into a harsh environment as a heel and reacting naturally to it, feeding off of it to enhance his antagonism is one thing, but having to brush it off and perform at the highest level without letting the jeers get to him is a different ballgame. Teams play better with a home court or field advantage for a reason. Cena does not have one arena in the world where he can absorb and be fueled by fan adulation (not even his hometown). It is either he is getting ridiculously booed or he is getting a mixed reaction. He has had to go into some raucous environments to wrestle over the years. Chicago set the standard at *WrestleMania 22,* emerging as the new measuring stick for WWE crowds and beginning the trend of it being completely acceptable to outright despise Cena. Its people, a microcosm of the WWE Universe, boldly stated that they were not ready to go back to the days of the whitemeat babyface. Chicago edges out New York City and Toronto as the two most anti-Cena towns in the world.

John Cena is one of the more fascinating cases to study in pro wrestling history. How someone can be so good and get treated like they are so terrible is beyond me. At *WrestleMania 29* in New York, my buddies Tony and Jeff both said to me, "I don't get why everyone hates Cena; I like Cena." It is a good question that does not have a particularly easy answer. I have a theory that relates to comic book lore. Cena is wrestling's version of Superman, but we no longer live in a world where people want to see Superman. People have a hard time relating to a guy with only one weakness and who is as pure of heart as they come. In modern times, people prefer Bruce Wayne/Batman, a tortured soul who has no special powers, but gets by on resourcefulness. Christopher Nolan's *Dark Knight* trilogy produced two of the highest grossing superhero films of all-time, accordingly, while *Superman* films cannot keep pace.

Era specific hero preference aside, we - as a society – probably need an enduring symbol of purity and hope like Cena. It is good for the world. Austin's era was far too raunchy to be sustainable for the long haul. Wrestling needed to redefine itself once that era ended and Cena has done well to help reestablish WWE's core values. He has granted more wishes for the "Make-A-Wish Foundation" than anyone else and has helped the WWE pioneer anti-bullying campaigns and programs to encourage more kids to read, in addition to spearheading an effort to get the WWE involved with the Susan G. Komen Foundation for cancer research. He is a genuinely good guy and represents professional wrestling as well as anyone ever has.

As a long-time fan, it would be different for me if Cena had been having average matches (or even just merely good matches), but ever since a 2007 match with Bobby Lashley at *The Great American Bash* that had no business being as good as it was, we have had a top star that can literally have an excellent match with anyone. Seriously, in that match with Lashley, it appeared as if Cena had unleashed everything that he had learned from working with Jericho, Edge, Triple H, and

Shawn Michaels in the two prior years. He has never looked back. He may never be listed amongst the greatest workers of all-time, but I am not sure that he does not deserve to be. If it were not for his performance level over the years, I might have become disinterested a long time ago.

His failure to make that core, on-screen shift to the bad guy is the only thing that you can levy against his career, really; the lone knock against his case for being #1 all-time. Remember Tom Brady's 2007 season when he threw 50 touchdowns, passed for nearly 5,000 yards, and led the Patriots to 16-0 in the regular season? He had already won three Super Bowls, but he had never before had that statistically dominant season that earned him NFL MVP honors. The heel turn is Cena's equivalent. Everything else on his resume is awesome.

I wrote in the first edition that "the fact that he is in the main-event all the time hurts (him) because it puts him in a position where he always has to look strong to the broader audience, preventing him from dropping down into the mid-card to have stellar matches with emerging talents on television like the Guerreros, Angles, HBKs, Punks, and Brets could routinely do. He has to wait for everyone to reach his level." He has evolved, in that respect, since I wrote those words in 2013. He had consecutive TV Matches of the Year with Cesaro and his US Championship Open Challenge in 2015 was an avenue to extremely competitive matches on TV that gave his opponents high profile spotlights in which to advance their careers.

I appreciate what Cena brings to the table; make no mistake about that. He is a very engaging talker, historically. He excels wrestling a variety of different athletes with various styles. I am particularly fond of his work against Randy Orton, Edge, CM Punk, Shawn Michaels, and The Rock. Cena and Orton have had many memorable battles, most notably the *Summerslam '07* main-event and a series in the summer and fall of '09 that included a phenomenal "Anything Goes" Ironman match at *Bragging Rights*. Both he and Edge became main-event players around the same time, elevating each other throughout 2006 while trading the WWE title from January to September in a personal war that spanned the main-events of three PPVs, including *Summerslam* and their classic TLC match at *Unforgiven*. His two WrestleMania main-events with The Rock confirmed Cena's ascension to one of the top four draws in wrestling history. No one can ever take away his involvement in the biggest WrestleMania buyrate of all-time (especially now that the PPV model is gone). Rock pushed him creatively in the storyline of Cena's career, to date. As much as Rock pushed Cena to new heights creatively and financially, Punk and HBK pushed him just as much in the ring. There have never been two wrestlers that pushed Cena quite so much to excel as a performer.

The list of classic Cena matches, in addition to those already mentioned from TV or PPV, also includes top notch bouts with Umaga, Batista, Rey Mysterio, Brock Lesnar, Daniel Bryan, Bray Wyatt, Rusev, Kevin Owens, and Seth Rollins.

It is almost scary to think that he has accomplished so much, yet could conceivably be around for another decade. I would rather see him turn wrestling into a young man's game like most competitive sports. The peak is the late twenties to the early thirties, the decline starts in the mid-thirties, and retirement hits by no later than the early forties. The profession would be better off that way, allowing for the most gifted athletes to rise to the top early on like he did while keeping somewhat of a cycle going. While I may be appreciative of what he has done and will continue to be until his last night in the ring, I do hope that his retirement is sooner rather than later.

Whenever he does retire, he will have done so as the man that lifted a floundering WWE brand onto his back and carried it to a really good place. I do not believe that the WWE ever intended for its television shows to be as risqué as they became in the late 1990s and early 2000s, but were rather forced into going that route because of WCW's ratings. Cena brought the WWE back to its roots. Though he gets criticized for the decline in television ratings, I think that most analysts tend to see the Nielsens through 90s goggles. Undoubtedly, the WWE would rather pull in domestic 5-7s rather than 2-3s, but since *Raw* is broadcast in over 150 countries and in 30 languages, the product has never been more internationally visible. I, myself, have readers for my column from India, Dubai, Ecuador, Australia….all over the world. It is pretty cool. The WWE business is doing just fine.

One very important thing that Cena has done for the business is help turn WrestleMania into all that Vince McMahon always dreamed it would be. Every year, it is a huge financial boon to both the WWE and the host city, bringing in tens of millions of dollars in event related revenue to the local economy. They set attendance records in football stadiums across the country and they have turned the week of Mania into a fan festival. It is no longer just the Super Bowl of professional wrestling, but it is a pop culture event on par with the actual Super Bowl. That happened on Cena's watch. The trend began in 2007 when *WrestleMania 23* was held in Detroit's Fold Field. Cena vs. Michaels was the main-event. They drew 80,000 people and set the PPV buy record with an assist from Donald Trump. With Cena as the #1 star, five WrestleManias drew over one million buys. Cena vs. Rock was this generation's Hogan vs. Andre, fiscally.

Ranking in the Top 5 of every statistical category, John Cena is unquestionably one of the greatest wrestlers ever. How he continues to keep himself motivated, along with his health, will define the next several years of his career. Perhaps he is destined to take over Undertaker's role as the guy that all the emerging stars want to topple at WrestleMania. Maybe he finally turns heel and pens the "Hogan in WCW" chapter of his career. One thing that is for certain is that the only goal left for Cena is becoming the #1 star of the WrestleMania Era.

#2: Triple H

The coronation ceremony for the 1997 King of the Ring was the official start to the all-time great career of the WWE's successor to Vince McMahon, then known as Hunter Hearst Helmsley and forever to be known as Triple H. Though he started with WWE in 1995, his first two years were best known for the "Curtain Call," the incident in which he, Shawn Michaels, Kevin Nash, and Scott Hall unsuspended the Madison Square Garden faithful's disbelief that wrestling was full of people that legitimately disliked one another and hugged in the middle of the ring. The "Kliq's" show of solidarity as Hall and Nash were leaving the company came at a price for young Hunter, as his push up the proverbial ladder was postponed.

It was Mick Foley who put him over in the '97 King of the Ring Finals and it was the ensuing feud with Foley that put him on the map. No one would have cared that HBK paired up with Triple H to form Degeneration X that autumn if it had not been for Hunter's matches with Foley. Both the Cage match at *Summerslam '97* and the Falls Count Anywhere match from *Raw* in September were quite memorable, making Hunter's alignment with Michaels a dangerous combination.

Through their real life friendship, Trips and HBK set out to do racier, edgier interviews that took their backstage antics onto live TV. They were actually very funny, especially to the WWE's new target market of young adults. As the WWE shifted its focus from little kids to pre-teens and teenagers, Degeneration X (and Triple H's status) took off. Hunter got comfortable with a microphone in hand and started working more important matches that upped his confidence as a performer. Before long, it was noticeable that it would be "when" – not "if" – Trips would become a top star. When Michaels was forced to retire, there were some people who thought that DX would end, but it was on Triple H's merits earned while under HBK's wing that it was a no-brainer for the WWE to hand him the reigns and let him run further with it.

Triple H is not given nearly enough credit for the Attitude Era's success. DX was the brainchild of both HBK *AND* Hunter. When The New Age Outlaws and X-Pac came aboard the DX train, it was Trips that conducted it. As the sarcastic, quick-witted leader of DX, he was an excellent rebellious-type hero for the expanding WWE fanbase. The Rock and Steve Austin get the majority of the accolades when people talk of that era, but Trips was guiding arguably the most popular faction in wrestling history. There was no denying that Stone Cold exploded in 1998, but victory was achieved in the Monday Night War through several emerging top talents in the WWE. WCW had nothing new and interesting but Goldberg, while the WWE product featured the combination of Austin hitting it big *and* The Rock *and* DX, plus Foley, Taker, Kane, and others. Triple H was a huge part of that success.

1998 saw Hunter rise in parallel with The Rock, who was the leader of The Nation of Domination. Their rising of the ranks to the heads of their respective factions even took place on the same night – the *Raw* after *WrestleMania XIV*. While Austin was busy with others, Trips and Rocky were each considered trendsetters in the sport and used the summer to solidify themselves as unquestionable future rivals for Stone Cold. It was basically a race to see who would get there first, culminating in the best match, to that point, in either of their careers at *Summerslam*. In a Ladder match for Rock's Intercontinental Championship, they stole the show and had one of the most underrated matches in the gimmick's long and storied history. It was a preview of one of the great main-event rivalries of the era. They each put their bodies at risk, they each took uncharacteristic chances, and they both showed great creativity in a match that put them neck-in-neck for the next shot at the WWE Championship.

Triple H was about nine months behind The Great One on reaching the main-event, but he kept the DX gig going full steam ahead, never too far behind Rock and Austin. At *WrestleMania XV*, DX, having run its course, ended as we had known it. Triple H went into the show as their leader, but was curiously booked in a match well below the standards that he had presumably earned with the previous year that he had. By the end of the night, he was on the precipice of breaking out as the next big star. An elaborate, all night story was told to reunite Chyna, who had turned on DX earlier in the year, with the rest of the group. The regrouped, refocused DX did an interview together backstage, but at the climax of X-Pac's headlining match with Shane McMahon, Triple H snuck into the ring and gave his stablemate the Pedigree, abandoning DX and joining the hated Corporation. It was a transition for Trips into a top heel – a role he would play very well for seven years.

For Hunter, DX had been a launching pad. He grew into a main-eventer through co-inventing the DX concept and spearheading it during its most successful run. In a way, that has actually become a somewhat forgotten time in his career for many of the fans that kept watching from the year 2000 on. He was *so* good as "The Game" and so different that it overshadows what he accomplished as DX's leader.

The McMahon-Helmsley faction – the hybrid of the two heel groups that had been the primary antagonists for the two previous WrestleMania main-events - was an excellent continuation of The Corporation, combining the firmly established evil qualities of wrestling's First Family with the betrayal felt by the fans when Trips joined and married, in storyline, Stephanie McMahon. Trips and Steph had great on-screen chemistry that wound up translating to life off camera, putting wrestling's future in the hands of the real world's Helmsley (Levesque)-McMahon family.

As the year 2000 approached, Triple H was firmly established as the lead heel in the WWE. He had one of the best years in history, beginning with matches regarded as two of the best of the decade with Cactus Jack that retired Mick Foley and his alter egos and pulled Trips neck and neck with The Rock in the race for the #1 spot in the company while Austin was recuperating from neck surgery. *The Royal Rumble* and *No Way Out* come and go every January and February and never cease to bring back memories of the epic HHH-Foley bouts. The momentum earned from his two defeats of Foley prompted the WWE to keep the WWE Championship on him through the main-event of *WrestleMania 2000*, the first and only time that a heel had retained a title in the last match of the biggest show of the year.

A month later at *Backlash*, Triple H defended the strap against Rock in another defining match in their rivalry. It had been less than two years since their Ladder match and there they sat at the top of the mountain, figuratively toasting to each other's success in the form of running high knees and spit-infused punches. That was the height of the McMahon-Helmsley regime, as all the prominent McMahon characters (Vince, Steph, and Shane) were on Triple H's side, involved in trying to keep the title around his waist. The Rock had the odds ridiculously stacked against him and there was no conceivable way that he should have won the title. Stone Cold showed up, though, wielding a steel chair and blasting every McMahon or Helmsley in sight, helping Rock win the title. Before Austin went under the knife, he had started a heated storyline with Trips over the title. It would eventually be revealed in the fall that The Game was behind the on-screen hit-and-run that had put The Rattlesnake on the shelf, but as of the spring it was purely speculative.

On the business side, it could be argued that The Game was as big a star in 2000 as Rock. He was the focal point of the show, be it in his stories with Foley, Rock, Chris Jericho, or the love triangle with Stephanie and Kurt Angle. The Rock unquestionably got more attention from the mainstream and was the face of the company, but Trips was debatably carrying the product.

In the ring, Triple H was tearing it up. With a variety of different matches against several stylistically unique wrestlers, he earned critical acclaim the likes of which we had not seen since HBK in 1996. His Street Fight with Foley at *The Rumble* was the top singles match of the year, with their Hell in a Cell match a month later not far behind. The Triple H vs. Rock Ironman match at May's *Judgment Day* was a great piece of work that built believably and progressed logically, featured eleven falls, and showed impressive stamina from each. At *Fully Loaded* in July, he tore the house down with Chris Jericho in a Last Man Standing match. Against Kurt Angle and Chris Benoit at consecutive PPVs in September and October, he displayed his sound technical ability against two of the best grapplers of all-time. Throw in a knockdown, drag out brawl with a returning Austin at *Survivor Series* and his leading role in the 6-man Hell in a Cell match from *Armageddon* and you have got a highly regarded period that has and will continue to stand the test of time. Triple H 2000 was one of the most impressive single years ever produced by a wrestler.

Ending the year locked in a feud with Austin, Triple H found himself in the unenviable position, specific to the Attitude Era, of needing a critically acclaimed series of matches with Stone Cold to avoid the rest of his brilliant year being rendered less significant. His feuds with Rock and Foley were undeniable in their historical implications, but he had to successfully combat Austin in a multi-chapter story for his Attitude Era career to be complete. All the other greats of that time (Rock, Foley, Taker) had gone toe-to-toe with Austin on numerous occasions. A storyline with The Rattlesnake that reached a satisfying conclusion was necessary, for he could not argue being the top heel of the era without facing its unquestionable top babyface.

Trips and Austin had three PPV singles matches that spanned a seventeen month period from *No Mercy* in October '99 to *Survivor Series 2000* to February 2001's *No Way Out*, the last of which was the most important. Sometimes it just takes a few tries before everything falls into place. The first two matches were really good, but they did not live up to lofty expectations. The Three Stages of Hell match to conclude their saga was where everything came together. They produced one of the finest matches of that era, renowned by some as one of the greatest of any era. In a move that spoke volumes about his status, Triple H won the match. It was just six weeks before the most financially successful WrestleMania of the most financially successful era in wrestling history and Triple H got the victory in the payoff match against the man that ultimately won the main-event for the WWE title. His record against Austin in their three match PPV series was two wins, *no losses*, and one no contest. Though Trips would go on to team with Austin just a few months later, then tear his quadriceps for the first time and take a year off, what he took away from the Austin saga was an unquestionable spot at wrestling's roundtable of the biggest stars. It also made him the unquestionable choice to take over as the #1 guy when Austin and Rock left wrestling in the years that soon followed.

The transition to Triple H as the face of the WWE was odd. The McMahons had always favored a hero to be their long-reigning champion and most recognizable force. Yet, they began the "Triple H era" by having him commit the ultimate act of betrayal. After returning from the quad injury to glorious fanfare at MSG in January '02, winning the Royal Rumble match, and closing out *WrestleMania X-8* as Undisputed WWE Champion, they had him go against the incredibly loud reactions he was getting as a babyface and turned him heel. It seemed that he and his old pal, HBK, were going to reform DX. Just as

Trips was doing his signature shtick, doing his best Michael Buffer impression and proudly exclaiming, "Let's get ready to Suck It," he turned and kicked HBK in the gut, following with a Pedigree.

 It was a bold move. The WWE was hitching their wagon to a modern day Ric Flair and traveling their first leg of the new journey with a HHH vs. HBK feud that produced some of the finest matches of modern times. The *Summerslam* match instigated by the bogus DX reunion was, in my opinion, the best match in the history of the Summer Classic. Their in-ring chemistry should have been predictable given how natural they were at playing off of one another as on-screen friends. They went onto several high profile matches from 2002-2004, including the original Elimination Chamber, a Three Stages of Hell match, a Last Man Standing match, and Hell in a Cell. While my favorite of theirs remained the Non-Sanctioned "Fight" from *Summerslam*, I am also quite partial to their match from the final *Raw* of 2003, which I rank as the top bout in the history of that program. Their Hell in a Cell match, upon first viewing, was an incredible story told, in its own right. Someone once asked me if there was *ever* a match that I *never* wanted to end. HHH vs. HBK from *Badd Blood '04* was my answer. Inside the Cell, they recreated bits and pieces of all their previous matches. Lasting 47-minutes, the bout kept adding layer after layer. I had actually hoped for Trips vs. HBK to be the last match of Shawn's career. I was quietly rooting for it to take place at *WrestleMania XXVI* in 2010, but the honor was, instead, given to Undertaker.

 From 2002 until 2005, Triple H was "The Man." It was during the height of "his" era that I started following LOP and other websites dedicated to pro wrestling news. There has been a strange, disproportionate loathing for Triple H by the vocal minority over the years. Though his time at the top solidified his case for being arguably the greatest all-around wrestler in history, his status subjected him to the variety of criticism that do the year in, year out sports franchises that stay at the top. Backstage political maneuvering is to wrestling what money is to baseball. The New York Yankees outspend the other franchises and draw the ire of all other baseball fans, accordingly. Triple H, so it was frequently rumored, used his clout with the McMahons to keep himself in all the main-events and the vocal minority hated him for it. In reality, there is a lot more to the Yankees than their payroll when they are consistently in World Series contention and there is a lot more to Triple H being in seven consecutive World Championship matches at WrestleMania than corporate politics.

We have seen it recent years with John Cena, and we have seen it in the past with Hulk Hogan, that if there is one guy who always finds himself in the cushiest spot, the people are going to ravenously turn on him. Triple H was one of those guys and the animosity has not gone away. The Internet Wrestling Community, in particular, will nitpick Trips to death in online forums from Dubai to Buenos Aires to Los Angeles. It started in 2002 when he was handed the WCW Championship belt, rechristened as the World Heavyweight title that was, at the time, exclusive to *Raw*. From that moment forward, he was labeled as a political powerhouse who hogged the spotlight and did not put anyone over. Never mind the fact that he was the last remaining star from the Attitude Era responsible for carrying the flagship program of the WWE as the leader in a transition phase of wrestling history. He could do nothing right.

I remember the laundry list of criticisms like they were spoken yesterday. "He was handed the title so that he could dodge putting over Brock Lesnar. He would not lose to anyone but his friend, Shawn Michaels. He would not put over Booker T. He begrudgingly did the honors for Goldberg, but then he wormed his way back to the belt. He made sure all the good talent ended up on *Raw* and screwed over *Smackdown*. He married Stephanie McMahon so he could stay in the main-event forever. He buried Randy Orton. He tried to put himself over

John Cena. He would not put over Jeff Hardy. He did not believe in helping new talent." On and on it went. Of course, very little of it was true, but perception is reality.

In recent years, I have often wondered if Hunter was purposefully feeding the rumors that made him so hated on the net. That was a time when the internet faithful were becoming more vocal and influential with live audiences. They could not stand him, but they were emotionally invested in seeing him lose because of it. If he ever writes a book and confesses to being behind all the unconfirmed dirtsheet gossip about himself, I will give him a giant pat on the back. I think the internet had a lot to do with the success of *WrestleMania XX* in New York City. On a night where Trips dropped the title to Chris Benoit, he not only put the notion to rest that he would not put anyone over, but did so for somewhat of a vocal minority hero. That was an internet-friendly crowd if there ever was one. The triple threat also involving HBK was one of the best matches of all-time, to that point, and finally gave Trips a critically acclaimed main-event at Mania to hang his hat on.

Evolution was a major factor in Triple H's success as the post-Attitude Era torchbearer. During their run at the top, they were an excellent faction formidable throughout history when compared to other groups. The Horsemen, The New World Order, and Degeneration X were certainly ahead of them, but they are right at the top of the second tier. The intent of the group had been to keep Trips looking strong at the top of the card while simultaneously creating future top stars in the process in Batista and Randy Orton. All four members rank inside the Top 17 of the WrestleMania Era, so it is hard to argue with its success. The Game racked up a third of his 14 total World Championships during that time. Orton and Batista became icons in their own right, each top rivals in Hunter's career.

Never did Hunter remind me of The Nature Boy more than he did then while feuding with Batista. Naitch had been known for carrying lesser talent and teaching them while working their matches. Before the storyline with Trips, Batista was a very average talent. By the time that their Hell in a Cell match at *Vengeance '05* was complete, Bats was a completely different wrestler. Trips deserves a ton of credit for what Batista accomplished during the first six months of 2005. It was Hunter's finest work as the top character in the business, capped off with one of his best in-ring performances. Hell in a Cell had started to become *his* gimmick, taking it from (or at the very least sharing it with) Undertaker. He thrived in an environment where he could be as dastardly as possible. I re-watched that match in preparation to write this chapter and was struck by his durability (outside of his two quadriceps tears) considering what he put his body through in two of the most physically taxing periods in wrestling history. He bled buckets during his time in the main-event. In almost every major match, he would do a hell of a blade job. Few were better at it. He wore the proverbial crimson mask with honor in putting Batista over decisively for a third time in an awesome battle to end their war. When that match was over, the Triple H era ended with it. The transition away from Attitude was complete.

After Evolution, Trips reinvented himself a bit. He became a hybrid of all of the different characters that he had played since 1998. He could be ruthless, as he showed when he and Flair ended their multi-year on-screen partnership. He could be arrogant and cocky, as he was while putting over John Cena at *WrestleMania 22* in one of the most underappreciated matches of all-time. He could be funny, as he was when he and HBK brought back DX in 2006. He got to pick and choose which part of his persona he needed to be, while slowly transitioning from the consistent World title threat that dominated the 2000s to part-time headliner and full-time WWE Executive being groomed to aid his wife in keeping the business as we know it alive and well once Vince McMahon steps down in the coming years.

From *Summerslam 2013* to the present, Trips has been as good as ever as a personality, taking the best of his antagonistic traits and combining them with the fantastic character of his oh-so-easy to dislike spouse for a modern take on the evil corporate empire, The Authority. Words cannot do justice how cerebrally they have gone about earning the jeers of the audience. The internet fanbase continues to grow and WWE's focus will undoubtedly shift to greater placate its desires. WWE Network needs the revenue generated by its most ardent supporters, many of whom access the growing wrestling media online to supplement their social media cravings. It is just a sign of the times. Hunter and Steph will be invaluable assets given how both are so adept at riling up the diehard fans.

When I look at HHH's overall legacy, I think about WrestleMania. He holds several distinctions at wrestling's Super Bowl. He currently ranks behind only Hulk Hogan with seven main-events. He is #1 on the list of superstars with the most World Championship matches (nine). Of all the stars that sit at wrestling's "best of all-time" roundtable, he is the only one to have main-evented a WrestleMania in his own era and three others (the Attitude, Cena, and Reality eras). Combine those Mania stats with his World titles, list of classic matches, etc., and it should come as no surprise that he wound up #2.

What he lacked, up until the latter part of his career, was the undeniable, generally thought to be 5-star caliber match at WrestleMania. An almost unanimously agreed upon four-five star match is like throwing a touchdown with seconds left to play in the Super Bowl. It is what separates Tom Brady from Peyton Manning. Winning the big game or, in wrestling's case, being in the biggest match, is not enough to separate yourself from the pack. You have to do it in grand fashion.

Triple H had numerous matches that were well-regarded at Mania – the brawl with Undertaker at *X-Seven* and the match with Cena in Chicago are good examples. Yet, nobody would ever mistake them as contenders for the best ever. The triple threat at *XX* was excellent, but most of its credit was given to the other two combatants (plus history is trying to forget it because of Benoit). Triple H *needed*, in the twilight of his career, to knock one out of the park. I would have been satisfied with his rematch with Undertaker at *WrestleMania XXVII* in Atlanta, but what they did a year later in their third Mania match was a "greatest match of all-time" contender that solidified his legacy and forced the remainder of his critics to shut their pie holes. In Miami, on the same night that titans of two eras collided in one history's most epic encounters, Triple H and Undertaker had the match that earned "best of the year" honors. He earned another "Match of the Year" award, from me, with his work at *WrestleMania XXX* against Daniel Bryan.

    He and I will both have grandkids by the time that he passes the torch to whomever ends up succeeding him and Stephanie McMahon as the heads of the WWE. When he is done, I hope that he writes a book. He is a wrestling genius and I would like to take a peek inside his mind for a few hundred pages.

#1: The Rock

In the end: Dwayne "The Rock" Johnson is the #1 wrestler of the WrestleMania Era. The numbers reflect it and I support it.

His journey to the status of "all-time greatest" has been unique to all his competing peers. He has and always will be no less than the most polarizing WWE Superstar to ever step foot in a ring. Unlike Steve Austin and Ric Flair, he is not universally loved. Whatever the reason, critics have flocked to The Rock since the day he debuted at the 1996 *Survivor Series*. Upon his debut, he was too vanilla of a hero in a time when wrestling's definition of heroism was changing. He promptly channeled the arrogance of his 1991 National Championship-winning University of Miami football team and became one of the best heels of all-time. Then, the people thought he was so great that they, in turn, cheered him into one of the most popular babyfaces of all-time, with the decibel level of the millions (…and millions) of "Rock's fans" chanting his name knowing few rivals. Later, the criticism turned toward his leaving the WWE for Hollywood from 2004 to 2011. He came back, though, to help the industry that made him a star produce three consecutive box office-smashing WrestleManias. Then, the fans decided that he was taking a top spot from someone who wrestled all year long. It has always been something. Yet, beyond a shadow of a doubt, the people have always cared. Nobody has ever generated emotions from the audience quite like The Rock.

It goes without saying that my choice for the top spot in the hierarchy will draw a response. While you sit there, either nodding in approval or wide-eyed in disbelief, you have an opinion that you want to get off your chest. The Rock evokes a reaction. Whether or not it makes you want to pull out the DVD and reminisce in the days of singing along with The Rock or it makes you so hot under the collar that you audibly begin your own, personal chant of "Die, Rocky, Die," indulge me and look at the proof that he really is "The Great One."

Business Factor

Hulk Hogan and Steve Austin were always the most hotly debated in the argument for top money-maker in wrestling history until recently. Thanks to his 2011-2013 return to the WWE, The Rock has forcibly inserted himself into that conversation on the heels of three consecutive WrestleManias drawing over one million buys, including the current record 1.3 million for *WrestleMania XXVIII*. Tackling the challenge of launching and sustaining a successful Hollywood acting career allowed Rock to become the type of celebrity that the WWE seeks to further promote their biggest event of the year. Subsequently, he has brought more mainstream attention to the product than Hogan or Austin ever did. Even as merely a guest at *WrestleMania XXVII*, his presence helped garner the fourth biggest PPV figure ever. Despite the loss of numerous top stars and during a period where WWE was elevating a lot of new top tier players, The Rock helped *WrestleMania XXVII* score numbers that were up 30% domestically and 15% internationally from the previous year.

Before 2011, Rock was widely regarded as the #3 draw of the WrestleMania Era, but –even then – the difference between his place and the top two was closer than people realize. Austin clearly overshadowed Rock's impact on the industry during the Attitude Era, but when given the chance to shine on his own for a solid year while Stone Cold was out recovering from neck surgery in 2000, The Rock did not just merely keep business steady - he expanded the WWE's mainstream profile. His rivalry with Triple H actually increased TV ratings to a consistent level above 6.0 and often into the 7.0 (or above) range. When Rock teamed with Mick Foley to form "The Rock and Sock Connection," the segment forever known as "This is Your Life, Rock" was the highest rated *Raw* segment ever (8.4). Rock and Austin shared in the responsibility of launching the WWE's second weekly program, but it was telling that the WWE decided to name it after one of Rock's catchphrases: *Smackdown* (which is now a word in the English dictionary).

2000 was Rock's year, as the product was largely built around him similar to how 1998 and 1999 were built around Austin. *WrestleMania 2000* earned the highest number of PPV buys ever to that point. He was also the host of "Saturday Night Live" and did so well that he began receiving offers from Hollywood to begin an acting career. He had a New York Times #1 bestselling book released. Television media avenues were stretching to record numbers, opening the door for someone as charismatic and people-friendly as Rock to spread the WWE's visibility to new levels that were not possible for Hogan and unattainable for Austin. Those same opportunities ultimately took Rock away from wrestling and into movies, but they also allowed him to build his name to the most recognizable in the business's history, permitting him to come back years later and bring unprecedented attention to the WWE product.

<u>Wrestler Score</u>

The Rock ranked 1st in this category.

On the microphone, he was the evolutionary step up from Ric Flair. He was a superstar that drew you in with the creativity of his words; his personality like a magnet for praise. The Rock is the single most entertaining character in sports entertainment lore. It is really not even close. He can do it all on the stick. He can get right up in a guy's face and bring all the intensity required to sell a PPV main-event. He is the master of hamming it up, getting the live audience involved like no one else can. His work with Mick Foley and Chris Jericho, two men who pushed Rock to the limit as much verbally as they did athletically, was legitimately funny in a business where there is a lot of scripted comedy, but very little of it is legitimately comedic.

In terms of his appearance, The Rock redefined how the WWE wanted a top talent to look and act. By '99, Rock had sculpted himself into what was often described as "like a Greek God." He always had a good look, with his 6'5" frame, 250 plus pounds, Samoan mixed with African American features, and million dollar smile, but when he hit the gym, reduced his body fat, and put the effort into his physical health, he gave the WWE their new description for the physique of a blue chip prospect. His calves were so big that they seemingly had to cut out the upper back half of the traditional wrestling boot to get people's eyes on his legs. Also, in stark contrast to Austin and Triple H during the Attitude Era, he was a sharply dressed man. He had an affinity for the immaculate grooming made famous by Flair.

In the ring, he had an unusual style and, once he found his groove, it translated to supremely underrated work as a performer. From his Ladder match with Triple H at *Summerslam '98* onward, there was never a combination like his size, strength, speed, athleticism, bumping, charisma/showmanship, and intensity. He threw one of the best punches in wrestling. He had an appreciation for the history of the wrestling match, frequently breaking out the old school sleeper hold sell where his arm nearly dropped thrice and paying tribute to Bret Hart by using the Sharpshooter.

Main-Event/Headliner Factor

Unquestionably, the fact that his main-event career spanned just 2.5 consecutive years, followed by small bursts of headlining activity since 2001, hurts him in this category. It is the only factor where other wrestlers are definitively ahead of him. When he has been around, he has been on top, but it is a cumulative statistic. Nevertheless, he has main-evented five WrestleManias, including all three during the most competitive stretch in the history of the WWE from 1999-2001 (and, honestly, everyone knows that 2002's Rock-Hogan match was the real main-event of *Mania X-8*, even the participants in the match that actually went on last, Trips and Jericho).

The race for the #1 spot in the WWE was a compelling storyline during the Attitude Era. Other periods have seen two guys compete for it, usually with a clear cut alpha rendering the beta a distant second. The Attitude Era had Trips playing the role that Macho Man occupied in the 80s. Rock and Austin were both legitimate alphas. Consider that when Austin went down in late '99, the WWE had just become a publicly traded company on the New York Stock Exchange. The Rock assumed the throne that, earlier in the year, Austin had indisputably stamped as his at *WrestleMania XV* when he defeated Rock. After Rock expanded the WWE's profile in Austin's absence, Stone Cold returned to a show in late 2000 that was no longer his. The Rock had snatched the brass ring and did not seem at all willing to let go, even though Austin would naturally be given the opportunity to take it back. It created for a dynamic that we have never seen before or since, with two guys legitimately being able to lay claim to being "The Man."

The Rock entered *WrestleMania X-Seven* as the WWE Champion, with Austin winning the Rumble match. It was the first time that the WWE had done a stadium show since 1992, with Houston's Astrodome playing host to a match for the ages pitting two stars against each other seeking validation for one being the go-to guy in the WWE at the other's expense. Rock winning meant that he had surpassed Austin and that there would no longer be any disputing his status as the #1 guy in the industry. Austin winning meant that Rock would always be remembered, to a degree, as the #2. Austin losing would have meant that his time was essentially over in the WWE's mind and that he might always look back on his neck injury with regrets. Rock losing meant that his accomplishments might always be overshadowed. The pre-match video production featuring Limp

Bizkit's "My Way" and an awesome sit down interview with Rock and Austin mediated by Jim Ross perfectly highlighted the stakes. "I will give you every drop of sweat, every drop of blood, every ounce of everything I have; you are going to get the absolute best of The Rock at WrestleMania," said Rock. "I need to beat you Rock; I need it more than you can ever imagine," countered Stone Cold.

All the while, Trips was pushing hard to take their spots. If we look just at that era (1998-2001) as a sample size, Rock and Austin tied for most Mania main-events at three while Trips racked up one, they all tied for Summerslam main-events with a pair apiece, and Austin beat them both with two Royal Rumble wins to Rock's one and Hunter's zero. Ultimately, Triple H outclassed both of them in the headliner category due to his longevity, but he main-evented just six of seventeen WrestleManias, while Rock main-evented five of nine and still has room to grow as a forty-one year old as of publishing time.

Championship Factor

"The People's Champion" initially made his name as the self-proclaimed "best damn Intercontinental Champion that there ever was" with an almost nine month second reign with the title. As one half of "The Rock and Sock Connection" with Foley, he also amassed three short runs with the Tag Team titles to go along with even shorter fourth and fifth reigns in short-lived duos with Undertaker and Jericho, respectively. Where he shined was his ten reigns as World Champion, which included becoming, at the time, the youngest WWE Champion in history and becoming just the second wrestler ever to capture the World Championship in three different decades (Hulk Hogan was the other).

Like many of the champions from his era, he never did have a WWE title reign that lasted longer than four months. The Attitude Era popularized moving the title frequently, which deemphasized the importance of actually having the physical belt to be the face of the franchise. We now see it with John Cena, who has been "The Man" for years but has not always carried the strap to signify it.

The Rock was always in the championship mix, but since there was so much talent on the roster, it put the WWE in a position where they could use the title to elevate a new main-event player to the next level. Rock was very smart in the business sense, never allowing ego to stand in the way of what was best for the overall product. Of all his rivals in the Attitude Era, he was the one that put over more new stars for the WWE title than anyone else. He was responsible for the rises of both Kurt Angle and Chris Jericho, dropping the belt to them at consecutive *No Mercy* PPVs in 2000 and 2001. He was also the most instrumental superstar in establishing Brock Lesnar. To end his seventh WWE title reign, Rock laid down for Brock at 2002's *Summerslam*. By that point, it became apparent that Rock was never going to be a full-timer again. He did well in his first starring role in the movies and action stardom was in his near future. He would be leaving wrestling behind, but just as he was creating a void, Lesnar came into the WWE and took it by storm. While Austin "took his ball and went home" over being asked to put over Lesnar and Triple H was rumored to have had him sequestered to *Smackdown* to avoid his path, Rock became his good friend and the two had a strong drawing Summerslam main-event.

When he came back to the WWE recently and won the title again, he did it so that he could drop it to Cena at *WrestleMania NY/NJ*. By putting over Cena clean in the middle of the ring for the WWE Championship, Rock gave back to the business that made him and officially passed the torch from one generational icon to another. For all those that like to claim that Rock in some way did the business a disservice by leaving it for the entertainment industry, they ought to take a close look at how many guys he put over. Four former champions in the Top 15 of the WrestleMania Era owe many thanks to The Rock.

<u>Performance Factor</u>

The Rock is in a rare class of wrestlers that got to the top of the mountain and did not settle for just going through the motions in the ring. His appreciation and love for working wrestling matches translated to absolutely classic confrontations, especially on the biggest stages. He could work with anyone of any style. Young or old, big or small, fast or slow; it did not matter. When he was in his "I'm here to prove that I'm the best that the industry has ever, ever seen" mode, he did amazing things on that canvas.

He has three bouts that rank in my top ten in WrestleMania history. Rock-Austin II at *X-Seven* was the best match of the Attitude Era, period. No other match from that time had the intensity or the atmosphere. Investing in their characters was so easy. It was suspension of disbelief at its finest, for you were not looking at the two of them as men with a real life beef, but as polar opposite characters played beautifully on television that locked you into their dramatic story. They battered each other to bloody messes and had one of the greatest and most dramatic matches of all-time. It was a leap forward for Rock, performance-wise. He had been in some great matches by then, but nothing quite like that. It was the bout that took him to the elite level in the ring. April 1, 2001 started his journey to "Greatest of the WrestleMania Era." It was the night where he seemed to realize that WrestleMania was the only stage where he could forge the legacy that he wanted.

The following year, his journey continued with the spectacle that rewrote the definition of a "dream" match. A dream match is a bout that you literally thought would never happen. It is the rarest thing in wrestling when one of them actually becomes reality. In the WrestleMania Era, I think we have seen only three legitimate dream matches. The first was Hulk Hogan vs. Ric Flair. The second was at *WrestleMania X-8* when The Rock faced Hulk Hogan. After Hogan left the WWE in 1993 and became the leading man on WCW *Nitro*, helping the rival company to unprecedented success, I think we all assumed that we had seen his last WrestleMania. Yet, there he was in a WWE ring again in February 2002. It honestly did not register, right away, what that could potentially mean. It was not until The Rock interrupted Hogan's promo in Chicago that it sunk in. "You talk about headlining, main-eventing, WrestleMania after WrestleMania after WrestleMania; well The Rock says, 'How bout headlining one more WrestleMania with The Rock!?'" It was the most electrifying segment in "The Most Electrifying Man in Sports Entertainment's" career.

A decade later, Rock gave us the third dream match. Over three WrestleManias, he and the modern face of wrestling, John Cena, told an incredible story. The people were his reason for coming back, but Cena was who The Rock targeted on behalf of the people when he returned to host *Mania 27*. The night after costing Cena the title in Atlanta, he laid down the challenge for *Mania 28* in Miami: Rock vs. Cena. There have never been two more polarizing top superstars in wrestling and the announcement for their match was an incredible cliffhanger that had me awash with anticipation for the entire year that followed.

With all due respect to everyone else mentioned or detailed in this book, it was during the fall of 2011 that I determined Rock had everyone else beat if he could deliver at *Mania XXVIII*. If he could encompass an engaging storyline, a great match, and a smash hit at the box office, then I would be proud to rank him #1 if the numbers added up. Sure enough, he delivered in spades. The Rock had to live up to enormous hype from the superstars to the WWE brass to himself and his family to the media to the fans. He had to knock one out of the park. I wrote in my column that anything less than a match in contention for the top 5 in WrestleMania's history would be a disappointment; not that it would be fair, but that it was simply the nature of the yearlong build. The match was everything that it was destined to be. In defeating Cena, he also became the one wrestler in history to have defeated, at WrestleMania no less, the three other top moneymakers in the modern era (Hogan, Austin, and Cena). It was one of my all-time favorite matches. I will watch it with my kids one day and talk about it like many would a Super Bowl won by their favorite team.

The Rock is the Greatest

By returning to the WWE, The Rock erased all the remaining questions about his legacy, adding one more WWE title, two more Mania main-events, one more iconic victory, and three of the top drawing PPVs in history to his name.

So, there you have it. Finally…The Rock has achieved #1. The "Jabroni beating, pie eating, trail blazing, eyebrow raising…ahead of the Hulkster, better than the rapper from Boston, even greater than Stone Cold Steve Austin." Your People's Champion of the WrestleMania Era: The Rock. IF YA SMELL….WHAT THE ROCK…IS COOKIN.'

Appendix C
The Bret Hart Wrestler Score

#	Wrestler	Look	Mic	In-ring	Total
1	The Rock	10	10	9	29
2	Triple H	9	9	9	28
2	John Cena	9	9	9	28
4	Ric Flair	6	10	10	26
5	Kurt Angle	7	9	10	26
6	Randy Savage	8	9	9	26
6	Undertaker	9	8	9	26
8	Chris Jericho	5	10	10	25
9	Hulk Hogan	10	9	6	25
9	Shawn Michaels	6	9	10	25
9	Randy Orton	10	6	9	25
9	Brock Lesnar	10	6	9	25
13	Steve Austin	7	9	9	25
14	Edge	8	8	9	25
15	Ted DiBiase	7	9	9	24
16	CM Punk	4	10	10	24
17	Eddie Guerrero	5	9	10	24
18	Ricky Steamboat	8	6	10	24
19	Batista	10	7	7	24
19	Bret Hart	7	7	10	24
21	Big Show	9	8	7	24
22	Roddy Piper	6	10	7	23
23	Sting	8	7	8	23
24	Mick Foley	3	10	9	22
25	Lex Luger	10	6	6	22
26	Roman Reigns	9	5	8	22
27	Chris Benoit	6	5	10	21
27	Ultimate Warrior	10	6	5	21
29	Kevin Nash	9	8	4	21
30	Goldberg	9	4	5	18

The Performance Factor

#	Wrestler	Total Score
1	Shawn Michaels	47.5
2	Ric Flair	46
3	Undertaker	45.25
4	Kurt Angle	45.25
5	The Rock	45
6	John Cena	45
7	Triple H	45
8	Bret Hart	44
9	Steve Austin	43.75
10	Edge	43.75
11	Ricky Steamboat	43.5
12	CM Punk	43.5
13	Chris Jericho	43.25
14	Chris Benoit	42.75
15	Mick Foley	42.5
16	Eddie Guerrero	42
17	Randy Orton	42
18	Brock Lesnar	41.75
19	Sting	39
20	Randy Savage	38.5
21	Batista	38.25
22	Roman Reigns	38
23	Lex Luger	37.5
24	Hulk Hogan	36.75
25	Big Show	33.5
26	Ultimate Warrior	31.5
27	Ted DiBiase	30.75
28	Kevin Nash	30
29	Roddy Piper	29.75
30	Goldberg	27.25

(Total score is based on the top 10 star-rated matches of each wrestler's career)

The Business Factor

#	Wrestler	Comment
1	Hulk Hogan	Very close between him and Austin
2	Stone Cold Steve Austin	Unbelievable numbers for 1 era
3	The Rock	Hollywood helped him here
4	John Cena	On top as Mania has ascended
5	Macho Man Randy Savage	Underrated in this category
6	Triple H	Also underrated in this category
7	Shawn Michaels	Turned it on late in his career
8	Ric Flair	Not bad for mostly NWA events
9	Undertaker	Resume has improved in recent years
10	Bret Hart	Carried WWE during rough times
11	Roddy Piper	Founding Father of WM franchise
12	Mick Foley	Goes to show how big "Attitude" was
13	Ultimate Warrior	Perfect fit for a cartoon generation
14	Goldberg	"As big as anyone ever was" – AA
15	Sting	Benefitted from Monday Night Wars
16	Ted DiBiase	Kept WM momentum going in 1988
17	Batista	Helped WrestleMania rebound in '05
18	Brock Lesnar	High profile matches post-MMA
19	Edge	A great secondary player, financially
20	Big Show	Been a featured part of major events
21	Randy Orton	Could have been much higher
22	Kurt Angle	Counted on during a declining period
23	Kevin Nash	Big TV ratings with WCW
24	Chris Jericho	Good numbers as a secondary draw
25	CM Punk	May struggle to climb this list
26	Roman Reigns	Impressive Network Era statistics
27	Lex Luger	Never hit it big in right place, time
28	Eddie Guerrero	Extremely popular at his peak
29	Ricky Steamboat	More a tertiary financial contributor
30	Chris Benoit	Similar to Steamboat, economically

(Ranking is based on best buyrates, buy numbers, and TV ratings)

The WrestleMania Era: The Book of Sports Entertainment

The Main-Event/Headlining Factor

#	Wrestler	Total Score
1	Undertaker	174
2	Triple H	171
3	John Cena	159
4	Shawn Michaels	129
5	Hulk Hogan	128
6	Randy Orton	115
7	Edge	89
8	The Rock	88
9	Ric Flair	84
10	Chris Jericho	81
11	Steve Austin	79
12	Bret Hart	74
13	Batista	71
14	Kurt Angle	67
15	Big Show	62
16	CM Punk	57
17	Randy Savage	56
18	Lex Luger	53
18	Mick Foley	53
20	Sting	50
20	Kevin Nash	50
22	Brock Lesnar	47
23	Chris Benoit	46
24	Roman Reigns	33
25	Goldberg	30
26	Ultimate Warrior	30
27	Roddy Piper	28
28	Ted DiBiase	23
29	Eddie Guerrero	18
30	Ricky Steamboat	8

(Total is based on cumulatively weighted score)

The Championship Factor

#	Wrestler	Score
1	Ric Flair	108
2	John Cena	71
3	Hulk Hogan	70
4	Triple H	60
5	Edge	58
6	Bret Hart	52
7	The Rock	43
8	Chris Jericho	42
9	Randy Orton	40
10	Steve Austin	39
10	Kevin Nash	39
12	Sting	37
12	Chris Benoit	37
14	Lex Luger	35
14	Randy Savage	35
16	Big Show	32
17	Shawn Michaels	30
18	Batista	28
18	Undertaker	28
20	CM Punk	27
21	Kurt Angle	25
22	Ricky Steamboat	22
23	Ultimate Warrior	21
24	Mick Foley	18
24	Eddie Guerrero	18
24	Brock Lesnar	18
27	Goldberg	15
28	Roman Reigns	11
29	Roddy Piper	10
30	Ted DiBiase	9

(Total score based on "Title Formula")

The WrestleMania Era Wine Cellar

One of the things that I love about *The Book of Basketball* (which inspired this book) is that I get something new out of it each time that I read it. Parts of the Bill Simmons epic are read every year (The Hall of Fame Pyramid) and parts only every other year or less, but in my most recent revisit, I came to more thoroughly appreciate the "Wine Cellar" section, in which Simmons poses the hypothetical question, "If a basketball game was to decide the fate of the world between us and an alien race and we had the ability to create a team utilizing a time machine to go back and get the best versions of players from any year, who would we chose to be on a roster tasked with saving our species and our planet?"

I was discussing the same concept as it would apply to professional wrestling with Rich Latta, a popular columnist, podcaster, and frequent guest host on my podcast, "The Doc Says," who also so happens to have read *TBOB* a dozen times. We asked, "If aliens were wiping out all humans and taking over the earth unless we were able to entertain the hell out of them with a WrestleMania-style pro wrestling card and we had similar access to time travel as in the Simmons query to pick the best versions of each wrestler, what would we book?"

Rich's podcasting co-host on One Nation Radio, James Boyd (another multi-time *TBOB* reader) joined us for several life-enhancing conversations about this crazy hypothetical in which we suspended our collective disbelief and pretended that we had been tasked with a *Men in Black*-style mission to be the first, last, and only line of defense against the worst scum of the universe. We had to put together the greatest wrestling card imaginable and our lives literally depended on it. Fortunately, we have the best vintages – hence the "Wine Cellar" – of all the greats from the WrestleMania Era at our disposal through the power of time travel.

We began our world-saving endeavor by choosing the preeminent year of each wrestler we would consider booking. In most cases, this was fairly simple, narrowing it down to two but, in a select few circumstances, we chose a superstar vintage because of a need we had to fill on our card. Using the *WrestleMania Era* rankings, here are the vintages that we picked:

The '03 Hollywood Heel Rock – The Rock's three month run to start 2003 is my favorite iteration of any wrestling character in history. This was a no-brainer to Rich and James as well.

The 2000 Triple H – Evolution HHH was in the conversation, but McMahon-Helmsley, pre-quad tear was the most confident and athletic HHH ever to grace the main-event. There have maybe been five better vintages of any wrestler since 1983.

The 2015 John Cena – Though generally agreed upon that the '07 was superior, we chose this version to give our card variety despite legitimate concern that '15 Cena would attempt a springboard Stunner, totally botch it but demand that he and his opponent sell it like he nailed it, prompting those of us sitting with the aliens to distract them long enough to avoid any awkward confusion.

The '89 Ric Flair – If putting together the ultimate wrestling TV show, then we might have gone with the '85 or '86 Horsemen-era Flair, but '89 Flair was supremely confident as a performer and offered one of the Top 5 individual years ever.

The '08 Undertaker – The Deadman peaked athletically in 2008, which was also his most psychologically sound and most versatile year.

The '05 Shawn Michaels – We were concerned that any mid-90s HBK would create such conflict in the locker room that he might sap the energy needed among his fellow wrestlers to save the world. The '05 produced at just as high a level when it mattered, but could put the stakes in proper perspective and would lead a healthy pre-show prayer.

The '87 Hulk Hogan – On a balanced card, we need great heels, so James and Rich tried to talk me into '96 New World Order Hogan. I swayed them by arguing that we needed on our card the purist symbol of good in our arsenal – the '87 Hulkster who preached that we train, say our prayers, and take our vitamins. Plus, '87 Hogan had an all-time-level aura.

The '97 Steve Austin – The '98 would have been a logical choice, but Austin after breaking his neck was not the same caliber of wrestler that he was prior to 1997 until 2001, but in '01 he was a heel for most of the year. '97 was picked because Austin was still at his in-ring best *and* he was approaching his peak as a character; that was better to us than '98 or '99 Austin who was nowhere near as good a wrestler even though his persona was peaking. We had to choose a babyface version.

The '94 Bret Hart – From a technical wrestling perspective, no wrestler was ever better than '94 Bret.

The '92 Randy Savage – The choice was between '92 babyface Liz protector and '89 heel Liz protector. Either way it was all about Miss Elizabeth, but '92 worked to our advantage when it became crystal clear that the mid-2000s offered the perfect opponent to stir up his jealous rage in a sympathetic manner.

The '05 Edge – There were a lot of really good Edge vintages – '05, '06, and '08 especially – but we went with '05 for two reasons: first because he was the perfect fit for a specific spot on our card and second because he was the healthiest post-neck surgery version.

The '08 Chris Jericho – The chenin blanc mentioned in the intro? Henry de Fontenay Vouvray for future reference – the single most underrated bottle of wine in my twenty years of wine drinking. That is the '08 Jericho to a "T" – the single most underrated individual year in wrestling lore.

The '09 Randy Orton – Crazy, psychopath Orton from 2009 was character-wrestling at its finest; nobody got absorbed into their act quite like he did.

The '02 Kurt Angle – Another all-time great vintage, '02 Angle was the most athletically dynamic performer during the most athletically dynamic period in wrestling history.

The '02 Brock Lesnar – We all had a great appreciation for 2014/2015 Brock, but when the human race depends on it, we wanted the highly motivated 25 year old version from '02 that still felt like he had to prove himself to the world; not to mention that '02 Brock is the greatest athletic specimen in wrestling's entire history.

The '92 Sting – '97 Sting could have occupied a headlining spot, but '92 Sting was a much more accomplished and resourceful *wrestler*.

The '07 Batista – The Animal in 2007 had rounded into a more than dependable commodity on a grand stage.

The '99 Mankind – If we needed a participant for a crash-bang sort of match, then we would want the smartest and highest profile version of Mick Foley.

The 2012/2013 CM Punk – He was "Best in the World" at the time; his attitude was a major concern for me.

The '96 Outsiders – Kevin Nash and Scott Hall were better performers while working for WWE, but they had a much more tangible and unmistakable presence when they first debuted for WCW. That said, their inclusion on the card was contingent on using heel "N.W.O." Hogan.

The '89 Ricky Steamboat – Ric Flair called Steamboat the "best babyface of all-time" because of their series in 1989.

The '04 Eddie Guerrero – Much consideration was given to the '97 heel vintage, but a combination of HBK '05-type reasons and a specific match we had in mind for him led us to choose the '04 version that won the WWE Championship.

The '90 Ultimate Warrior – I wanted to pick the '91, who was the superlative worker, and James and Rich wanted to go with the '89, who was reaching the peak of his powers. The '90 was a cross between both vintages.

The '85 Roddy Piper – The Hot Rod was a tough pick because you would want to use him more for his personality than his in-ring acumen, but he at least warranted a look.

The '98 Goldberg – Maybe not the guy you need to deliver on the greatest wrestling card ever assembled but, with presence to spare, he had to at least be considered.

The 2013/2014 SHIELD – There is a local winery that just opened in North Carolina in the last few years; they make absolutely fantastic wines, but it has not yet emerged as my go-to vino. Maybe it will someday. Pretty well describes Reigns, Rollins, and Ambrose when considered separately. As a unit? They are all-time great.

The '96 Rey Mysterio – Smarter versions of Mysterio were considered, but '96 was the vintage that made you feel like you were watching something you were never going to see again.

The '99 Kane – A less characteristically-robotic iteration of the '98 heel Kane, the '99 would make for a good utility player on the card, filling a gap that needed a top quality wrestler.

The '06 Booker T – I felt very similarly about Booker T as I did Kane in that I was certainly not sold on using him on the card, but felt quite confident that he would deliver if we needed him.

The '09 Jeff Hardy – A wildcard similar but not equal to Mick Foley, the '09 Jeff Hardy cleanses a particular palate – the extreme grappling arts.

The '93 Vader – Beyond Undertaker, you will find no more consistent and impressive a big man in modern wrestling lore than '93 Vader. His position in the *WM Era* hierarchy betrays how important we thought him to be for our card, which we absolutely thought needed a "Big Man" match.

The '98 Diamond Dallas Page – The best year of a vastly underrated performer. DDP looked like a bottle of wine with a screw cap covered in dust and with a half-peeled label, but God he was really good.

The '90 Mr. Perfect – He would embrace his spot and work his tail off as a bumper extraordinaire who would help, as my pal Samuel 'Plan would say, "make instead of steal the show."

The '01 Rob Van Dam – A little bit like Hardy or Foley but with an added aesthetic quality, the '01 RVD would make for an ideal choice in the opening match.

The '89 Terry Funk – One of the most transcendent vintages of any wrestler ever, the '89 Funker could be used anywhere on the card from a headlining position to the opener and thrive.

The '94 Owen Hart – Another star whose position in the *WM Era* rankings failed to do justice how badly we wanted him wrestling with the fate of the world on the line.

The '91/'92 Jake Roberts – Specifically, we wanted sadistic heel Snake to be involved in some fashion.

The '92 Brian Pillman and The '97 Dean Malenko – Both were "change of pace" picks should we have decided that a cruiserweight-style opener or second match was needed to dazzle the aliens with innovative moves.

Our next challenge was building the show. The perfect wrestling card would feature a series of stylistically distinct performances. What made events like *Summerslam '02*, *WrestleMania X-Seven*, and *WrestleMania XIX* – considered by many the three greatest PPVs ever – so extraordinary was the variety on display. Booking a card full of nothing but 20-minute main-event-type matches would tire an audience full of diehard wrestling fans, much less our novice alien viewers. Therefore, we carefully crafted a show full of emotional peaks and valleys with four matches designated as headliners, a clash of the titans, a technical marvel, a character-driven six-man tag, the ultimate tale of jealousy, an athletic exhibition, and a hot opening tag team match.

We would put the alien leaders in all the luxury suites at AT&T Stadium in Dallas, Texas and fill the remaining 100,000+ seats with carefully screened enthusiasts who fully comprehended the part they needed to play on this show (passionate and capable of being fully sucked into the presentation). We were a little leery that certain fans would hijack the event and start chanting a bunch of nonsense that would agitate the extraterrestrials and potentially seal our fates; the last thing we needed was a group of jaded fans yelling "CM Punk" at various points since we made a tough call not to use the Second City Saint. We would make the operators of the giant, football field-sized screen for *WrestleMania 32* (who incessantly kept using the world's greatest big screen TV as an inane prompt for crowd chants and weird, triple-split-screened replays) tend to the aliens wearing tiny cowboy hats (think Kurt Angle in the spring of 2001) that would hopefully amuse our guests. The luxury suites would be fully equipped with speakers to relay the commentary from Jim Ross and Bobby "The Brain" Heenan, our All-Star duo from 1998 and 1992 respectively.

The opening match would see the pairing of excellent Canadian characters in '94 Owen and '08 Jericho, the former the best whiny brat heel ever and the latter one of the best heels of all-time, period, cut from the pompous mold of Nick Bockwinkel of AWA fame. Anything short of phenomenal chemistry as partners between those two would be surprising and they would readily establish themselves as the clear antagonists despite their aesthetically-pleasing athleticism. In the opposing corner would be '04 Eddie and '96 Mysterio, a duo we would trust to effortlessly combine innovation and savvy.

A pre-match hype video package, a hallmark of this show considering the aliens would not have watched any of the television shows in the lead-up, would paint the simple picture of the Latinos holding the (early 90s-model) Tag Team Championships and the deceitful Canadians having won the right to challenge for them in a #1 contender tournament. Then the heels would hit the ring first and utilize a brief promo running down the audience and taking a subtle jab at the aliens, with Jericho referring to them as "unearthly sycophants" and drawing a furrow from the alien leader where a brow might reside on a human. The mid-match domination by Hart and Jericho would have human and otherworldly being alike itching for a high-flying comeback, which they would receive during the climax of a 14-minute contest that would end when Owen tripped Mysterio allowing Jericho to roll the Luchador up with a handful of tights for the three-count to win the gold.

The alien leader's stoic expression would be betrayed by the tapping of his gigantic foot as the eerie funeral march added the audio soundtrack to the stunning visual of '08 Undertaker's fiery entrance. The Brain and JR would run down the Tale of the Tape on Taker vs. '93 Vader; JR would note that The Deadman's uncanny attributes make him almost "alien" to his peers as Heenan would suggest that the new potential rulers of the earth clone Vader and use him as a defender for the planet, both comments making the match seem like a battle more between Gods than men.

A balance of control would be quickly established, but just as JR mentioned the agility of both giants, the gargantuan wrestlers would take to the skies. Taker would perform Old School; the Mastodon would come back with a Vader Bomb from the second rope. The Phenom would dive over the top rope to outside the ring and clobber an unsuspecting Vader; Big Van would connect with a stunning moonsault a few minutes later. Vader would literally have Taker on the ropes when he clubbed him repeatedly with his forearms and opened a gash under The Deadman's left eye, a reminder of the performer's mortality not lost on the approving captain of the extraterrestrials, but Vader would make a costly error when he attempted to add leverage by accentuating his blows from the height of the second turnbuckle in the corner; Taker would take advantage and plant him with a Last Ride Powerbomb. Vader would try to mount his own comeback with a powerbomb in response, but Taker would escape and land a chokeslam-Tombstone Piledriver combo for the win in 12-minutes.

After an intricate, move-heavy first match, the Vader-Taker battle would be the change of pace necessary to showcase a different sort of assault on the senses, the opener about finesse, the follower about power united with finesse. The purely physical power-struggle would be told in a different story on this night, but up next to round out the first hour would be the culmination of the deeply personal blood feud of the card. A video package would reveal the story of '05 Edge (with the full support of '05 Lita) developing a predatory lust for '92 Miss Elizabeth much to the acute dismay of '92 Macho Man. Edge and Lita sought a twisted triple-tiered relationship with Liz, whose innocence would be on full display as Randy savagely fought for her purity right from the opening bell.

Macho Man would be atypically brutal in his assault, busting Edge open mere minutes into the match, but his maniacal attitude would resonate with every being in the audience; the Rated R Superstar was clearly the scum of the earth and not even those born beyond earth's atmosphere could deny how easy it was to hate him. Edge would turn the tide thanks to assistance from his sinful vixen, Lita, who would attack Liz in an assault that drew considerable ire from fans so appreciative to see her early 90s-self alive and well in the present. By the final minutes, Savage too would be a bloody mess and would only be able to escape the jaws of humiliating defeat when Liz valiantly attempted to return serve against Lita, distracting Edge and allowing Macho a roll-up victory. The catharsis would be fleeting, however, as Edge and Lita would leave WWE's all-time greatest couple lying.

With human and alien alike feeling dejected by Edge and Lita's antagonistic display, out would come the ever-positive '15 John Cena reminding us to "Never Give Up." In a match very similar to the work that Cena put in during his U.S. Open Challenge in 2015, he and '90 "Mr. Perfect" Curt Hennig would let loose for 13-minutes in a rapid fire encounter that would exhaust every move in their respective arsenals, but also add a touch of early 90s savvy; ring positioning would be utilized rather strategically to avoid the numerous finisher-kick out sequences that have had a tendency to earmark Cena's matches (a conscious effort on the part of Vince McMahon behind the scenes to save such substantial near falls for the main-events). The alien leaders would not be able to help but root for Perfect given the overwhelming support he garnered during the match and would seem quite satisfied that Cena took the loss despite Hennig's use of brass knuckles to assist his Perfect-Plex.

A graphic would then display that '00 Triple H was about to face '13/'14 Daniel Bryan and the ensuing video would suggest a storyline not unlike the one they had in 2014, with The Game wielding his considerable influence to hold down Bryan's desire for upward mobility. To avoid confusion between similarly chorused themes for HHH ("My Time") and Cena ("My Time Is Now"), we would bring Lemmy and the Motorhead crew from 2001 to play Hunter to the ring with "Time to Play the Game." For those of you that have seen the Trips-Bryan match from *WrestleMania XXX*, the match on this night when the fate of the world was at stake would be just a slightly better version thanks to a younger, healthier Triple H; the pace would quicken to account for the depth of the card, though, and the match would be several minutes shorter, concluding at the 22-minute mark.

Triple H would do well to sell his surprise at how proficient Bryan would be with his comebacks despite the heavy-handed offense utilized to keep his energy lower and thus his strikes and submissions weaker. The alien leaders would show their own version of surprise at Bryan's resiliency, as the slightly-framed submission specialist would continue to try and take Hunter to the mat for a tap out. Scouting would clearly have played its usual role in The Cerebral Assassin's pre-match routine, however, and he would be consistently able to escape and re-establish control with a powerful blow or a ring-shaking display of superior strength. Nevertheless, Bryan would have the crowd in the palm of his hand and they would be thrusting their arms skyward in a massive, "this could be our last time watching wrestling"-fueled "Yes" chant while he set up in the corner for the Knee-Plus. Triple H would counter with a vicious clothesline and connect with the Pedigree for the win, much to the dismay of even the extraterrestrials, who would seem genuinely caught up in the underdog story.

From David vs. Goliath, we would move to the irresistible force meeting the immovable object as The Next Big Thing, Brock Lesnar ('02), would make his way to the ring with Paul Heyman to try and take down '87 Hulk Hogan. A hype video would show Hogan attempting to befriend the young monster, only for the evil Heyman to coerce his client into betraying the WrestleMania Era's greatest super-hero; Lesnar would prefer to be the villain. In the second of four main-events, it would be Hogan vs. Lesnar.

Nobody stirs up patriotism quite like the Hulkster – or shall we say that nobody's *theme* stirs up patriotism quite like Hogan's "Real American"; the iconic entrance music would take on greater meaning that extended beyond the borders of its home country on this night. Hulkamania would try to run wild, but would find its leader quickly snuffed out. Lesnar would truly be a Beast Incarnate. '87 Hogan had been thrown around before; never so effortlessly, though, had he ever been subjected to the kind physical decimation that Lesnar would impose.

It would look like the most realistic Hogan-formula match of all-time when the Hulkster began his classic "Hulk Up." Surely, Hogan would deliver the boot, follow it with the leg drop, and the hero would emerge victorious. When Lesnar stopped in mid-stride and grabbed Hulkster in position for a capture suplex, it would seem obvious that this would serve as a lesson to the aliens of human capability and would find them considering bringing Lesnar back with them should Earth be lost. Yet, Hogan would "Hulk Up" again and this time connect with the boot and the leg. Violently and without remorse, Lesnar would kick out at one-and-a-half. It would be later, only when Brock rammed his own head into the steel post and knocked himself silly, that Hogan's classic physical retort would prove its worth as he valiantly slayed the Beast in 12-minutes.

A fervor of anticipation, a buzz of eagerness would begin to settle in as the graphic previewing the next match begged the simple question: "Who is the greatest technical wrestler ever?" No video required, the match between '02 Kurt Angle and '94 Bret "Hitman" Hart would pit against each other an Olympic Gold Medalist and the Excellence of Execution, the Ankle Lock and the Sharpshooter, and the two most gifted grappler-storytellers of consecutive generations. It would spark a different sort of atmosphere in the building, one predicated upon the promise of athletic achievement instead of emotionally dramatic constructs. Hart vs. Angle, the third of the four matches on the marquee, would live up to every expectation possible in its 24-minute timeframe. Why would we expect anything less?

The first half of the match would be dedicated to a game of one-upmanship; think of a cross between Owen vs. Bret at *Mania X* and Angle vs. Michaels at *Mania 21*, with the pace favoring the Bret-Owen encounter capped off by Angle's missed moonsault, which would create an injury to his midsection that Hart would attack to set-up for the Sharpshooter. A desperation counter to the Ankle Lock would be less a move for the kill by Angle and more a chance to create some space and wound his opponent for a later assault. Such mutual respect existed among the fans for both men that the result almost would seem irrelevant. Near tap outs would be met with gasps that suggested a desire to keep watching rather than concern for a potential finish.

In the end, it would be Angle whose simply brilliant lock on the ankle would earn the victory. He would have countered the Sharpshooter in mid-move to latch hard onto the appendage and somehow twist just enough to cause Bret to release his hold and fall victim to Angle's. "Awed by athletic supremacy" might would be the best way to describe the satisfied looks on the alien leaders' faces, as well as the faces of every human-being in the crowd, but the hype video package signaling the next match would change the tone in the stadium considerably. The rebellious gambit led by '97 Stone Cold Steve Austin against the flamboyant, arrogant, pro-establishmentarian '89 Ric Flair would be to be the ultimate example in sports entertainment lore of the everyman vs. societal superiority.

Flair would accentuate his air of pre-eminence by entering AT&T Stadium in a stretch limousine that would be parked JBL-style on the entrance ramp. Austin's introduction would be expectedly muted, but would stir up a great deal of positive energy from the audience. Stone Cold would start the match with a furious series of right hands, the Thesz Press, a running elbow, and stomps in the corner of the mud-hole variety. He would be totally in control until a well-placed thumb to the eye foiled his momentum and allowed the ever-cunning Nature Boy to go to work.

During the climax of what one fan in ear-shot of our suite would prominently refer to as a "better version of a 1980s Flair vs. Dusty Rhodes match," Austin would make his second comeback (the first would end by a low blow out of the referee's field of vision) and attempt the Stone Cold Stunner, but Flair would counter with an elbow to the knee he had so diligently worked over (legally and illegally) and lock on the Figure Four. Blood from an earlier wound streaked down Austin's face ala Austin-Hart at *Mania 13*; passing out, though, would not be an option on this occasion. The Texas Rattlesnake would break the hold and connect with the Stunner for the 1-2-3 at just under the 18-minute mark. Austin's combination of true grit, intensity, and passion would seem to have won over the aliens.

Sierra, Hotel, India, Echo, Lima, Delta…The '14 Shield. The Hounds of Justice would make their way through the crowd as Austin was finishing his final salute on the ramp. As Rollins, Reigns, and Ambrose stood tall in the ring, a quick video would play revealing various historically reviled acts by their opponents: '89 Terry Funk, '91 Jake Roberts, and '09 Randy Orton. Jim Ross would nickname the evil trio, "The Shining," as Heenan filled in the details of the classic film for the extraterrestrials. It at first would appear that the sadistic villains would quite easily put down The Shield, but Reigns would use a hard shove to send Funk into Roberts, who would then crash into Orton. The Hounds would pounce the Funker and the Snake and soon the Viper would join into help them, enraged from even being inadvertently struck by his teammate. Once Orton had laid out Funk and Roberts with RKOs, Ambrose would catch him with Dirty Deeds, which would bounce him right into a Spear from Reigns. Rollins would follow with the uber-impressive Phoenix Splash for the pin and the win just 5-minutes after the opening bell had rung.

As preparations began for the main-event, we would see dozens of photographers line the massive entrance ramp and a digitized red carpet graphically rolled out. It would look as if someone really important was about to come out. We would then cut backstage to '89 "Mean" Gene Okerlund standing by with The '03 Hollywood Heel Rock, who would proceed to tell both human and alien alike how inferior they all were compared to him and that how, if life were a game of chess, then the people would be the pawns, the aliens would be the knights, and he of course would be king. A hype video would air immediately afterward that showed Rock mocking "E.T." and talking down to '05 Shawn Michaels, who would implore the two competing races to find peace and who would suggest that a victory over The Rock would serve as an olive branch extended.

In an amazingly athletic 22-minute contest, Rock and HBK would tell the story of the man apart from all other beings in the universe being humbled by the simple man of faith. Though The Great One certainly would exude an aura of otherworldly ability, a simultaneous kip up would show

Michaels to be every bit the competitor. A Rock Bottom might have signaled the end if the earth's survival were not at stake. Each HBK kick out – one would even come after being Rock Bottomed onto a steel chair – would carry with it the hope of a planet and, as we eventually came to understand, the admiration of a previously destructive alien race. Neither one nor two super kicks would put The Rock down for the count either, though. In the final moments, Rock would have HBK in position for the People's Elbow, but Michaels would kip up in mid-Rock stride and blast him with Sweet Chin Music for the victory. It would be a masterpiece, as would be the entire show; and it would save the world!

Acknowledgements

I have spent the past several years working on this book. It has been tremendously fun. Writing about pro wrestling has always been a refuge, but I can honestly state that these nearly two hundred thousand words were the most rewarding that I have ever written.

In addition to, again, thanking my family for their support, I also want to recognize a few others. I will forever appreciate Mattberg for pointing me in the direction of the online world of wrestling. My analytical mind needed an outlet to cultivate my sports entertainment fandom in the same way that ESPN.COM has cultivated my team sports fascination. Mattberg's brother, Sac, has been my best friend since 9th grade and continued to watch wrestling with me throughout our college years. I think that he kept watching for my sake more so than for his own enjoyment of WWE, so thanks, buddy. Shaun regularly split the cost of PPVs with me in professional school when neither of us had two nickels to rub together (and took many a picture with me doing various wrestler poses, most notably Randy Orton's). Jeff is "The Man." I am not sure I would have been alive to write a book if was not for him and his wife. Forever grateful, brother. Tony continually reminds me that it is OK for doctors to love pro wrestling. He is an inspiring guy. Chris has been my most recent wrestling viewing pal. An old school wrestling fan dating back to the pre-WrestleMania Era, he has been a loyal friend and supporter of this book. I have to give a huge thank you to Calvin Martin, owner of Lordsofpain.net, for giving me a place to write about wrestling for all these years. It has meant more than he knows.

Finally, thank you to the pro wrestlers around the world. I respect the hell out of your profession, your dedication to your craft, and to the sacrifices that you make so that guys like me can analyze and write books about it.

www.ingramcontent.com/pod-product-compliance
Lightning Source LLC
Chambersburg PA
CBHW060231100426
42742CB00011B/1509